Third World Environmentalism

Third World Environmentalism

Case Studies from the Global South

N. Patrick Peritore

University Press of Florida
Gainesville/Tallahassee/Tampa/Boca Raton
Pensacola/Orlando/Miami/Jacksonville

04 03 02 01 00 99 6 5 4 3 2 1

Library of Congress Cataloging-in-Publication Data
Peritore, N. Patrick.
Third World environmentalism: case studies from the Global South /
N. Patrick Peritore.
p. cm.
Includes bibliographical references and index.
ISBN 0-8130-1688-6 (cloth)
1. Environmentalism—Developing countries. I. Title.
GE199.D44P47 1999
363.7'009172'4—dc21 99-28827

The University Press of Florida is the scholarly publishing agency for the
State University System of Florida, comprised of Florida A & M University,
Florida Atlantic University, Florida International University, Florida State
University, University of Central Florida, University of Florida, University of
North Florida, University of South Florida, and University of West Florida.

University Press of Florida
15 Northwest 15th Street
Gainesville, FL 32611–2079
http://www.upf.com

This book is dedicated to my wife and partner in many adventures in the field, Dr. Ana Karina Galve Salgado de Peritore.

Contents

Preface ix

1. Studying Environment in the Global South: Hypotheses and Methodology 1

2. Millenial Politics: Postmodernism and Post-Fordism 19

3. The New Politics: Postmodernism Left and Right 45

4. India: Greens Facing the Impossible 60

5. Korea: New Democracy and Environmentalism 91

6. Brazil: Developing the World's Arboretum 111

7. Mexico: Neoliberal Sustainable Development 145

8. Puerto Rico: From "Operation Bootstrap" to Ecodisaster 175
   Rafael Albarrán and N. Patrick Peritore

9. Romania: Candidate Democracy, Vulnerable Environment 193
   Steven D. Roper and N. Patrick Peritore

10. Iran: From Revolution to Ecological Collapse 209

11. The New Environmentalism in the Global South 228

Appendix: National Q-Sort Data 247

Glossary 283

Notes 293

Bibliography 305

Index 327

Preface

This book models the attitudes of key decision makers in seven countries of the Global South on the issues of environment and development. Please note that the term *Global South* is a new usage replacing *Third World*, for countries which are developing, are dependent on the rich, high-tech Global North, but hold most of the world's genetic diversity, unique species, and fragile ecosystems.

When I commenced fieldwork in India in 1990 I expected that each country would have a unique answer to environmental questions based on its particular history and culture. It turned out that the seven countries, India, Korea, Brazil, Mexico, Puerto Rico, Romania, and Iran, produced the same attitude types. Environmentalism has become a truly international issue.

Elite thinking shows the impact of the globalized high-tech economy (post-Fordism) and of postmodern values such as concern for subjectivity, personal autonomy, quality of life, risk aversion, community, participation, feminism, lifestyle engineering, multiculturalism, and environmental and global social problems.

I expected to find that elites would be divided according to the sector of the society they controlled. Thus, government, business, environmentalists, scientists, and journalists should have very different attitudes about environment, and these differences should be correlated with the old left-right political spectrum. In fact, the seven attitude types to emerge mixed all of these occupational sectors. There is a high level of consensus on environmental issues in the Global South, much higher than is reflected in the press or political systems of the countries concerned.

Most of these countries have large and growing environmental movements and have created significant legislation and regulatory systems. But all are beset with typical problems of the Global South:

debt, overpopulation, inability of the government to effect real changes at the ultimate local level because of resistance from powerful elites. Environment is a new issue, increasingly urgent, and will no doubt become the crucial issue of the next millennium. The countries of the Global South will require a great deal of scientific help, international treaty law direction, and financial aid if they are to bring their population and productive systems into line with their ecological carrying capacities, which is what sustainable development is all about.

The hopeful element in this story is that there is a new politics emerging that goes beyond the old left-right politics, which was concerned with which social classes controlled the output of industrial production. This class viewpoint is outmoded in a global technology-driven economy. The unhappy part of the story is that the global economy shows few signs of ecological sensitivity. All the new environmental treaties are being overridden by free trade instruments like NAFTA, GATT, and MAI, the Multilateral Accord on Investments.

But public opinion on a world scale is demanding that governments provide environmental balance as a natural right. Sooner or later governments and corporations will have to listen to this increasingly urgent message, and the press and party systems will have to adapt to the deep attitude changes that are coming.

The consequences of destroying the unique and fragile environments in the Global South in order to provide a few more decades of excess consumption for the rich include the crash of human populations, and widespread war and social breakdown, as we clash over scarce resources and as global warming shifts the livable productive zones, causing waves of migration. The attitudinal and political changes are at hand, but so is the emergency.

Ecological succession through natural selection overrides economics, politics, culture, ideology, and religion. Survival dictates that we outgrow the fantasy of controlling nature and begin to live within our ecological means. We evolved as short-lived small-group social specialists; let us see if we can extend our evolutionary inheritance and learn to plan for the long term. If not, we will become extinct like the many other species incapable of adapting to rapidly changing circumstances.

My wife Ana Karina Galve-Peritore shared the fieldwork and data collection on the Mexico chapter and is its co-author. She also prepared the endnotes and bibliography and provided a lot of support during nine years of fieldwork and writing. This book is dedicated to her. Thanks are due to Dr. Emilio Aguilar and Senator Matias Cruz for their assistance and friendship over the years.

Professor Rafael Albarrán, the chair of political science at University of Puerto Rico, did the fieldwork and data collection in his own country. Marissa Pellisier aided Rafael in the fieldwork. He is first author of the Puerto Rico chapter. Professor Steve Roper of Pace University did the fieldwork in Romania and is first author of that chapter. Steve was on a Fulbright Fellowship, and the Pace University Scholarly Research Committee provided release time. Rector Demetru Cicoi-Pop and Professor Eugen Gergely of Lucian Blaga University of Sibiu were of enormous help to Steve and me and made our research and teaching in Romania an excellent experience.

I did Indian field research with the help of a University of Missouri Alumni Grant and a Fulbright-Hays Fellowship. Thanks are due to the Karlekars for their inspiring tour of the Calcutta Social Project, a brilliant and humane example of grassroots development using local resources and community input.

David Fleischer and Luiz Pedone of the Universidade de Brasilia and Sidney de Miguel, the lone Green Party deputy, were of great assistance in my Brazilian fieldwork, as were all of the important people who generously gave their time.

Fahimeh Hosseinzadeh, a professional survey researcher in Teheran, translated, cross-checked, and pretested the protocol and utilized her extensive contacts to develop a person sample reflecting the greatest opinion diversity on the issue. I analyzed the data with help from some Iranian specialists. It must be noted that Fahimeh could not participate in analysis of the data and the writing of this chapter because of telecommunication problems, so that all analyses and conclusions are mine alone. Because I have not been back in contact with her since she sent the raw data, she is not in any way responsible for any statements or analysis in this chapter. But I owe her thanks for making the Iran chapter possible.

In 1993, Professor Kim Young-Khee applied our research protocol to a sample of environmentalists, scientists, governmental officials, businessmen, and journalists in Korea, with the aid and advice of the research team at Lucky Goldstar Advertising Agency. For his dissertation he ran a large sample of journalists, which was cut out of the data run for my chapter. An Soon-Cheol was of great assistance in translating Korean sources.

I owe great thanks to Barry Gustafson, Andrew Sharp, Chris Carson, Carmen Schweiger, and all my colleagues at the Tamaki Campus of the University of Auckland for making my stay there such a rich and rewarding experience.

Since I conceived the Q-method protocol, ran and analyzed all the data, and wrote all the chapters either by myself or in conjunction with Karina Galve-Peritore, Rafael Albarrán, and Steve Roper, the responsibility for errors, misunderstandings, or omissions falls on me alone.

Thanks are due to Chris Hofgren at the University Press of Florida for seeing the potential in this book and shepherding it through the acceptance process. Thanks are due to the 241 leaders in government, business, environmental movements, science, and journalism who generously gave me their time and information and shared their attitudes on some sensitive issues. I found them to be an impressive font of judgment and knowledge, and I wish them the best in their efforts to move their countries forward toward sustainability. It is our hope that this book will be a contribution to that effort.

✿ 1

Studying Environment in the Global South: Hypotheses and Methods

The way that decision-making elites in India, Brazil, Puerto Rico, Korea, Mexico, Romania, and Iran think about environmental issues is examined in this book. This country sample presents a wondrous diversity of cultures, languages, and religions. It seems logical that each country should have its own unique approach to the problem of mixing environment and development.

Surprisingly this is not true. We applied a Q-method protocol (psychological modeling, as explained later in this chapter) cross-nationally to 241 top leaders in government, business, and environmental groups. From this data came seven factorial attitude types that explain elite environmental attitudes in the Global South. The new environmental politics is truly international. Global environmentalism overrides differences among the widely varying cultures and economies.

This new environmental politics also fits very well into predictions of a postmodern culture shift and a post-Fordist global economic restructuring, which are explained in the following chapters. Our results show that environmental issues raise a strong consensus. Government, business, and environmentalists in the Global South are not seriously in conflict. Each of the seven attitude types mixed environmentalists and business and government elites (with a smattering of journalists and scientists), showing a broad overlap in their attitudes. Moreover, the seven attitude types—Greens, Political Greens, Sustainable Developers, Postmodern Managers, Developmentalists, Bureaucratic Nationalists, and Cultural Traditionalists (see glossary)—were all open to compromise and to a nonpolitical, data-driven debate about environmental policy.

We found that Global South environmental elites are moderate, seek consensus, and have international postmodern attitudes on environmental issues. The seven attitude types found in our data form a new political spectrum that is pulling politics away from the old modernist left-right division into a postmodern "new politics." Even in the Global South, elites recognize the choice they face among a green society, hypercapitalism, green capitalism, or chaos, the four alternatives of the new politics.

How This Study Was Done

I began this study in 1989, by assembling statements from the world literature on development and environment. A representative sample of these statements was converted into a psychological profile and translated and run, by myself in India and Brazil and with collaborators in Mexico, Korea, Puerto Rico, Iran, and Romania, between 1990 and 1995. Colleagues in South Africa, Jordan, Ethiopia, Thailand, and Argentina were not able to complete the Q-sorts, but fieldwork in the Global South is notoriously difficult and even hazardous, so this is understandable.

Our seven-nation sample represents 11 percent of the world's landmass and 23 percent of the world's population. Catholic, Orthodox, Protestant, Confucian, Hindu, Buddhist, Islamic, and shamanistic religious cultures and capitalist, colonial, revolutionary, and postsocialist economies are found in the sample, providing an interesting range of conditions for testing the hypotheses developed in this study.

These countries are here organized through the chapter sequence on a scale of most to least environmentally concerned. The aforementioned seven factorial types recurred persistently despite profound cultural, linguistic, religious, and political differences among the countries. These types are seen in the following national case studies and are discussed further in the conclusion. Let us examine the hypotheses that were confirmed and disconfirmed in this study.

Hypotheses

All studies begin with explicit or implicit hypotheses. The hypotheses implicit in the formation of the Q-method instrument and in the thinking leading up to the project are interesting because they show how our best intuitions often fail to capture complex social realities.

1st Hypothesis: Because the Global South does not play the leading role in the new world economy, elites there will not show postmodern values. Their environmental politics will be stuck in the old modernist left-right spectrum. Each country will have a culturally unique approach to environment, with no postmodern attitude shift.

This "culturalist" hypothesis was disconfirmed. Fieldwork showed that the attitude types within and between these "culturally unique" countries were almost entirely the same. Despite the dozens of languages and cultures in the sample, and extreme religious and political economic diversity, some of the same seven attitude types recurred in the different countries. The "political culture" model had to yield to data showing a truly international elite culture. I would argue that "political culture" is no longer useful in the new global economy and emerging international postmodern culture.

2nd Hypothesis: The three major sectors studied—environmental groups, government, and big business—should each have a distinct approach to environmental issues. Environmentalists and business should be enemies, with government playing a mediating role.

This hypothesis was also disconfirmed. The data in all countries showed a strong mixing of occupational sectors within each attitude type. The occupations of members of elites did not significantly determine their attitudes toward environment. There was broad consensus between and within types.

3rd Hypothesis: Environment is a divisive issue, which should create high levels of partisanship and social division.

This too was disconfirmed. Field data showed large areas of agreement on environment among postmodern elites. Data showed that the entire issue spectrum had already shifted from the old left-right politics into a postmodern new politics.

These findings were not presupposed in construction of the protocol. Quite the contrary, the statement set (sample) was built around a modernist vision of Global South politics, with "left versus right," "environment versus development," and "business versus environmentalism" indicators. Yet even this implicit scale—"developmentalism/business/right" versus "environmentalism/social movements/left," with a neutral government in the center—produced attitude types arranged in a postmodern new politics spectrum that transcended the old left-right divisions. Discoveries like this are the payoff for the discomforts of field research.

4th Hypothesis: The closed nature of most Global South political systems would require creation of Green parties or mass movements to bring environmental issues before elites.

This was disconfirmed, because we found that elites were already strongly concerned with environment and incorporating it into their decision making, probably because of international contacts, educational backgrounds, environmentalist pressure, international treaty standards, environmentally linked aid, and the seriousness of their own local environmental situations. Also, as poll data shows, there is a high level of concern and increasing popular mobilization around the environmental issue on the part of the mass public.

A recent Canadian poll of thirty-five thousand people in thirty nations (representing two-thirds of the world population) showed that a majority in twenty-eight countries (ranging from 54 percent to 91 percent) want tougher government regulation and environmental protection. Seventy-five percent showed high levels of concern, and a majority of people in nineteen countries believed that industry generated the environmental problem.[1]

In our data, elites seem receptive to non-ideological discourse and scientific data about environment and seem willing to change positions and cooperate with other social forces. Despite high levels of environmental concern in the mass publics, the party systems, mass media, and social hierarchy in the Global South do not readily allow such new trends to change the way politics is conducted. None of the seven countries studied has the political flexibility in its party, electoral, or campaign finance system to allow for a large Green party or to adjust policy quickly to changing public opinion. But elites are taking an active interest in the issue. Postmodern elite attitude shifts are significant in pointing out future trends and allow some hope, especially when combined with this new mass consciousness.

5th Hypothesis. The transitions from modernism to post-modernism, and Fordism to post-Fordism, provide axes for a model on which the shift from old to new politics may be mapped.

This hypothesis was strongly confirmed in the cross-national data but requires some explanation. The same model is used in each of the seven countries to map the attitude types. In the last chapter we summarize the attitude types found in the Global South using an overall model of postmodern transition. The trend line moves from Fordist modernism upward into post-Fordist postmodernism, as becomes clearer after going through chapters 2 and 3.

I elaborated a sample of key statements out of the international literature and interviews in various countries and arranged these into blocks, each bearing on a major environmental issue. The statements were printed on numbered cards and given to 241 key members of elites to sort into a normal curve representing their deep preferences. The actual sample in this book consists of these 8,767 acts of prioritization or preference ordering (done by 241 people on 36 statements). This is not a small sample.

These 241 Q-sorts were entered into a matrix so that every person could be correlated to every other. Factorial types were drawn from this sample and rotated to simple structure (Varimax rotation), producing the seven factorial attitude types modeled in this study. The last section of the present chapter explains the Q-method and its differences from survey methodologies, which should prove interesting to social scientists.

The Statements

The following are the statements used on cards in the study.

BIOCENTRISM

1. All living things have a right to exist.

4. Biological diversity must be treated as a common heritage of mankind, to be indexed, used, and above all preserved.

5. Life on earth is a single organism which modifies the atmosphere to serve its own needs.

ANTHROPOCENTRISM

3. The view of man as the infallible creator, whose salvation lies in his own technology, is the origin of cosmic vandalism.

6. Humanity is doomed to extinction. Our main effort must be to preserve maximum diversity so nature can carry on after us.

11. Environmental collapse and violent conflict over resources destroyed most ancient civilizations, and will surely destroy the West.

SUSTAINABLE DEVELOPMENT

18. The only alternative is a Green economy, with grassroots democracy, voluntary simplicity, sustainable production, and recycling.

2. Sustainability was the original economy of the species. To restore it now will require a revolution as great as the industrial revolution.

7. Traditional farming mimics nature and is more sustainable than Western monoculture. But we kill natives and their knowledge.

Critique of Developmentalism

21. Maximizing GNP means maximizing cost, resource waste, pollution, and inequality.

8. Development means the rich redistributing natural resources in their own favor.

9. Foolish international development programs caused most third world poverty, revolution, and environmental damage.

12. Western development plunders and destroys nature, and uses the third world as a dump site and laboratory.

Environmental Policy Making

19. Economic development on a sound environmental basis is possible and cost effective.

13. If government gave business information and incentives, not command and sanction, the market and entrepreneurs would protect the environment.

14. Environmental policy is piecemeal and defensive, not global as required by the urgency of the problem.

15. Democracy cannot meet the challenge of imminent ecocatastrophe, because it acts slowly and through compromise.

International Treaty Regimes

16. East and West are converging toward a social democratic model with a mixed economy, equity, and control of environmental damage.

17. European Community legislation, Law of the Sea, and Antarctic treaties show growing international consensus about environment.

20. If the West enforces and pays for high environmental standards, then the world's nature will be conserved.

Energy issues

25. Investment in energy efficiency and recycling can reduce fossil fuel demand without sacrificing growth.

26. The world economy of the next century will not be powered by coal, oil, gas, or uranium.

27. Nuclear power's long-term cost in waste disposal, accidents, and terrorist threats far outweighs its benefits.

10. Poor countries must develop without fossil fuel dependency, thus avoiding the cost, pollution, and alienation of the West.

BIOTECHNOLOGY

31. Biotechnology is the next step in human evolution. Our destiny is to control evolutionary advance on this planet.

32. The hidden ethical basis of biotechnology is eugenics.

33. Biotechnology replaces free scientific information with secrecy, collusion, and research geared toward corporate needs.

34. Biotechnology offers cheaper, quicker ways to improve third world diet than costly mechanical-chemical technologies.

35. The risks posed by release of engineered microbes or plants into the environment far outweigh commercial gains.

36. Biotechnology research is not a luxury for the third world but a strategic necessity for avoiding permanent underdevelopment.

GLOBAL WARMING

28. Why spend large sums to avert greenhouse effects that may not happen? Better to adjust if climate changes appear.

29. Greenhouse radiation and acid rain will disrupt oceanic and land food chains and dramatically change the climate.

30. Greenhouse warming will lead to death by flooding, famine, of up to a billion people.

POPULATION

22. Third world population will not decline naturally due to rising affluence; if not forced down it will prevent even basic development.

23. Respect for women should not be based on having children. Women's rights are the key to population control.

24. Stop environmental degradation and population growth will decline by itself.

The elites who participated in this study were chosen in the field by "respondent pyramiding" (asking who is important in this area and zeroing in on individuals named by two or more people). The elites in this study consist of truly important persons. There are ministers of environment and planning, former presidents, major environmental lawmakers, top national and state bureaucrats, some well-known scientists and journalists, heads of environmental groups and political parties, some powerful national and transnational businessmen, and managers of international agencies and interest groups. But because politics in the Global South can be cruel and unforgiving, the names,

Table 1.1. The Seven Principal Types of Environmental Attitudes

Person Sample Per Country

	Gr	SD	PM	D	PG	BN	CT
India	15	7	12	—	—	—	—
Brazil	10	11	7	7	—	—	—
Puerto Rico	13	6	—	—	10	11	3
Korea	13	9	16	—	—	10	—
Mexico	8	6	16	—	7	—	—
Romania	—	—	—	11	—	5	—
Iran	—	6	—	9	—	3	10
Total	59	45	51	27	17	29	13

Total person sample = 241 Women = 24% of sample
Total Q sample = 241 persons x 36 statement placements = 8,676 decisions.

Key: Gr = Greens, SD = Sustainable Developers, PM = Postmodern Managers, D = Developmentalists, PG = Political Greens, BN = Bureaucratic Nationalists, CT = Cultural Traditionalists.

Breakdown of the Person Sample by Sector

	Gr	SD	PM	D	PG	BN	CT
NGOs	25	15	4	1	2	11	2
Government	10	10	19	11	6	8	5
Business	13	7	24	4	3	8	2
Scientists	15	9	6	10	6	5	1
Journalists	1	2	—	1	—	—	2
Women	19	12	3	7	7	5	4
Men	40	33	48	20	10	24	9

Note: Totals are not the same as in the chart indicating the person sample per country because of some sectoral overlap, hence double counting.

and sometimes the positions, of these individuals are masked in my data, so that they could freely express their attitudes without repercussions.

Table 1.1 summarizes the numbers of people in the elites of each of the countries by attitude types, and by the sectors they represent, so that the reader can appreciate the nature and quality of the person sample.

The seven factorial types emerging from this study are roughly summarized in the following for guidance through the country studies. They take on slightly different nuances in each country but are recognizably similar transnationally. Types were given names for ease of discussion and to indicate their content.

Seven Principal Environmental Attitude Types in the Global South

GREENS

- Biocentric, in favor of a decentralized, pluralistic green economy.
- Popular grassroots participation in environmental management.
- Do not oppose growth, but are risk averse, oppose hard power, high technology.
- No apocalyptic world view, but are concerned with global warming effects.
- Do not conceive population as an urgent problem. Only mildly favor feminism.
- Moderate critique of Western developmentalism.
- Politically moderate, open to dialog among sectors, open to change based upon scientific evidence. Non-ideological.

POLITICAL GREENS

- Aware of environmental concerns at a rhetorical level, use the discourse but lack concrete knowledge or clear policy positions.
- Ambiguous views due to high-visibility political positions, will move as directed by the strongest political pressures.
- Critical of Western imperialism, but not of international programs and loans.
- GNP growth using hard power is necessary, but support conservation. Neutral about nuclear power.
- Neutral about market incentives and the role of business.

- No concern with overpopulation or global warming.
- Neutral regarding efficacy of democratic decision making.

SUSTAINABLE DEVELOPERS

- Anthropocentric humanists. Reason, technology, democratically regulated markets will best preserve nature.
- Mildly distrust big business. Business should adopt clean technologies; main emphasis on clean, green capitalism (intensive development).
- Not as risk averse regarding fossil fuel, nuclear power, biotechnology as Greens.
- Only mildly critical of Western Fordist modernism.

POSTMODERN MANAGERS

- Capitalist humanists. Environmental question must be rationally managed.
- Risk averse regarding fossil fuels, high technology.
- Capitalism is changing, GNP maximization no longer the main social goal. Favor intensive development. Great concern with global warming.
- Neutral about promoting market mechanisms and incentives for environmental protection. Distrust motives of big business.
- Support democratic decision making.
- Support international treaty regimes in environmental protection.

DEVELOPMENTALISTS

- Modernists, Fordists; rational management of technology for growth.
- Rational use of markets and pricing mechanisms for conservation.
- Global warming, overpopulation, hard power high-technology impacts can be managed.
- Oppose Greens and Sustainable Developers as utopians. For greener capitalism as by-product of GNP growth.
- Strongly pro-democratic, strongest support for women's rights of all types. Women's rights more likely seen as economic, as developmentalists oppose feminism and postmodernism.

BUREAUCRATIC NATIONALISTS

- Technocratic, bureaucratic authoritarians on environmental issues.

- Oppose markets, incentives; anti-business.

- Pessimistic about the human future, critique Greens as utopians.

- Sound development is possible with massive system change, but are very critical of business and governmental capacity to modernize.

- See little risk in fossil fuel and high technology. Give GNP growth priority.

- Strongly critical of Western modernism, developmentalism.

- Nationalists: purely national solutions to environmental problems—import substitution, industrialization. Strongly critical of international treaty regimes or external pressure.

- Neutral or hostile to women's rights, population control.

CULTURAL TRADITIONALISTS

- Outliers on our model, the type is essentially premodern.

- Humanity is doomed; strongly apocalyptic expectations.

- Organic conservatives, potential allies to Greens and sustainable developers on a few issues.

- Highly critical of Western developmental models and culture for destroying traditional values, pillaging nature. Hostile to transnational business.

- Environmental problem has low salience. Neutral about energy, population, and technology issues.

- Women's rights acceptable, but low social justice orientation. Will actively oppose postmodern lifestyle issues.

To summarize, data from seven countries of the Global South allow us to discard some conventional wisdom. Global South environmental politics no longer fully corresponds to left-right thinking but shows clear elements of postmodern new politics. Global South elites are not distinguished by culturally unique approaches to conserving the global and national commons; political culture is not a useful model because of internationalization of the environmental question. Despite differences of language, culture, religion, and political economy, the elites in the seven-country sample all fit on the same political spectrum (Fordist modernism to postmodern post-Fordism) as the Global North. Culturally specific modeling is not a useful way to approach international issues such as the environment.

Instead of conflict between government, business, and environmentalists, there is broad consensus in the seven factorial attitude types across a mixture of occupations. There is strong elite agreement about many environmental fundamentals. The division within Global South elites lies between fractions still holding to pre-modernism (Cultural Traditionalists), on the one hand, and, on the other, Fordist modernists (Bureaucratic Nationalists, Developmentalists) or postmodern post-Fordist types (Greens, Political Greens, Sustainable Developers). Postmodern Managers straddle the three types of greens and seem to hold the balance of power.

There is evidence of high concern among mass publics about environment, and our data shows that elites are already engaged in international discourse and show heightened awareness of these new issues. These are interesting discoveries that bode well for the future.

A major finding of this book is that a postmodern/post-Fordist value shift, including environmental concern and risk aversion is occurring in the Global South, but this shift deemphasizes the lifestyle, feminist, libertarian, and multicultural dimensions found in the Global North. This finding is proved in the country case studies and by their aggregation and comparison with Western trends in the last chapter.

All about Q-Methodology

As noted, this description is for readers interested in methodological issues or who want to comprehend in depth how this study was done, and those more interested in the countries and results can safely skip it, as the statistical apparatus was largely removed from the text for readability. The Q-data are provided in the appendix.

The method used is the exact opposite of survey technique and is designed to elicit a profile of deep attitudes, or "operant subjectivity," underlying the transitory opinion found in surveys. William Stephenson's Q-methodology applies the presuppositions of quantum physics to the study of subjectivity. It parallels Neils Bohr's "no model" option in physics, in that Q advocates no theory of mind or human nature. Consciousness is a *non ens*, not reified into an entity, and thus thought and feeling are probability states, pure communicability. Feeling states can be quantized into a set of self-referent statements and sorted by participants into a scale of relevances to model their perspective. The individual is treated as a "complex configuration of events" for which factorial regularities in the attitude states can be experimentally discovered.

The subject reorders the randomized set of Q-statements into a forced normal distribution (the Q-sort), ranging from positive to negative, based on different hypothetical or experimental conditions of instruction. Each Q-sort results in a matrix, in which the individual models his or her own subjectivity. These matrices are intercorrelated, factor analyzed, and rotated to simple factorial structure to model the scale of operant attitudes in the universe of discourse. The factor types represent deep structures of subjectivity—enduring attitudes instead of transient opinion—and provide a systematic account of operant subjectivity or the real basis of individual decision making.

Operant subjectivity, or factorial structure, an artifact of measurement, provides an interactive, contextual, and complete explanatory frame. The Q-method is a useful tool for understanding the structure of discourse in other life worlds and is a powerful way of drawing comparisons across diverse cultures. The emergence of seven common ideological types across the very different countries studied demonstrate this power.

The statement set provides the source of "quantum stuff"; the Q-sorting or manipulation of these statements by the subject is a "quantum detector"; and the resultant factors are artifacts of a positional and theory-grounded measurement process. As in physics, all knowledge is positional and measurement based.

Factoring of self-accounts changes subjective events into objective factor structure; it is analogous to the collapse of myriad superimposed probability wave functions into one probability as a result of experimental measurement in quantum physics.[2] The Q-method reveals types that are remarkably stable. A replication I performed on liberation theology in Brazil showed 85 percent stability in factor types in retesting after two years.[3] Q-results are robust.

The Q-method is preeminently a fieldwork methodology, designed for developing, field-testing, running, and interpreting a protocol in close collaboration with central participants in the universe of discourse. Its result is discovery and arrangement of knowledge into a new abductory understanding, recognizable by both research subjects and researcher as an extension and deepening of their comprehension of themselves and others.

How was the protocol elaborated?

Q-statements are developed in interaction with the subjects and literatures being studied. Statements are translated and back-translated with the aid of native speakers and are pretested in a small sample. When possible, finished factors are taken back to the key subjects who produced them for interpretation. The attractiveness of the Q-method for cross-cultural understanding is that the researcher interacts with the data, discovering new understandings, and feeds them back to the subjects who created the data in order to discover which of these understandings offers the richest, most nuanced, and most accurate presentation of their point of view.

The thirty-six statements used in this study, each one a scalar, represented the main issues in this area, as can be seen from the statement blocks already given. The statements comprise the sample; the reverse of survey methods. The statements are inductively drawn from a universe of discourse—in this case the literature on environment and development and interviews made in the field during studies of the Brazilian and Mexican left parties and in Cuba and Nicaragua. Some 350 statements were collected on three-by-five cards, until repetition showed that there was no significant subjectivity uncaptured by this sampling of the universe of discourse on environment and development.

The statements were laid into piles and the piles into groupings of subject matters, and statements were selected to represent best the range of opinions within each block. The statements were edited for clarity and self-reference and to ensure that each represented only one feeling state or issue.

The set of Q-statements are arranged in an experimental design reflecting the hypothesized effects and levels that the researcher expects to find operative in the population. The statements, printed on separate numbered cards, are shuffled and then sorted by the subjects into a normal distribution representing their emotional weight relative to that person. These cards are sorted by each respondent into a scale of affective response representing a normal curve:

    -5   -4   -3   -2   -1,   0,   +1   +2   +3   +4   +5
         (Disagree)   (Neutral)   (Agree)

The concepts and assertions in the statement set have no meaning (or have equipollent meaning) except within the context the subject creates by normalizing their distribution—that is, by prioritizing them according to subjective feelings. The subject ranks the items according to his or her own frame of reference; the interrelation of statements provides a context that assigns them meaning and significance.

Subjects are given the materials needed to model their own attitudes. The statements are sorted by all participants into the same normal curve (-5 to 0 to +5) so that they can be compared. The statements have meaning in relation to the whole Q-sort.[4]

The subject controls the meaning of the continuum, the rank and contextual significance of each statement item, by placing them in a context relative to themselves. The Q-sorts of diverse individuals can be compared because they are all constructed on the same normal curve with the same midpoint (0 valence) and endpoints, -5 (strongly disagree) and +5 (strongly agree). The forced normal distribution ensures that the means and standard deviations of all Q-sorts will be the same.

Thus, all individuals model their own subjectivity and place themselves within the universe of discourse. The range of these placements, the factorial attitude types, represents a few underlying deep structures of feeling or belief. These factorial ideal types, obtained experimentally, are modeled in terms of ideal-type Q-sorts; as if the persons who weighted on the factorial types were made into a committee and forced to agree on one Q-sort to represent their common attitudes. Individual factor weights show the closeness or divergence of individuals within that type to the ideal-type Q-sort representing the whole; that is, factor weights (Spearman's w) indicate the closeness of approximation of individual Q-sort to the ideal-type Q-sort that represents the type.

Who Was Chosen to Participate?

The participants in the study comprise the "tests" to which the sample of statements is subjected. The sample of persons is chosen for their "theoretical saturation," or ability to represent a variant of attitudes within the universe of discourse being studied, and not for their statistical representativity of a larger population.

In Q-methodology, we study the attitudes, not the sample of persons who produced them. The subjects are the variables, and the statements are the sample (of a universe of discourse). The sample (N) is the number of persons times the number of statements, because this total represents the number of acts of prioritization by persons expert in the area.[5]

The proportion of persons in the larger population holding these attitudes is a question the Q-method is not designed to answer. Q is a method of discovery that creates a detailed model of the attitude spectrum in a universe of discourse, as drawn from decision operations performed by a diversity of key individuals in this universe.

The survey method requires validity and reliability tests and a large sample because it tests a researcher's hypotheses, a scale of traits formed intuitively or externally to the universe of discourse, against a sample of the population supposedly exemplifying these traits. The Q-method differs from surveys in utilizing relatively small numbers of respondents (35–65) because the hypothesis is discovered in the factor analysis of the Q-sorts (respondents' presentation of their own perspectives). The statements are the sample, and the persons are the variables or tests to which it is submitted. Subjects determine the meaning of the statements by putting these in a context relative to themselves. Statistical tests would be out of place because there is no validity criterion for a person's point of view. The Q-method always leads to discoveries and surprising results, because it allows the subjects to speak in their own voices. The factors simply structure the subject's response into types.[6]

The small number of persons (cases) in Q often raises questions of generalizability. The factor is an abstraction drawn from the values of the individuals statistically related to it. Statistically reliable factor scores can be obtained from five or more persons; larger numbers would not provide more information or make modeling any easier.[7]

The actual sample of this study consists of 8,676 prioritizations of statements—the placement of thirty-six scalars (statements) by 241 decision makers (in seven countries), for a total of 8,676 acts of subjective prioritization.

The sample of decision makers by type, sector, and country has been indicated. For an optimal study, the person sample is chosen theoretically; that is, by constructing a block design of respondent characteristics (sex, status, position, etc.) and seeking individuals who exemplify those characteristics to do the Q-sorting procedure. However, since this was pioneering fieldwork in Global South countries, in which access, communication, and personal security of the participants and researcher were all sensitive matters, the participants were found by "respondent pyramiding" in the field; as already noted, if a person was mentioned by two other members of an elite as being important in this area, that person was interviewed. Individuals who weigh weakly or whose weights are confounded (weigh on more than one factor) can be dropped from the study as insignificant; however, no one was dropped from this study.

In the overall data set, names are never used, and some job descriptors are masked; the minister of planning or environment may become a "high government official." In the Global South politics can be cruel and retribution swift; the first ethical concern of the investigator is to protect respondent identities. Especially because the Q-method probes deep subjectivity, cooperation could potentially expose participants to serious political problems. Fieldwork on political topics has gotten me into trouble with the secret police of two countries.[8] Thus, respondent names are not kept.

A full list of the participants would reveal how important most of them are in government, business, and environmental groups; a large proportion are top executives and officials, so that their placement of statements is ipso facto highly significant. We must appeal for trust in our word on the significance and range of the person sample; the statistical summary given is a helpful indication of its significance and importance. For each country study the person sample, factor weights, item loadings, and ideal-type Q-sorts are listed, so that the reader can replicate the argument.

What Do the Factorial Attitude Types Signify?

Factors are discoveries, abductions. The factor structure that emerges from the matrix (correlation of each person's response on each item against that of every other person, leading to Piersonian correlation scores between individuals) is inherent in the subjectivity of persons performing the Q-sort. Deep attitudes are not always conscious; the operant subjectivity underlying the facile and often contradictory expression of "public opinion" is what the Q-method is concerned to measure.

The factors represent natural categories of thought operant in the universe of discourse in question. Explanation must square with the actual Q-sorts and factors derived from them. Subjects can help the researcher interpret the meaning of factors and the complementarities and subtexts that often emerge in them.[9]

There are three levels to this procedure: (1) Opinions are self-referent statements expressing deeply held beliefs. A number of statements about an issue is the "population" from which a Q-sample (inductive statement sample from a universe of discourse) can be drawn. (2) Attitudes are operantly defined as factorial models derived mathematically, by factor analysis and rotation, from the data set of Q-sorts (or individual placement of the statement set into a normal curve relative to themselves). And (3) beliefs—values—are the deeper theoretical explanatory level for the spectrum of factorial types defining the universe of discourse.[10]

The seven data sets in this book were analyzed in the same QUANAL program (a 10,000-line Fortran program) and were given Varimax (objective mathematical) rotation to simple structure (instead of judgmental or hand rotation). Factor scores are dependent variables, the values of which are altered with each rotation. Rotation is an experiment that does not change the relation between scores but only provides a new theoretical perspective on the data set.[11]

With these methodological considerations in mind, let us examine the specific studies of India, Korea, Brazil, Mexico, Puerto Rico, Romania, and Iran, to monitor the emergence of postmodern environmental consensus among Global South elites in business, government, and environmental groups and to explain how seven common factorial attitude types model the new environmental politics.

Millenial Politics: Postmodernism and Post-Fordism

The end of the Cold War in 1989 accelerated the globalization of capitalist culture and the economic integration of the Global South. Postmodern cultural values are evident among younger educated elites in both North and South. The national fragmentation, weakening of state control over the economy, and integration of key regions of the Global South into the North's economy are proceeding apace.

In this chapter I examine critically the different ways of conceptualizing these millennial changes. Postmodern philosophy is dramatic, nihilistic, schematic, often insightful, but it offers no guidelines for political action. The postmaterialist model of a new political culture cannot explain the tidal wave of environmental concern and mass movements in the Global South, because it relates post-materialist values to affluence. Post-Fordism offers a clear description of the new globalized economy but rarely points to the dangerous trends it contains.

I look at these models and try to extract from them some workable insights for understanding the changes we are fated to live through. Postmodernism, in its environmental guise, and post-Fordism, both criticized and qualified, provide the axes on which we can model the international attitude types found in seven nations of the Global South.

Postmodernism: Nihilist Philosophy, Fragmentary Politics

Postmodern philosophy grows out of the failure of the Paris Revolt of 1968, an event that led European intellectuals to reject New Left doctrines of social and sexual liberation. The New Left was the avant-garde of modernism. Modernist culture advocated the control of history and nature by reason, material progress, development through technology, the primacy of capital and consumer good production, grand systematic political theories, hierarchically ordered mass movements (parties, unions, interest groups) designed to change social structures, and a mixed economy with state regulation. Modernism was divided into right and left, mainly a conflict of elite versus mass interests, markets versus state, social conservatism versus personal liberation.

Post-1968 postmodernism took a radical tack in its rejection of the entire modernist project. Postmodernists argue that reality is made of signifiers (signs, symbols, images)—in effect saying that reality is virtual. A world of signs endlessly refers to other signs but never constructs larger meanings. History is stripped of myths of origin, grand narratives, projects and goals, structure and meaning, and the ends and means that lead to political action. Sign, symbol, image, and event production (advertising, Internet, MTV, political campaigns), and media interpretations of events (spin), fill our conceptual world. This "knowledge-production" serves an anonymous network of power, which increasingly controls us by manipulating consciousness, bodies, and social relations and by channeling dissent into the sale of symbolic commodities.

Postmodernism rejects grand social and political theory. These are dissolved into mere signs with no grand context to justify and organize them. In Todd Gitlin's definition, "'Postmodernism' usually refers to a certain constellation of styles and tones in cultural works; pastiche; blankness; a sense of exhaustion; a mixture of levels, forms, styles; a relish for copies and repetition; a knowingness that dissolves commitment into irony; acute self-consciousness about the formal, constructed nature of the work; pleasure in the play of surfaces; a rejection of history."[1]

The philosophers of postmodernism, Jacques Derrida, Michel Foucault, and Jean Baudrillard, relish their millennial pessimism. Deconstructive analysis hovers somewhere between scholastic quibbling and gossip. The great "master narratives" of modernist rationalism—science, systematic history, political theory, and philosophy—are fragmented into digitized bits, to be taken up and used in networks of signs and power. The world is only a "text," signs cut free from reference to reality and open to endless deconstruction. Politics is only talk about talk, an endless game of spin.

Postmodernists argue that history is made of petty malice, vicious intentions, evil motives, the clash of wills, domination, strategy and tactics. There is no dominant subject or social elite directing the whole. Power constantly redefines social relations, the social field in which knowledge is generated and used to dominate the body, to force it to emit signs and ritualized behaviors. Modernism, the project of which was to conquer the world and human society with reason, has simply augmented the network of unfreedom. But there is no hope of liberation. Deconstruction cannot free us from the network of power, which is anonymous, serves no one's interests, and twists all discourses, practices, and disciplines of the body into intensified control and manipulation. Deconstruction only criticizes the signs of power and thus creates new discourses, which are reabsorbed into the network of power. "Liberation" is only a sign in this theory.

In postmodern hypercapitalism, individuals exist to move commodities, which serve as signs of status, wealth, power, competence, sexuality, intelligence. Having is being. Exclusivity and snobbism create social hierarchies based on the immediate consumption of the newest set of fads in architecture, interior design, cars, clothing, recreation, schools, etc.; that is, on the latest "lifestyle engineering." Ideologies, ideas, analyses, myths, religions, media messages, all float in hyperreality. History loses meaning and is digitized into models of models; there is only catastrophe, random slippage, meaningless interpretation. Lost meaning cannot be restored, and hyper-capitalism creates wealth for the few, while marginalizing the vast majority into an ecological wasteland. The ultimate fate of the postmodern world is entropy, chaos.[2]

Postmodern philosophy is dramatic, incisive, and pretentious. Postmodernists dismiss history and political theory, but in effect they are themselves writing the same type of linear history and grand theory. Their questionable "caesura," or decisive "break" in history, between modern and postmodern, cannot be defended without constructing the same grand historical narratives that they reject. In fact, their systems are based on illicit metaphysics—illicit because these thinkers reject metaphysics and systematic theory while engaging in those very enterprises. Like the logical positivists, their rejection of metaphysics is itself based on metaphysics. They "write in order to have no face," but their strong personalities and metaphysical presuppositions keep breaking through their texts.

Postmodernism has a history in French post-1968, post–Frankfurt School thought influenced by Nietzsche, Saussure, and structuralism. But postmodernists deny their own origins and are thus blind to their own presuppositions and metaphysics. Their philosophies are not artistic productions (*jouissance de texte*), because they would then be open to deconstruction, endless supplementation, and fragmentation; that is, their own methods would be applied to their texts. If deconstruction can be deconstructed, then it can say nothing absolute about history and society. But postmodern philosophers clearly want to say something universal about this new epoch, to clear away modernist ideological narratives and prescribe a new set of discursive rules. They end up creating grand metaphysical systems that violate their own deconstructive method.

Metaphysics that denies metaphysics, philosophy that denies philosophy (logos, telos, *arché*), is simply contradictory. A social theory that denies theory and any possible social action (except textual criticism) should be subject to a final deconstruction, which should liberate philosophy from deconstruction. If deconstruction itself cannot be deconstructed, then it is not a methodology; that is, if a method cannot be applied to itself, then it cannot be defended or justified. So deconstruction becomes an attitude, a pose, hip sophistry incapable of changing social reality.

The apparent radicalism of deconstruction is illusory. In actuality it is profoundly quietistic and socially reactionary. Inverting hierarchy only creates new hierarchy. Deconstruction is only reasoning by analogy, with no anchor in world process and therefore no chance of changing reality. If there is at least one fact that can be established (a glance at any scientific journal will yield many), then the world is not merely a text (signs, symbols). The signifiers postmoderns chain together must ultimately be tested against a signified (concept) and referent (fact)— against some sort of reality. But then linear temporality is once again valid, events become concrete, and master theory is restored to its rightful place. High science—evolution, quantum physics, genetics—once again serve as models for knowledge and action.

Nor does deconstruction succeed as rhetoric. Nothing is more metaphysical than saying that "the world is a text" operating in our collective unconsciousness. If this is true, then it cannot be said without violating its own premise. How did these authors discover an unconscious, unknown, but universal textuality hidden to everyone else? How can deconstruction discover the hidden universals underlying discourse? What is the relation between language, signs, symbols, and the subconscious?

Denial of reason (logos, arché, telos, causality, linear thought) is a denial of the capacity of language to communicate. Signifiers (without signifieds pointing to referents in some reality) become unreadable hieroglyphics that destroy the possibility of grammatical rules. Universal textuality lacks meaning and cannot construct meaning from within by chaining signs together. Signs can be linked by "differences"; but such a theory eliminates meaning and communicability. Juxtaposition of signs is not grammar; juxtaposition of texts is not critique. Deconstruction allows no reconstruction. Postmodern nihilism is so profound that it cancels postmodern philosophy altogether. As the joke goes: "Who put the 'con' in 'deconstruction?'"

The only defense for these philosophies is honestly to admit that these are semiotic critiques (drawing on Fernand de Saussure, Vladimir Propp, Theodor Adorno, French structuralism) of the Frankfurt School's failed project of sexual and social liberation; that is, critiques of left modernism. In fact, postmodernism draws its central themes from the Frankfurt School: the critique of modernist reason, Adorno's "constellations" of meanings (compare Foucault's epistemes), the pervasive nature of power relations, pessimism about finding social agents of liberation.

Jacques Derrida's critique of "logocentrism" mechanically reverses Edmund Husserl's theory of meaning. Postmodernism substitutes scholastic textual interpretation for the incisive negativity of Herbert Marcuse's dialectics and thus loses all predictive capacity. Postmodernity's nihilism reflects its own methodological shortcomings. There is a great deal of philosophical continuity between modernity and postmodernity, but postmodernism lacks the creative speculative imagination of the Frankfurt School and even the poetry of Nietzsche's manic depressive narcissism. Perhaps for this reason it hotly denies any roots in modernity and claims to be an absolute break with the past.

This claim is rubbish. There are no decisive "breaks" in history; this is merely a literary device. Postmodern philosophy does not provide a secure foundation for a new world view or culture. It represents the despairing critique of a failed New Left, which is already fading in relevance as we retreat in time from the events of the 1960s.

The Political Implications of Postmodernism

This rather critical look at postmodern philosophy makes it seem extreme and schematic. These it is, but it does reflect a mood and an attitude shift in a mass public of the Global North facing the loss of affluence, intractable environmental limits, complex social conflicts, and lack of clear answers to major problems; in effect, a failure of nerve.

Developed nations, those having knowledge/information economies, show increased concern for personal autonomy, quality of life,

risk aversion, community, participation, feminism, lifestyle engineering, multiculturalism, and environmental and global problems; all elements of the postmodern temper. Not all aspects of postmodernism
are constructive, however, and we should be disturbed by its nihilism,
which reflects the political dangers of the millennium.

Allow me to sketch some political and social implications of postmodernism. Postmodern hypercapitalism is dedicated to rapid con-
tinual turnover of crucial indicators of power and status, without considering the costs to nature. As Pierre Bourdieu noted,

> Aesthetic intolerance can be terribly violent. Aversion to differ-
> ent life-styles is perhaps one of the strongest barriers between
> the classes; class endogamy is evidence of this. . . . Economic
> power is first and foremost a power to keep economic necessity
> at arm's length. This is why it universally asserts itself by the
> destruction of riches, conspicuous consumption, squandering, and
> every form of gratuitous luxury.[3]

Elite status is symbolized by the ability to purchase expensive islands
of safety and comfort in a sea of social breakdown, violence, and pollution. The virtual realities of computer networks, interactive mass media,
drug-induced states (Prozac), lifestyle engineering, and psychosocial
services create an elite economy. A transnational underground economy
run by criminal syndicates (Mafia, Camorro, Ndrangheta, Triads, Yakuza,
Mafiya, and many national groups) operates at the expanding margin
of the global economy and controls a piece of the world's GNP equal to
the oil trade. The drug trade is estimated to equal the U.S. federal budget, and money laundering runs at $500 billion a year. This nightmarish
dynamic of ecological destruction could accelerate social breakdown,
violent conflict over reduced resources, epidemiological crisis, human
population crash, and major species extinctions. Many bioscientists
whom I interviewed hold such a pessimistic assessment of the human
future.[4]

The old Cold War ideologies, right and left, reactionary and radical,
are too exhausted to do the work of mass mobilization and organization. Nor is corporativist mass mobilization politics useful in today's
disintegrated and disarticulated global economy. Postmodern politics is
based on fragmented, localized single-issue groups without permanent
or tangible organization; business, community groups, greens, women,
pro-abortion and pro-life groups, Indian, black, gay, animal rights groups,
AIDS and victim groups. It also includes libertarians, anarchists, terror-

ists, militias, ecstatic religions, ultranationalists, racists, fascists, and various types of pathological marginals. All of these have web pages on the Internet.

Single-issue politics leads to fluid opportunistic coalitions, built around sophisticated information networks. Groups use symbolic action and media events to lever state resources and commitments or to veto the initiatives of other powerful groups. Spectacle, media events, psychodrama, violence, terrorism, all present images of power. Such virtual politics leads to no permanent change or coherent policy but is reactive, Machiavellian. The political continuity of such groups is provided not by organization but by a widespread if thin consensus on postmodern feelings and values.

Since the state plays the same game of event-creation, to maintain the illusion of being in control, these fragmentary groups have great power potential. The state cannot repress or manipulate such evanescent groups, but it can co-opt their symbols, discourse, and minor demands. Official politics is reduced to the lowest forms of crisis management. Legislators appeal to such a diversity of groups and transnational corporations that they must continuously adjust policies and allegiances to changing group dynamics. Instead of being leaders they are ciphers, and their illegitimacy increases with time. Politics becomes a series of catastrophes and escapes; soap opera for the mass media. Democracy, without a coherent civil society or common socialization in agreed values, is impossible.

Ramashray Roy's description of Indian politics may provide a model for the postmodern state.

> The merry-go-round of factional fights puts one faction in power, but then rival factions immediately mount a campaign to dislodge the winner from office. For such a campaign, any issue will do as it is usually a proxy for a personal drive for power and position. . . .
>
> Unsatisfied demands for access to resources force aspirant groups to mobilize traditional sociocultural referents of identity formation to seek political advantage. . . . The gate barring political violence is opened. Finally, in the acutely competitive game of politics, survival and ascendance depend upon . . . bringing about a nexus between politics and corruption.[5]

The old political ideologies, increasingly out of touch with these changes, become reactionary, realigning their rhetoric to capture xenophobic, ultranationalist, anarchist, fascist, and fanatical religious movements, which have been following their own weird agendas by organizing into cults, street gangs, and militias. Contestatory, violent, or terrorist single-issue politics is ultimately impossible for elites to manage. Negotiated balances of interest are disallowed by passionate mobilization, extreme positions, and group impermanence. Politicians become adept at symbolic mediation, co-opting the rhetoric and signs of contradictory movements, granting the most minimal popular demands, while mainly satisfying the demands of powerful transnational corporations and banks, which can punish states with disinvestment, liquidity crises, destabilization, and depression.

International environmental groups are masters of the new politics. Amassing large funds through emotive appeals to mass constituencies—one cannot say memberships as there is little reciprocity, organization, or member influence on leadership policy—these "checkbook organizations" pursue conservation pilot projects and litigation. They have, over time, moderated their interests and language to fit the logic of corporate power. The big ten environmentalist groups and establishment elites have a great deal in common, both being parts of the postmodern information bourgeoisie. There is a growing distance between highly credentialed and well-paid leaders and their members, who are more radical, passionate, and consistent than the elites claiming to represent them. Environmental issues require sustained global regulation of production, consumption, transportation, and waste disposal and are ill-served by the virtual politics of postmodernism.

I believe that we are justified in taking a rather dark view of the impacts of postmodern transition on civil society, economy, and the state. Capitalist elites that have fostered this globalized economy and culture are either dangerously naive in thinking that capitalism is self-regulating and social equilibrium automatic or vicious in not caring about the social effects of their actions as long as they can purchase safety and comfort amidst the social breakdown they themselves have fostered.

Nonetheless, the philosophers of postmodernism have pointed to new trends in public opinion that correspond to the creation of a new knowledge/service elite and its insertion into a globalized economy. A new set of attitudes has arisen, and these have both negative and positive indications for the future. At least postmodern culture, among its central values, does give priority to environmentalism and risk aversion, on which the philosophers, usually the vanguard on such issues, have missed out.

Postmodernism/Postmaterialism: A Look at the Data

Let us look at the data about this transition to postmodernism (or its polling proxy, "postmaterialist" culture), to see whether this view of postmodernism finds empirical support. There being no poll data directly addressing the broader implications of postmodern cultural values, I turn to the more narrowly cast postmaterialist poll data as an indication of this transition. If we can model the postmodern value complex, and map this transition in the Global North and South, then we can explore its implication for environmentalism and the new politics.

Postmodern values, such as personal autonomy, quality of life, risk aversion, personal autonomy, self-expression, libertarian lifestyles, community, participation, confessional subjectivity, multiculturalism, and environmental and global concern, are popular but not uniform across social sectors or generations. So the picture is complex, and there are measurement and definitional problems in this poll data. Shifts in mass values are quite difficult to measure and change with the choice of definitions and variables, so that postmodernism is neither easy to characterize nor easy to utilize as a longitudinal variable.

Polls on environmental attitudes have been run in most developed nations, and there is an extensive database of Eurobarometer surveys spanning two decades, all of which attest to a postmodern/postmaterialist attitude shift. Ronald Inglehart's analyses of opinion in developed nations since the 1970s show that each successive generation is less "materialist" and more "postmaterialist," so that population succession creates a large shift in values. Inglehart offers two hypotheses. The "scarcity hypothesis" argues that prosperity leads to increased postmaterialism, but that this should fluctuate with short-term economic swings or "period effects." The "socialization hypothesis" argues that values reflect preadult experiences, so that there are long-term "cohort effects" in which gradual population turnover leads to value change. The cohort effect may be overwhelmed by period effects, but in the long term, cohorts (generations) do not become more materialist as they age. Between 1880 and 1965, the ratio of materialists to postmaterialists shifted from 53/5 percent to 22/26 percent in Germany; from 45/5 percent to 22/15 percent in Britain; and from 67/2 percent to 27/20 percent in Spain. Controlling for inflation and unemployment, there is a significant trend toward postmaterialism in eight countries of Europe.[6]

American surveys show the older cohort retaining materialist values to a higher degree than Europeans but younger generations rapidly making the postmaterialist shift. Europeans have shifted rapidly, adopting to the new information economy, while the United States is stagnant: in the 1980s, materialists and postmaterialists were roughly equal in number. But postmaterialists are more educated, articulate, and politically active and have influence disproportionate to numbers.[7]

There are several criticisms of the postmaterialist opinion shift. Inglehart's statement indicators of postmaterialism are drawn from Maslow's hierarchy of needs, which presuppose that rising affluence lessens the need for sustenance and safety and increases postmodern demands for autonomy, belonging, self-esteem, and aesthetic-intellectual pursuits. While there is a correlation between affluence and postmodern values, it is not clear why elites, who have always been affluent, have not always been correspondingly "postmaterialist." Were not postmaterialist values such as self-realization, aesthetics, and recreation age-old pursuits of the aristocracy?

Albert Weale opposes the use of a slow-moving variable such as "political culture" to explain rapid changes in voting patterns. Kitschelt and Hellemans agree that supporters of "new politics" parties are largely postmaterialist, but they find Inglehart's causal argument for value change indeterminate. Green party post-materialism could also be explained by generational, period, or life-cycle effects. Inglehart's battery of questions is a "very crude measure of the extensive, complex value system it is supposed to tap," according to Oddbjorn Knutsen, who goes on to argue that "it is, of course, not formally correct to make inferences of value concerns by comparing value priorities that are based on rankings from different sets. Each value is ranked only in relation to other values in the same battery."[8]

The "materialist-postmaterialist" scale is too rigid, historical, and deterministic to capture the complexity of changing attitudes, according to Bo Reimer. His factor analysis of Swedish youth attitudes shows a "multitude of different, personal directions" a "plurality and ambiguity" of values, which cannot be aligned on a single scalar. Liisa Uusitalo found that Finnish youth, although interested in environmental protection, were the least willing of the age cohorts to support collective measures because of their libertarian and hedonistic outlook. Knutsen found that the association between age and political values became weaker in Scandinavia from 1975 to 1987, and that these "period effects" cast doubt on Inglehart's contention that the postmaterialist proportion of the public will necessarily increase in future. There are arguments about the dimensionality of this value shift. When a rating method is substituting for ranking, people hold both types of values, according to Bean and Papadakis. De Graaf and Evans argue that postmaterialism is not correlated to formative affluence, and that it is a measure of progressive liberalism rather than of postmaterialism. The debate surges back and forth on these methodological issues.[9]

Jorgen Goul Andersen's study of Danish Greens found a postmaterialist dimension but no generational effect and only very weak associations with education and social class. There was no relation between postmaterialist values and affluence; the division really lies between wage earners and the self-employed. Controlling for education, class, and age make attitudinal differences between workers and the new middle class disappear; unskilled workers are even slightly more environmentalist than the middle class. The "new politics" model was also disconfirmed, as a ranking of parties on a scale of environmentalism corresponds almost exactly with the left-right scale. Inglehart's "dilemma of the left" was likewise disconfirmed: environmental issues did not divide the Danish working class. Bernt Aardal found that postmaterialist values were declining in Norway, from 9 to 7 percent between 1981 and 1987, and that the relationship between political values and age has grown weaker in all Nordic countries in the 1980s. Sixty-eight percent of those supporting environmental protection also supported economic growth. "Old politics" issues of welfare and employment were decisive in the electoral fate of three parties supposedly representing postmodern new politics.[10]

Markus Kreutzer finds that postmaterialists spread their votes more evenly than expected between left and right, and that there is a low youth vote for Swiss Greens. The "unconventional political behavior" of the new politics finds acceptance among materialists as well as postmaterialists. But the dimension of opposition to or support for the social order does not correspond to materialist/postmaterialist cleavages. An added dimension measuring dissatisfaction with party or government performance or the incapacity of government to meet new needs is required to explain why postmaterialists do not slip into apolitical privatism, and why new politics parties also capture materialist votes. Hofrichter and Reif argue that cognitive/emotional attitude dimensions are different from actual behavior. Austrian Greens provide a vehicle for postmaterialist demands and for voting against the system. Green politics canalizes participation by symbolizing threats to collective goods, fear of dangerous technologies, and personal stress.[11]

Postmodern/postmaterialist survey data show strong attitude shifts in the mass public, but the question is open as to whether this effect is evanescent and transitional or the harbinger of a new culture. The same question was asked about the Renaissance: Is it the decay product of Medieval culture or a new stage in history?[12] Such attitudinal shifts may prove to be temporary conjunctural effects, rapidly superseded by other more immediate issues, or may be absorbed into a thin postmaterialist consensus, which can be cynically used by elites to update the creaky left-right ideologies of the Cold War.

Postmodernism may be a transitional phenomenon as the post-Fordist globalized economy impacts the economies of major world regions and makes full employment a thing of the past. The current wave of neoliberal ideological hegemony, beginning with the collapse of the Soviet Union in 1989, will naturally be accompanied by postmodern values of subjectivity, libertarianism, hyper-consumerism, stress on social differentiation through lifestyle engineering, deemphasis on social class politics, multiculturalism concomitant with a globalized economy, calls for deregulation, and so forth. As the social problems inherent in this model begin to manifest themselves, there could well be another swing of the ideological pendulum in the direction of state regulation and international treaty regimes to control the effects of transnational corporate power on socioeconomic and environmental factors.

Environmental Concern North and South: Is It Postmodern?

Environmentalism, although a good postmodern indicator, is more fundamental than a culture shift because it is based on serious global threats to life on this planet. Ideologies may surge and flow across the face of these realities, but environmental issues are not merely "social constructs" and cannot be argued or deconstructed away. The test of this proposition is that the Global South countries surveyed in this book evince few signs of a postmodern shift in values, yet their mass publics show high levels of environmental concern, and the elites of these countries are fully aware of coming environmental crises and are actively moving to meet these challenges.

There are three perspectives on the question of the underlying motivation of environmentalism. The first is Inglehart's postmaterialism, the view that environmentalism stems from a shift of values from materialism to postmaterialism, as a result of sustained affluence. The second is the sociological perspective that the decline of the industrial working class from a post–World War II high of 50 percent of the work

force to under 20 percent today opens space for new middle-class social movements embracing feminism, environment, peace, and antinuclear views.

The third is the economic view that environmental quality is a luxury
good purchased only after a population has attained affluence. The
negative side of this view is that the Third World poor are the worst
polluters because survival dictates a high discount rate on the future
value of nature. This view is found in the Brundtland Commission and
Garret Hardin's "tragedy of the commons" thesis.

All three of these views support the neoliberal conclusions of
the United Nations Conference on Environment and Development
(UNCED) in Rio de Janeiro 1992: that sustainable development can only
be attained through GNP growth and free trade, which will (eventually) bring the poor the affluence needed for them to conserve nature.
In this view, environmental concern is a luxury for the Global South.
Economic growth must not be limited by environmental regulation.

The three theories—political, sociological, and economic—underlying this neoliberal view of sustainable development are wrong. The
data show that the poor of the Global South are intensely concerned
about environmental issues. A 1993 international Gallup survey showed
high levels of environmental concern in both industrialized and developing nations, with the latter manifesting stronger concern about the
issues. The proportions of "great" versus "moderate environmental
concern" were the following: Canada 32/57 percent, United States 38/
47 percent, Britain 28/53 percent, Japan 23/43 percent, Mexico 50/33
percent, Brazil 53/27 percent, Korea 22/58 percent, Russia 41/37 percent, and India 34/43 percent. Note that in all cases the total percentages of environmental concern are exceedingly high.[13]

Between January and April 1997, Environics Ltd. of Canada ran the
largest survey yet, of twenty-seven thousand people in twenty-four
countries. The results show strong support for environment in both
North and South. "A majority of people in 15 of the 24 countries agreed
with the view in one question that 'we should assume the worst and
take major action now to reduce human impacts on climate, even if
there are major costs.' In another seven countries, pluralities share this
view. No majority or plurality in any country took the opposite view."[14]

In contrast to U.S. opinion, which divided evenly on taking action
on climate change (46–46%), the percentages of respondents "in favor
of strong action on climate change are: France, 74 percent; Germany,
71 percent; Italy, 71 percent; Switzerland, 70 percent; Japan, 69 percent;

Korea, 69 percent; Australia, 67 percent; New Zealand, 65 percent; Canada, 61 percent; Chile, 61 percent; the Netherlands, 58 percent; Finland, 54 percent; United Kingdom, 52 percent; Mexico, 50 percent; Spain, 49 percent."

Environmentalism stems from strong health concerns. "Asked if their children's health has been affected, overwhelming majorities (84 percent to 97 percent) in twenty-three of the twenty-four countries replied 'a great deal' or 'fair amount.' Only in Japan were results significantly lower at 70 percent."

Differences between the Global South and North emerged in the relative weight to be given environmental protection versus economic growth. "Asked if environmental protection is more important than economic growth, those in agreement comprised just 27 percent of citizens in Nigeria (down from 30 percent in 1992), 32 percent in Poland (down from 58 percent), 39 percent in Hungary (down from 53 percent), 44 percent in Mexico (down from 71 percent), and 47 percent in Russia (down from 56 percent)." These countries are all heavily impacted by economic recession.

"Countries with the largest percentage of people who agree that environmental protection is more important than economic growth include: Canada (73 percent), Switzerland (73 percent), the Netherlands (72 percent), Germany (71 percent), Finland (70 percent), United Kingdom (69 percent), USA (69 percent), South Korea (63 percent) and Japan (60 percent). In each of those countries, the result was virtually the same or significantly higher than in 1992." Furthermore,

> Majorities in 23 of the 24 participating countries agree with the statement: "The clean-up and protection of the environment, in itself, will contribute significantly to the growth of our economy." Some 75 percent of the populations in 10 of the 24 countries agreed with this statement.

> People in the survey gave bad marks to most governments for their environmental efforts. Majorities in 17 of the 24 countries rated their national government's performance in addressing environmental problems "very poor" or "poor." The Ukraine and Italy (81 percent), South Korea (77 percent), Japan (76 percent) Russia (76 percent) and Hungary (71 percent) have the largest majorities of people who disapprove of their national government's efforts.

> Governments receiving the best environmental performance ratings from their citizens were The Netherlands (just 34 percent said "very poor" or "poor"), Nigeria (41 percent), Switzerland

(41 percent), the USA (43 percent), Chile (45 percent), China (48 percent) and Canada (49 percent).

Note that the approval ratings for government action on environment are low at best. These results did not vary greatly by gender, age, income, or community size.

Riley Dunlap ran a survey of twenty-four nations and found that low-income countries expressed more concern for environment than did high-income nations. People in poor nations (under U.S. $5,000 per capita income) were more likely than the affluent to see negative health impacts from environmental degradation and were more likely to favor specific environmental protection measures. This is not surprising, as 1 billion people lack access to clean water and 1.7 billion lack adequate sanitation. There are 900 million cases of diarrheal disease per annum and 3 million children die from these disorders. Some 200 million suffer from schistosomiasis or bilharzia and 900 million from hookworm; not to mention typhoid, paratyphoid, tuberculosis, dengue fever, cholera, and AIDS.

Majorities in twenty-one nations, and pluralities in two, chose environmental protection over economic growth. Dunlap concludes that postmaterialism and new social movements may explain environmentalism in the Global North but cannot explain the widespread public concern and grassroots movements in the Global South, which are driven not by lifestyle issues but by survival. He concludes: "The old assumption that non-industrialized nations will not worry about environmental protection until they have achieved economic development is incorrect."[15]

Robin Broad cites studies showing that 1 billion people live unsustainably at or below subsistence levels, 3 billion live sustainably at or below carrying capacity, and 1.25 billion of the world's population are unsustainable overconsumers. His extensive Philippines fieldwork showed that peasants were strongly future oriented and became environmental activists when they had roots in the area and had some form of land tenure, when civil society was organized and politicized, and when the subsistence base was threatened either by migrants or by corporations forcibly enclosing the commons. Corporate extraction of resources for immediate sale on the global market reduced the peasants to desperation and created strong political mobilization. The corporations were engaged in the very short-term pillage of which they accuse the peasants.[16]

His findings are backed by ethnographic data showing that tribal peoples pillage their environment when outsiders begin enclosing it or introduce a monetary economy. But tribal peoples also learn to conserve their resources when there is an economic, cultural, or survival motive to do so.[17]

Inglehart's 1993 World Values Survey of ninety-six countries shows that 96 percent of the people were favorable toward the ecology movement: 62 percent "strongly approved" of it and 34 percent approved. Tax increases for environment were approved by 65 percent of the sample. He argues that postmaterialism is a weak factor in low-income countries because few people hold these values. Materialist concern with environment is more prominent, given that pollution is life threatening. Industrializing countries show more pollution (i.e., survival motivation), while affluent countries show higher levels of postmaterialism. "The result is that, in global perspective, neither high pollution levels nor high levels of postmaterialism appear to have significant impact on support for environmental protection." He argues that postmaterialist values are correlated to affluence and negatively correlated with pollution and underdevelopment. Inglehart admits that the materialist-postmaterialist shift is itself only one aspect of a much broader value shift.[18]

The problem with the postmaterialism value-change perspective goes even deeper. Postmaterialists average 22 percent of citizens in low- to middle-income countries and 39 percent in high-income countries, a 17-point spread. Yet the percentage of the population with postmaterialist values, minus the materialists, does not attain the status of a positive number. Materialists in low- to middle-income countries show a mean support for environmental protection of 2.8, while postmaterialists show a mean of 2.9.

Twenty-two percent of citizens in the Global South are postmaterialist, but 62 percent score high on the environmental index. Affluence is clearly a poor predictor of environmental concern within both developed and underdeveloped societies, cutting to the core of Inglehart's affluence thesis based on Maslow's hierarchy of needs. According to the postmaterialist, sociological, and economic theses, environmental concern should directly correlate to national income. It does not.

Inglehart's model does not characterize any country as postmaterialist or materialist; there is only a trend toward the former. Does higher concern and willingness to pay for environmental protection indicate that environment is a materialist value in the Global South? The argument that poor countries are environmentalist because of a combination of pollution plus a high percentage of postmaterialist values (Lee and Kidd) cannot be proven from the survey data. Arguing that pollution accounts for materialist environmental concern is a logical fallacy that makes the postmaterialist thesis nonfalsifiable!

Riley Dunlap stated that "rather than creating a false dichotomy in which environmental concern must be attributed either to post-materialist values or to exposure to environmental degradation, we should concentrate on 'unpacking' the diverse ways in which people form environmental perceptions and how those perceptions are influenced by conditions at varying geographic scales and differing time horizons."[19]

Dunlap is right, and the Q-method protocol in this book was designed precisely to differentiate the types of environmental concern in the Global South. These resultant seven types are arrayed on some indicative statements that point toward postmodern environmentalism and post-Fordist globalized economy. This general model is admittedly imperfect because fieldwork could not be designed in 1989 to account for the changes that would occur by 1999, but the array is consistent with ideological shifts in the North and has explanatory value in the nations of the Global South examined in the present work. Independent of the overall model used here, the factorial types are robust across countries and cover the range of environmental attitudes.

Thus, environmental concern is strongly generalized in both northern and southern publics. The prevailing thesis, that environmental concern comes only with affluence and that therefore development and free trade are essential prerequisites to environmental regulation, is simply wrong. The data have piled up against such assertions. Inglehart's postmaterialism does not account for environmentalism because environmental concern does not correlate with income. The sociological argument about new social movements in affluent middle-class countries does not explain the plethora of active contestatory environmental movements in the poor Global South. Economic arguments that environment is a luxury good, and that peasants are the main polluters, are false because they lump all primary producers together in one utilitarian set of motivations. Economics has a bad habit of mistaking doctrine for reality, and short-circuiting field investigation into empirical realities with spuriously "scientific" models. The discount rates of peasants with roots in the area and land tenure turn out to be quite low; they care about future generations and their local ecology. Field studies show that peasants and tribal people can destroy nature when they must compete with corporate enclosures of their commons, but they also can learn to conserve and use nature sustainably, even when they are forced into a market economy against their will.

Political science, sociology, and economics have all contributed to the neoliberal error of postponing environmental regulation until the entire world reaches some requisite level of affluence.

Our findings run contrary to this consensus. Our field data show that despite the linguistic, cultural, religious, and political diversity of our seven-nation sample, environmental elites held common transnational attitudes as the basis of their decision making. Elite attitudes toward environment were truly international rather than culturally specific and could be captured in seven transnational attitude types; thus, the political culture model does not function.

The government, business, environmentalist, scientific, and journalistic elites interviewed in this study were in most cases foreign educated, internationally networked, and fluent in English. This internationalization was less obvious in Iran and Romania, which have been marginalized from the global economy up to now, but even in these countries there was heightened perception of the international dimension and responsiveness to cross-boundary pressures and international treaty regimes and standards.

Thus, postmodernism is not important as a new philosophy, nor as a new form of national political culture, but represents the reception of some new values and themes in the postwar cohort in the developed world and by internationalized elites in the Global South. Inglehart characterizes postmaterialist values as "protecting freedom of speech; giving people more say in important government decisions; a less impersonal, more humane society; giving people more say on the job and in their communities; a society in which ideas count more than money."[20]

These sorts of "left-libertarian" values are rare in the Global South. But we speculate that the environmental component of postmodernism is the most permanent value in the ensemble because it is driven by threatening objective conditions, which can only become worse and which pose evident problems of national (and elite) security and continued economic viability. Other postmodern values—concern for subjectivity, personal autonomy, quality of life, risk aversion, community, participation, feminism, lifestyle engineering, multiculturalism, and global problems—may or may not become salient in developing nations, but the environmental problem cannot be ignored or superseded by other concerns, and it must become increasingly central to international discourse as time goes by.

We utilize postmodernism as an elite value dimension, a vertical axis, in our model of transition to a new environmental politics. Postmodernism should be read not as postmaterialism or deconstructive philosophy but rather as an "environmental post-modernism," cautious, risk-averse, concerned, active, and aware about ecology. The horizontal axis is provided by the post-Fordist model of a globalized hypercapitalist economy. To this model we now turn.

Post-Fordism: The New Globalized Economy

Postmodern philosophical analyses and postmaterialist poll data are superstructural to millennial political economy, the transition from Fordism (economic modernism) to post-Fordism (the global economy of knowledge, sign, information, and event production within world networks of production and communication).[21]

Post-Fordist political economy offers a rich description of the ongoing globalization of world economy and civil society, driven by the new technologies of the quaternary sector—supercomputing, artificial intelligence, global telecommunication, remote sensing, robotics, biotechnology, fine chemistry and engineering, new materials sciences, complexity theory. A sophisticated successor of Dependency theory, post-Fordism as yet lacks causal analytic explanation or alternative policy prescriptions. But given that no other economic theory offers deep explanatory or policy dimensions, its usefulness in englobing these rapidly changing times is beyond doubt.

Since the 1970s, the developed world has been in transition to a post-Fordist form of production. *Fordism,* a term coined by Antonio Gramsci, was based on a triangular relationship of corporate business (mass production), big labor (mass consumption), and the welfare-warfare state (which provided socioeconomic regulation, full employment, and Cold War ideological pressure). Alain Lipietz defines Fordism as a mode of capital accumulation based on constant technical change, which incorporates workers' know-how into mechanized production. Taylorization systematized work into a microscopic division of labor and separated technical conception from unskilled execution. Fordism's welfare state raised mass consumption to meet the productivity gains of increased capital intensity. Workers' nominal income steadily improved to allow mass consumption of standardized commodities and to support monopolistic pricing by corporations that created and controlled demand for their own goods through advertising.[22]

Maintained by U.S. hegemony and the cultural terrorism of the Cold War, Fordism created a stable culture and world economy from 1914 to 1980. The welfare state stabilized the business cycle using Keynesian countercyclical fiscal and monetary stimulation and contraction and incorporated big business and organized labor into corporativist forms of dispute resolution. Developed Fordist states encouraged "sub-Fordist" regimes in Third World countries under the ideology of "modernization" or "developmentalism," claiming to pull all nations along the same historical trajectory through aid programs, controlled technology transfer, debt leverage, and political or military intervention.

This world economy was stratified into core, semiperiphery, and periphery, with multinational corporations and banks acting as agents of the core in creating "associated dependent development" in developing nations.

Peripheral sub-Fordist regimes engage in "import substitution industrialization." As Lipietz describes the process, "the object was to accumulate primary export incomes in consumption goods industries by buying capital goods in the core and by protecting these fledgling industries by customs barriers. The hope was that it would then be possible to move upstream toward the production of capital goods."[23] Peripheral societies adopted Fordist mass production and consumption, without modernizing social class or land tenure. Industrial growth was confined to urban centers and regional enclaves, without forward or backward linkages to the rest of the economy.

Lipietz argues that technology transfer did not create modern labor relations in the Global South, and thus international competitiveness was not attained. Once the early gains of "easy import substitution" (extensive development) declined, peripheral states were unable to fund the technological transformation of industry (intensive development). Highly stratified societies could not provide enough market demand to drive capital accumulation. Exports of raw material and low-tech goods into protected core markets were insufficient for capitalization or debt service.[24]

By the late 1960s, Fordism had fallen into crisis. The United States, driven by bureaucratic momentum and strategic and economic misconceptions, lost its hegemony in the Vietnam War, spending $131 billion dollars to kill 1.9 million Vietnamese. U.S. abrogation of Bretton Woods monetary agreements and floating of the dollar marked the end of U.S.

hegemony and the beginning of serious competition from Japan, the NICs or Newly Industrializing Countries (Korea, Taiwan, Singapore, Hong Kong), and the European Community.

The postwar curve of growth and productivity peaked in the 1970s, as the cheap energy subsidies that drove the system were withdrawn. World War II technology began to age, environmental problems increased, and a wave of revolutions (Iran, Nicaragua, Grenada, El Salvador, Guatemala, Panama, Libya) led to expensive countermeasures like low-intensity conflict, destabilization, and invasion. Iran and Libya are oil powers and Guatamala has oil reserves equal to 10 percent of U.S. demand, but the rest were ideological rather than strategic conflicts, which helped delegitimize U.S. hegemony and induce a fiscal crisis of the state.

The modernist Keynesian-Fordist welfare state was beset by simultaneous stagnation and inflation, declining corporate productivity and profitability, a fiscal crisis of the state including the bankruptcy of major cities, and unregulated offshore wildcat banking. The state was "overloaded" by demands and protest from antiwar, black, indigenous, solidarity, feminist, gay, anti-abortion, and religious right movements and stooped to repression (Cointelpro, Watergate, Irangate, low-intensity conflict), thus losing some of its legitimacy.

Elites responded to the mass mobilizations of the 1960s and 1970s with reactionary social policies. Corporations successfully used mass media to deflect popular anger from themselves to the state, which neoliberalism was designed to dismantle. The "capitalist counterrevolution" assimilated New Left personalist rhetoric in order to convert liberation into Yuppie consumerism. In the 1980s, Reaganism-Thatcherism imposed on developed countries the same authoritarian neoliberalism that had failed to "modernize" the Global South when promoted by the International Monetary Fund. Neoliberalism succeeded in breaking the power of organized labor, facilitating speculative-financial rather than productive uses of capital, globalizing corporate production, eliminating welfare benefits, and creating an "informal economy" of the under- and unemployed, minorities, the poor, street people, and criminal gangs.

Monetarism refused to share profits with the working class or Global South and made workers pay for capitalist globalization by holding their wages below inflation. Deindustrialization of the core, and industry transfer to the Global South, broke union power to bargain collectively for consumption shares and benefits. Drastic cuts in welfare state benefits, elimination of job tenure, widespread temporary contract labor, and high structural unemployment followed. The U.S. stock market crashed in 1987; a liquidity crisis led to a 1994 bankruptcy in Mexico and several other countries, threatening debt repayment and therefore the viability of Northern banks.

This crisis of Fordism and neoliberal reaction mark the emergence of *post-Fordism*, which transformed global industry with information systems, automated but nondedicated assembly lines, elimination of middle management in favor of computer networks, small-batch production of specialty products for niche markets using just-in-time stocking, and the proliferation of nontraditional and speculative financial services. "Multinational corporations," housed in the North and serving its political interests, became truly "transnational" or independent of national policy objectives and regulation.

Advanced telecommunication and computer nets allowed corporations to separate geographically their management-finance-design operations and skilled labor, which remained in the "headquarters countries," from deskilled execution and assembly, which were relegated to the periphery. Transnational corporations have dematerialized into information networks dedicated to creating and saturating micro markets and are rapidly conglomerating in hostile takeovers using virtual capital (derivatives, junk bonds). Corporations respond to rapidly changing fashions, using automated assembly lines, but are no longer identified with a specific product. Hypercapitalism produces "virtual products," intangible positional goods for the world middle class, and these symbols of status and power have tapped an insatiable market. The half-life of modernism's mass produced goods was five to seven years, while the half-life of postmodern goods is under eighteen months. The turnover of status goods, capital, and labor is accelerated, as is environmental damage.

Capitalism has burst the confines of state boundaries. The World Trade Organization, North American Free Trade Association, the European Community, Asia-Pacific Economic Cooperation, Mercosul (Market of the Southern Cone), and so forth are the regional economies of the future. Nation-states are economically unviable, their markets too small and homogeneous to subsidize global production with steep differences in living standards and resource endowments.

Many mass-production industries were closed as the state could no longer subsidize their inefficiencies on Keynesian grounds of providing full employment. Old industrial regions of the core were devastated. The world economy became regionalized as free trade zones, outwork, homework, and *maquiladora* (sweatshop) assembly plants converted key peripheral areas from import substitution to export promotion strategies; what Lipietz calls "Bloody Taylorization."[25] Corporate multisourcing maintains unequal labor relations, as it is possible for TNCs to pass design, development, and production costs to subcontractors, disciplining them through "just-in-time" inventory delivery systems. Corporations engaged in automated small-batch production for niche markets, maintain a near zero stock level by reducing circulating capital and the capital turnover time, with frequent small batch deliveries of needed components from suppliers.[26]

Peripheral assembly industries are Taylorized but with low capital or technical content. They operate with temporary labor, usually youth, women, and minorities. Disadvantaged groups are organized in domestic-patriarchal forms of exploitation backed by terroristic state repression. Transnational corporations ignore the social and environmental costs of production because they deal at arm's length with their subcontractors. Global South regions compete with one another to provide cheap labor and lax environmental, health, and safety standards, to subsidize gentrification of the West's postmodern new class.

Stable-demand commodities are produced in the core with high-tech processes, while peripheral subcontractors satisfy fluctuating demand with the lowest-wage and least capital-intensive processes. Transnational corporations avoid union pressure for homogenization of wages by subcontracting to companies with low wages and high working hours, eliminating highly paid labor in core industries and forcing core workers to compete with Global South labor. Corporations provide little in the way of services, benefits, and security to their employees and pay little heed to the labor conditions or environmental practices of their subcontractors.

A two-tier labor force is created with the major class division between the under- or unemployed, temporarily employed, and low-wage working class, on the one hand, and high-salary workers with job tenure and benefits, on the other. In the North, differences in educational levels between workers and unemployed people is not great. The difference between the employed and unemployed is therefore arbitrary and helps enforce rigorous labor discipline, poor working conditions, low real wages, and steeply increased working hours in advanced nations. The number of workers receiving seniority, sick pay, health care, paid holidays, and retirement is also cut through subcontracting. Lifetime job tenure has now disappeared, as technical and managerial positions have become temporary jobs without benefits. Permanent unemployment remains high, although masked by fraudulent statistics, and leads to a growing sub-minimum-wage and criminal service economy.

Labor conditions have dramatically worsened in both the core and peripheries of the world economy, now that the maquiladora is the model of labor-management relations. Because of the abundance and desperation of labor in the Global South, capitalists no longer pay to reproduce labor power. Children are the main victims in hyper-capitalism. Deregulation and the disintegration of civil society into possessive individualism has left children to be sold for adoption, cheap labor, and prostitution or as organ donors. Thailand has about 800,000 child prostitutes, India about 500,000, Sri Lanka 20,000, Brazil about 200,000; the United States and Canada have up to 300,000. In the post– Cold War era 2 million children were killed, 5 million disabled, 1 million orphaned, 12 million left homeless, and 10 million psychologically traumatized by the incessant petty warfare in the Global South. In the United States, 22 percent of children live in poverty, child abuse and neglect doubled between 1986 and 1993 to 2.8 million cases, serious injuries quadrupled to 570,000, and the percentage of cases investigated declined dramatically.[27]

Global South regions with large middle and trained working classes, substantial capital, natural resources, and markets can enter the world economy as "Peripheral Fordist" areas. These regions are allowed limited import substitution in low-technology industries, making commodities low on the product cycle, and can export capital and secondary goods useful to Northern markets. Thus Mexico's northern border, with more than fourteen hundred maquiladoras, is undergoing Bloody Taylorization while Mexico City develops sophisticated manufactures for export.

Peripheral Fordist regions all hope to emulate the NICs—Korea, Hong Kong, Singapore, Taiwan—by converting dependent industrialization into autonomous growth. But corporations do not transfer high technology, research and development, transportation, communication, infrastructure, or world marketing capacity; the corporations thus perpetuate "associated dependent development" in client regions. Also, most of these regions lack the historical advantages of the Four Little Dragons: land reform, rational agriculture, universal education, high capacity to absorb technology, large capital markets, a modern bureaucratic state (a result of British and Japanese domination), zero population growth, and disproportionately large foreign investment. Thus, their hope of emulating the NICs will remain largely unfulfilled.[28]

The USSR collapsed in 1989 because its technologically backward heavy industry and military-industrial complex were unable to globalize and convert to an information/service economy. Oil recovery costs spiraled upward, and environmental mismanagement became economically devastating. The USSR could not transform an extensive import-substitution (Fordist) economy into an intensive knowledge-based export-driven (post-Fordist) economy.[29]

Permanent unemployment, legal and illegal immigration to the core, and the rise of an underground economy everywhere disarticulate and criminalize civil society and politics. The deregulated neoliberal nation-state grants large shares of public power to corporations, the managers of which serve no constituency or national interest. Democracy becomes a fruitless exercise in electing alternative cliques of crisis managers, a "virtual government" that dare not touch the levers of corporate power.

Postmodern culture provides spectacle, distraction, ephemeral fashion and image, "difference," a virtual reality or simulacrum of culture. Political symbols become part of this hypertext, and political discourse becomes strident nonsense unrelated to policy and incapable of explaining increasingly intractable social problems. The exhaustion of political symbols and discourse is a sign that the very ideologies that led to economic growth and hegemony have become a burden on elites who would invent new solutions to complex social problems—but not to elites driven by greed.

Computer networks provide a simulacrum of democracy and community, as millions of people organize their virtual communication around the "information highway." The mass media come to specialize in sensationalistic personalism, organizing and interpreting the nonevents of crisis politics using pop psychology; producing virtual intimacy with the virtual stars of our times. Stars rise by gaining access to media through extreme or outrageous behavior, and since the media have created them, the same media have the right to savage and exploit them as the cost of keeping their images before the public. The media replace democracy with expensive advertising and image manipulation, requiring politicians to take office burdened by major financial compromises with corporate capital.

The old civil society and ideologies inevitably meet diminishing returns, and their decline causes social chaos in the very societies whose expansion they used to promote. Conservatives advocate using state pressure to restore the "good old days," and "liberal" reformers centralize state power, thereby giving corporate elites undue influence. Revolutionaries end up fighting against their own false analyses rather than against the real power holders. Postmodernism shows all the signs of being the cultural and socioeconomic decay of Fordist modernism, or at least a transitional product, rather than an avant-garde renaissance.

Post-Fordist economy has reverted to early capitalist *Verlagindustrie*, patriarchal domination in small-scale contractor industry. It accelerates extraction of surplus value but excludes most of the world's people from the high-tech marketplace. Post-Fordism may not be a new stage of capitalism at all but a further internationalization of capitalism, globalization of accumulation, intensification of exploitation, and constriction of benefits to all but global elites. Capitalism has historically grown by exporting its crises and out-sourcing its material and labor needs. Post-Fordism may not be a change in kind as much as in scale.

Hypercapitalism may accelerate system breakdown by creating an extremely complex global economy, which is fragile, subject to chaos, and riddled with positive feedback loops that magnify impacts on society and nature way out of proportion to causes. The financial crises of Mexico in 1994, the Barclay's Bank derivatives scandal, and the fiscal problems of the Asian "tigers" in 1998 are symptomatic of the fragility of economies based on speculation.

Will post-Fordism produce a technological ensemble causing take-off into an ascendant long wave of development? Or does it represent the global retrenchment of a failing Fordist modernism? In neither case is the environmental prognosis encouraging. No one can predict the future of the post-Fordist economy, but the theory will be utilized in this book as the most useful first pass at understanding the emergent global economy.

Post-Fordism provides an interesting description and analysis of a transitional global economy and installation of a quaternary sector of information- and knowledge-based production. As a global description it is theoretical and difficult to measure, but it does predict the rise of a new class of postmodern elites and the realignment of party politics to take into account the shift of values. There are data pertaining to these effects, and we will turn now to these data.

3

The New Politics: Postmodernism Left and Right

The millennial change in the world economy and in global attitudes, the shift to post-Fordism and postmodernism, will undoubtedly swing the political spectrum into a new realm of issues and concerns. In this chapter I examine some of these changes; the development of a post-modern new class or information bourgeoisie and the shift in the political spectrum from the old left-right politics to new postmodern ideologies. I focus on the emergent Green parties as examples of the new politics.

These political shifts in the Global North are important, because our field data show that a new political spectrum is also emerging in the Global South and that of the three different kinds of Greens, the new class we term Postmodern Managers holds the balance of power.

Is There a Postmodern "New Class?"

New-class theory holds that post-Fordism—the dominance of service and high-tech sectors, the global production and processing of signs, symbols, knowledge, and events—involves a cadre of women, youth, and information managers who are concerned with lifestyle engineering and environmental issues. This supposed new class stands between owners of capital and the proletariat, between state and citizens, old and new professions, and establishes its distinctive status through lifestyle management. "Its expertise in symbolic communication enables its members to assemble a bricolage of goods and symbols into customized packages that are in some sense unique: the constituent elements came from the commercial marketplace but their uniqueness resides in the ensemble and acts as a symbolic assertion that the New

Class is self-created." Constant creation of "minutely differentiated status distinctions" heightens competitive consumption in hypercapitalism.[1]

This new class manipulates virtual reality and purveys postmodern culture. This "information bourgeoisie" grows rich on wildcat banking, finance, high-tech industry, design, marketing, research and development. Intellectuals and subintellectuals in the service sector cook the symbolic stew of virtual civil society. New postmaterialist elites oppose the old bourgeoisie of modernist Fordism and the new petite bourgeoisie of hustlers and *arrivistes* whose postmodern ideology consists mainly of resentments.

Lifestyle engineering—the attempt to create a holistic life world from the fragmented pieces of postmodern culture—leads its practitioners to ironic self-reference, nihilism, hyperconsumerism, multi-culturalism (a form of intellectual tourism), feminization of culture ("emotional labor") as feelings are publicly self-monitored ("deployment of the private self"), and to media gate keeping of ideologies and public attitudes. The new class mediates a disaggregated world to the bewildered consumer.

Postmodern feminization of culture allows more voice for women, minorities, and the less educated but does not necessarily indicate a new or coherent politics. Pierre Bourdieu's surveys of French social class and lifestyles found that "the more questions deal with problems of daily existence, private life or domestic morality [t]he smaller becomes the gap between men and women or between the least educated and the most educated, and sometimes it disappears completely." The more abstract, political, and scientific a poll question, the greater the gap in response rate between men and women, least and more educated.[2]

Let us examine the data relevant to this new-class model. Ronald Inglehart's Eurobarometer data shows that postmaterialists, candidates for the new class, have better education, higher status, and better jobs and income than materialists but give priority to quality of life over material gain. Salary and job security do not motivate postmodernists as much as do self-esteem, job prestige, and congenial work relations. Postmodernists seek interesting, meaningful work, self-expression, good social settings, status more than income, and intangible goods that publicly manifest quality of life and status.

Materialists and postmaterialists are roughly balanced in top management and civil service, but postmaterialists predominate among younger professionals and managers. Materialism predominates among small business, farmers, and manual workers. Elites are more post-materialist than the mass public. Postmaterialists comprise some 13 percent of the European general public and 33 percent of the European Parliament. Most elite groups in West Germany, for example, are post-materialist: civil servants, university and research administrators, media executives, union and political party leaders. Only business, farm association, and corporation and bank executives, Christian Democrat politicians, and top-ranked military were predominantly materialist.

American survey results showed conflict between modernist economic elites and postmaterialist media, research, and service sector elites regarding which values will be used to socialize the public. The "new politicians," who emerged in the 1970s, differed from modernist politicians in being fiscally conservative, progressive on social issues and provision of public goods, more tolerant of alternative lifestyles and minority rights, populist in style, distrustful of parties, and skill-ful in using mass media to contact their publics.

The new class is interesting theory, but the postmodern service sector it inhabits turns out to be vertically stratified in complex ways. According to Gosta Esping-Anderson, the service class comprises, first, business services—design, engineering, legal, financial, accounting, marketing, system, and software; second are social, health, education, and welfare services, which monetarize the "free" household services of women absorbed into the job market (by downward real wage pressure on the middle class); third are providers of consumer services organizing leisure and surplus income.

Her national occupational classification is the following: (1) The Fordist hierarchy: managers, proprietors, clerical-administrative-sales; skilled manual production workers; unskilled workers; (2) the post-Fordist hierarchy: professionals and scientists; technicians and semi-professionals (teachers, nurses, social workers, laboratory technicians, etc.); and (3) service workers, skilled and unskilled. Esping-Anderson argues that the postmodern economy favored women in the United States but led to gender segmentation in Sweden and Germany. However, ethnic minorities such as American blacks have moved into mid-level services, while Hispanics, like the *Gastarbeiters* in Germany, staff the new postindustrial proletariat.

With high chronic unemployment and temporary employment, the new "job poor" minorities—welfare claimants, housewives, students, pensioners, minimum-wage workers—have no social leverage or basis of social solidarity from which to pressure the system to create jobs. The very existence of an alternative economy worsens work conditions for the employed. The post-Fordist economy has not been successful in creating employment: Argentina, for example, after years of neo-liberal economic adjustment, faces an unemployment rate close to 19 percent, and far from being frictional unemployment, this rate represents a permanent structural loss of jobs. This is typical of post-Fordist nations North and South.[3]

Besides complex vertical stratification, the new class also demonstrates horizontal cleavages. Steven Brint's reanalysis of 1974–80 U.S. survey data showed that new-class theorists have created a fiction by mistaking the confluence of several "period effects" in the late 1970s: "the liberalizing effects of a much expanded higher-education system, the traditional liberalism of a growing category of social and cultural specialists, and the coming of age of a notably liberal cohort." Brint found that education was most correlated to political and personal liberalism, but that the value shift was relatively minor. The new class was not notably egalitarian or anti-business, and social-cultural professionals manifested weak and personalistic, rather than political, dissent from the system.

Thus a significant split exists within the new class between sociocultural services, professional-managerial, and technical occupations. Professional and managerial strata tend toward traditional conservatism but show little sympathy with the radical new right; they are less conservative than standard businessmen. The new right finds support among less educated, blue collar, and small business people, farmers, small town or rural inhabitants, western, older, religious, Protestant males, and those with strong Republican Party identification.[4]

James Savage's reanalysis of Inglehart's 1970s surveys also shows a split between materialists of the left (28%, or 1488/5314 sampled) and right (36%), and postmaterialists of the left (22%) and right (14%). Left postmaterialists double in number as one passes to younger cohorts, while rightist postmaterialists show the same percentages. Left postmaterialists tend to higher-status occupations (69%) than right postmaterialists (59%) or right materialists (57%). Poorer leftists tend to be materialist (50%). Rightist postmaterialists favor economic growth and strong national defense and are more satisfied with life than leftists but less than right materialists. Lower education levels, higher church attendance, and Republican Party identification tend to create rightist postmaterialists. But rightist parties often hold the parliamentary balance and thus are more powerful than their low popularity suggests; rightists also tend to vote more than leftists.[5]

Both right and left postmoderns participate in a shift in the ideological spectrum. There is an unusual commonality of discourse between the new right and new left; both reject central planning as economically irrational; both are critical of the welfare state, but neoliberals want to dismantle it while neoleftists wish to change its orientation. They disagree over self-interested versus social orientations. Both value personal autonomy and freedom, although the new right conceive the crucial split to be market versus state, while the new left wants a democratized civil society to take over more state functions.

Bernice Martin's study of British market researchers finds a paradox in this postmodern new class: they lead single-issue social movements opposing market forces, and yet their personal hedonist consumption ethos serves as a postmodern version of the Protestant work ethic, a point also made by Jean Baudrillard. Thus, "The current Western governments of the New Right have set themselves the problem of how to reprogram the young inheritors of the hedonistic consumption ethic so as to suppress certain desires (for drugs, for instance) and to reestablish the old bourgeois value of restraint."[6]

Feminism, environmentalism, self-realization, subjectivity, personal liberty, and multiculturalism appear to have been co-opted by the capitalist system, and the stratum I call Postmodern Managers uses the new values of autonomy, identity, teamwork, self-expression, participation, quality of life, eccentricity, and irreverence toward tradition as tools for restructuring the workplace and defining desirable commodities to be marketed to the public.[7]

Data on the new-class argument are contested. The model masks a high level of stratification, both horizontal and vertical, within elite blocs, and differing levels of adherence to postmodern values. But new-class arguments usefully point to changed perceptions and a realignment of roles and power relations within elites.

The data in this book show that many Global South elites hold post-Fordist roles and postmodern attitudes toward environment. The data also show a serious split within elites, between a bloc of what we have called Developmentalists, Bureaucratic Nationalists, and Cultural Traditionalists and a bloc of Greens and Sustainable Developers. Postmodern Managers bridge these conflicting blocs and mediate their policy conflicts. This new stratum of managers has an international rather than a nationalistic understanding of its role and is committed to post-

Fordist globalization and many postmodern values, among which are risk aversion and environmental concern.

Given these attitude and cleavage structures, the most striking effect should be realignment of party systems to fit into the new postmodern attitudes and post-Fordist elite roles. Let us examine the data regarding party realignment in the "new politics."

Postmodern New Politics: The Green Parties

Postmodern values differ from the old modernism so significantly that a new spectrum of political parties should emerge to replace the old left-right cleavage of the Cold War period. According to Ronald Inglehart, postmaterialism places the old materialist left in a paradoxical position. Postmaterialist elites tend to vote left, quite against the socioeconomic indicators. They do not respond to class-based ideology and raise issues such as environmentalism, women's and minority rights, antinuclearism, antimilitarism, personal liberty and nonconformity, and urbane lifestyles.

The social base of the left has shifted toward postmaterialism but left ideologies remain materialist, nationalist, and class oriented; a contradiction accounting for the left being fragmented and marginalized. The old left labor union–based parties take materialist positions that downplay the importance of new politics issues. Thus, they support Fordist modernism: economic growth, job security, military strength, nationalism, and domestic order. There is no general right- or leftward shift in this electorate but rather a fragmentation into issue-focused parties and movements. Materialists, including many of the old working class, are likely to support extreme right, nationalist, or fascist parties—Reagan, Thatcher, LePen.

Postmaterialists are single-issue oriented and allergic to the hierarchical corporatist organization of unions and left parties. Thus, the European Greens have a latent electorate as large as 47 percent and pose a threat to the old left. Left votes come increasingly from middle- and upper-middle-class postmaterialists, while the old working class shifts to the right. The Workers' Party, PT (Partido dos Trabalhadores), in Brazil, a postmodern conglomerate of left parties, factions, unions, Church-based communities, and popular movements, finds its greatest vote in Rio de Janeiro within the affluent beach suburbs: Copacabana, Ipanema, Gavea, Leblon, Barra de Tijuca.

Yet, looking at the data, a postmodern attitude shift is not sufficient to explain concrete political realignments in several countries where

Green parties have emerged. There are intervening factors, such as voting systems and party cleavage structures. Evart Vedung makes the point that

> stressing the importance of central political institutions, like political parties and party systems, does not engender the discounting of general, cross-national ideological trends and belief systems. It means that the importance of general ideological trends is translated through the national political party system. . . . The way established institutions and, most notably, the traditional party systems react on new issues are crucial in the establishment of new political parties. If the existing institutional systems provide favorable opportunity structures for new popular movements, there will be no new parties.[8]

Markus Kreuzer's data show that Swiss Greens have a high proportion of left electors but are a moderate, practical environmental party. Because Swiss federalism provides strong citizen initiative, the Green Party of Switzerland, GPS, provides a protest vehicle against neglect of environmental issues by sitting parties, rather than an antisystem vote. In contrast, the VGÖ/ALÖ (United Austrian Greens/Alternative Austrian Greens), with a heterogeneous electorate and large white collar vote, attracts antisystem votes against a restrictive corporatist political system. Finger and Sciarini's study of the Swiss Greens concludes that the left-right party spectrum has co-opted the new environmental politics by redefining traditional platforms. "If this hypothesis is correct, the future cleavage will be less and less about the role and the importance of the state in the organization and the management of society and economy, but about ecology as opposed to economy, regardless of the degree of state intervention."[9]

Evert Vedung shows that Sweden's Green Party was founded in 1981 because of the failure of the five-party system to respond to environmental issues. The Center Party coalition elected in 1976 skillfully incorporated environmental concerns into its program but was forced to compromise on agrotoxics and nuclear power to hold together. The entire party system fell into disrepute during the 1980 referendum on nuclear energy, in which the phrasing was unfairly manipulated. Deliberate confusion of the issue led to defeat of powerful antinuclear forces and the continuation of nuclear power. Antinuclear and Green forces, feeling excluded from the system, formed an autonomous party in 1981 and broke the five-party monopoly by entering parliament in 1988. Their 5.6 percent of the vote represented young urban protest voters; and popular environmental concern rose from 7 to 46 percent during 1982–88.

Bennulf and Holmberg found that Swedish Greens and Communists are the only parties with a majority of postmaterialists. Green voters were 33 percent postmaterialist, and 22 percent materialist in 1988. Green voters could be characterized on a combined left-right and environmental scale. On left-right socioeconomic issues, Greens tend toward the center but distrust politicians and politics. On environmental issues they have strong, coherent, and radical positions.

The Green dimension crosscuts the left-right dimension among Swedish elites. As Bennulf and Holmberg argue, "If one talks about a green alternative dimension in Sweden, it is an elite phenomenon. Until now, constrained green attitudes only exist among educated people highly involved in politics. The green breakthrough in Sweden has not yet created a coherent green dimension in the mass public." Green deputies ranked parties along a Green dimension, while Green voters ranked parties along a left-right continuum. Parliamentarians showed a correlation of 44 percent between self-rankings on left-right and Green scales: that is, the Green continuum crosscuts the left-right continuum transversely.[10]

Bernt Aardal showed that the failure of an independent Green Party in the 1988 Norwegian elections resulted from the lack of political space, the Socialist Left and Liberal parties having already taken up the environmental issue. Norwegians show high environmental concern but low and declining postmaterialism scores (7 percent in 1987), with 68 percent of the population supporting economic growth, productivity, and environmental protection; a mix of modern and postmodern values quite similar to the stance of the Brundtland Commission headed by their ex–prime minister. Left-right conflict over welfare state benefits is still salient. Environmental issues are not decisive for voters but accounted for a shift from the Liberals, who were weak on left-right issues, to the Socialist Left Party, which has a red-green profile, and for the exclusion of a new and untested Green Party.[11]

Jorgen Goul Andersen's study of Danish Greens shows that environmental issues were already captured by the Left Socialists and Socialist People's Party, leaving little political space. Danish left culture is strongly antinuclear and environmentalist with clear generational effects in the expected directions. Ranking of Danish parties along the environmental dimension corresponds almost exactly to the left-right ranking, and this is also true of a self-placement test among parliamentarians. The environmental scale does not crosscut the left-right spectrum but actually reinforces it. Andersen concludes that "it is plausible to suggest that environmentalism is perhaps about to become just another aspect of the left-right dimension—not because it is structurally determined to become a left-right issue, but because of the political articulation of the political parties."[12]

In their study of Belgian Greens (Ecolo/Agalev), Kitschelt and Hellemans show that militants place themselves on the left or far left (54 percent), center left (36 percent), and center right (10 percent). Militants are largely postmaterialist (86 percent), with 1 percent materialist and 13 percent mixed. "By blending postmaterialist, ecological, leftist, and libertarian demands together, ecology parties constitute a 'second left' which defies the conventional alternatives of bureaucratic, statist socialism and liberal free-market capitalism." But old issues of state versus markets are not superseded; "they are transformed and resurface in ecology parties as cleavages concerning the desirability of anticapitalist reforms."[13]

Ferdinand Müller-Rommel's review of European new politics parties found that electoral success depended on the type of party system. Polarized multiparty systems with proportional representation divided new politics votes among small left and more established parties that could take up the issues. In multiparty systems with blocs, separate Green parties existed as vehicles for protest voting against system inflexibility. New politics parties realign and redefine the left-right spectrum by creating conflict within the left. Socialist parties are caught between a centrist majority, a militant new politics constituency, and old left materialists, who could be lost by adoption of postmodern issues. New politics parties can flourish by stealing these divided constituencies. Agile older parties will rebuild themselves around new politics issues, changing their social base but gaining new adherents.[14]

Emergent new politics parties challenge the left as potential competitors as well as allies and could significantly shift the political spectrum toward postmodern issues. Thus Italian Radicals and Greens and the Dutch Political Party of Radicals, Pacifist Socialist Party (both with 90 percent postmaterialist electorates), the Dutch Communist Party, and Democrats (with 60 and 50 percent postmaterialists) are all pulling the spectrum in a new direction. However, in Greece with a strong left-right dimension and a dominant petite bourgeoisie, small parties are marginal and fit comfortably into the old left-right dimension.[15]

Vincent Hoffmann-Martinot's comparison of German and French Greens shows that both have postmaterialist electorates: young, highly educated, new service sector, middle class, urban, in environmental or antinuclear struggles, members of alternative unions, with high political interest and desire for participation, and self-placed on the center-left. German electors are more radical and homogeneous in their postmodernism than the French, who are more nationalist, moderate, and less pacifist.

But the difference in partisan orientation, the radical Germans versus the pragmatic French, is also due to differences in electoral system. The French two-ballot majority system discourages new parties, unlike the personalized proportional representation found in Germany. Although there are broad similarities in electorate, system constraints create structural-ideological differences between the two Green parties. Guillaume Sainteny's interviews with French ecologist leaders show a rhetorical refusal of the left-right distinction. But their voting behavior, union memberships, and New Left ideology clearly situate them as part of the alternative left. This contradictory ideological definition may be a factor in the electoral weakness of *Les Verts* among French voters, who do situate themselves in terms of the old left-right politics. Herbert Kitschelt noted that generally postmodern left-libertarian values are a precondition for Green Party success, but Green parties must broaden ideologically to include socioeconomic issues, and must continuously differentiate themselves from left parties that would absorb their message.[16] Recent lack of voting success among French, Australian, and Scandinavian Green parties shows their unwillingness to include social issues and the ability of other parties to capture their rhetorical flag.

Postmodern pressure on the old politics spectrum is not only a developed world phenomenon. In 1985–86, during the Brazilian democratic transition, I used a Q-method protocol to map the emergent political left: thirteen legal and clandestine parties of the Leninist, Trotskyist, Eurocommunist, and socialist left, including the aforementioned workers' party PT (Partido dos Trabalhadores). The PT is a truly postmodern party, supported by the liberation Church, labor unions, Leninist and Trotskyist parties, and a number of left factions; artists and intellectuals, the service sector bourgeoisie, black, women's, and gay rights groups; slum dwellers, landless peasants, pro-Indian groups; and a Green party. As a participatory democratic alternative, the PT shows the same "ideological diversity stress" as German Greens. Despite its intense internal political life and high turnover rate, the PT has come within a few percentage points of winning the Brazilian presidency in the last two elections and has been "occupying political space" at all electoral levels and among all strata of the populace.

The PT has absorbed more Communist parties and factions since my fieldwork, but the three factorial attitude types structuring thirteen parties and factions in 1986 showed that instead of a left-right continuum, there was a triangular relationship among three poles: the Eurocommunist PCB (Brazilian Communist Party) and its outliers, the centrally located socialist/PT grouping, and the clandestine Leninists and Trotskyists. The PT, like other left libertarian parties, occupied the center-left with radical outliers.

Four Communist formations and one moderate Trotskyist group fell within or near PT (factorial) political space, showing that the possibility of their absorption already existed in 1985. Ranking these parties on the basis of their ideological coherence, I found that the more ideological cohesion there was, the less the proclivity to enter into coalition with similar parties, and the less cohesion prevailed, the more possible coalition partners there were. These data predicted inclusion of the Eurocommunist and moderate Trotskyist left into the PT some six years before the event. Less militant parties were more pluralist and practical and thus more liable to form lasting alliances and attract members from other parties and groups.

The Brazilian left has borrowed European ideologies of little local relevance to the closed elitist politics maintained by a manipulative electoral system and a strong military/security complex. Despite system constraints, the PT was able to create a model "new politics party," which occupied the electoral space held by the old Communist Party, absorbed the Communists, Church, and unions into its postmodern framework, and became the only antisystem party.

Indeed the PT is now the only nationally organized grassroots party in Brazil, where parties tend to be shifting coalitions of notables. Whether the military, security services, or the United States will ever allow the PT to take power and make the agrarian and political reforms necessary to modernize and democratize civil society is an open question. The economic conditions of affluence are not met in Brazil or the other Global South countries studied in this book, but postmodern values exist, at least among elites, and are slowly eroding structural system constraints, which are far more powerful than those found in European electoral systems.[17]

An example of postmodern values restructuring a neo-corporatist authoritarian one-party state is found in a field study my wife and I ran of activists in Mexico's PRI (Partido Revolucionario Institucional) during the 1988 election of Salinas de Gortari. Factor analysis of sixty Q-method interviews among party elites yielded three factorial attitude types. "Modernizers" followed Salinas's neoliberal economics but supported authoritarian one-party dominance. An "Opposition" supported the internal democratization of PRI and renovation of its historical social democratic political project and aligned with expelled factions, which supported the social democratic candidacy of Cuauhtémoc Cárdenas. The "Discontents" represented the 48 percent who abstained from voting. Discontents, largely rightist postmaterialists, decried PRI's corruption, the opportunism of its candidates, the high cost to consumers of its corporatist control of labor and the peasantry, and the irrelevance of its social democracy and pro–Third World foreign policy. They supported Salinas's neoliberalism but thought that it would fail because of the PRI's corruption and political incapacity.

Mexico's system strongly discourages the emergence of new politics movements, so that the discovery of factorial divisions within the dominant party-state demonstrates the capacity of postmodern value shifts and post-Fordist economic restructuring to fragment modernist authoritarian corporatism. In the 1988 election, the Cardenista movement rallied a host of alternative unions, indigenous, youth, feminist, and slum dweller organizations, small left parties, and ex-PRI cadres into an antisystem coalition. Leftist exit polls indicated that Cárdenas may actually have won the presidency, although he was formally defeated by questionable vote counts and local coercion. This new politics mobilization persisted and ultimately Cárdenas won as mayor of Mexico City.

If the PRI is divided into left and right postmoderns and moderate socialists, the policy issues are so complex, and crosscut one another so thoroughly, that the PRI can continue to exist and maintain policy initiative despite its growing fragmentation. As our study concluded, "Because these issue cleavages crosscut any putative left-right ideological spectrum, there are ample grounds for complex coalition behaviors between different combinations of attitude sets within PRI and between PRI, PRD (Democratic Revolutionary Party), and PAN (National Action Party). . . . Thus, it can be concluded that while PRIista attitudes divide into Modernizers, Opponents, and Discontents, these cleavages recombine on different issues, and that complex policy coalitions will replace the superseded unifying revolutionary ideology of the Partido Revolucionario Institucional."[18]

The "new politics" model posits a shift from the old left-right spectrum of modernist parties, oriented around social class control (bourgeois or proletarian) of Fordist mass production, to a new set of postmodern parties, which may be left, libertarian, multicultural, environ-mentalist, single-issue coalitions or right libertarian neoliberals. This shift comes from post-Fordist globalization and postmodern attitude shifts in postwar generations, and it is modulated by structural vari-ables such as voting systems, the exclusivity of sitting parties, and the agility of the old parties in taking over postmodern themes and sym-bols in their propaganda.

Data from our transnational study clearly support this shift of the political spectrum and make it possible to map this transition in terms of environmental ideologies and Global South elite attitudes.

Conclusions

1. Postmodern philosophy is schematic, extreme, dogmatic, and melo-dramatic, but its nihilism does point to some serious social problems in the new global economy. Deconstructive method cannot create a new culture, but it does point to new values, which survey data show are taking hold in the mass public.

Data on postmodernism and postmaterialism are mixed. They point to new values of personal autonomy, self-expression, libertarian lifestyles, participation, confessional subjectivity, feminism, multiculturalism, and environmentalism in a plurality of the mass public and elites. Shifts in values are quite difficult to measure and vary with the choice of defini-tions and variables, so that postmodernism is not going to provide an easy explanation of attitude changes. The national "political culture" model is not confirmed by our data, which show that elites are tied into an international network and attitude set that is broadly postmodern in tone and is a function of post-Fordist economic transition. Postmodern attitudes may be transitional "period effects," which disappear in the next century with the crystallization of a new ideological and political spectrum. This would be the optimum outcome.

2. Postmodernism does not explain the explosive growth of envi-ronmental awareness and movements in the Global South. The neo-liberal version of sustainable development argues that affluence is a prerequisite of environmental concern, because clean environments are a luxury good. Peasants are the worst polluters because of their high discount rate on the future. These rational choice, new social move-ment, and postmaterialist models all fail to explain the data showing in the Global South high and growing awareness and willingness to pay for environmental remediation. The postmaterialist/materialist dimension cannot explain attitudes that have many more dimensions.

The data in this book show that there are seven attitude dimensions (or types) to the environmental issue in the Global South. These dimensions are international and cross-cultural, showing that elites and economic sectors of these differing nations have postmodern or modernist views of environment as an international question in the global economy, and not as a problem framed in terms of local political culture.

Environmental postmodernism is driven by threatening objective conditions, which can only become worse and which pose evident problems of national security and economic viability. Other postmodern values—concern for subjectivity, personal autonomy, quality of life, risk aversion, community, participation, feminism, lifestyle engineering, multiculturalism, environmental and global problems—may or may not become salient in developing nations, but environment cannot be ignored or superseded by other issues and must become increasingly central to international discourse as time goes by.

We utilize postmodernism as an elite value dimension, a vertical axis, in our model of transition to a new environmental politics. The Green value indicator used as a proxy for postmodernism is admittedly imperfect, but few good measures of postmodernism have been developed to date. The factorial attitude types found in our data show a clear transition from modernism to postmodernism, and from Fordism to post-Fordism. When these types are arrayed on these axes, the trend away from the modernist left-right to a postmodern left and right is striking. A new politics is clearly in the offing. Postmodern Managers in all seven countries hold the balance of power among left and right postmodern environmentalism (Greens versus Sustainable Developers) and modernists (Developers, Bureaucratic Nationalists).

3. Post-Fordism provides a good descriptive model of globalization and the installation of the quaternary sector of knowledge- and information-based production. Post-Fordism may not be a new form of capitalism at all but only its further internationalization and intensification.

Capitalism grows by exporting its crises. Post-Fordism creates extremely complex global economic relations, which are fragile and prone to chaos.

Post-Fordism provides a useful conceptualization of the new globalized corporate economy of regions, not nations, and provides a horizontal axis for our model of transition to a new political spectrum.

4. The data seem to show that there is no univocal postmodern new class of managers, but there is complex horizontal and vertical stratification of elite blocs, with different levels of adherence to postmodern values. New-class theory is useful in pointing to changing perceptions among elites and ongoing realignments among power groups.

The data developed in the following chapters show that Global South elites are adopting post-Fordist roles and postmodern attitudes toward environment. Members of this new stratum of Postmodern Managers and Greens see their role in global, not national, terms and are committed to post-Fordist globalization and several postmodern values including environmental concern, risk aversion, democracy, and moderate feminism.

5. The new politics model posits a shift from the old left-right spectrum of modernist parties, oriented around social class control of Fordist mass production, to a new set of postmodern parties, which are left, libertarian, multicultural, environmentalist, or right libertarian pro-corporate neoliberals. This shift is motivated by post-Fordist globalization and postmodern attitudes, moderated by structural variables such as voting systems, open or closed party systems, and the agility of old parties in taking over postmodern themes and symbols.

Data from our transnational study clearly show this shift of the political spectrum from old to new politics in terms of Global South elite environmental ideologies.

India: Greens Facing the Impossible

In the 1990s, a series of unstable coalition governments has been trying neoliberal adjustment to integrate India into the global post-Fordist economy. This goes against the grain of India's nonmaterialist religions and its Fabian socialist pattern of state-led import substitution industrialization; that is, the leftist Fordist modernism that has guided development since independence. However, the attitude types emerging in 1990 interviews with Indian environmental elites—Greens, Sustainable Developers, and Postmodern Managers—form model types that recur consistently in the other countries in this study. In fact, Indian Greens are the most advanced in the developing world due to Mohandas Gandhi's ethos, religion, and method of nonviolent resistance.

Indian Greens provide a standard against which to measure the progress and sophistication of Greens in the other countries, even though they have been largely co-opted into a closed bargaining process, which moderates their demands and impact on policy. The gains of the movement, in terms of complex laws enforced by the Ministry of Environment and Forests, are often lost in implementation at the state level. India has created a sophisticated regulatory infrastructure, but this has had little impact on overpopulation, desertification, deforestation, overfishing, and the ecologically damaging drive for development.

In this chapter we review the four alternative political economic models of India's future generated by Mohandas Gandhi, Jawaharlal Nehru, neoliberals in and outside Congress-I, and the environmental movement. We then examine the political problems encountered by these sophisticated environmental groups and analyze their relation to the attitude spectrum discovered among India's decision makers.

Gandhian, Nehruvian, and Neoliberal Visions of Indian Development

India has generated four economic models in its post-independence history: Gandhi's village utopia, Jawaharlal Nehru's Fabian socialist state-planned import substitution regime, the current neoliberal adjustment regime begun under the late Rajiv Gandhi's prime ministership and continued under successor coalition governments, and neo-Gandhian environmentalism.

1. Mohandas Gandhi's utopian system mixed idealized Hinduism with Western anarchist and utopian theories drawn from Kropotkin, Tolstoy, Morris, and Ruskin. There are a number of key concepts in his theoretical vision.

First, Gandhi argued that the originary Vedic society was organic and cooperative and that the *varnas*, which later degenerated into the caste system, originally provided a socially harmonious division of labor. Gandhi argued that India could again realize *sarvodaya*, spiritual development for all, unlike the West, which was lost in hedonistic materialism. Voluntary simplicity and spiritually disciplined consumption allow all basic needs to be met within a village economy. Spiritual reform underlies national strength and independence, his concept of *swaraj*. The related idea of *swadeshi*, rejecting the overvaluation of things Western and advocating a return to Indian values and local products, allows national autarchy and disconnection from international entanglements.

Second, Gandhi's commitment to *ahimsa* (nonviolence, respect for life) and *satyagraha* (nonviolent resistance) was central to his political methods, but the two are situational policies rather than absolute values. He opposed absolute pacifism and argued that in certain circumstances—when under physical attack, for instance, or threats from noxious animals—violence was necessary. Satyagraha was viable as an expression of disciplined mass moral outrage, civil disobedience, and self-sacrifice only in order to resist oppression and realize freedom and justice. Satyagraha was an instrument of the moral oppressed that allowed smoother subsequent political resolution of conflict than did violent means.

Third, in the economic realm, Gandhi opposed class war and undisciplined mass action. Instead of redistributing wealth, Gandhi talked of convincing the rich to accept an ethic of trusteeship and service. While recognizing differences in innate intelligence and skills, Gandhi believed in guaranteed minimum subsistence and a maximum amount of allowable wealth. Although not egalitarian, Gandhi foresaw a more equal division of wealth than existed in India, primarily because of his emphasis on the dignity of "bread labor" or self-provisioning.

Fourth, Gandhi opposed Fordist mass production and consumption and instead supported appropriate, decentralized village-scale technologies. National-level large-scale production was justified only in support of this village economy. Gandhi distrusted the state and large cities and envisioned a regenerated village commune as the base of autarchy and self-rule, *panchayat raj*. His vision of the kingdom of god (Rama) on earth, *ramrajya*, was essentially village-based anarcho-syndicalist, moralistic, and spiritual.[1]

Perhaps Gandhi's vision was utopian, in that it succeeded within a few ashrams stocked with his followers but could not be generalized in a complex, overpopulated country facing severe economic and military challenges and upheavals in public order. The closed static economy Gandhi projected as an ideal conflicted with modern values of democracy and individual liberty. Gandhi's vision was not properly ecological, but his simple village economy has low impacts on nature. Gandhi's spiritualism is essentially anthropocentric; a localized society would be more in harmony with nature than would Western urban state-led development. Environmentalist concerns are not central to his spiritualism and can be overridden by human and religious concerns.

2. A modernist alternative to Gandhi's premodern vision was articulated by his disciple Jawaharlal Nehru. Nehru supported Fabian state planning, import substitution industrialization, a large state sector, strong protectionism, and urbanization. Beginning with the Second Plan, the drive to build heavy industry and the subsequent neglect of agriculture created inflation and foreign exchange shortages. Between 1951 and 1989, four five-year plans and four annual plans pushed India's GNP up 3,774 percent, with annual growth rates as high as 17.8 percent. High increases were noted in basic materials, consumer durables, and social welfare indicators such health, literacy, infant mortality, life expectancy.

The state sector grew from 25 to 43 percent of total investment, while the private sector declined from 75 percent to 57 percent during this period. India became self-reliant in agriculture and industrial production, with the lowest direct foreign investment in the semiperiphery. Conservative fiscal policy ensured that debt was a modest 11.9 percent of GNP in 1980. However, the state sector was plagued with inefficiency and corruption, and subsidies to outmoded industries took increasing shares of GNP. India's rapidly increasing population consistently blocks creation of sufficient jobs or alleviation of structural poverty and has brought environmental problems to crisis proportions.

3. Neoliberal policies first emerged under Rajiv Gandhi's leadership (October 1984 to December 1989). The government invested heavily in modernizing railroads, telecommunications, and power generation, cut industrial license fees and taxes, and deregulated many sectors, leading to rapid industrial growth in the 1980s. Deregulated capital markets tripled their transaction volume, leading to a large number of mergers and acquisitions. Imports of foreign technology and local R&D were aggressively pursued, leading to a 98 percent increase in capital goods imports in the 1980s—but also to balance of payments shortages and increasing debt. India selected a number of key sectors for export promotion using fuel and fiscal subsidies, and the rupee was steadily devalued. From 1986 to 1988, exports increased 43 percent, especially in labor-intensive manufactures, chemicals, engineering, and arts and crafts.

But 9 percent of domestic capital remains tied up in 160,000 outmoded "sick industries," the subsidization of which creates shortages of loan capital and savings. Low R&D budgets, weak linkages with industry, and pervasive oligopoly make intensive development (technological conversion) of industry difficult. Liberalization failed to introduce domestic competition but increased the debt (U.S. $60 billion in 1989), balance of payments deficit, and debt service ratio (30 percent). In 1995, popular revolt against Western transnational corporations like Coca-Cola and Pepsi led to their withdrawal and cancellation of some important construction contracts. There is growing religious and cultural hostility to globalizing India's economy, which politically benefits the conservative Hindu party (Baratiya Janata) and its coalition partners.

Defense expenditures, state subsidies, and budget deficits have grown under liberalization, and most employment growth now takes place in the informal economy. Consumer durables are the fastest-growing sector, supplying a tiny affluent urban elite, while the impoverished majority cannot supply the necessary domestic demand to drive growth.

The benefits of India's growth have accrued to a tiny elite. From 1950 to 1985, the GNP share of the top 10 percent of the population grew to 70 percent, including black market profits. India's 1986 per capita income was U.S. $260 despite an average 3.6 percent GNP growth since 1950. Industry grew at an annual average of 6 percent, while agriculture grew at 0.05 percent. The top 10 percent of households own

56 percent of the land, while the bottom half of the population own 6 percent. In the cities, the top 5 percent control 75 percent of the property. India has the worst income distribution and lowest agricultural productivity among developing nations.[2]

Indian planning has begun accommodating environmental problems with new legal and administrative structures. Under Indira Gandhi, various environmental acts were passed and in January 1980 the Department of Environment was created. The department was elevated to the Ministry of Environment, Forests, and Wildlife in 1985. The Environment Protection Act of 1986 led to specific enabling rules and regulations. Environmental impact assessments are now required for all government projects.

The Forest Conservation Act of 1980 mandated reforestation, reclamation, restrictions on fuelwood and grazing, elimination of forest contracting to loggers and swidden (slash-and-burn agriculture). Desert and island biomes came under legal protection. The Sixth Plan (1980) prioritized energy conservation and renewable sources, including biogas, solar, and geothermal energy sources. However, planners are urban technocrats lacking necessary scientific training, and funds are insufficient: the Seventh Plan allotted only 0.43 percent of the budget to environmental issues.[3]

India is nowhere close to resolving its population and environmental problems. Despite favorable institutional and legal factors, the major policy changes, required by India's rapidly approaching crisis, cannot be applied nationally. Why is this so?

Population growth is so rapid that it cancels the benefits of development and is overloading the subcontinent's carrying capacity. India's population will increase from an estimated 850 million in 1990 to one billion persons by 2000. The 1985 production of food and seed, some 171 million tons, must increase to 297 million tons to meet projected demand in the year 2000. Similarly, production of firewood and green and dry fodder must increase from 737 to 1,636 million tons. Such increases are not likely when deforestation exceeds 1.3 million hectares (ha) per year, and desertification is overtaking the productive semiarid lands wind-shadowed by the Western Ghats.

India's land area of approximately 300 million ha contains 13 percent rocky, glaciated, or settled land, 55 percent private land, and 28 percent government land. Total forest cover has declined 91,710 square kilometers (sq km) between 1972 and 1982, and Landsat satellite data show India to be losing 1.3 million ha of forest per year. Closed forest cover has declined from 14.12 percent to 10.96 percent of the total, while open-canopy and degraded forests have increased from 2.67 to 3.06 percent. Mangrove forests have declined from 0.099 to 0.081 percent of total forest cover.[4]

4. The fourth alternative model to Nehru's Fabianism and current neoliberal globalization of India's economy is being articulated by over 950 local and international environmental groups and the Ministry of Environment. The most sophisticated environmental group is Chipko Andolan, the Movement to Hug the Trees, which is worth examining in order to see why a powerful popular movement, with significant elite and international connections and strong support in the national Gandhian ethos, ultimately has so little influence in making national policy and was converted to a popular movement for local statehood and forest development.

Chipko Andolan arose in the Tehri Garhwal and Kumaun districts of the western Himalayan foothills, in response to drastic ecological degradation. Flooding and sedimentation were caused by predatory deforestation, destructive resin tapping, and forest fires in the Himalayan catchment. Himalayan forest canopy has dwindled to 35 percent against the historic optimum of 64 percent. Deforestation and erosion cause groundwater subsidence rates up to 46 percent. Population pressure and erosion cause peasant migration up the slopes and farming on landslide fans, increasing erosion and subsidence. Livestock graze the forest beyond its regenerative capacity. The ecological tragedy of the Himalayas affects India, Pakistan, China, Nepal, Bangladesh, and Bhutan and requires complex regional planning.[5] But given the region's history, this effort will not come soon.

Chipko's emergence was made possible by the simplified Himalayan caste system, with Doms, the farm servant and artisan group, Khasa or indigenous peasant farmers, Thuljats or later immigrant Brahmins, and Rajputs from the plains. The open economy and constant pilgrimage to the shrine of Badrinath allows a high degree of social mobility and moderates class divisions.

Although socially subordinate, women were equal economic partners in agropastoral work, with additional tasks of childrearing and collecting fuel, fodder, and water. Both princely and British taxation and control tended to be weak because of village autonomy, 90 percent private land ownership, and strategic placement on the Nepalese and Tibetan borders, which allowed peasants the option of flight. Further, the mountain agropastoral and collecting economy did not generate the requisite surplus to support a royal court, nobility, or British plantation or colonization schemes. Extensive sacred groves, rotational cutting and grazing of commons, and customary sanctions on lopping and gathering of wood all operated to promote cooperative forest management by the villagers.

Gradually, however, market penetration and ecological degradation made inroads into the hill people's autonomy, prosperity, and equality. Fragmented holdings and environmental change made subsistence farming untenable. Poverty led to overpopulation and increased livestock holdings as survival strategies; strategies which only accelerate environmental and economic degradation. In eighty years, population increased 119 percent while cultivated land increased only 54 percent. Crop yields declined. Of the 34,042 sq km of land officially declared to be forest, only 6.6 percent has decent tree cover, 23 percent and 14 percent are medium and poor forest respectively, and the rest is wasteland.[6]

A dual economy emerged, with up to 60 percent of the male population migrating to the plains to work and provide cash remittances and females remaining to perform marginal agriculture and increasingly difficult gathering of fuel, firewood, water, and fodder. Familial authority, village self-governance, and management of the commons all disintegrated under these cross-pressures. Local ecological knowledge was lost as the villagers adopted the Western view of forests as a nonrenewable source of cash income.

Chipko Andolan originated in protests against the commercialization of village commons by outsiders. The traditional form of rebellion in the hills was *dhandak,* forceful reassertion of customary rights with a simultaneous appeal to the Raja (prince) to restore paternal governance. In 1921 a movement against coolie labor grew out of these local protests, with the help of Mahatma Gandhi's disciples. Major protests occurred during the Civil Disobedience movement of 1931 and the Quit India Movement of 1942, and in 1949 protest ended the Raja's rule.

The Gandhian movement maintained a strong presence in the western Himalayas. Mira Behn, Sarala Behn, and Sarla Devi, close associates of Gandhi, set up ashrams in Garhwal, Kumaun, and Almora and organized satyagraha around traditional village and women's rights. Today, Sunderlal Bahaguna, a Gandhian activist, and ecologists and intellectuals like Chandi Prasad Bhatt, Vandana Shiva, and Jayanto Bandyopadhyay synthesize Gandhian nonviolent social change with the latest environmentalist and feminist thought.

The Chipko Andolan or Hug the Trees Movement grew out of two

Gandhian popular movements, the Dashauli Gram Swarajya Sangh (DGSS), a Chamoli district production cooperative movement, and Uttarakhand Sarvodaya Mandal. Both movements, created in the 1960s, pushed for temperance, women's rights, and local forest-based industry. Public meetings demanded replacement of the contractor system with local cooperatives.

In 1973, the DGSS resisted imposition of a Symonds Company monopoly of their ash groves by hugging the trees, interposing their bodies between the trees and contractor's saws. Other demonstrations followed in December in Purola and over the next few days in Uttarkashi and Gopeshwar. Bahaguna and the villagers followed the contractors throughout the forest, encouraging successful local opposition to cutting in several places.

The government formed two committees to investigate the situation and issued reports connecting fellings with landslides, criticizing destructive resin-tapping practices, and reviewing the Star Paper Mill leases. Committee reports supported Chipko, and the government ended private contract felling, creating the Uttar Pradesh Forest Corporation in 1975. But this state corporation continued predatory extraction, leading to popular direct action to stop all pine tapping and to repair damaged trees. Throughout the 1970s, local protests were organized like community festivals, with religious ceremonies sacralizing the repaired trees.

In April 1981 Sunderlal Bahaguna began a long fast to ban all felling in the Himalaya above 1,000 meters in elevation. The government commission whitewashed the Forest Department, but after meeting with Bahaguna, a charismatic and persuasive man, Indira Gandhi ordered a fifteen-year moratorium on commercial felling in Uttarakhand. Later moratoria applied to the western Ghats and Vindhyas.

Chipko won a relative victory. From 1971 to 1981, forest produce in the eight hill districts fell from 62,000 to 40,000 cubic meters of timber per annum. Chipko entered a new phase with regular marches; resistance to the Tehri Dam project; and summer camps funded by international environmentalists, involving environmental education, reforestation, creation of small biogas plants, and establishment of women's cooperatives to manufacture efficient smokeless wood stoves.[7]

Chipko won international fame, intellectual influence, and publicity and engendered many like movements. But the specific Himalayan cultural factors that made this success possible also limited national spread of the movement. Chipko, and other local movements like it, suffer the defects of their virtues.

First, Chipko is a modern environmental group speaking the language of peasant moral economy and claiming traditional rights to ecological subsistence. These elements do not blend easily. Chipko is Gandhian, nonviolent, traditionalist, and moralistic. It aims to raise popular environmental consciousness and restore folk wisdom about nature while reaffirming traditional culture through popular poets and singers, readings of the Bhagavad Gita (a Hindu holy book), and religious ceremonials resacralizing the forests.

Women, being principal agents in the household economy, repositories of local tradition and religion, and an oppressed group with direct economic interests in environmental maintenance, play a central leadership role. Chipko's ecofeminism, skillfully articulated by the physicist Vandana Shiva, has caused male resentment, especially the 1984 campaigns against liquor, to abolish dowry (which allows men to spend women's inheritance), and for equal participation in politics.

Second, like Gandhi, Bahaguna and his followers teach by example but cannot articulate resistance to neoliberal international pressure on the central government to emphasize deregulation and export-led growth. Sunderlal Bahaguna's asceticism and capacity for sacrifice (marches, fasts in the snow), as well as his incorruptibility, make him the ideal spokesman for village demands and critic of the contractor/bureaucrat/politician mafias cutting the Himalayan forests. But like earlier dhandak protesters, Bahaguna appeals to higher state and national authority figures to set the situation right, restoring moral order. He is apolitical, mixing the discourses of ecology, popular morality, and Brahmanic religion, but is careful not to question the legitimacy of state authority.

Third, Chipko has successfully exploited the ambiguities in Indian state ideology by claiming Gandhian inspiration. Chipko upholds the ideals of the Founding Father against those who have distorted his message. The Himalayas, with the shrine of Badrinath, have strong religious resonance, and movements there have not faced the same violence as other movements involving non-Hindu tribals. Other local movements lack Chipko's sophisticated intellectual leadership capable of pressing demands and raising money in international fora.

Fourth, although it is led by internationally connected environmentalist intellectuals, villagers see Chipko as the vehicle of a simple struggle for survival, without philosophical overtones. Environmentalism, feminism, and Gandhian ethics are complex abstractions, which hold villager attention only as long as they mesh with immediate local demands. As a movement against state control of forest revenues and contractor clear-cutting—both of which denied the benefits of small scale forestry and fuel and fodder to locals—Chipko had a strong developmentalist component. The Ghandian dimension was cultural, and the ecological dimension was an addition by outside intellectuals to local traditions.

Developmentalism in India includes demands for social equality, economic access to natural resources, political attention to local demands, and self-management, and thus has a popular component. Some critics argue that movement intellectuals endowed a simple folk resistance with higher ecological consciousness than existed on the ground. Large-scale education, reforestation summer camps, and a youth movement have no doubt created much more such consciousness than previously existed, and as noted Chipko has provided a model for many similar movements. But it has failed to become institutionalized and has suffered from its own success.

Indira Gandhi responded to the movement because it was articulated in terms of the official vocabulary of development and democracy and in the moral vocabulary of local native traditionals versus greedy outside capitalists. Mrs. Gandhi had a prior interest in environment, but Chipko appealed to her image as Mother of the Nation and promised to build positive popular support and provide powerful regulatory instruments for her drive for centralization, control of industrialists, and patronage. She had just finished a successful war with Pakistan, had a majority in parliament, and was surrounded by party loyalists, so that environmental initiatives, both by her and by her son Rajiv, sailed into law.

Water, air, and forest laws, and a general environment act that became the basis for the Ministry of Environment and Forests (Paryavaran Bhawan), created a complex regulatory regime. The Indian Forest Conservation Act of 1980 required permission to cut forests of over one hectare, and imposed a fifteen-year ban on felling above 1,000 meters in the Himalayas. Uttar Pradesh state government responded with acts against felling protected tree species and set up a new forest corporation, which was supposed to operate through local cooperatives. A constitutional amendment prevented state governments from converting large tracts of forest without central government permission—the states having cut 4.3 million ha of forests between 1950 and 1975.

The ironic outcome of this strict preservation regime was that natives were once again excluded from the forests, cooperatives were disbanded or were riven by rivalries, and unemployment worsened. Since two-thirds of Gharwal is forest, natives were excluded from fuel, fodder, and small forestry industry, especially since they lacked political access. Tourism revenues were captured by lowlanders, and real estate prices in hill towns soared. Heavily armed timber mafias, using Nepalese labor, began clear-cutting and illegal liquor distilling.

Popular enthusiasm switched from Chipko to a strong popular movement, with revolutionary dimensions, for the creation of Uttaranchal, a new state including the eight Himalayan districts of Uttar Pradesh. This demand is unlikely to be met because U.P. is the most populous and politically powerful state in the federation. The core of this new state demand is popular control over developmental resources, against strict national and state regulations constraining local use of the forests. So far, the movement has met either symbolic or violent responses from the state and has attacked police stations in order to arm itself. The area may be ripe for violence.[8]

Chipko and the national environmental movement have successfully articulated an alternative model of sustainable development and placed it on the national agenda. But since the assassination of Rajiv Gandhi, who was at least open to such concerns, and with neoliberal stabilization policies—beginning with Narasimha Rao's government and continuing with subsequent Janata Dal and Baratya Janata coalitions—there is little hope of it being widely adopted. Let us examine this policy model, as articulated in preplanning documents for the Eighth Plan, and the interests which oppose it.

In the environmentalist model, the common definition of "development" is no longer GNP growth, industrialization, and urbanization. "Development must . . . satisfy the basic needs of the poorest; promote equitable income distribution and social justice; provide employment; encourage participation and involvement; and build institutions and infrastructures. And, of course . . . has to be sustainable."[9]

Because half of India's population is in the primary or subsistence sector, poverty is redefined not as lack of cash but as a shortage of biomass for subsistence needs. The environmentalist priority is the regeneration of GNaP (Gross Natural Product), or a sustainable increase in the biomass base drawn down by "development."

This model intends to reinstate village commons under reformed local institutions. Village councils (*panchayats*), although elected bodies, are riven with caste, partisan, and class divisions, dominated by wealthy elites, economically dependent, and alienated from their own resource base, which they pillage like outsiders. Village boundaries have not been revised since the British Raj and are obsolete because of population growth. The Forest Department has taken over much of their commons as "protection forests" but frequently auctions grass or trees to outside contractors, leading, by 1993, to popular resistance and state repression.

The environment is in the hands of complex and elephantine bureaucracies, which apply contradictory policies, and of local elites connected to national parties, contractors, and mafias. Outmoded colonial laws treat villagers as strangers in their own land and criminalize actions creating autonomy. Government permission, requiring years of legal battles and large bribes, is required for villagers to reforest their own catchment watershed or commons or to build small dams and modify village water tanks.

Thus, the environmental movement advocates that the *gram sabha* or general village assembly make collective management decisions regarding protected commons designated for exclusive village use. Enabling legislation, like the Rajastan Gramdan Act of 1971, which gives executive and legal powers to registered village gram sabhas, is required for local management of natural resources and grants local power to judge and punish offenders. Women form a parallel council with clear rights and access to funds, because women are usually reticent to speak up in mixed public assemblies. Environmentalists also want delimitation of village boundaries and commons and limitation of commons to biomass production. Sales of surplus biomass and creation of village sideline industries could expand local investment in reforestation and water conservation.

Training in ecological management blends traditional production with new techniques and biotechnologies. Extension agents teach villagers new technologies and restore neglected native agro-forestry systems, which successfully intercropped some forty species of trees and cultigens for maximum biodiversity and resistance to climate and pathogen stress.[10]

In 1990, before the assassination of Rajiv Gandhi, the environmental movement articulated a model of decentralized bioregional planning in preparation for the draft Eighth Five-Year Plan. The Eighth Plan discussion paper spoke of decentralizing planning to local governments and environmental groups, of guaranteed minimum wages, small and intermediate industries, land reform and restoration of village commons, and giving village panchayats control over commons and finances. Austerity, progressive taxation of incomes, and anticonsumerism are central to this change. Non-tied block grants with government monitoring would replace direct planning.

Hydroelectricity, nuclear power, and plantation monoculture projects already in place would be completed but no new ones initiated, as planning would come to give priority to small and medium-sized industry and agriculture. Growth of small and medium towns would buffer big cities from migration. Women, scheduled castes (former "untouchables"), and tribals would be specially protected and their participation encouraged. Education, higher marriage ages, job creation, and public health input would reduce birthrates. Improvement of women's social condition would mean less population growth. Mandatory environmental impact statements and strong sanctions for pollution or waste were part of the draft plan.

The program was strong and positive, but it ran contrary to the neoliberal adjustment and world market integration avidly pursued by India's coalition governments in the 1990s, under considerable pressure from foreign governments, development banks, and corporations. It was, for obvious political reasons, not adopted.

Indian Administrative Politics: Prestige, Patronage, and the Frustration of Environmental Regulation

Significant resistance from vested industrial, state corporate, bureaucratic, partisan, and regional interests, within the framework of neoliberal policies and world market integration and enforced by unsteady coalition governments beginning with Prime Minister Narasimha Rao's (elected on June 21, 1991), neutralized many environmental movement demands. The national political conjuncture is anything but favorable to environmentalism; it is instead concerned with deregulation, stabilization, and market opening toward an export profile.

There are a number of structural factors in the Indian political system making implementation of environmental regulation difficult. This critique could be applied to most other governments of the Global South. India's federal government is fractionated and subject to informal elite bargaining, which favors powerful interest groups and the status quo. Many commentators note an increasing criminalization of Indian politics. Political power means wealth, privilege, patronage, so that criminal thugs, who before served politicians in election rigging, have themselves entered politics and business. The underground economy is taking over the legitimate. Communal violence spawns ecstatic fundamentalist movements, in some instances fueled by the failure of technocratic solutions, like the Green Revolution in Punjab, which created massive economic dislocation and environmental damage.[11]

Government has neither the interest nor the power to institute sweeping changes in environmental policy.

The Ministry of Environment and Forests (MEF), established in 1985 under the patronage of Rajiv Gandhi, was charged with regulatory functions, the coordination of other agency policies, enforcement of environmental impact statements for large industrial or infrastructure projects, wildlife conservation, research and development and information system creation, and promoting international cooperation. In three years its staff rose to 1,171, with fifty-eight subagencies and two independent directorates (Project Ganga and Wastelands Development) reporting to the ministry. Under a United Nations program there are 51 water quality monitoring stations, and an Indian program added 232.

The Ganga Action Plan deals on an urgent basis with pollution in a river basin that includes 37 percent of the population and 47 percent of irrigated land. Passing through 29 major cities, 23 small cities, and 48 small towns, the Ganges receives 900 million liters of untreated sewage daily and a heavy load of industrial effluent. Sewage treatment, waste diversion, closing noncompliant industries or forcing them to install treatment equipment, and ending the dumping of human and animal corpses and animal processing wastes are major aspects of this program. MEF reported that in 1998, 253 out of 261 projects had been completed and that of 2,137 units without effluent treatment, 106 complied and 480 were closed, while 1,457 were slated to be closed.

MEF has set up important environmental monitoring infrastructure, legislation, and educational programs but has not made a major impact on pollution, deforestation, or desertification. The main problem is that any policy and budgetary initiatives are overwhelmed by the brute fact of India's population explosion. With a growth rate of 2.2 percent per annum, India will top one billion persons by 2000. India's main concern is development, and environment is clearly subsidiary. Irrigation takes 8 percent of the central budget, rural employment and health care take 1.9 percent each, urban development takes 2.4 percent, water supply takes 3.6 percent, and small-sector industry takes 1.5 percent; the environment receives only 0.2 percent.

As Renu Khator astutely pointed out, "The government is able to achieve a balance between its developmental goals and environmental goals by glorifying procedures, and as long as these procedures do not directly threaten the developmental goal, the government faces no political challenge by committing itself to environmental activities."[12]

MEF's problems are similar to those of any Indian bureaucracy. India has a centralized federal system in which policy is made centrally but implementation and finance are local. Central policy is prestige oriented, without clear time limits, technical standards, or much central financing. The ministry lacks information, clientele, and legal support and thus has trouble competing with other ministries for scarce resources or to implement policy. The cost of environmental protection is often quantifiable and high, while the benefits are long-term, diffuse, and intangible—stopping siltation, better air and water quality, lower disease rates, maintenance of biodiversity. Any MEF program is bound to accrue powerful enemies with tangible financial interests in the outcome, but its clientele base is diffuse and hard to mobilize.

The laws MEF implements are complex and lack enforcement provisions. The Environment Protection Act of 1986 uses sixteen center agencies and local state councils to enforce its provisions. Although it does mandate fines and imprisonment for violations and allows third party suits, though not in civil courts, it disallows any suits against the government and also clears company or departmental executives from full legal responsibility. Missing are set standards, a clear timetable for implementation, strong punishment, centralized power to regulate, and public involvement in surveillance and enforcement.

Indira and Rajiv Gandhi passed the enabling legislation and created the ministry almost without opposition, because these did not threaten the goal of growth, and they offered international and national prestige as well as new sources of patronage. The cost of its creation was its relative inefficacity.[13]

Because India in the 1990s is ruled by neoliberal coalition governments, finding powerful patrons in the Cabinet or among party bosses is difficult at best. MEF's mandate is to coordinate other ministry decision making to protect environment. But without strong exact legislation or a clear clientele and patronage base, and with ministries that are highly competitive and place emphasis on neoliberal development, MEF has little chance of influencing policy.

India's bureaucracy works on a patronage system, which augments the conservatism of administrators; procedures and rules are applied differentially to get benefits and concessions for patrons and local clients. Industry has the ear of party bosses, who directly intervene in administrative processes. MEF exists for the international prestige, and the appearance of action, but is too young and politicized to be an effective regulator. Thus, MEF has created 9 biosphere reserves, 84 national parks, 447 wildlife sanctuaries, and 22 state parks; has passed laws regulating biotechnology; has banned import of wastes with heavy metals and forced 1,261 highly polluting industries to install pollution controls—a not inconsiderable set of accomplishments. But impacts on air, water quality, and other problems have not been as expected.

MEF benefits from the growing environmental movement and rising environmental awareness in India. Fifty-two percent of the public shows "a great deal of concern" about the environment, and 54 percent think that environmental laws "do not go far enough" toward solving the problem.[14] Elitism, patronage, corruption, the priority given to neoliberal adjustment and development, and the lack of technostructure and budget for environment will cause increased frustration with MEF.

Policy may be national but the politics of implementation is strictly local. Local officials, who do the actual work of implementation, see central policy as an imposition. They are not responsive to the same international and national pressures as the center, being patronage appointees beholden to local power brokers and industrialists.

Bureaucrats are unpopular because of their technocratic urban middle-class origins, ethos of political neutrality, arrogance, and excess love of regulations and formal procedures. Bureaucrats are accountable for following procedures, not for getting results. Industry is usually defiant and would rather pay bribes to regulators, pay fines for noncompliance, or engage in drawn-out litigation than pay the costs of compliance. Industry sets up personal relations with bureaucrats who enforce policy, because it is largely excluded from policy making. Corruption is considered a business cost. Business is hostile to the environmental impact statement process—and may have good reason. Khator found that a major venture could require three EIS clearances, each of which required seven stages of bureaucratic process; the process could require three to seven or more years.

States lack finance, technical personnel, data, and clear means of enforcement. There is animosity between state and central bureaucracies, but both benefit from it: states accuse the center of inadequate funding, and the center blames the states for failing to implement laws. Both levels have automatic excuses for nonperformance.

State governments are anxious to attract investment and must compete with one another to lower environmental standards de facto and to show "flexibility" in enforcement.[15]

As is no doubt true in most Global South nations, complex constitutional, legal, and policy instruments are created to meet international, national, and fragmentary local demand. But the actual implementation of policy, or its effectiveness on the ground, are missing. Throughout these case studies we see that governments overreach their own implementation ability in creating complex environmental regulation. Overpopulation, economic constraint, corrupt administrations, patronage politics, unrepresentative political parties, and mass passivity all work to defeat implementation.

Indian political parties see environment as a moral rather than a practical issue; it conflicts with development and the patronage development brings, the very basis of their local power. Environment is seen as a fragmentary local issue risky for national parties. Congress as a mass party strives for consensus and is loath to take on controversial issues. The support base of smaller parties is too narrow for them to profit from environmental issues. The safest strategy, then, is to use environment as a moral, rhetorical issue and to ignore the politically dangerous area of implementation.

Mass protest is often locally considerable but can be demobilized by government passivity or by providing a quick injection of emergency resources. Local discontent with national policy can be isolated and contained, and the public role of surveillance and protest can be carefully controlled. Nationally, powerful interest groups are mobilized to give policy input. But the trade-off is that they must search for consensus and moderate their demands in bargaining with conflicting interests. The optimum solution from the government's point of view is not the ecologically maximum one. Equilibrium environmental policy tends to be nonscientific, politically feasible, reconciliatory, and gradualist.

Environmental elites in all countries and sectors of this field study show great moderation and accommodation, and this reflects the fact that they have been captured by the consultative process. Environmental groups, who helped make the policy, cannot then oppose the government's implementation of it. This co-optation helps explain the paradox that the environmental movement—large, vocal, extensive, and networked as it is—has limited policy impact. Extensive grassroots efforts are filtered into a conservative prestige-oriented showcase policy that preserves the elite patronage system.

Growing mass frustration with this highly organized inaction has no channels of expression, as the party, interest group, administrative, and legal channels are all jammed by ineffective actors. Thus, as Khator notes, "the intensity of the governmental effort did not result in a similarly intense level of performance."[16]

Once policy making, implementation, and impact are separately measured, few nations of the Global North or South find equal success in all three measures. Policy making, the most visible and politically profitable, receives all the emphasis. Implementation is left to bureaucratic infighting over unclear mandates, scarce resources, and inadequate legal instruments. Patronage and corruption are logical choices for bureaucrats caught between pretentious mandates and utter lack of resources; political survival becomes the key environmental policy. Impact goes wanting; governments publish plans, position papers, targets, "gee-whiz" statistics, media spin, and clever public relations to hide the lack of real progress in the impacted biomes.

Powerful vested interests, bureaucracy, state corporations, contractors, international banks, and aid agencies favor large projects such as the Tehri Dam, which would increase area seismicity to 9.0 Richter. Similar large-scale endeavors are the 3,435 Narmada Valley dams, which would have submerged over 100,000 ha in order to irrigate 120,000, in the process displacing 200,000 people; the Baliapal missile range in Orissa, which required removal of fifty-five villages and 100,000 persons; and the six Kaiga nuclear reactors in Karnataka to be sited in a virgin rainforest. Environmental groups have arisen to resist these megaprojects: Chipko against logging and the Tehri Dam in Uttar Pradesh, Narmada Bachao Andolan against the Narmada dams, Khepanastra Ghati Pratirodh Committee against Baliapal missile range, and Keralal Sastra Sahitya Parishad against the Silent Valley dams.

The two largest dams in the Narmada system posed a threat of "reservoir-induced seismicity" in an area that is moderately seismic and laced with faults and fractures through which dammed water can percolate, leading to waterlogging. The habitats of rare and endangered flora and fauna, inhabiting 40,332 ha flooded by the Narmada Sagar dam, would have been destroyed, as would a flourishing riverine fishery. Irrigation works in India typically generate large cost overruns and are almost never completed within a plan period; by 1990 over 181 irrigation projects from prior plans were still under way and were creating large losses.

Narmada project estimates of 60,000 rupees per hectare in irrigation costs are absurd in a poor country, and the local government, which is seriously overburdened, is responsible for raising 67 percent of the project's costs; costs equal to all irrigation outlays in the Seventh Plan. The official benefit-cost ratio was calculated at 1.51 and 1.84 for the two major dams, but when environmental costs were added in, the benefit-cost ratio fell to 0.11. Locally managed lift irrigation using simple technology could provide most of the benefits of this megaproject at a small fraction of its costs—but would not provide payoffs for large transnational corporate and local construction firms or for central and state bureaucrats. The Narmada project was finally canceled because of local and international pressure.

The Baliapal Missile Testing Range in Orissa is another example of the infirmities of megadevelopment. Baliapal is one of the most prosperous farming areas of India, with 126 villages cultivating rice for the domestic market. The missile range, which admittedly has no economic value, will destroy 400 sq km of riceland and displace 100,000 people. Projected "model villages" for refugees will in turn displace 1,500 scheduled caste families. It is evident that India's planning is economically irrational but not solely because of the state's inefficiencies. Megaprojects are driven by local business, transnational corporate, and bureaucratic interests willing to sacrifice large numbers of settled villagers as well as ecosystems to "pork barrel" payouts.

Environmentalists question Western and Indian elite-driven peripheral Fordism, heavy dependent industrialization involving dams, nuclear power, urban middle-class consumerism, and bureaucratic centralization of decision making; all this supported by powerful transnational corporations, aid agencies, and banks. However, critique of the corporate capitalist model of development is not easy as India adopts a neoliberal free-trade posture. Recession and fiscal crisis promoted policy emphases on exports and job creation instead of environmental conservation, which in the long term provides the crucial underpinning of further growth.

Despite environmentalist influence in the Eighth Five-Year Plan, such plans are often decorative. India is the land of pilot projects, a style of work skillfully promoted by international aid agencies as well as by the environmental movement. But generalization of a locally successful pilot project to a nation of 850 million with fourteen languages and hundreds of dialects, cultures, and religions poses intractable administrative and financial problems. Even a resolute neoliberal government with strong international support cannot shake established bureaucratic-political-corporate linkages, leaving little hope for popular environmental movements to shake the system.

India's environmental situation is critical and requires a dramatic recommitment to the balance and simplicity of traditional sustainable production. Despite large popular movements backed by Gandhian ideology, and despite the resources of 950 environmental groups, the existence of a stubbornly corrupt administration, the international conjuncture, and unstable neoliberal governments promoting market-driven and export-led GNP growth all bode ill for a nation facing desertification, deforestation, and the need to feed one billion people early next century.

Indian Elite Environmental Attitudes

India has a widespread environmental movement, strongly influential in government with a capacity for building mass movements, an excellent intellectual infrastructure, and roots deep in native culture and the Gandhian ethos. Yet the movement's politics is largely defensive. It fights rearguard actions against a corrupt and elephantine government, extraordinary linguistic-cultural complexity, persistent economic and political crises, and ecological and population problems among the world's worst.

In July and August 1990, I administered the Q-method instrument to thirty-four key persons in government, business, and environmental organizations in New Delhi, Udaipur, Jaipur, Calcutta, and Bombay. Three factorial attitude types emerged from factor analysis; Greens (N = 15), Sustainable Developers (N = 7), and Postmodern Managers (N = 12).

Three consensus statements emerged in the analysis. Indian environmental actors agree on some significant core values: the value of life, its right to exist in its full diversity—essential to Hindu philosophy—is strongly affirmed by all subjects (with valences of +4 +4 +5). The statements are: "Biological diversity must be treated as a common heritage of mankind, to be indexed, used, and above all preserved"; "All living things have a right to exist"; and "Investment in energy efficiency and recycling can reduce fossil fuel demand without sacrificing growth."

The *Green* attitude type includes political scientists and economists from the Center for the Study of Developing Societies, the Indian Institute of Public Administration, and the Institute of Economic Growth in New Delhi; teachers from Value Orientation and Environmental Education in Calcutta; and ecologists and environmental activists from Lokayan, INTACH, Developmental Alternatives, the Center for Science and Environment (New Delhi), an environmental magazine and the Save Bombay Committee (Bombay); Seva Mandir in Udaipur; and the Indira Gandhi Institute for Environmental Science in Jaipur. Of the fifteen persons showing this attitude type, eight are women.

Greens respect life and natural diversity and dislike the technological hubris of Western developmentalism. Greens distrust large dams, nuclear power, and biotechnology because of their environmental risks and are alive to future dangers of global warming. They advocate a sustainable Green economy mixing traditional and modern production methods with recycling to cut energy use, favor Gandhian voluntary simplicity and women's rights, and support tribals and scheduled castes who bear valuable traditional knowledge. Only grassroots economic development mobilizing these sectors can be environmentally sound.

Greens disagree that the West bears responsibility for enforcing environmental standards or that there is growing maturity in the international community regarding ecological issues. They reject the apocalyptic notion that "Humanity is doomed to extinction. Our main effort must be to preserve maximum diversity so nature can carry on after us." They think that democracy, despite its inefficiencies, is the best means for creating a Green economy.

Greens are realistic about the limitations of the famous Chipko Andolan movement. A political scientist and an environmental activist both see Chipko as a popular resistance movement in the western Himalayas giving priority to immediate survival over Gandhian or ecological philosophy. However, Chipko's impact and a growing consciousness of India's environmental degradation have led to an alternative vision of the future, to a questioning of Western elitist high-energy, urban, technocratic development. Greens anticipate the spread of their perspective because of the exigencies of the Indian environmental situation. As an activist told me, "Thousands of groups like Chipko are evolving a new political process, an alternative vision of the future which is humane, respects natural limits, and questions the socioeconomic organization of the last two hundred years. It is an emotional experience to work so closely with them, instead of the coldness of the planners I know."

But there is significant sentiment within this type against forming a Green party out of such grassroots groups. As the activist said, "The constituency of the environmental movement is the powerless. Consciousness is not widespread enough or profound enough to form the basis of a party. The green ethic must pervade all parties, and life itself, and shouldn't specialize politically." The publisher of an influential magazine argued that "at every meeting of groups about Narmada we talk about a Green Party. But to accept the system and strive for domination would be wrong. It is better to inoculate all the parties with Green thinking."

Greens adhere to the Gandhian legacy of nonviolent resistance. As the publisher said, "Gandhi spoke of self-sufficiency and equal distribution of resources. Nehru wanted development and military power to match the West. But no ideology understands environmental limits. Development means improvement of land, air, water, human potential. We must strive for human and women's rights, and for ecological goals, with nonviolent means, with Gandhian tactics. The reverse of technology is humility. We need humility instead of seeking to dominate and manage nature. It is impossible to manage complexity."

An economist in rural development argued: "We are disenchanted with technocratic development models. We know how to develop but not how to eliminate poverty. Welfare won't work when the vast majority is poor. We must abandon Western and elite notions of 'the good life.' There can be no prosperity or consumer society here. The poor want only incremental improvement, economic security. Western media bring in consumerism and irrelevant notions of the welfare state. This influence, along with our democracy, makes it hard to build consent around the idea of enforcing sacrifice among the elites."

Greens favor native, grassroots, popular development grounded in bioregional and cultural diversity. Economic models must be developed by villagers, scheduled castes, women, and tribals who directly manage the environment for production. Viable ecomanagement traditions are to be combined with the latest ecology and conservation biology into a sustainable mixed economy that is egalitarian, nonconsumerist, and popularly managed.

The people are to be empowered through local nonviolent mass movements, against megadevelopment projects and for local control over commons. Movement politics replaces appeals to corrupt state and national politics and provides the basis for lasting social change. India is well positioned for creation of a Green economy, argue Indian Greens, because much of its traditional and tribal knowledge base is still intact and because there is growing national and international consciousness about its environmental crisis. Also, the fiscal crisis of the state, and the exhaustion of planned high-power, urban industrial development models make conversion to sustainability a necessity.

The *Sustainable Developer's* perspective is represented by seven individuals, three being women and four men: directors of INTACH, the Indian National Trust; ecologists in Developmental Alternatives, the Center for Policy Research, and the Bombay Natural History Society; and a pharmaceutical firm CEO involved in urban environmental issues.

The Sustainable Developers fear humanity's technological hubris and disagree that our destiny is to control nature. They are wary of the risks of nuclear power and biotechnology and concerned about conscious planning for industrially induced climatological change. But SDs believe that environmentally sound development is cost effective and can be done with a mix of fossil and alternative fuels.

Sustainable Developers see current environmental initiatives as piecemeal and defensive but believe in the possibility of development respecting environmental parameters. As a pharmaceutical executive and ecologist stated, "We should see no more megaprojects like the Narmada Dam. They waste intermediate inputs. We should change to a 'small is beautiful' stance rather than the old TVA model, which was fine for America which had the technical base from which it could spring. Such models cannot be transplanted. India has a good technical base compared with the rest of the Third World, but there is no reason to jump into large projects without local experience. Especially under the influence of international agencies and local contractors who have a very short-term view."

As an economist noted, "The Nehruvian development model was hi-tech in the 1950s–60s, but its high-energy extensive development is no longer sustainable. Now there are too many interests supporting import substitution; they would like to keep the economy slow-growing and closed. But India must open up to the world economy."

Given a growing international consensus on environmental regulation of production, it is possible to turn economic growth in a new direction. Global South problems cannot entirely be blamed on international developmental programs. As the economist said,

Indian politics is populist. Politicians must woo the poor with left slogans even though their policy is right of center. But now we need growth to abolish poverty. The population is eating our economic growth. NGOs debate growth versus distribution, but there is no good debate on inflation, corruption, population.

Now we face the fiscal crisis of the state. We fought inflation but at the cost of low production. Now we face large slack capacity and a drying up of foreign aid. This could be a blessing in disguise because foreign aid encourages inefficiency, and we could have fast growth with little investment by using our large slack capacity. Growth is no longer correlated to foreign investment.

Sustainable Developers do not believe that population growth is linked to environmental degradation or that women's rights are the key to cutting population. The Bombay CEO thought women's rights the key to population control, but the female economist thought that "women's education is the key to population. Women's rights are not antagonistic to men; these issues require mutual decisions. Indian feminism is moderate." A female executive in INTACH said, "The feminist view in [statement] number 23 is bullshit. Women do not feel complete in this individualistic way of life. If we know ourselves, we can balance home, private, and worldly life."

Sustainable Developers do not think population control will be automatic; it must be planned. Nor do they agree that development represents a transfer of natural resources from the poor to the rich; that is, they reject class analysis. As the Bombay CEO said, "Politicians use the poor's anger against the rich. They don't take advantage of upper-class concern. And we are concerned, not blind. The poor can't be helped without our support." The implication is that environmental concerns are consensual issues, not class issues.

In summary, Sustainable Developers envision converting India to environmentally appropriate intensive development. This new model can include a just distribution of resources, population planning, women's education, and consensus among social classes. Given perceived international maturity over environmental issues, the end of the Cold War, and the exhaustion of India's economic model, a limited opening to the international market, to encourage further growth, is seen as beneficial.

Sustainable Developers and Greens, many of whom work together within the same environmental groups or governmental agencies, maintain different emphases on key issues. Sustainable Developers, who tend to be executive officers in the environmental movement, wish to utilize the gains of Western development, tempering economics with environmental responsibility. They are political realists ready to operate within the system for incremental environmental gains.

Sustainable Developers and Greens are neutral (with a different polarity) on growing environmental maturity in the international community—and on the idea of the West's responsibility for funding and promoting environmentalism in the Global South. Sustainable Developers do not blame Western development agencies for Global South ecological damage and are neutral about Western developmentalism as imperialist plunder, unlike Greens. Maximization of GNP can be achieved without polluting and without increasing social inequality, according to Sustainable Developers, but Greens show little interest in GNP growth as a social goal (21: -5, +1). Sustainable Developers in turn are neutral about some central Green values. They are relatively neutral regarding the Green economic model (18: -1, +5) and population control based on education and sociopolitical rights for women.

The *Postmodern Managers'* perspective is the third to emerge from the data. Twelve men and one woman are included in this type, all of them managers, either in environmental groups such as MARG (Multiple Action Research Group, New Delhi), Developmental Alternatives, Seva Mandir (Udaipur), and World Wildlife Fund or in corporations like INFAR Ltd. (Calcutta), and two are Cabinet-level executives in the Ministries of Planning and Environment.

Managers give priority to human needs and rational management of environmental processes. As the minister of planning told me, "India has systematized management of the environment, in fact, no country has made such progress. Our Environmental Protection Act is comprehensive and tough. We have made amazing progress, despite a lack of money. But poverty drives us to produce. The West produces for no reason, creates waste for consumerism. But in the Third World, poverty is the main cause of pollution."

Postmodern Managers give no credence to apocalyptic visions of ecological collapse, believing that human beings have the rationality to save themselves through democratic and pragmatic management of environmental problems. As a manager at World Wildlife Fund argued, "Environmental policy is piecemeal. But hope for a green environmentalist regime is only a dream. Until then we must fight a rearguard action. We must maintain tight control over environmental damage. There is a whole generation of wrong values; we need to control the situation until they die out, and a new generation takes over." A growing environmental consensus on the international scene is positive, but the West should not control India's situation; local elites have the capacity to manage their own problems.

It is possible and cost effective to have a balanced economy, with recycling and traditional and modern technologies. GNP growth need not be sacrificed, and it is possible to include distributive justice. As a biotechnologist and pharmaceutical executive in Calcutta said, "Development means enriching our capability, capacity, ability to produce for a better life. Redistributing natural resources isn't enough. We must create new wealth-making mechanisms, and a strong infrastructure like

Japan, Korea, and Taiwan. A high level of wealth will benefit everyone."

Technology can be managed and its environmental effects controlled. Even nuclear power, biotechnology, and large dams can be useful. As the World Bank Narmada Project manager said, "I am not so pessimistic about big projects or environmental changes. We can perpetuate and even enhance the environment while serving human needs."

Postmodern Managers believe that global warming and population growth can be controlled, the latter through recognition of women's rights; indeed managers score more positively on women's rights (+4) than do Sustainable Developers (-1) or Greens (+3).

In summary, Postmodern Managers believe in rationally managing economic growth and incorporating environmental concerns. Pragmatists who give no credence to apocalyptic or utopian visions, they are willing to utilize Western technology for development and to control its negative effects. Their concern is that India's economy continue to grow to meet the exigencies of a rapidly spiraling population.

Postmodern Managers differ from Sustainable Developers in their emphasis on the primacy of human needs (including women's) and human management of the environment. Sustainable Developers believe that our Promethean technocratic ideology is the source of cosmic vandalism, a proposition such managers ignore. Managers are stronger on the issues of women's rights, about which Sustainable Developers are largely neutral (+4 versus -1).

Postmodern Managers believe in large-scale high-energy technologies and thus support nuclear and hydroelectric power and biotechnological transformation of agriculture. Sustainable Developers believe in small-scale intensive models and distrust high-power extensive development. The largest area of disagreement between the two types is on this extensive versus intensive development issue, specifically in the application of high-energy or high-risk technologies.

For example, the idea that biotechnology is the next step in human evolution, and that our destiny is to control planetary evolution, is strongly rejected by Sustainable Developers but weakly acceptable to Postmodern Managers. Sustainable Developers are neutral about biotechnology being superior in food production to chemical technologies; managers are weakly positive. Developers think the risks of biotechnological experimentation outweigh potential benefits, while managers are neutral. Similarly, these developers see some risk in nuclear power while the managers see only its benefits.

Thus, Sustainable Developers embrace developmental economics with a biocentric perspective, while Postmodern Managers believe in the pragmatic incorporation of environmental policies into extensive high-tech models of growth, and they believe in the priority of human needs over nature.

The differences between Postmodern Managers and Greens are even more pronounced. Greens are biocentric and antitechnocratic. Their interest lies in restoring the lost balance with nature and creating a Green economy based on sustainable production, simplicity, participatory democracy, and recycling, instead of managing the environmental effects of technocratic growth models. Greens want grassroots movements that train the disadvantaged majority for environmental and economic self-management, and empower them to oppose technocratic planning.

Greens reject the Western hard-energy model as plunder rather than progress. The strongest disagreement between Greens and Postmodern Managers is over biotechnology and nuclear power. Greens oppose biotechnology as the inevitable evolutionary step for human beings (-4 versus +1). Greens oppose the notion that biotechnology is superior to chemical food-production methods and disagree with the managers that biotechnology research is essential to avoid dependency. Greens and Postmodern Managers are strongly polarized on the risks of nuclear power (+4 versus -4).

The attitude types we have called Greens, Sustainable Developers, and Postmodern Managers overlap occupational categories utilized in elaborating the survey—government, business, scientists, and environmental groups. There is room for compromise between sectors on environmental issues, because attitudinal cleavages crosscut sectoral cleavages in complex ways. This complexity may be a sign that environmentalism is more congenial to India's heritage than in the West, where it forms a recent and novel ideological addition, and that there are grounds for broad elite consensus on the issue. But this consensus is also forced by government co-optation of the movement into complex insider bargaining to make policy. The moderation and empiricism of the environmental types is at once testimony to their maturity and a sign of their lack of power apart from government fora.

Figure 4.1 graphs these attitude types on modern/postmodern and Fordist/post-Fordist spectra, using statement 18 on the Green economy and statement 13 on business and market incentives as indicators. Greens fall into postmodern/post-Fordist factor space and are the most advanced on these dimensions of all countries, showing that Gandhi's mixture of native religion, philosophy, and forms of social action, when added to sophisticated science and international political perspectives of environmental elites, yields perhaps the Third World's most advanced Green movement.

India's Sustainable Developers lie in modernist/Fordist factorial space and are the most conservative of the SDs in all the countries we studied. This type comprises environmental executives, a pharmaceutical executive active in Bombay environmental issues, and a number of scientists, who all reject the Nehruvian developmental model in favor of export-led free trade; that is, they are in line with the international neoliberal model of sustainable development enunciated in Rio de Janeiro at UNCED. They reject large-scale international agency projects, which have proven so damaging to India's environment, in favor of smaller-scale, cost-beneficial sustainable growth.

Sustainable Developers fear nuclear power and biotechnology and think that intensive development, technological efficiency, and recycling will solve many of the problems of fossil fuel cycles. They want a consensual and nonpopulist approach to environmental politics but are neutral about relying solely on market incentives. In fact, they criticize India's democracy for inefficient regulation. India's Sustainable Developers accept free trade but are not enthusiastic about deregulation. They mix localist community development with the Gandhian ethos.

India's Postmodern Managers are postmodern and post-Fordist because four of them work for international organizations (UNEP, World Bank, WWF), one is a cabinet minister, and another is a deputy minister. Anthropocentric optimists, these managers believe in environmentally intelligent use of all means for development but are negative toward government and business. As the World Wildlife Fund executive said, "There is a whole generation of wrong values; we need to control the situation until they die out and a new generation takes over"—a most characteristic postmodern attitude.

Postmodern Managers differ from Sustainable Developers on the scale of technologies and projects, and they differ from Greens in accepting nuclear power and biotechnology. Postmodern Managers are strongest in support of women's rights, take the strongest stance on preventing global warming, and are the most avid of the types in believing that environmentally sound economic development is possible.

India's environmental elites show a largely postmodern consensus, a spectrum of attitudes running obliquely across the left-right continuum. They are international in perspective and in tune with Western environmentalist and attitudes, while utilizing Hindu/Gandhian traditions with great affective force.

However, India's environmental movement, for all its national and international cachet and its impact on planning, is frustrated by the nation's sheer linguistic, cultural, and environmental complexity. The Gandhian ethos provides environmentalists a coherent ethic, metaphysic, and method of struggle and strong legitimation on the national political scene. But the official Gandhian ideology is largely ignored

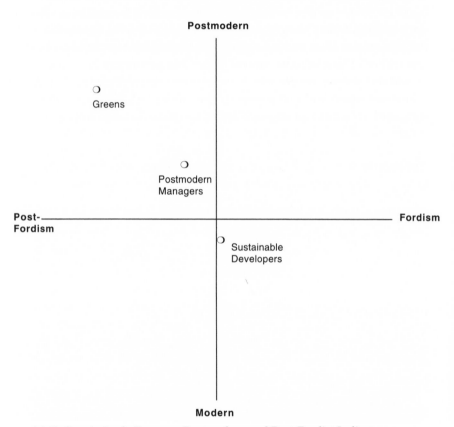

4.1. Indian Attitude Types on Postmodern and Post-Fordist Indicators
Postmodern indicator is a positive score on statement 18. The only alternative is a green economy, with grassroots democracy, voluntary simplicity, sustainable production, and recycling.
Post-Fordist indicator is a negative score on statement 13. If government gave business information and incentives, not command and sanction, the market and entrepreneurs would protect the environment.

by powerful corporate, family, national, and state government elites and by increasingly powerful criminal elements.

Thus, the environmental movement is in the unusual position of gaining significant victories in terms of national policy and local resistance movements but ultimately having little impact on the national environmental situation. The government it pressures is largely unable to promote the profound long-term changes required to remedy India's slow-motion environmental collapse.

India's environmental movement has the advantages of Ghandian religion, strong links to native ecomanagement practices, an excellent intellectual and political infrastructure, sophisticated international support, and multiple points of access to national and local government. But its sophistication and strength are dissipated by a corrupt and bureaucratically tangled government, a declining economy, and an ecological and population crisis that surpasses known techniques of environmental repair and management. The movement, far from being a vanguard, is fighting a rearguard action for cultural and ecological survival.

Conclusions

1. India has experienced four socioeconomic developmental models: Mahatma Gandhi's village-based appropriate technological economy; Jawaharlal Nehru's Fabian state-planned import substitution, which created growth and urbanization but is defeated by government incapacity, population pressure, ecological problems, and international conjunctural changes; the neoliberal deregulation and free-trade posture of Congress and the later coalition governments, under pressure from Hindu traditionalists because of culturally invasive corporate impacts; and the environmentalist paradigm blending ecological science, mass movements, international scientific and interest group input, and Gandhian philosophy into a powerful resistance movement against state megadevelopment and neoliberalism.

2. There are three environmental attitude types among Indian elites: Postmodern Managers, who believe in sustained yield from nature; Sustainable Developers, who wish to convert the technocratic hardpower model to more environmentally balanced development; and Greens, who are creating a Gandhian mass movement for a localized sustainable economy mixing traditional and Western technologies.

3. These types crosscut government, business, scientific, and environmental group membership. Postmodern Managers are found in the

executive strata of government, business, and international and national environmental groups. Sustainable Development represents a politically and economically pragmatic orientation within business, government, and environmental groups. The Green orientation is largely found in grassroots organizations but is shared by some scientists and government and business personnel. Environmentalist consensus among elites aligns India with Western postmodern thinking despite significant economic and cultural differences. Environmentalism will remain on the political agenda, and the sophistication of its proponents and the weight of its 950 environmental groups mean that this voice cannot be ignored by planners.

3. India with its interlocked environmental, population, political, religious, and ethnic problems is not likely to make a transition to a post-Fordist knowledge/information-service economy in the foreseeable future. Yet India has the advantage that environmental concerns were part of traditional village ecomanagement and the Gandhian worldview, so that elite postmodern values connect to resilient premodern traditions.

But India's widespread environmental movement also faces the disadvantages of extreme cultural and political complexity and of interlocked crises driving the biological erosion of this lush subcontinent. However enlightened the elites, the masses are locked into parochial localism, so that India's extreme multiculturalism, augmented by its recent commitment to neoliberal free trade, will cause this elite environmental consensus to have influence but little power to remedy the country's extreme environmental situation.

5

Korea: New Democracy and Environmentalism

The Republic of Korea has achieved remarkably rapid economic growth and, as a model Newly Industrialized Country (NIC) and new democracy, provides an important case study of transition to sustainable development. Korea's recent democracy allows a rising crescendo of popular environmental concern to be expressed, and the government has created a Ministry of Environment and a suite of sophisticated laws to counter the awful pollution arising from some thirty years of unbridled industrialization.

Korea intends to join the developed nations by internationalizing its economy and creating higher environmental standards. Korea entered OECD, the Organization for Economic Cooperation and Development, in 1996 and must now meet the common environmental standards of these countries. With a GNP ranking tenth within OECD, the resources to do so are available. The financial crisis of 1997 put Korea under International Monetary Fund discipline at the same time that it was experiencing an effective democratic opening, but this may be only a temporary setback in its regulatory momentum.

Current Korean democratization must transform the legacy of forty years of Fordist developmentalism driven by military dictatorship. Popular environmental concern coincides with business and government interests in globalization and democratic legitimation, to motivate considerable progress in Korean environmental standards in the 1990s. But Korea's environmental deficit and rising tide of consumerism require massive and costly remediation.

In this chapter I examine Korea's rise to prosperity and the environmental costs of its aggressive military Fordism. I explore Korea's developmental path, its new environmental administration and law, and the attitudes of decision makers in a period of democratic transition and globalization.

Environmental Crisis and Response: The Rise of a Modern Regulatory Regime

South Korea occupies 99,392 sq km of the Korean Peninsula, two-thirds of which is mountainous and possessed of few natural resources. Its population of 44.9 million is well educated and 97 percent literate. Ten percent of GNP is spent on education. Population increase is only 0.97 percent per annum, but density ranks third in the world at 452 persons per square kilometer. The intensity of cultivation ranks first in the world.

In 1953, when the Korean War ended with partition along the 38th Parallel and an uneasy armistice, South Korea was in ruins, with 60 percent of its industry and 25 percent of its infrastructure destroyed. Per capita gross national product was only sixty-seven dollars. Until the early 1960s Korea "was considered to be in dire economic straits with poor prospects."[1]

Since 1963, Korea's economic achievement has been remarkable. Within a single generation, Korea advanced from a war-shattered economy to a high-tech upper-middle-income country. In the period 1970 to 1993, Korea's GNP advanced from thirty-third to fifteenth in the world (U.S. $8.13 to $308.9 billion), and per capita GNP increased from U.S. $252 to $7,435 in current dollars. External trade volume increased from thirty-second to tenth in the world (from U.S. $12.3 to $170 billion). Korea experienced not only rapid quantitative expansion but solid qualitative growth in terms of income equality. A model NIC, Korea had a U.S. $12,200 per capita GNP and $546 billion GNP in 1996 and is the world's fifteenth largest economy.[2]

However, Korea's "economic miracle" resulted from decades of state promotion by repressive military regimes, a bureaucracy insulated from civil society, collusion with giant conglomerates, patronage, corruption, repression of labor, and co-optation of the peasantry. Recent democratization and negotiations toward reunification with the North have begun to change this picture, and Korea is moving rapidly to modernize its civil society and environmental legislation.

Japan's colonial rule (1910–45) produced land reform that made Korea an important rice producer within its sphere of influence. The 1920s saw the beginning of light manufacturing, and Korean heavy industry grew rapidly after 1937 in order to supply materiel for Japan's conquest of China. Japan's legacy of commercial agriculture, a rationalized bureaucracy, and extensive light and heavy industry became the structural basis for later autonomous growth. After the fall of Japan in 1945, worker, peasant, and youth organizations attempted to democratize Korean politics but were defeated by the U.S. military occupation, which suppressed the left and supported the rise to political power of the bureaucracy, police, and military.

The Korean War (June 1950 to July 1953) and partition devastated the country and required massive U.S. aid, which between 1953 and 1961 financed 70 percent of total imports and 75 percent of total capital formation. Seventy-five percent of this aid was in the form of commodities and surplus agricultural goods and formed an indirect subsidy to U.S. producers. But in return for this aid, the United States extracted privatization, fiscal and monetary stabilization, United Nations command over the Korean army, U.S. military occupation, and normalized relations with Japan.

Syngman Rhee's dictatorship pursued import substitution industrialization using foreign capital and co-opted business by rationing loans and government contracts, through exchange and import licenses, and with frank graft and corruption. The student revolt of April 1960 led to the short-lived Chang Myon government, which was overthrown by a coup on May 16, 1961; this put Park Chung Hee into power and brought a shift to export-promotion strategy.

The Park regime purged the bureaucracy and attacked business corruption in order to break the Rhee patronage machine. Having brought big business to heel, and managing popular protest through martial law, Park began aggressive state promotion of exports using subsidies, cheap credit, tariff protection, devaluation, and foreign capital investment. An increased state role in banking and foreign loan allocations mobilized and controlled the uses of investment capital. Efficient taxation, foreign capital investment, and loans all worked to offset declining U.S. direct aid. Light manufacturing was considered the leading sector, until the downturn of the early 1970s. President Nixon's withdrawal of a combat division led to a policy of "industrial deepening"— promotion of heavy industry, for defense production.

Under a state of emergency, which closed the universities and repressed growing student and labor protest, the dictatorship began promoting steel, machinery, electronics, shipbuilding, and oil and chemical industries, motivated by national security and export-promotion considerations. This policy of state-programmed heavy industrial development, funded in large part by foreign loans, did not improve competitiveness and sparked foreign debt, inflation, and a high corporate debt-to-equity ratio, which made Korea vulnerable to international economic downturns. It was also the beginning of the massive environmental pollution that has led Korea to its current ecological crisis.

Large conglomerate firms (*chaebols*) emerged, favored by the 1971 National Security Law, which broke up the unions, by the 1972 freeze on private debt, and by preferential governmental credit. Fifty conglomerates were responsible for 43 percent of GDP in 1978. Nine major conglomerates—Samsung, Hyundai, Dao Woo, Pohang, Goldstar, Yukong, Sunkyong, Sangyong, and Korean Air—account for 80 percent of Korean GNP. In the 1980s Japanese investment surpassed the U.S. share, although the U.S. market for Korean goods is twice the size of Japan's.

The regime collapsed with the assassination of Park Chung Hee on October 26, 1979, but already growth rates had declined from 9.9 percent in the late 1970s to 2.2 percent in the early 1980s, and inflation had risen to 26 percent, with high current account deficits and debt.

A coup d'état by Chun Doo Hwan in June 1981 instituted a neoliberal adjustment program, which cut the governmental sector and public enterprise subsidies, cut real wages, imposed monetary restraint, and supported strategic small and medium high-tech export industries such as semiconductors, computers, aerospace, and telecommunications. Banks and the capital market were privatized, investment restrictions were lifted, and antimonopoly laws curbed some conglomerate abuses.

But this combination of neoliberal market reforms and state repression failed to curb popular demands for democratization, and opposition from industrialists, farmers, and the middle class could not be met by patronage or corporativist measures from a "downsized" state.

Large-scale labor action and widespread popular protest led to the presidential election of December 1988, which brought Roh Tae Woo's conservative transition regime into office. Facing continuous street protest and strong opposition pressure, Roh used repression. Tight money led to bankruptcies and falling stock prices, while the current account deficit reached U.S. $9.5 billion. The high-cost Olympic Games combined with chaebol speculation in real estate, stocks, and financial markets led to extravagant consumerism, redistribution of income to the upper classes, and increasing violent crime. Korea is now the fourth most expensive country in the world in terms of basic living costs.

In the 1990s, Korea has been modernizing its legal and constitutional structures and civil society, democratizing national and local government, and liberalizing its economy. In December 1992, the new president, Kim Young Sam, began purging corrupt bureaucrats, military, and politicians; attacked the underground economy; and began liberal economic reforms, privatizing government enterprises and acceding to U.S. pressure to accept the terms of GATT and to open his market.

Korea has begun actively promoting Asian Pacific Economic Cooperation, a free-trade regime for the Pacific Rim. The election of December
18, 1997, made opposition leader Kim Daejung president. Kim is pro-
environment, but he has no majority in the legislature, and he inherited a banking crisis that is leading to many bankruptcies. Unemployment went from 2 to 9 percent, and Korea was forced to accept a tough
IMF stabilization program in return for emergency loans.

Confucian countries grant small legitimacy to private profit making, and Korean corporate capitalism remains tainted by its collusion
with Japanese imperialism, repression of labor, corrupt and speculative misuses of state-donated capital, dependence on foreign capital,
technology, and markets, and its environmental irresponsibility. Given
the current economic crisis due to irresponsible bank loans to the giant
chaebols, popular attitudes toward business are negative, causing corporations to be concerned with legitimating themselves by taking active environmental measures.

Environment is a paramount issue in Korea. A 1998 survey showed
that 39 percent of Koreans showed a "great deal of environmental concern," and 69 percent thought that environmental laws "did not go far
enough." Nineteen percent (up eight points from 1992) thought that
environment was the most important issue facing the nation. Seventy-
seven percent of the public are in favor of major action on climate
change issues.[3]

Fifty years of rapid development have pushed Korea to the environmental limits of its export-promotion development model, and
Koreans are experiencing serious pollution and biosphere degradation.
The Environmental Administration was established in 1980, based on
"harmony between development and environmental protection." But
as major environmental problems were brought to light in the mid-
1980s, policy shifted to a conservationist balance of development and
environmental protection. In 1990, the Ministry of Environment was
established, and subsequent aggressive initiatives have begun to improve the situation.

Korea faces four major environmental problems: air quality, waste
disposal, water quality, and nature conservation.

Air pollution is a serious problem, which is being addressed through
an innovative mix of regulation and incentives. Coal briquettes were
widely used in urban centers for heating, and coal for electricity generation. Industrialization has led to a ninefold increase in Korea's energy
supply since 1970. Energy intensity per unit of GDP is significantly higher
than in Japan or Europe. Coal, oil, and gas are all imported; oil pro-

duces 62.5 percent of primary energy, coal 18.7 percent, and nuclear power 11 percent.

Automobile pollution is a serious problem. Freight transport rose 532 percent from 1980 to 1994, passenger transport 505 percent, while GDP increased 213 percent. There will be 13 million vehicles by 2000 and they emit 2.1 million tons of pollutants, or 49 percent of the total and 25 percent of CO_2. There were 1,533 oil spills at sea, 72 percent of them willful or the result of negligence. The economic loss from traffic congestion is above 3 percent of GDP and the death toll from accidents far above OECD averages.

The Ministry of Environment (MOE) has produced some creative regulatory programs. Fuel prices are no longer subsidized and are reaching true costs. A road tax is charged proportionate to engine size, and registration costs double for each additional car. Large facilities are taxed for generating private traffic, but if they adjust work hours or provide shuttle buses and ride sharing, the tax is cut 70 percent. A congestion charge is paid by each car entering Seoul on weekdays. More subways are being built.

MOE now requires three-way catalytic converters, annual inspections, and higher quality fuel, and is attempting to reduce carbon monoxide, hydrocarbons, and nitrous and sulfur oxides in the air. MOE also regulates fuel production and consumption, with low-sulfur solid and liquid fuels and Liquefied Natural Gas reducing SO_2 pollution from 0.062 ppm in 1988 to 0.023 ppm in 1993.

SO_x (sulfate) emissions decreased 5 percent from 1990 to 1995, NO_x (nitrates) increased 25 percent, suspended particulates dropped 3 percent, but CO_2 emissions increased 53 percent and are more than double the 1985 level. Emission of CO_2 per unit GNP exceeds the OECD average and draft programs are being considered to cut these Greenhouse emissions. Ozone emissions have also increased.

A serious component of pollution in Korea is the transboundary flux from China of SO_x, NO_x, and loess (fine red desert sand). Korean cities still experience significant acid rain and snow, with Seoul at 5.4 pH, Pusan 5.3 pH, and Daegu at 5.5 pH in 1993. Particulates have almost halved in major cities due to aggressive programs, but in spring Chinese loess doubles the concentration. MOE has begun regulating the siting of dirty industries such as cement, brick, glass, and steel, requires scrubbers for factory smokestacks, and applies tough standards for construction sites. Since 1986, particulate pollution has decreased in all major cities; in Seoul from 150 mg/m^3 in 1990 to 88 mg/m^3 in 1993.[4]

Tough air quality laws and enforcement have rendered clear results.

The MOE wants renewable energy to form 3 percent of total energy by 2001, and the lowest WHO quality values are mandated in law. Unlike in U.S. regulation, which requires new legislation to ratchet up standards, Korea modifies its air and water standards in each five-year plan and tightens them yearly.

Now 233 types of industry and business require air and water quality permits to operate. Energy efficiency standards are imposed on domestic appliances and energy labels on consumer goods. Asbestos is being eliminated; construction sites must be covered and trucks washed. Industry needs dust collectors and smokestack monitoring devices, and dirty industries can expect frequent inspections. In 1995, 54,504 inspections were done and 1,521 indictments handed out. Some 33,855 workplaces were inspected for dust, and 2,473 were out of compliance, leading to fines, prosecution, or closure. Emission charges levied for noncompliance are equal to the cost of cleanup. This is an economic incentive that removes the profitability of imposing environmental costs on others. Also, large businesses are charged based on the amount of fuel used for heating and cooling.

Korea is spending 0.3 percent of GDP on air quality measures, matching a growing public demand for cleaner air. Industries are moving toward ISO14000 (U.N. International Standards Organization) quality control standards. A country that imports its primary energy sources must become more efficient, so energy prices are moving to reflect market costs, the fuel mix has changed to cleaner forms, and aggressive inspection coupled with economic incentives, have all shown significant results in the 1990s. Environmental measures are also good business practice.

Industrial and domestic solid waste pose another serious problem for Korea. In 1989, 57,645 tons of industrial waste per day were discharged from 9,822 industries, but by 1994 this amount had fallen to 54,000 tons. Of this waste stream, 67 percent came from industry, 33 percent from municipal and commercial sources, and 3 percent was considered hazardous. In 1989 Korea ranked first in the world in home garbage discharge, with 78,021 tons per day, which is 2.2 kg per person, compared with 0.9 in Germany and the United Kingdom, 1.0 in Japan, and 1.3 kg in the United States. MOE and many environmental groups have attempted to raise public awareness, with apparent success. By 1995 this home waste had fallen to 1.1 kg per day due to recycling. But the waste stream has changed due to rising consumption, so combustible waste has doubled, and packaging waste is 32 percent of the municipal stream.

Between 1991 and 1995 hazardous industrial waste increased at an annual 8 percent, and Korea lacks facilities for treatment. In 1995, 4,444 tons per day of hazardous waste were generated. Half of hazardous waste was recycled, 16 percent incinerated, and 5 percent landfilled. Polychlorinated biphenyls (PCBs) have been banned from import, and 118 items are under permits and tight restriction. Tough fines and enforcement ensure that waste is tracked (it must be transported in yellow trucks) and stored in identifiable ways. The "polluter pays" principle is applied as a strong economic incentive; polluters will pay 100 percent of waste management costs by 2001. The many subsidies to industry waste production are being cut. Contaminated soil around industries and U.S. military bases is removed and processed, with the polluter paying the costs.

MOE has been moving aggressively to recycle 35 percent of municipal waste, incinerate 20 percent, and cut landfill in half by the millennium. Government gives soft loans, R&D grants, subsidies, and tax exemptions to promote recycling industries. The government uses recycled goods and is promoting demand. Recycling rates are high—53 percent for paper, 57 percent for bottles, though only 13 percent of plastics. Seventy-two percent of scrap iron, 90 percent of tires, 66 percent of silver oxide batteries, and 80 percent of lubricants were reclaimed by 1995. Government promotes refillable containers in most areas and bans the use of disposable goods in restaurants, baths, and lodgings over a certain size. Large restaurants have cut food waste by half in four years. Household waste fell 27 percent between 1994 and 1995, as recycling gained popularity, in line with high environmental concern shown in polls.

Composting plants are being built in the major cities, and eleven incinerators are being built. Large businesses are responsible for their own disposal under stringent regulation. Some seventeen items are subject to deposits, and producers and importers of nonrecyclable goods must pay a waste disposal charge.

Korea has moved aggressively, combining regulation and economic incentives, and has seen some gratifying results. But industrial waste in 2001 will be 74 percent higher than in 1994. Most landfills are substandard, while 63 percent will be filled by 2000 and 873 are now closed. Korea needs twenty-one large new landfills, but there is strong public resistance. A 1995 act created mechanisms by which communities and promoters must agree on siting, and property owners must be bought out or compensated for losses, unlike in the United States, where large transnational corporations unilaterally impose landfills on poor people of color. Industrial waste is being generated faster than GDP growth, and standards need to be tightened.

Korea has nine nuclear plants, which produce half of the country's electrical energy, and five are being planned; the antinuclear movement is concerned with siting, safety, and waste disposal. After a brief flirtation with the French in the mid-1970s, Korea decided against producing nuclear weapons and signed the Non-Proliferation Treaty in 1985, although it has not agreed to implement treaty safeguards. The nuclear program generates 4,200 drums of low-level radioactive waste and 248 tons of spent uranium fuel rods per year. By 1995 Korea had accumulated 50,000 drums of low-level waste and 2,623 tons of spent rods, creating a serious problem of storage and security.

Water pollution is a serious problem in Korea, and despite strong legislation, there has been no improvement in the 1990s. Four major rivers—the Han, Keum, Youngsan, and Nakdong—show serious pollution problems. Of some nineteen thousand lakes, most show serious pollution; many are unsuitable for swimming due to high *E. coli* counts. At most locations monitored, levels heavy metals, cyanogen, and lead and eutrophication because of fertilizer use all exceed standards. Precipitation varies widely from year to year, but a high 34 percent of available water is utilized. Per capita water use exceeds OECD levels. Agriculture uses 63 percent, the public 26 percent, and industry 11 percent of water. The four major pollutants of water are domestic sewage (13,972,000 m^3/day), industrial waste (6,412,000 m^3/day), rural human waste (44,652 m^3/day), and livestock slurry. Red tides occur annually on the shallow coastal shelf of the Yellow Sea, and bottom sediments are heavily contaminated.

Industrial point discharge has doubled between 1986 and 1994, and 15 percent enters the Han River, 18 percent the Nakdong. Despite several MOE initiatives, little progress has been made in reducing the biochemical oxygen demand (BOD) in the four major rivers, except in the lower reaches of the Han River. BOD statistics for the four rivers are not encouraging: for the Han River, this was 3.1 mg/liter in 1993, down from 3.4 in 1990; for the Naktong River 3.8 mg/l in 1993, up from 3.2 in 1990; for Keum River 3.1 in 1993, down from and 3.2 in 1990; and the Youngsan River had a BOD load of 3.3mg/l in 1993, against 3.8 in 1990.

Coastal waters receive heavy effluent discharges from four heavily industrialized coastal towns. Livestock production has risen 45 percent from 1988 to 1994, and fish farming, rice paddies, and agriculture based on heavy pesticide and fertilizer use all contribute to serious water pollution.

Important legislation was passed in the 1990s, and inspections have been stepped up in an aggressive effort to reverse a serious situation that is creating a lot of public pressure. Water quality regulation uses 0.8 percent of the budget, which amounts to three-quarters of environmental expenditure. In 1994, 128,000 plant inspections were made and found 8,000 firms were noncompliant. Some 660 firms had their licenses removed, 88 were prosecuted, and 112 were canceled. Over 30,000 companies are under a permit system, but standards need to be tightened.

Domestic water prices are approaching market level, but irrigation water is delivered free by the government, because Korea intends to become agriculturally self-sufficient. Sewer and storm water systems are being separated, and sewage treatment is creating a problem of sludge disposal. Factories must pretreat waste water before disposal.

Korea has modern legislation and administration in place, and is rebuilding hydroelectric, sewer, and waste treatment networks. But with a dense urban population, and high growth in industrial production, and fragmented administrative responsibility, water quality is not responding either to regulation or to incentives. Korea will have an uphill battle ahead in the area of water quality.

Korea has made a commitment to reforestation and is seriously entering into nature conservation. The country used to be 65 percent temperate deciduous broadleaf forest, but massive clear-cutting and war reduced the forest cover to minimal amounts. Since the 1960s a considerable reforestation effort has restored 32 percent of the prior forest, and by 1995 most of the remaining forest had regrown; but the composition has changed to 46 percent conifers due to replanting. National forests, 21 percent of the area, are carefully managed, but in the 71 percent of private forests, an unsustainable 8,000 ha have been clear-cut in the last five years.

Korea supports 28,500 species of flora and fauna, with 45 endemics, and 179 species rare or on the way to extinction. Some 203 species are listed for special management by MOE. Excessive or illegal hunting affects 180 species, and Korea has moved to ban hunting. Snakes, bears, and tigers are threatened because of their illegal use in traditional medicine. Korea signed CITES in 1993 and is working against the huge illegal Eastern market for animal products.

Large fishing fleets from China, Korea, and Japan are exhausting fish stocks locally and in the Pacific basin. Between 1963 and 1988 major species on the Yellow Sea coast have declined from 145 to 24, while the human population rose to 400 million. Korea has one of the worst records for predatory fishing and trawling practices. A new Ministry of Maritime Affairs and Fisheries plus some new legislation should help the situation, although nature preservation commands a very small budget. A coastal management act is expected and badly needed. Korea shelved plans for agricultural reclamation on 129,000 ha of Yellow Sea coastal shelf, but airport reclamation used 46 sq km of tidal flats near Seoul. Most inland wetlands are now used for agriculture.

Public lands represent 23 percent of forest lands, twenty national parks cover 6,473 km², and there are 723 protection areas and a 2,345 sq km marine park. MOE is creating a network of ecological corridors to facilitate animal migration, and 5,400 sq km of green belts have been mandated in the cities. But only 7 percent of Korea's territory is protected up to IUCN standards, and protected areas are not representative of all ecosystems in the country. National parks have banned cooking and are periodically closed in rotation to recover from tourist impacts. Golf courses and ski slopes were prohibited in national parks after a heated controversy.

Enforcement is weak as the park authority has only seven hundred personnel, and most regulation is done by the newly created local governments, which lack budget and capacity. Nature conservation is divided among several ministries, and ecological surveys have been mandated but not yet implemented.

Environmental groups, the Ministry of Environment, and many governmental figures are attempting to educate industry and the public about necessary changes in behavior. As of 1994 there were more than 160 environmental groups in Korea, over half founded in the 1990s, and their efforts are far-reaching. Korean environmental groups can be divided into three different categories. Eighty-four groups are closely linked to governmental policy and initiatives (e.g., Environmental Preservation Association, Council for Environmental Science, National Movement for Environmental Preservation). Forty-three social organizations participate actively in the environmental movement (Korean YMCA and YWCA, Consumer Association, Press Association). And there are thirty-three independent environmental groups organized by intellectuals and scientists (Alliance of Environmental Movements, Baedal Environmental Union, Society for Environment and Pollution). In addition to these groups, there are a number of small local NIMBY ("Not in my back yard") groups in the movement. The Korean government gave 506 million won (U.S. $640,000) to government-affiliated groups in 1993, with nonaffiliated groups receiving less than U.S. $10,000.

Korean Elite Environmental Attitudes

With Korea's new affluence and democratization, postmodern demands are emerging. As Donald Macdonald noted,

> Having largely been freed from extreme poverty and the threat of war and possessing a high educational level, south Koreans are throwing off the shackles of traditional deference and acquiescence to authority. As they acquire a stake in the national society, in property ownership, and employment, they are demanding a greater share in political decision-making and a larger measure of political freedom. As early as 1980, a public opinion poll showed a reversal of the economic and political priorities of the 1960s. . . . Such matters as protection against foreign imports, women's rights, environmental regulations, financial policies, and the special needs of medium and small businesses, which received little political attention in the past, are now coming to the fore.[5]

Growing public awareness of and concern over environment was reflected in our sample of seventy-four Korean government, business, scientific, and environmental leaders. Four distinct attitude types emerged from this sample: Greens, Political Greens, Sustainable Developers, and Postmodern Managers.[6]

Greens are an attitudinal composite of executives in the Kwanju Environmental Pollution Research Institute and Korea Peace Research Institute, two female workers and two members of the National Alliance of Movements for the Expulsion of Pollution, a manager and a member of the Environmental Conservation Association, a member of the Society for the Study of Environment and Pollution, two researchers and two life science students from Yonsei University, and an employee of Sangyong Engineering.

The majority of Greens emerged from the antinuclear movement, so that opposition to nuclear power is their first priority. As a female executive in the Kwanju Environmental Pollution Research Institute said, "The nuclear power plant is a live bomb." A female executive in the National Alliance of Movements for the Expulsion of Pollution considered nuclear energy "the most urgent issue," noting that "nuclear power should not be regarded as a necessary evil providing a substitute future energy source. It is just evil."

Greens are strongly anti-Western. The West has plundered the Glo-

bal South and international development programs have caused ecological damage, so the West has no moral claim to finance and enforce
international environmental standards.

Greens dislike the Western Fordist obsession with GNP growth. As
a member of the Environmental Conservation Association said, "The
priority on technological development in Western countries results in
inequality between countries as well as environmental destruction."
Specifically, "Advanced countries have capitalized on the Third World
as a nuclear testing ground and toxic waste dumping site," as a person
in the Environmental Planning Institute argued. He continued that "as
shown in the formula for calculating GNP, destruction and construction simultaneously heighten GNP, and the GNP index gives the people,
particularly the underclass, false consciousness." Recycling and conservation can reduce fossil fuel dependency and provide for growth,
although ultimately these fuels must be replaced with sustainable alternatives.

Korean Greens are concerned with global warming and strongly
oppose the passive policy of simply adjusting to climatic changes as
they occur. People in this type do not believe that the market will protect the environment, even given the right mix of incentives and information, nor are they sanguine that Korea's emergent democracy can
meet the challenge of its serious environmental problems. A member
of the Society for the Study of Environment and Pollution notes that
"environmental destruction has been caused by our materialist value
system, which has been accelerated by monopoly capital's ruthless
pursuit of profit and commercialism. Piecemeal alternatives or publicity campaigns cannot restore the environment. The full realization of
democracy is the only hope."

Korean Greens are weak adherents to the standard articles of international green ideology. They are neutral about the possibility of real-
izing a sustainable democratic green economy, neutral about the Gaia
hypothesis "Life on earth is a single organism which modifies the atmosphere to serve its own needs," and mildly negative about avoiding fossil fuel dependency, restoration of traditional farming practices,
and a sustainable economy.

Korean Greens have no regard for feminist concerns, which are usually part of environmentalist demands, and seem unaware of the
ecofeminist critique of industrial capitalism; these concerns do not resonate in Korea's Confucian culture. Greens have no distinct position regarding population control, which is not an urgent problem in Korea

where twenty years of population planning have produced near zero growth. Greens disagree that world population must be forced down in order to maintain basic development, but they also disagree that world population will automatically decline with rising living standards.

Having emerged from the antinuclear movement, these Greeens oppose Fordist developmentalism and are technology averse. Yet, they have not developed a complete green ideology or articulated the deep opposition to Korean neoliberal democracy implied in their stance.

Political Greens include a member of the Korea Anti-Nuclear Anti-Pollution and Peace Research Institute, an executive and member of the Kwanju Environmental Pollution Research Institute, an executive of the Catholic Farmers Federation, an employee and high-level executive of the Hankook Environmental Technology Corporation, a member of the Ministry of Environment, and employees of Lucky Goldstar and of the Seorim Environmental Development Corporation.

The tone of Political Green thought is quite different from that of the Greens. Political Greens are strongly committed to the proposition that humanity is ultimately doomed to extinction and that we must preserve nature to carry on after us. All living beings have a right to exist; but our excessive faith in technology has vandalized nature. "The degradation of nature is the same as the degradation of human beings, who are a part of nature," notes an employee of Hankook Environmental Technology Corporation. Holders of this attitude type believe that environmental collapse has caused the violent end of other civilizations and will overtake those who have adopted the Western model, which has been used to plunder and exploit the Global South. A member of the Kwanju Environmental Pollution Research Institute notes that "modification of nature has been nothing but destruction. Leaving the natural environment as it is, is the best basis for human survival."

Restoration of the original sustainable economy of the species and restoration of sustainable farming would require a revolutionary change in social organization and value systems. A director of educational programming in the Kwanju institute argued that "every life form on earth should respect other life forms in nature. Anyone who does not follow this natural relationship will be driven out of nature. Human beings' arbitrary worldview has dictated our relationship with nature. Remolding a sound worldview is a necessary condition for survival. Thus, the only alternative is first to overthrow imperialism and monopoly capital, which have violently exploited nature and other life forms, including human beings, and then the mass of people should organize around a new life-centered worldview in which they become masters."

Political Greens, unlike their Green counterparts, believe that ecologically sound economic development is desirable. A Green economy, with recycling, sustainability, and democratic bioregionalism, is strongly supported by this type. They are the only type positively supporting traditional organic farming.

They are second to the Greens in their critique of nuclear power and rejection of fossil fuel cycles but are the weakest of the types in support of recycling and fuel efficiency. Political Greens are neutral regarding the economic and ecological risks of biotechnology and mildly negative on women's rights. Their concern for global warming is high, but they are undecided about its potential for disruption of food chains, climate change, and causing migration.

Political Greens do not trust the West or growing international consensus over environmental issues to ameliorate the situation, and they strongly distrust business and the market as environmental regulators. They have little faith that democracy by itself can resolve environmental issues because it produces piecemeal and defensive policy through compromise.

Political Greens think that there is no way to reverse environmental degradation in Korea. They no longer believe that economic development produces human well-being and see little possibility of transforming society for sustainable living. Political Greens would like to convert the economy to a green model of sustainable development but cannot envision political or legal instruments capable of doing so. They distrust both business and government. They believe that humanity has ultimately doomed itself through improvidence.

Sustainable Development is a composite encapsulating the attitudes of two professors from Seoul National and Yonsei universities (one is also a member of the Friends of Nature), four business persons from Sangyong Engineering, Lucky Goldstar, and Seorim Environmental Development Corporation, four members of the Friends of Nature, Society for the Study of Environment and Pollution, and the Kwanju YWCA, which is environmentally active.

Sustainable Developers are essentially conservationist, proposing a model of green capitalism. They believe that development can proceed on a sound environmental basis through governmental stimulation of market forces and a national popular campaign of recycling. Among the four attitude types, Sustainable Developers are the most pro-democratic.

A professor in the Graduate School of Environmental Study stated that "if a government is trusted by the people, the government will not hesitate to open information to the people. And this will lead the people to feel the necessity for environmental protection activities, based on voluntary participation. Rather than enforcement by authority, national education campaigns are more important for environmental protection."

Sustainable Developers show great respect for life and natural diversity, because, according to a Seoul National University professor, "If humanity is responsible for the future of the earth, the most fundamental responsibility is for the protection and conservation of other life forms." Nevertheless, Sustainable Development is not feminist; for example, a professor at Yonsei University and activist in the Friends of Nature believes that "overpopulation has nothing to do with discrimination against women."

Even though Sustainable Developers oppose exaggerated technocratic claims, technology is generally seen to be the solution for ecological loss. Consequently, Sustainable Developers believe that "economic development on a sound environmental basis is possible and cost effective." Also, they believe the results of development will be justly redistributed, showing that holders of this type have faith in the economic system and that their green capitalism has no redistributional or social justice component.

Sustainable Developers are worried about global warming but do not see it as catastrophic. "Human extinction is nonsense. A technology to reduce greenhouse effect will be developed in the near future," said an assistant manager in Sangyong Engineering, an environmental consulting firm.

Sustainable Developers are neutral about predictions of environmental catastrophe (environmental collapse, human extinction, the Greenhouse effect) and unconcerned with fossil fuel depletion and the dangers of nuclear power. They are optimistic about the possibility of technological repair of the environment and believe that Korea can successfully democratize its capitalist system and regulate the environment while providing for growth. Sustainable Developers believe that Korea's Fordist technological base can be modified in a conservationist direction through democratization of decision making and through public education. Sustainable Developers are anthropocentric technological optimists, who believe that Korea's economic system can repair the environment with minimal regulatory and educational changes.

Postmodern Managers are an attitude composite of eight managers from Lucky Goldstar, L.G. Advertising Agency, and the Korea Incinerator Manufactory, seven persons from the Ministry of Environment, and one Seoul University environmental scientist.

Managers were surprisingly neutral about the idea that government should give business information and incentives so that the market can protect the environment. Holders of this attitude type reject the green social model but think that environmentally sound development is possible and cost-beneficial. They are the strongest supporters of recycling and energy efficiency.

Postmodern Managers are the most worried of all types about global warming and give high priority to government planning and regulation to minimize ecological, economic, and social effects. Environmentally sound development, recycling, and energy efficiency are necessary, but fossil fuels and nuclear power clearly must provide the energy basis of industrial growth into the next century. "GNP growth can be maximized without worsening the environmental situation," asserts an executive in the Ministry of Environment.

These managers are not critical of Western Fordism, nor do they blame foreign developmental programs for environmental degradation. An MOE official states that "advanced agricultural technology allowed self-sufficient agricultural production by enhancing productivity, as in the Green Revolution." An employee of the L.G. Advertising Agency adds that "poverty, revolution, and environmental destruction resulted from indifference and immorality, rather than Western programs."

This type only mildly supports the use of agricultural biotechnology, which is surprising given that Korea has venture capital firms in this dynamic area. However, Postmodern Managers seem to have lost faith in much of the export-led developmental paradigm (the Korean "miracle") and accept the idea that human technological hubris has vandalized the planet.

The environmental problem has forced its way into Korean public attention because of serious incidents of pollution and growing health hazards. Thus, there is a overtone of pessimism among Postmodern Managers, compounded by fear of global warming effects. This type is most adamant regarding planning for global warming but also seems to think that it may already be too late to save humanity from extinction. Members of Korea's managerial elite, although modernist and Fordist, have come to realize the serious environmental externalities of the so-called Korean miracle and have become pessimistic and technologically risk averse. They seem to be evolving toward a postmodern and post-Fordist value stance as Korea emerges from authoritarian state-led developmentalism into a democratic, liberal, export-led economy.

Conclusions

1. Four distinct attitude types emerged from a person sample of seventy-four Korean opinion leaders in environmental movements, government, business, and the sciences. Figure 5.1 arrays these types on postmodern/post-Fordist indicators.

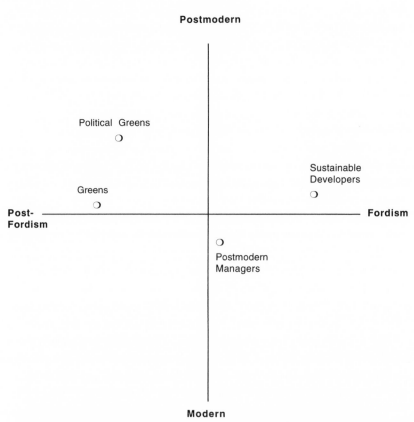

5.1. Korean Attitude Types on Postmodern and Post-Fordist Indicators
Postmodern indicator is a positive score on statement 18. The only alternative is a green economy, with grassroots democracy, voluntary simplicity, sustainable production, and recycling.
Post-Fordist indicator is a negative score on statement 13. If government gave business information and incentives, not command and sanction, the market and entrepreneurs would protect the environment.

Greens oppose nuclear power and the Western developmental model and are concerned about global warming. They are the most post-Fordist of the types. However, this type is neither ideologically mature nor consistent. They have yet to think through issues like women's rights, alternative energy, and agriculture, and are cynical regarding governmental regulation of Korea's monopolies and the new democracy's ability to meet the environmental challenges left by the Korean miracle.

The Political Greens, strikingly similar to the Mexican and Puerto Rican types, seem to be the most advanced on postmodern and post-Fordist dimensions because of their adherence to a green vision of society. But they have not formulated concrete alternatives to Korea's export-led development, nor can they envision the political or legal mechanisms of transition. They are not vitally concerned with nuclear power risks, fossil fuel dependency, global warming, or women's rights. They have lost faith in government, social movements, and democracy as potential agents of change and seem convinced that ecological degradation has proceeded so far that humanity is doomed to extinction. These two green attitude types can work in concert, as they occupy the same political space, but they could face policy conflicts in articulating a green platform.

Sustainable Developers, Fordist postmoderns, believe that mass education, recycling, government stimulation of the market, and democratization will spark popular participation in environmental concerns. Although their enthusiasm is muted, they still see technical solutions as the only option for environmental problems, and they reject concerns about resource depletion, global warming, nuclear power, and environmental collapse. Sustainable Developers believe most strongly in market solutions to environmental problems and exhibit the most faith in democracy. Their postmodern but Fordist placement shows that they are going to be adherents of green capitalism rather than of an intensive restructuring of the economy in a green direction.

Postmodern Managers believe that government planning and regulation are required for environmentally sound development, to control global warming effects and counter the risks from fossil and nuclear fuel cycles. The Western developmental model has benefited Korea in the past, but there is an attitude of pessimism among government and business elites regarding its continued efficacy. Postmodern Managers fall in the bottom boundary of the international type and are moving upward out of the modernist/Fordist quadrant into postmodern/post-

Fordist political space, because of their risk aversion and concern for environmentally sound development.

2. It can be expected that Sustainable Developers and Postmodern Managers will work to reform Korean capitalism in a sustainable direction but will oppose green social visions or environmental justice. Greens should seek coalition on specific issues—public education, recycling, regulation of chaebols, and so forth—with Sustainable Developers and Postmodern Managers but cannot expect them to support a deep postmodern value shift toward a green bioregional paradigm.

The Korean environmental problematic shows polarization between post-Fordist Greens and Political Greens on the one hand and Fordist Sustainable Developers and Postmodern Managers on the other. There are tactical issues on which these attitude types can unite, but the depth of opposition should not be minimized. This is clearly a new politics dimension rather than a left-right issue, but it could be mistakenly ideologized in terms of the old politics, thereby clouding the large issue-specific consensus possible between these attitude types—consensus that can be propelled by high and persistent public concern about the environment. Now that Korea is experiencing democracy, this public concern should find more direct expression.

Korea's Greens and Political Greens may be well advised to plumb the traditions of Buddhism and Confucianism to find philosophical anchors for their nascent idea structures. Although these worldviews seem to have accommodated capitalism, logically this should be an uncomfortable union, and a Green movement would be strengthened by blending Buddhist and Confucian cultural traditions with the latest environmentalist thought and ecological science into a potent program of transformation toward sustainability.

Brazil: Developing the World's Arboretum

Brazil has the world's most biodiverse environment and the largest rainforest. Since 1930 Brazil has been pursuing predatory industrial development under various dictatorial, populist, or military regimes. Environmental issues have come to the fore only in the New Republic of 1985, but without deep changes in this highly stratified and regionalized society, environmental policy remains subordinate to economics. In August 1993 I administered an environmental Q-sort to a sample of thirty-five key legislators, high governmental officials, business leaders, scientists, and environmental group executives in Brasilia, to model elite thinking on key issues of environment and development.

In this chapter I describe Brazil's diverse ecology, outline the legal and bureaucratic structures evolved in the New Republic to manage environmental issues, and model the spectrum of attitude types that emerged from a study of key decision makers in the Ministry of Environment; Ibama (Brazilian Institute of Environment and Renewable Natural Resources) and Embrapa (Brazilian Agrarian Enterprise); deputies from five main parties; leaders of five environmentalist groups; and three scientists and a science journalist.

The Brazilian Environment

Brazil possesses some of the world's richest and most fragile ecologies. Devastation of the Amazon has attracted world attention and a great deal of political pressure. But there are four other ecosystems threatened with degradation in this continentally proportioned country, besides Amazonia.

The Littoral and Mata Atlantica are Brazil's coastal areas, 8,000 km^2 in extent and containing 60 percent of its population. The mangrove swamps, gulfs, lagoons, dune systems, coral reefs, and beaches are degraded by raw sewage, industrial toxins, trash, port and shipping discharge, nine oil and chemical terminals, and predatory industrial fishing. The Mata Atlantica is the remnant of a 1.3 million km² closed canopy forest, of which only 12 percent remains in coastal and inland patches. It is still impacted by urbanization and industrialization, although belated attempts are being made to save significant remnants of its biodiversity. Of Brazil's fifty-five species of New World monkeys, the world's largest assemblage, many inhabit the patch ecology of the Mata Atlantica, and twenty-five are threatened with extinction.

Second, the Pantanal, or wetlands of Alto Paraguai, located in the state of Mato Grosso, represents 150,000 km² of aquatic and semiaquatic environments, forming a transition between Amazon rainforest (*hileia*) and the savanna (*cerrado*). The world's largest and most biodiverse wetland, the Pantanal is contaminated by mercury from wildcat goldmining and is subject to predatory hunting and fishing, hydroelectric projects, urban pollution, and agrotoxics and fertilizers.

The Cerrado represents 200 million ha of savanna, with more than 2,000 plant species and 430 species of birds, most of which have never been studied. Over 25 percent of Brazil's territory, equal in size to Western Europe, this complex system forms part of the agricultural frontier and has been rapidly urbanized. Its rain-fed and relatively poor soils are seriously eroded and polluted. The Cerrado is a heavily threatened ecosystem, occupied without planning or even understanding of its proper uses.

The fourth threatened ecosystem, the Pampas and Matas in southern Brazil, consists of 160,000 km² of rich groundwater-fed grasslands and savanna. Clear-cutting, agriculture, and burning of pasture has led to the desertification of 36,000 ha of these rich lands.

Amazonia is a rainforest ecosystem covering 5.5 million km² and bordering five nations. Most of it is in Brazil, 3.3 million km² of Amazonia forming 60 percent of Brazil's territory. Rainforest or hileia covers 74 percent of the Brazilian portion of the Amazon Basin, 14 percent is cerrado or savanna, and 12 percent is under human occupation. The forest contains some 2.5 million species of plants; a single hectare contains up to 25,000 species of all genera. The Amazonian hydrographic basin (6 million km²) produces 20 percent of the world's riverine flow, with 175 million liters per second flowing into the Atlantic Ocean at its mouth. The Amazon, which stretches a distance equivalent to that from New York to Rome, contains more species of fish than the Atlantic Ocean.

A climax forest system living within a constant evapotranspirative cycle, Amazonian hileia recycles all of its energy and nutrients, including oxygen, and is one of the world's major carbon sinks. That is, it uses atmospheric carbon in its growth cycle and thus helps counter global warming. By 1990 13 percent of the Amazon forest had been cut, while the burned area was two and one-half times larger than this. Between 1978 and 1988, 21,000 km^2 per year of hileia were cut, while in 1990 the cut was equal to 15,000 km^2, a reduction deriving from cuts in financial incentives and from economic downturn, rather than because of effective government policy. Degraded forest is subject to fire. In the twenty years prior to 1990, 52,000 metric tons of biomass were burned, increasing the atmospheric CO_2 load and thereby contributing to global warming. Taking into consideration the annual burning of pastures, the Amazon contributes 6 percent of the world's carbon emissions.[1] Drying due to the El Niño effect led to massive and long-term forest fires in 1998, which the government has been unable to stop.

Sixteen million persons, 10 percent of Brazil's population, inhabit the Amazon, living primarily in large urban centers where they earn a per capita income of U.S. $1,271, about half of the Brazilian average. With the highest urban fertility rate in the world, this population will grow 62 percent to 26 million by 2010. Forty-four percent of the population is under fifteen years old, and 47 percent have no education. Fifty percent of employment is in extractive industries and 33 percent of women work in domestic service, while 31 percent of men earn below Brazil's (sub-) minimum wage.[2]

The Amazon's primary industry is wildcat goldmining (*garimpagem*), which employs a million people and supports another 4.5 million; thus, mining impacts 28 percent of the Amazonian population. Pollution of rivers with sediment, massive physical destruction of watercourses and forest, the spread of serious disease, and most seriously, massive mercury poisoning of the Amazon Basin all result from this mining. On the Tapajos River, 1.2 kg of mercury are used to extract 1 kg of gold. Between 1983 and 1987, 250 tons of mercury were cast into the ecosystem from three hundred mining centers. Mercury can even be detected in the Pantanal over a thousand kilometers to the south. Fish show twice the acceptable mercury load, and the majority of persons in Itaituba, Pará, for example, show perverse mercury diarrhea, the first step toward irreversible damage to the nervous system and brain and ultimate death from Minamata disease.[3]

Half a million peasants engage in slash-and-burn (swidden or shifting fallow) agriculture, and in so doing have degraded 10 million hectares of forest. Large clear-cut swatches cannot revert to forest and so are converted to low-productivity cattle pasture. The soils supporting this system are full of acids and aluminum salts. Dystrophic soils, like podsols and latisols, make up 88 percent of the region, while fertile or eutrophic soils make up only 12 percent.

Predatory logging has extracted 24.6 million m³ of timber. While 16 percent of trees are selectively cut, 26 percent of the remainder are damaged or destroyed, and thus the entire ecosystem is compromised. But there are many benign and sustainable uses of this standing forest. Some fifty-five thousand *serengistas* or rubber tappers work in Acre, many in newly created extractive reserves. Despite a local regime of exploitation and violent repression, the serengistas are pursuing a sustainable productive use of the rainforest.[4]

The military dictatorship (1964–85), backed by transnational corporations and banks, embarked on massive predatory development of Amazonia. Considerations of geopolitics—stabilizing borders with its five neighbors, redirection and absorption of urban migration, lowering pressures for agrarian reform, creation of showcase projects to generate more international aid and to enrich elite supporters, and commercialization of mineral wealth—were all crucial factors in the creation of various bureaucratic institutions and programs.

Extensive roadbuilding, colonization, large-scale state subsidization of the expanding agricultural and stock-raising frontiers, and expansion of transnational corporate mining and industry were all disastrous in their impact.[5] For example, half of the pasturelands established by the cattle industry in the last twenty-five years have reached advanced stages of degradation—about 100,000 ha of wasted land—and only about 10 percent have been reclaimed.[6]

The New Republic (1985–present), under significant international pressure, has launched more responsible programs, like Nossa Natureza (Our Nature), which eliminated cattle subsidies, and established thirty-four natural parks, twenty-three biological reserves, twenty-one ecological stations, thirty-eight national forests, fourteen protection areas, four extractive reserves, and Indian reservations. Unfortunately, many of these preserves and reservations remain unsurveyed and therefore unprotected from encroachment by miners and squatters. These conservation efforts total 31,294,911 ha or 3.4 percent of national territory, which is low even by Global South standards.[7]

The current tendency is to shift from extractive activities to agroforestry as subsidies are eliminated and the true costs of production, as well as rising land prices, are figured into Amazon production. But it remains to be seen whether sustainable uses or remaining forms of predatory extraction will dominate. The prognosis looks grim as population pressure, Brazil's depressed economy, and world market forces propel wildcat mining and logging, which the Brazilian government is largely incapable of preventing. Pacific Rim market pressures have increased wildcat logging, mining, and roadbuilding, which gives the cocaine industry free entry and brings further illegal settlement.

Serrao and Homma note that switching from predatory to sustainable forms of production could cause political conflicts with impoverished local populations. They argue that "day-to-day regional life includes high demographic densities, urbanization, the need for more employment, low income, and low quality of life. If poverty, unemployment, underemployment, and the lack of a basic infrastructure persist, conservation and preservation intentions will gradually lose the support of the population."[8]

Unfortunately, sustainable development preserves Brazil's paradigm of development without modernization, a model that continuously reproduces the power of the rural oligarchy, and a bureaucratic, conservative, and unrepresentative elitist democracy that have brought the New Republic to an impasse.[9] Nor can sustainable development claim to resolve Brazil's fiscal and monetary crises and massive indebtedness.

Nonetheless, sustainable development is the only available model for preserving the enormous future value of Amazonian biodiversity, while allowing reduced present utilization. The concept remains largely undefined, except in terms of neoliberal market efficiency. But continued predatory exploitation of forest resources, until the hileia and the regional climate are insulted beyond recovery, is unthinkable. Thus, any model of multiple ecological uses for local consumption provides an attractive alternative to market-driven sustainability or predation.

Indigenous knowledge and technique are valuable assets in finding sustainable uses of Amazonia. Indigenous peoples appeared in Amazonia about 12,500 B.P. and probably numbered some four million at the time of European contact. There are now about half a million indigenous people divided into some 180 tribes. Density is about 0.2 persons/km^2 and settlements vary from 50 to 250 people. For millenia, settlements moved as areas were exhausted. These peoples have long subsisted by biodiversity maintenance and sustainable harvesting of flora and fauna. Populations and intensity of exploitation—that is, ecological zonation—decline as one moves from the wetland *varzea* (sunken forest), and hileia (canopy rainforest), to terra firma, the drier grasslands.

Settlement relocation and selective taboos on animals and plants were forms of management. Slash-and-burn plantings were under a hectare and polycultured up to fifteen species. Manioc is the main plant because it tolerates ferralsols and acrisols and still produces high yields. Fruit, root, and tree crops are planted, and as the field is progressively abandoned, in two to four years, medicinal plants and species that attract animals are sown. In fifteen to twenty years the forest has regenerated in these small patches.

The dry savannas were peopled by nomadic hunter-gatherers, who occasionally cut plantations into the nearby forest. The varzea wetlands and coastal estuaries maintained dense populations ($14.6/km^2$) based on fishing and terraced crops. Through taboos, war, and exploitation of diverse ecological niches, natives kept their populations below carrying capacity and protected themselves from starvation.

There are a number of similar contemporary strategies for sustainable development. Fertilized fields with cereal/legume rotation are possible in the patches of rich nitosols. But fertilizer is expensive and markets are distant. Long-cycle tree and shrub crops recycle their own nutrients and need little fertilizer; coffee, cacao, rubber, *guarana*, papaya, oil palm, Brazil nut, and *copaiba* are richly productive and yield high value crops. But viral and fungal disease is common, and insect, bird, and mammal pests take 24–32 percent annually of such crops, unless they are intercropped into agrosilvapastoral systems.

The most advanced agrosilvapastoral models mix intercropping, recycling, and conservation and maintain biodiversity that mimics the forest ecosystem and protects farmers against both market cycles and the area's tenacious pests and weeds. Vertical stratification of the biome, maintaining the complexity of the food web, allows a rich variety of products to be produced from a relatively self-sustaining system.[10]

Highly successful Japanese-Brazilian farms intercrop perennial trees (cacao, rubber, *cupuaçu*, papaya, *gaviola*, avocado, mango, and Brazil nuts, with palms like *açai*, coconut, oil, and peach), with fruit-bearing shrubs (pineapple, cherry, banana, coffee, passion fruit, pepper, *urucu*) and annuals (cotton, beans, pumpkin, cassava, melon, cucumber, cabbage). These family farms cultivate about 20 ha out of their average 150 ha holdings, leaving most of the land in secondary or gallery forest. These farms utilize heavy fertilizer inputs, require high capital investments, are labor intensive, and face complex problems of managing equilibrium interactions among so many different species, but they do provide jobs and supply local markets, and they constitute the most sustainable use of the biome known to date.[11]

Sustainable timber extraction and tree plantations require research and investment, which local and transnational companies are unwilling to supply unless government regulation and taxation policies artificially raise production costs to make capitalization and sustainable production necessary. Biotechnology and other forms of plant improvement could be used to customize species to produce more efficiently in such systems. Unfortunately, Brazil's R&D capacity, although substantial by Global South standards, is limited by lack of infrastructure and personnel, low salaries, the politicization of science, and small-scale extension services.

Natural forest silvaculture manages rather than clear-cuts the forest cover, but requires a twenty-five- to fifty-year cropping cycle. Forest diversity is maintained and pest management is natural. Pre- and post-logging refinement of the forest (liberation thinning) can increase the commercial species within a natural stand of forest. But this long-range strategy is stopped by very short-term market forces, which would rather clear-cut the forest than invest in it.

Intensive livestock rearing on grass-legume pastures using tropical or biotechnological grasses is possible, but soil liming is needed; sulfur, zinc, molybdenum and other trace elements must be added; shrub invasion has to be controlled; and low-number rotational stocking is required.

Savanna and wetlands could be exploited for rice and sugar cultivation, but these crops release large amounts of methane and carbon. Fishing is potentially more productive than cattle rearing, but deforestation, dams, and pollution are depleting this resource rapidly. Aquaculture of some of the giant fish species and farming of wild species such as capibara, turtle, tapir, deer, peccary, and caiman are possible and probably profitable.[12]

Increasingly capital- and science-intensive land uses could displace extractive activities such as swidden, logging, collecting, and rubber tapping but may not influence mining. Agriculture can provide food and raw material for local markets and exotic products for world market niches—which are, however, easily saturated. Logging will undoubtedly increase to provision Pacific Rim demand but should be done on the basis of tree plantations outside the canopy forest, which would have the added benefit of providing carbon sinks. Agrosilvapastoral systems and pisciculture could prove richly productive but require investments in research and extension and carry high initial capitalization costs.

Science and technology, capital intensity, and qualified labor could ultimately displace the comparative advantages of cheap natural resources and labor, which have caused such serious insults to the region's ecology, biodiversity, and climate. These trends need to be augmented by carefully crafted political regulation and management and overt suppression of wildcat mining and logging, of drug traffic, and of predatory hunting and capture for the world trade in animals.

Unfortunately, indications are that the Brazilian government has a seriously limited capacity to provide this crucial programming of the Amazon's future. The Amazon is not the bonanza the government requires. Sustainable use of its resources will require complex ecosystem management, suitable utilization of small patches, and high inputs of local and scientific knowledge. In the long term, Amazonia could prove a world treasure. But the political short term dictates rapid extraction and urbanization, which will reduce Amazonia to a wasteland, like the formerly sugar-rich northeast interior, which is now a desert.

Brazil's Environmental Regulatory Structure and Politics

Brazil subscribes to a number of important treaty regimes and possesses a sophisticated system of constitutional and federal law, enabling legislation, and a cabinet-level Ministry of Environment (Ministerio de Meio-Ambiente), all created under the New Republic. However, planning, research, funding, and enforcement is hampered by Brazil's large debt, the fiscal crisis of the state, and a technobureaucratic structure weakened by neoliberal austerity and a tradition of legal formalism and bargaining.

Brazil's 1988 Constitution has advanced provisions that regard the environment as a commons (*bem de uso comun*) and provide for its management, preservation, restoration, and biodiversity maintenance. The wording of Article 225 is direct, strong, and progressive, in effect making the enjoyment of a decent environment into a human right: "All persons have the right to an ecologically equilibrated environment, as a good for the common use of the people, essential to a healthy quality of life, and imposing on the public power and the collectivity [of the nation] the duty of its preservation for present and future generations."

The Littoral, Mata Atlantica, Pantanal, and Amazon forest are national patrimonies, and all forms of utilization must assure their conservation. This article mandates the regulation of biological research and genetic engineering in order to preserve the integrity and diversity of the nation's genetic patrimony.

Articles 23 and 24 make environmental regulation the joint responsibility of federal, state, and municipal governments, with the strictest rule, at whatever level, prevailing. Federal laws implementing these constitutional provisions include a Forest Code, National Environmental Policy, rules protecting cetaceans in Brazilian waters, coastal management, protection of rivers and lakes, and creation of a national environmental fund. There are mechanisms at all levels for citizen action against anyone injuring the environment or national patrimony. Constitutional Article 61.2 allows direct initiative legislation, and Law 6.938 requires public powers to produce full information upon citizen petition.

On the international front, Brazil has ratified the Antarctica treaty, treaties regulating Antarctic natural resource use, conservation of Antarctic seals, and the Law of the Sea. It has ratified a treaty against atmospheric testing of nuclear weapons, has a side agreement with Argentina for pacific uses of nuclear power, and has ratified the Vienna and Montreal protocols protecting the ozone layer. Brazil has not ratified treaties regarding hazardous waste transport, fishing and marine conservation, and wetlands preservation.[13]

Sisnama, the National System of Environment, is headed by Conama, the National Environmental Council, which advises the president. A body of seventy-two members, Conama includes representatives of all ministries and principal environmental groups and is charged with defining national policy. It has the power to establish resolutions binding in law and has already required environmental impact statements and a program for controlling vehicular pollution.

The cabinet-level Ministry of the Environment reports to the president and is the strategic planning body of Conama. Ibama, the Brazilian Institute of Environment and Renewable Natural Resources, is the technical/enforcement core of the ministry and was formed in February 1989 by fusion of the Special Secretariat of Environment, Superintendency of Fishing Development, Brazilian Institute of Forest Development, and Superintendency of Rubber Development. Ibama has superintendencies in all states of the federation and manages national parks, conservation units, special projects, and research centers. It coordinates thirty-seven state environmental units and their counterparts at the municipal level.

A high-level female executive in Ibama explained the system as follows:

> The function of the Ministry of Environment is to coordinate policy between the ministries and local and international NGOs. Ibama is the technical executor of these policies. We have good

sophisticated laws, but must work with the business sector explaining and discussing the laws so that we can reduce direct oversight. Business always ignores laws and taxes unless you can show they are to their benefit or will not hurt their interests. Ibama has sections in each state, and decentralized enforcement. We oversee state laws and try to avoid conflict of laws. State laws must apply federal norms, but they can be stricter. We try to network, cooperate, conciliate between levels. We like to negotiate, to avoid court cases. The big enterprises are best controlled with federal and state cooperation.

Conama includes participation of some of the twelve hundred environmental groups. As the above executive explained, "NGOs play a direct role in Conama, and in open hearings on environmental impact statements. They can question decisions at the executive level. We work with them in pilot programs and they have helped decide about projects. They are in all the various councils dealing with specific environmental subjects. They can make direct denunciations of violations. Ibama has a special audience procedure."

This sophisticated and elaborate system is not without problems, as noted by many of the insiders whom I interviewed. The then minister of environment is worth quoting at length:

> Our legislation is very good and the institutions are reasonable, but we have no capacity to generate alternative scenarios or a new model of sustainable development. We only spend about U.S. $15 per capita in research compared to $1000 per capita in the first world and are thus very limited in identifying opportunities. Administration lacks means, technicians, finance, and must administer complex standing laws. The result is that the law is not followed. We turn in circles and can't solve any of the really large problems.
>
> Starting in the 1980s the technocratic bureaucracy left by the military regime was cut down by the debt crisis, and later by [ex-President] Collar's shock program. We have lost our capacity for strategic economic planning, sustaining national sovereignty, relating to civil society. Not only have there been firings for financial reasons, but a broad loss of experienced cadres who have retired. Bureaucratic salaries are so low that only people that are totally dedicated to environment, or people that are corrupt, can continue working.

The state is deteriorating; it is being eaten by debt, a heavy load of public functions and heavy social services. The internal debt is larger than the external debt by about twice—the state is undergoing a fiscal crisis. It is disorganized, has no logic or plan. Public enterprises make their own policy in their own interest and stop the state from modernizing. Ibama makes policy and does the politics instead of the ministry. Ibama is preservationist, not behind sustainable development.

A top executive in Embrapa, Brazilian Agrarian Enterprise, a large research and extension agency under the Ministry of Agriculture, argued the following:

The state is bankrupt and cannot even respond in areas of necessity. The Ministry of Environment is disorganized and cannot take the lead in these issues. For example, Ibama joined together four institutions, without any planning, and they diverge in viewpoint.

Ibama is defensive about environmental impacts. There is lack of communication in the ministry, no organizational policy. Each ministry should assume the environmental question in its own area and not pass responsibility onto the Ministry of Environment. Embrapa assumes responsibility for sustainable development policy, but we are part of the Ministry of Agriculture which does not. There is a lack of relation and communication and a lack of executive [i.e., presidential] leadership.

An analyst in Embrapa said former president Collar agreed

to destroy the national technobureaucracy and demobilize the public sector to gain international financial support. This makes the neoliberal prejudice that government is incompetent come true after all. Functionaries in Congress earn more than scientists, so we have a huge brain drain.

We reported to President Itamar Franco that we needed an intersectorial strategic plan, and he said that it wasn't important. He responds to television news programs and thus allows powerful conservatives to make the agenda. We are facing a global crisis of paradigms: political, cultural, scientific, religious, economic. Only knowledge intensive public policy is sustainable.

Enforcement seems to be a problem. As a high-level female executive in Ibama explained, "Ibama or a state agency regulates environment. We make agreements with state police as they have no autonomous power and can't act directly without delegated power from Ibama. We use Federal Police in the Amazon. The Secretariat of Strategic Subjects [secret political police] does R&D in this sector, but we need to change their mentality. Conama is at least discussing nuclear and military installations, which used to be top secret."

An environmental lawyer and lobbyist argued:

The bureaucracy is not in harmony with itself, and isn't ready to enter into conflicts. Funai (the National Indian Foundation), Ibama, and the Federal Police all act in the Indian question, and the Ministry of Mining is added in on the wildcat mining question. The military police have their own interests, a national, developmentalist viewpoint which does not fit in with the environmental issue.

There is a huge informal economy. About 40 percent of the GDP is outside law and regulation. Even the official economy is badly regulated because of inefficiency, corruption. Only 15 percent of the population pays taxes, only about 20 percent of the people get social services. Ministries and NGOs can't do much. Brazil is close to civil war because of social and economic breakdown and incompetence. Our laws are detailed, pretentious, sophisticated, ambitious. But they are unrealistic for this country. There is no possibility of compliance. The law is ahead of our capacity to apply it.

A former Ministry of Planning executive, now an environmentalist, said:

The Ministry of Environment was a Pyrrhic victory, it is [environmentalist José] Lutzenberger's Ministry. It was stronger as an advisory organ to the president; now it has to fight for budget with the other ministries. There is a crisis in government planning—everything is done week by week. But environment is a long-term question they can't handle. The economic crisis stops all concerted action, they only improvise, survive.

Large sectors of the government are refractory to the environmental question; they are into developmentalism and lack the capital for a technical transformation. The elites are not interested in correcting the government's incapacity. The parties see environment as just another platform item, and do nothing. The NGOs support the ministry but relations get strained when there are no resources to carry through on commitments. NGOs are upper-middle-class movements with a lot of charm, mainly urban, not popular. Most of them consist of a phone and fax and that's all. The Church is animating many NGOs.

State governments have their own budgets but ecology is secondary to the social question. Big states are the most environmentally devastated, and have the best programs. The military sees ecology as a maneuver of the first world to steal resources from the Amazon. We are close to Fujimorization [an authoritarian presidential regime as in Peru], but the military is weak and cannot return to power.

Brazil shares a historical peculiarity of Latin America: authoritarian presidencies and elaborate legal and administrative systems, the functions of which are hampered or blocked by informal social forces in civil society. Roberto Guimaraes, who worked in the earlier environmental bureaucracy, noted that environmental planning lacks relevance and is dominated by economistic models based on privatization of natural resources. Every public enterprise has a cosmetic and powerless environmental unit that creates environmental impact statements, which are formalistic and generally ignored.

Environmental issues are inherently conflictual because they restrain developmental activities pursued by powerful social interests and create jurisdictional disputes among bureaucracies. The results of environmental balance are hard to quantify, benefit common rather than individual interests, and impact the whole society or future generations, so that decision makers lack the legitimation of immediate gains. The bureaucratic response is to postpone decisions and negotiate the lowest-common-denominator solution: continued development with some environmental protection. Diffuse future interests without a strong political constituency must negotiate with powerful corporations enjoying elite and military backing. A minimal policy is written, a symbolic, underfunded, and politically isolated agency is created, which pursues studies and a few prestige projects. The bureaucracy protects itself from the potentially revolutionary impact of environmental planning with a prestige-oriented project, a simulacrum of action.[14]

Brazil's environmental bureaucracy suffers from rapid turnover of top administrators due to political pressure, insufficient funding for technical programs, and difficulties in enforcement in such a large, diverse country, where local power brokers control courts and police and do not shy away from corruption and violence.

Only 3.7 percent of Brazil is in conservation units, compared with a global 5 percent and 6.7 percent for South America. Only one-third of the 350 conservation units are operational, and only 20 percent are accessible to Ibama officials. These units were set up by decree before the Rio UNCED of 1992, but their full legalization would cost U.S. $1.2 billion. Price incentives and some zoning are in place, and laws are being strengthened along with enforcement, although there is an increase in illegal extraction of valuable tree species and there was gross inability to control the El Niño drought-induced forest fires burning out of control in 1998. Sustainable development gets less overall attention than does neoliberal economics.[15]

This rather pessimistic assessment applies to most countries of the Global South, many of which are creating sophisticated legal and administrative frameworks for environmental regulation but must still operate these frameworks in highly stratified and unjust societies, where popular concern is not translated into direct pressure for decisive action and is unable to counter powerful elites.

Brazilian public opinion has manifested strong concern about environment for decades. A 1975 Gallup poll in São Paulo showed that 80 percent of Brazilians considered pollution the most important problem, and 10 percent thought that the government was doing nothing to solve the problem. A 1986 poll showed that 85 percent thought Congress should take up environmental issues, as against only 58 percent in favor of (badly needed) agrarian reform. A 1989 poll showed that 54 percent were as concerned with environment as with development and 66 percent were concerned with the devastation of Amazonia.

A 1991 Brazilian poll showed a majority regarding the environmental problem as very serious. Awareness was higher in urban than in rural areas, and environmental demand goes down with age, while it correlates directly with education and income. Forest fires are seen as the major problem; industrial pollution is important in the developed urban southeast. Destruction of the Atlantic rainforest and the risk of nuclear power follow in salience. The majority criticized government actions and thought that international interests pressuring for Amazon conservation were really concerned with economic exploitation rather than with ecology.

A 1991 World Values Survey showed that 82 percent strongly approved of the ecology movement, 71 percent were willing to pay higher taxes for environmental protection, and 41 percent support taxation and concrete government measures. A 1998 world survey showed that 37 percent of Brazilians showed a "great deal of concern" for environment and that 62 percent thought environmental laws did not go far enough to remedy the situation.[16]

The Brazilian Green movement emerged in the 1970s in Rio Grande do Sul, São Paulo, and Belem, at first in a conservationist mode. In the 1980s, with the return to democracy, Greens shifted to ecopolitics. National fora were held by Rio Greens who wanted to form a national party, and from 1985 to 1988 a national mobilization was formed to participate, with moderate success, in the Constituent Assembly. As noted, the constitution that emerged includes a strong and sophisticated article about the natural right to a balanced environment. But the Greens were blocked in their push for land reform, antinuclear provisions, indigenous rights, and formal surveys of contested forest and Indian lands.

The ENEAAs (National Encounters of Autonomous Environmental Organizations) organized the Global Forum, an alternative popular meeting held at Rio UNCED in 1992, which attracted thirty thousand participants and drafted some thirty "peoples treaties" but which had little impact on the official proceedings. Green groups distanced themselves from officialdom and linked up with Church, peasant, union, professional, and scientific organizations to apply pressure and to conduct informational and symbolic politics in good postmodern style.

Brazil's environmental movement has grown rapidly, from 400 groups in 1985 to 700 in 1989, 1,300 in 1992, and some 2,000 currently, with a budget of U.S. $18.5 million. About 90 percent are located in the center-south, with one-quarter in São Paulo.[17]

Local mobilizations often have significant political impact, and several of their officers have ascended to high governmental positions; José Lutzenberger drafted the national pesticide law and eventually became minister of environment under Collar's presidency. Fabio Feldman entered Congress on a Green list, drafted the constitutional article on environment, and later became minister.

Local groups face financial difficulties, which can be resolved only by surrendering their autonomy to the Church, parties, or international environmental organizations. They want outreach to unions and agrarian reform, the Church, and peasant organizations, but fear having their issues diluted in the process. Often their members are successful at municipal, state, or national politics, but while needing legislative clout to solidify their political accomplishments, activists remain suspicious of politicians and the system. Ties to national parties involve Green politicians in wider issues and mobilizations but cause them to bargain away their issues, or lose focus. Environmental groups have professionalized and engage in permanent dialog with Congress and the relevant ministries.

UNI, the Union of Indigenous Peoples, representing the aforementioned 180 peoples, has also become a successful environmental lobby with international contacts and sophisticated tactics. It is estimated that almost half of the rural population of Brazil is involved in movements to preserve their natural resource base.

Amazon environmental groups have not been well integrated into the emergent national movement, despite local mobilizations blocking forest cutting, for extractive reserves, and for Indian rights. Brazilian Greens tend to be southern, urban, well educated, professional, and postmodern in values, and struggles by the Amazonian poor and marginalized often do not cross the threshold of attention.[18]

The military is an important player in Brazil's environmental policy because it considers the Amazon an area of national security, which must be colonized and utilized to preserve it from outside incursion. Large-scale mining, agriculture, and colonization were pursued by the military dictatorship from 1964 to 1985. But even in the new democracy, the National Security Council drafted the Calha Norte Project giving the military a 150 km strip along the Amazon border and some 6 million ha, about 14 percent of Brazil and 24 percent of Amazonia, making the military the region's largest landholder. This fief was ostensibly to discourage a Yanomami National Park, incursion of the drug trade, guerrilla activity, Venezuelan border revision, and foreign environmentalist and Church influence. Supposedly dismantled in 1991, Calha Norte may still be partially in place, and the military continues to act as a powerful veto group in Amazon policy.

The Kayapo Indians, rubber tappers, miners, and local farmers have all mobilized to resist military influence and have gotten the attention of the United Nations and World Bank, which blocked major development projects. The military responded by arresting lobbyists returning from abroad and declared the need for the "extreme expedient of war" against drug traffickers, Indians, and environmentalists. Special areas were set aside, perhaps for nuclear testing or fuel storage, and the military plans the "total integration [of the Indians] into regional society."

President Fernando Henrique Cardoso (1995–2000), brings a neoliberal cost/benefit approach to environment, which will not function because of the inherently low market price of Amazonian resources. Environmental impact statements are to be based on market values. The military persists in place and has set up an extensive radar and satellite surveillance system for "national security" motives, which involves remote sensing platforms, twenty-three radar installations, eight planes, and a network of "Regional Vigilance Centers." Neoliberal "sustainable development" puts all producers on a par in bargaining and is directed toward development with lower impact. There is a marked increase in illegal timber extraction, wildcat mining, and invasion of Indian reservations, which Ibama is powerless to stop because of resistance from mining, logging, and ranching interests.

Amazonia is now an "urbanized jungle," with 55 percent of its population in cities and close market links between town and bush. Successful local environmental projects are more evident in the affluent industrial center-south than in Amazonia.[19]

The Brazilian Catholic Church is an important player in environmental policy, but its "preferential option for the poor" emphasizes satisfaction of present human need over ecological balance. Natural law should lead to a more environmental attitude, but humanism and emphasis on the moral vices that give rise to ecological pillage lead the Church to a static stance on environment. The National Council of Brazilian Bishops (CNBB) frames land use as an issue of human self-realization. It criticizes dislocation of the Indians but defends its right to missionize. The environment comes into CNBB purview only if it affects the disadvantaged.

CIMI, the Indigenous Missionary Council of the Catholic Church, has been more consistent and militant in its defense of Indian political rights but sees the environment as an Indian resources base. The CPT, Commission on the Pastoral Land, defends smallholders, the landless, and rural laborers and has played a role in seizure of significant amounts of idle land, settling some 140,000 families. Environment is seen as an issue of social justice by this active, and often persecuted, agency. The sixty thousand CEBS or Christian Base Communities promote land reform, demarcation, education, and local social justice, which may or may not include local environmental policy. The Church, despite its large apparatus and progressive social politics, has not taken the lead on environmental issues. Because the Church has been divided over liberation theology, and many prominent activist clergy have been retired and transferred, it is unlikely to play a significant environmental role in future.[20]

Business, government, and military elites represent (or are checked by) some two hundred families who rule Brazil and who manage to frustrate the intent of sophisticated legislation and administration structures by control of local power and national politics. Brazil's unfortunate administrative incapacity bodes ill for the future of its fragile and wonderfully diverse ecosystem.

Brazilian Decision Makers' Environmental Attitudes

The Brazilian elites directly involved in making environmental policy can be characterized as being few in number, multifunctional, and strongly interlocked. That is, they tend to hold several key positions in the course of their careers, and they pass easily between environmental, governmental, and business sectors. For example, the sample of this study, carefully chosen by cross-checking with academics and environment and governmental officials, manifested strong overlapping functions. The thirty-five individuals held a total of forty-four positions in other sectors; eight as scientists, twelve ecologists, fifteen bureaucrats, six deputies, and three business representatives—an impressive 80 percent rate of intersectoral crossover.

The respondents in this study are key decision makers in their respective sectors. With expert local advice, I was able to interview key environmental decision makers. A listing of names would convince anyone of the importance of the sample, but anonymity was guaranteed as a condition of their participation and thus this information cannot be made available. Four factorial types characterize Brazilian decision makers' attitudes toward environment: Greens, Sustainable Developers, Postmodern Managers, and Developmentalists, ranging in the order of their commitment to environmentalist ideas.

Each of these types mixes individuals from government, business, science, and environment sectors, showing that there is a high degree of consensus and a high degree of overlap between sectors, instead of the expected polarization along the old left-right continuum. In Brazil, environment is part of the "new politics" but is largely restricted to a small group of well-educated decision makers. Brazilian respondents were not aware of the degree to which the various sectors broadly agree on environmental issues, especially because the press in Brazil tends to utilize a polarizing dismissive discourse, which is irrelevant in this issue. These findings are in line with data presented in chapters 2 and 3 showing a shift to a postmodern consensus regarding environmental issues, although Brazil's structural crisis precludes any early transition to a postmodern knowledge-service economy, and the value shift is seen only among educated elites. All the types but Developmentalists can be characterized as postmodern.

All four opinion types agreed on the following consensus items: "Biological diversity is the common heritage of mankind, to be studied, used and above all preserved"; "Economic development on a sound environmental basis is possible and cost-effective"; "Investment in energy efficiency and recycling can reduce fossil fuel demand without sacrificing growth"; "Environmental policy is piecemeal and defensive, not global as required by the urgency of the problem"; "Biotechnology replaces free scientific inquiry with secrecy, collusion, and research geared toward corporate needs"; and "The real goal of biotechnology is to engineer human beings."

These consensus statements indicate an important shift away from the developmentalism of the military regime (1964–85) and toward a new consensus on sustainable development, the definition and operationalization of which should be a central task for the New Republic. The four types showed the following intercorrelations: Greens 0.65 to Sustainable Developers 0.55 to Postmodern Managers 0.32 to Moderate Developmentalists. This is another indication of the signal consensus in Brazil on these issues, and structures the spectrum of attitude types.

Greens are a composite of the subjectivity of executive officers in the Institute for Society, Population and Nature (2) and CIMI (2); two deputies from the Brazilian Social Democratic Party (PSDB, which came to power with President Cardoso in 1994) and one from the PDT, the Democratic Labor Party; the CEO of the Ministry of Environment; and a science journalist. Three individuals in this type, the CEO, a CIMI executive, and the science journalist, also load significantly on the Sustainable Developer type, again showing emergent consensus.

Brazilian Greens are notable for their moderation. Philosophically, they believe that "All living things have a right to exist" and that "The only alternative is a Green economy, with grassroots democracy, voluntary simplicity, sustainable production, and recycling." However, they are not optimistic about constructing this alternative soon because "Sustainability was the original economy of the species, but to restore it now will require a revolution as great as the industrial revolution." Brazilian Greens are not necessarily inimical to GNP growth and do not believe that development solely benefits rich elites. However, they reject the idea that if given incentives, markets and entrepreneurs and not government regulation will protect the economy.

Greens reject the apocalyptic vision that "Humanity is doomed to extinction. We must preserve maximum biodiversity so that nature can carry on after us." They strongly support democratic methods, strongly rejecting the notion that "Democracy cannot meet the challenge of imminent ecocatastrophe, because it acts slowly and through compromise." To Greens, constructing a new civil society in Brazil's economically and politically stagnant New Republic is major political goal.

As an ex-national and state government official now working in an environmental group said:

> NGOs are improvising; the people have the ideas and these are interpreted by science. We need to speak a professional language, but also must decodify. Bring ideas to the people. We work with scientists, professionals, popular movements, unions, Indians and must move in state and even international circles. Environmentalism can't be based only on local movements or we will lose political space.
>
> The political process is exhausted; we have links with the parties but must keep a certain distance which gives us apparent neutrality and better capacity of penetration. Parties reduce action to only fragments of the question; but ecology is different than class struggle. Some rightists are more advanced than the left. Religious people and professionals in the bureaucracy are the most ecological, the entrepreneurs are pretty minimal. We have to maintain the biodiversity of ecologists.

The Green Party [Partido Verde] deputy disagrees.

> The Green Party's role is to dispute traditional political spaces, which we can't abandon or leave in the hands of traditional elites. We can't abandon the terrain saying that global policy is not possible; this would diminish the role of democratic institutions. Worldwide, Greens are more of a lobby than party, but with this new Ministry of Environment we can help construct institutions. We cannot remain outside. We must convince the environmental movement that a party is important. Look, for example, at the power of the apolitical vote that went to [ex-President] Collar.

Greens reject the developmentalist model imposed by transnational corporations and banks during the military regime, arguing that Western developmental models plunder and destroy nature, utilizing the Global South as a dumpsite and laboratory. Badly designed international programs have caused more poverty, revolution, and environmental damage than underdevelopment

An executive in Embrapa said, "We have a global crisis of paradigms, cultural, social, economic, and Brazil's internal problems makes it a mess. If our ruling class were serious and competent, which it isn't, we would still need fifteen years of political education to leave this crisis behind. In the 'knowledge society' of the future, research and public education are dominant factors in sustainability. In the 1980s Brazil joined the Third World. We have no conditions to confront the twenty-first century economy where natural resources and cheap labor are no longer crucial factors of production."

In line with the social consensus that led to cancellation of Brazil's nuclear program, Greens strongly reject nuclear power because of its waste disposal problems and high risk. Greens also believe that poorer countries must minimize fossil fuel dependency and are neutral concerning the costs and benefits of biotechnology.

This type strongly rejects the argument that spending to avert global warming is foolish, and that it is better to adjust to changes as they appear, but they are neutral when it comes to predicting concrete effects of global warming such as disruption of food chains, famine, mass migration, and flooding.

Greens accept the idea of demographic transition occurring as a consequence of development, reject reducing population through administrative measures, and reject the correlation between environmental degradation and population increase. But regarding one of the standard tenets of world Green thinking, "Respect for women should not be based on having children; women's rights is the key to population control," this type is neutral. The feminism that is a standard component of European Green thinking is lacking in Brazil.

An environmental group sociologist said, "We have high fecundity, but no national program of birth control or even debate on the issue. The old generation does not see this as a problem; development included population growth according to the old theories. Now, population is not *the* problem, but it is *a* problem. We lack funds and technology, and the Church opposes it, although many inside are for it. Even feminists reject it. Rio '92 showed the north-south split. The north uses far more of the world's resources with much lower populations than the south." As a PSDB deputy said, "Family planning without economic development is unfair. Only if we spread medical services nationally will population naturally decline."

In summary, Greens advocate a green economy and reject the developmentalism of the last twenty-one years. Development must be balanced, lowering dependency on fossil fuels, lowering the impacts of global warming, and it can lead to social equity and, ultimately, demographic transition. Greens are socially moderate, pro-democratic, neutral on feminist issues, and open to dialog with all sectors. Their project is to open political space within the establishment, without being identified with system parties or ideologies.

Sustainable Developers represent the composite operant subjectivity of three scientists; environmentalist executives in the environmental group IPSN, Funatura, the Institute for Amazon Studies, and the World Wildlife Fund; three administrators from the Ministry of Environment and Ibama; and an environmental lawyer. The minister of environment, a top executive in the missionary council CIMI, and a science journalist all weighted significantly on both this and the Green type.

Sustainable Developers believe that development on a sustainable basis is possible and cost effective, and will not require a revolution equal to the industrial revolution. The Green socioeconomic model is not the only viable alternative. Maximizing GNP should not necessarily cause waste, pollution, or inequality, nor would it solely benefit the wealthy and powerful. However, Sustainable Developers do not trust business and the marketplace to protect the environment, even under a regime of open information and incentives. As a female environmental group executive argued, "Business has the information, but they must be punished in order to change. In Minas Gerais, environmentalists published a 'dirty list' of industries, and over the years they have begun to clean up. Next year's list will mainly be state enterprises; the government can't even enforce regulations [*fiscalizar*] against itself."

Sustainable Developers are neutral as to whether democracy is incapable of meeting the environmental challenge. As a female technician in Ibama said, "Environmentalism demands a global theory because ideology and science are linked. With our serious socioeconomic problems there is great fear of social convulsion, and the problem grows daily. Our democracy lacks maturity; we are still learning."

As to Brazil's environmental movement, a female coordinator of the IEAA argued that, "NGOs here are weak, incipient, low on resources, with few technical people. We have little financing and no citizen consciousness or contributions. We depend on external resources, NGOs which are mostly conservationist, but weak on the issue of poverty or education, and which won't pay for lobbying. We must professionalize and mobilize. Of twelve hundred NGOs in Brazil only 15 percent are linked by communications, and few can afford headquarters in Brasilia where the political space is open."

Sustainable Developers are, however, concerned about global warming and strongly oppose a wait-and-see policy, because they believe that dramatic climate changes and disruption of land-based and oceanic food chains are in the offing.

Despite this concern, the Sustainable Developers' technology policy is relatively moderate. They believe that traditional, sustainable, farming methods could provide a practical model with further scientific elaboration. They reject the risks of nuclear power but do not reject the use of fossil fuels such as oil, gas, and coal for future development. As a high executive in Ibama said, "Nuclear power impedes investigation of other energy possibilities. Brazil has a wealth of hydro- and petroresources which could be used instead of high-tech, high-risk energy sources." Biotechnology holds neither the promise nor the risk projected in international debate. Sustainable Developers do not feel that the risks of biotech overshadow its commercial potential. Biotechnology does not represent anything as dramatic as the next step in human evolution and control of nature.

Sustainable Developers are inconsistent in their view on population. Stopping environmental degradation will not slow population growth; population must be forced down lest it block even basic development. Yet, they argue that women's rights, and presumably choice in areas of birth control and abortion, are the key to population control. Sustainable Developers have not decided between administrative and libertarian measures, but no doubt the issue is severely constrained by Church pressure; even the left PT does not raise the issue for fear of alienating its Catholic base community supporters.

Sustainable Developers are weakly critical of the Western development model. They agree that anthropocentric ideologies and Western development models plunder and destroy nature, and that ill-conceived aid programs have caused more poverty and environmental erosion than development. But their opinions in this area are not strongly held.

They believe that the Law of the Sea and the Rio UNCED treaties show growing international consensus about environment but reject, with some force, the argument that Western financing and enforcement of international environmental regulation would conserve nature.

In summary, Sustainable Developers believe in cost-effective environmentally benign growth with moderate use of fossil fuels and hard technologies and some planning to offset global warming. While supporting women's rights as the key to population control, Sustainable Developers believe that population must be forced down. They admit some international consensus on environment but only weakly criticize the prior dictatorship's Western modernist developmentalism. They are distrustful of business and skeptical about democracy's capacity to resolve crucial environmental issues.

Sustainable Developers differ from Greens in being less oriented to class and anti-developmentalist sentiments, being more moderate about fear of global warming. But they are more anti-business and more strongly favor women's rights. Greens have a firmer preference for grassroots transformation of the economy and are more negative toward nuclear and fossil fuel cycles but also more permissive regarding the population question. Greens are more optimistic about the human prospect and more enthusiastic about democracy.

Postmodern Managers are represented by high-level officials in Ibama, Embrapa, a PMDB (Party of the Brazilian Democratic Movement) deputy, a businessman and president of the Federation of Commerce and Latin American Chamber of Commerce, and an economist in Funatura. The type includes one woman.

Postmodern Managers believe that environmentally responsible development is possible for Brazil. They are moderate about social justice issues, but when it comes to the utilization of technologies, they are risk averse. They criticize the Western developmental model but think that a growing international consensus will facilitate environmental development.

Managers strongly believe that development can proceed on a sound environmental basis, with investment in energy efficiency and recycling. They support the model green economy—with sustainability, democratic participation, and voluntary simplicity—more strongly than do the Greens and reject the idea that creating sustainability will require revolutionary changes. As one environmental group scientist said, "A sustainable economy does not represent a return to mere survival. Sustainability can be comfortable and have levels of well-being superior to our economy."

An agronomist with Ibama agreed. "We cannot return to the original economy of the species as we have interfered with nature from the beginning. Nature has recuperative powers, but these are hampered by technology. We must educate people to see limits to their action. We need a cultural vision of nature as a spaceship, a system view. We must change our behavior so that we use the technology we have in a balanced way."

The environmental consultant said: "Few nations take ecology into account, it has a cost and low initial level of return. Business is beginning to think about the issue, for example in Germany. The world economy is turning to recycling as energy prices rise. Technology must show businesses how they will profit."

Postmodern Managers are moderately progressive and are in tune with environmental considerations. Their view of the available policy instruments is similarly moderate. Environmental policy is piecemeal and defensive, but democracy, despite its defects, can promote a rational legal regime. An agronomist from Ibama said, "Democracy is slow, but it builds civil society. The ecology is too complex and interlocked for centralized regulation. We need education as we have no grand development model."

Regarding the environmentalist role, a consultant and historical leader in the environmental movement said, "NGOs need to be technically able to specify goals. Laws are vague and general, and if they cannot be made scientific and specific they will demoralize society. We must prove the economic viability of environmental concerns."

An international business leader expressed some surprisingly postmodern sentiments on this issue—surprising given his position of power and place in the interwar cohort. "Capitalism as we know it has failed. We need a new capitalism, a profound change for the new millennium. The elites are outmoded, the old schemas are useless. We need new leaders, a sense of human fraternity. Frontiers are unnecessary. But we shouldn't let the multinational corporations enslave Brazil; we must ally with them and modify their impact."

Managers mildly distrust market forces and corporations when it comes to managing the environment and are also critical of the government. As the environmental group scientist said, "Governing sectors are refractory to environmental change. Elites want growing profits, and our industrial profile and lack of capital and technology transfer make sustainability difficult. The government is incompetent and the political-institutional-economic crisis makes it worse. We are incapable of planning."

Postmodern Managers are neutral about the goal of maximizing GNP but strongly reject the notion that development favors only the rich. An agronomist in Ibama said, "The development that we are looking for is sustainable, not merely for redistribution to the rich. Not even capitalists want this now."

While Postmodern Managers are not pessimistic about the human future, they tend to be strongly risk averse. Thus, they argue that both nuclear power and the experimental release of biotechnological products entail more risks than benefits. An administrator in Embrapa said, "We fear the manipulation of life, especially in the hands of corporations like Monsanto who are interested only in profits. We must plan to protect areas of great biodiversity. International treaty arrangements help with this."

Postmodern Managers believe that future development will require fossil fuel cycles and that traditional farming cannot be part of the effort. Women's rights are not the key to population control in their estimation; and they have no brief on the population question.

They worry about the possibility of global warming causing severe social dislocation and strongly oppose a wait-and-see policy. A program coordinator at Ibama said, "The Greenhouse effect is a grave preoccupation; it could be catastrophic, but it is not yet clear. There is no investigation showing the effects, so we must be careful with our policies."

Postmodern Managers criticize international development programs and Brazil's dependency, but do not reject the philosophy that humanity is ultimately the master of nature. There is a growing international treaty regime on environmental issues, and if the West enforced and paid for conservation, it would benefit the world commons.

A female PMDB deputy said, "Rio '92 was a series of compromises. We were conscious of the debates here, but it had no real impact on Brazilian legislation. The social problem makes us blind. But our social problem is linked to environment. A global environmental policy is impossible because of the immense differences between countries. There can only be general guidelines at the international level. But like the Greenhouse effect, we shouldn't be paranoid, but should study it and act before something awful happens [uma desgraça acontece]."

The consultant and environmentalist leader voiced the Postmodern Managers' critique of Green movements. "The Green Party is made of amateurs and consumers of nature; the able politicians and scientists are in other parties. It is a church—it is too closed. We must show the political importance of the question. The problems are larger and more long-term now. I don't believe in catastrophe. We can create conditions to resolve many problems. But changing a culture is a very slow process, while the changes in the environment are rapid."

In sum, Postmodern Managers support sustainable development with rational management to minimize the risks from biotechnology, fossil fuels, and global warming, and they reject nuclear power. Properly planned development can be generally beneficial and environmentally clean. Postmodern Managers criticize the conduct of business and government in Brazil and are interested in post-Fordist intensive development and industrial conversion; they show strongly postmodern values, except on women's rights issues.

Developmentalists are found among officials in the Ministry of Environment and Ibama, the CEO of Embrapa, a well-known deputy from the conservative PPR (Progressive Reformist Party), a deputy from the conservative PFL (Party of the Liberal Front), and the president of the environmentalist group IPSN.

Given its composition, one would expect this type to be conservative, pro-development and pro-market. Indeed, this type lies within the modernist and Fordist quadrants (see fig. 6.1). But while believing in market-led development, Developmentalists are generally quite temperate and non-ideological in their views.

As expected, the two rightist deputies in this type tend toward a more polarizing position. As the PFL deputy said, "Ecology is very partisan, the NGOs are ideological, not environmentalist, and are dominated by the far left. The issue shouldn't be politicized, but it is. Politics is first, science second." The PPR deputy, a historic figure on the right, said, "The new environmental consciousness veers toward exaggeration; there are ecologists, ecomaniacs, ecoromantics. The Indian question is romanticism. It is absurd to have 10,000 ha per Indian. Industrial exploitation can improve the landscape. The transnational corporations are more environmentally conscious than we are. The Trombetas bauxite exploitation done by C.V.R.D. (Companhia do Vale do Rio Doce) and the Japanese pays royalties, taxes, and gives health services to the Indians."

Perhaps more characteristic of the core of this type, a planner from Embrapa said, "We must trade off production for global livability [*vivencialidade global*]. Natural pest control can't compete with agrochemicals, but is an environmental gain. We have to transcend developmental economics. Extensive development means more headaches. We need sophisticated technology with new parameters and markets. It fits postmodern in-time production for custom markets, but here we must also feed the masses. The power to create Green and feminist ideologies is in the cities, but when they have to pay higher prices they will become more moderate."

Developmentalists believe that all living things have a right to exist, and that biodiversity is the common heritage of mankind, to be rationally used and conserved. Humanity is not doomed to extinction in their view, and there is no threat of environmental collapse and subsequent social breakdown.

Developmentalists do not fear the externalities arising from GNP growth and are neutral as to whether development favors only elites. They strongly believe that energy-efficient industry and recycling can cut fossil fuel use without sacrificing growth, and unlike the other types, they strongly believe that information and incentives, instead of command and control regulation, allow business and the market to protect the environment.

They believe that despite its inefficiencies, democracy can meet the environmental challenge, but they are also aware that environmental policy has been piecemeal and defensive and not global, as the case demands. Developmentalists are second only to the Greens in adherence to democracy. This represents an important shift, because the military definition of developmentalism, which reigned between 1964 and 1985, required a bureaucratic authoritarian state with severe restrictions on liberty and participation.

As a high Embrapa official argued, "Democracy itself is not incompetent, but our society is not organized, it is not fully democratic. The vote is not enough as the state is super-disorganized. The growth of NGOs helps civil society organize its own basis without vertical state action. A mature self-organized, participatory civil society should drive democracy. The left and right are still linked to corporativism, they see the solutions only from their own sectoral interests. We have no national project."

Developmentalists are not as critical of Western aid programs as the other types and believe that the growing international consensus and treaty regimes regarding the global commons, coupled with side payments from advanced countries, can help preserve nature.

Stopping environmental degradation will not halt population growth, according to Developmentalists, and thus population must be forced down to allow continued economic growth. As the CEO of Embrapa said, "The rate of population growth is falling, but we still need more control. Population is not the main factor, because we face bad developmental and distributional policies. Most development comes from the state, but the state cannot promote the economy further, and the economy is failing. The ecology is at risk from economic causes." It is perhaps surprising that of all four types, Developmentalists most strongly support women's rights as the key to population control.

They see no risk of global warming, denying that it could cause sea-level rise and subsequent disaster, and are neutral about taking initiatives or simply waiting to see what effects develop.

However, Developmentalists show themselves averse to the risks of hard power. They think that the risks of biotechnological releases may outweigh the economic value of the industry and strongly reject the notion that biotechnology is superior to mechanical-chemical farming or that it is a strategic necessity for developing nations. They argue that fossil fuel will be necessary to future development and reject a return to traditional farming along sustainable lines. But they do not believe that the costs of nuclear power, in terms of waste disposal and risk, outweigh its possible benefits.

As a planner from Embrapa said, "Sustainable agriculture needs more, not less, science, a more sophisticated relation to nature that takes out only what is necessary. Sustainable production doesn't mean primitive. Science can make the world more livable, but not through a return to the past. We must change the parameters of science from only productivity, which leads to the degradation of nature. But I am afraid that this will come down to an ideological battle and we will see an increasingly antiscience position."

In sum, Developmentalists show increased concern for environmental outcomes and believe in conservation, efficient energy use, and democratic means, including government cooperation with the business community and other market forces, to foster development. They are concerned about population growth but not about global warming, but are relatively risk averse in dealing with the fuel cycles driving development. Technical assistance from developed nations could enable more sustainable development. Developmentalists believe in a more democratic and environmentally responsible form of capitalist development.

Figure 6.1 models Brazilian elite attitude types on postmodern/post-Fordist dimensions. Postmodern Managers surpass Greens by one point along the postmodern scale, but are significantly more post-Fordist. They are critical of the military regime's "savage capitalism," of business and market conduct, and they are risk averse, while believing that technologically sophisticated intensive production can protect the environment. Postmodern Managers and Sustainable Developers are, surprisingly, twice as anti-business as the Greens. Managers and Greens share the goal of a green economy but differ about technical means, while Sustainable Developers are relatively neutral about the ideal

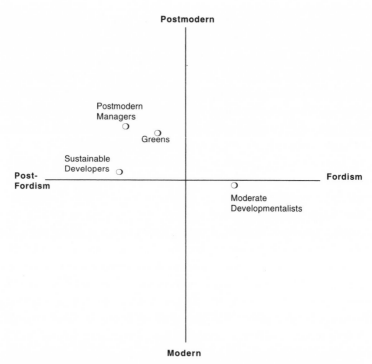

6.1. Brazilian Attitude Types on Postmodern and Post-Fordist Indicators
Postmodern indicator is a positive score on statement 18. The only alternative is a green economy, with grassroots democracy, voluntary simplicity, sustainable production, and recycling.
Post-Fordist indicator is a negative score on statement 13. If government gave business information and incentives, not command and sanction, the market and entrepreneurs would protect the environment.

green society. Greens are the most enthusiastic about democratic participation, while Postmodern Managers and Sustainable Developers have much weaker faith in the New Republic.

The Greens' social profile should indicate strong postmodern values and social radicalism. But even with this profile, they are center-left on social issues and not as radically consistent on environmental issues (e.g., they are neutral on women's rights and GNP growth) as would be expected from data on European Greens. Sustainable Developers, mainly environmental executives and scientists, have a more technical than postmodern value orientation toward environment.

Postmodern Managers, mainly top government and business executives, believe strongly in intensive development, industrial conversion, but are the most Postmodern because of their critique of GNP growth effects and their acceptance of a green model in broad outline. They differ from Greens in accepting feminism but in being weaker supporters of democracy.

Developmentalists—government and party figures, some of whom participated in the military regime—currently show only limited adherence to market-led growth as a goal and accept the cost-benefit nature of environmental management of the economy. They also have changed their attitude toward democracy, from the national-security stance of "sacrificing a generation" to modernization toward strong democratic adherence (second only to the Greens), and they show the strongest respect for women's rights. They remain Fordists and modernists, but shorn of the illusions of "economic miracles" and willing to help reconstruct a civil society eviscerated by twenty-one years of state terrorism.

This model is of importance in elucidating differences between the new environmental politics and the old left-right political continuum, which continues to dominate Brazilian official thought and mass media. It would be tragic if Brazilians did not realize that their environmental issue is much more consensual and much less politicized than it appears, that there is great scope for serious negotiation among sectors and a general willingness on all sides to change opinions based on scientific information leading to sustainable development.

Postmodern values are not fully embraced by any of the attitude types and, in the country's closed elitist politics, may not be a realistic alternative. But there is broad cross-sectoral agreement on sustainable development through industrial conversion, recycling, and rational resource management, and there is a common rejection of forced corporate-driven "savage capitalism."

Despite ongoing fiscal and monetary crisis, Brazil has the legal and intellectual infrastructure to deal creatively with its environmental tragedy. So this research concludes on a note of tempered optimism. The new Brazilian environmental thinking shows the way to a knowledge-based politics of consensus, which must replace the old dysfunctional ideological politics of modernism if Brazil is to recover and perhaps flourish.

Conclusions

1. Few national elites have the knowledge or interest group backing to place environment on the national agenda. The small environmental elite dealt with in this study is strongly interlocked; that is, its members move easily between government, business, and environmental sectors, with high job turnover. They tend to be overcommitted and overworked with little institutional support or infrastructure. Groups that fund and support popular outreach and lobbying have been most successful with local environmental issues but have yet to mobilize significant popular pressure in order to enter the national arena with Green demands.

2. Brazil's ideologically right-wing press frames environmental issues in terms of the old left-right politics, a polarizing, dismissive discourse strongly echoed in Congress. The major media and parties are doing a great disservice to the dialog needed to define sustainable development, which can easily be facilitated by the strong agreement, moderation, and sectoral overlap seen in the attitude types discussed.

None of the attitudes discovered among these key environmental decision makers is extremist or rhetorical, and all seem willing to reconsider positions on the basis of scientific data and workable technical proposals for more intelligently utilizing Brazil's ecology and resources.

3. Brazil's Constitution, environmental legislation, and new Ministry of Environment demonstrate a clear institutional commitment to the problem. However, Brazil's serious economic crisis, neoliberal presidents, conservative Congress, administrative incapacity, lack of technical bureaucracy capable of consistent planning and execution, poor salaries, and difficulties in enforcing regulation against government agencies, parastatal enterprises, and local elites all conspire to work against the success of sustainable development. The new legal-administrative structure tends to work in a vacuum, without the input and assistance of the environmental movement. This is partly the result of strong military and security police influence within Conama, the council incorporating environmentalists into ministry planning.

4. Brazil's rightist partisan press, and outmoded party system, do not reflect the salience of postmodern issues such as environment, feminism, indigenous and black rights, human rights, or urban issues. Both the party right and left are still immersed in statist corporativist models, or extreme neoliberal reactions to such models, both of which are counterproductive in Brazil's current fiscal, socioeconomic, and political-administrative crisis.

There appears to be no political space or mobilization push for a Green party in Brazil. Its only Green Party, Partido Verde, arose within the PT or Workers Party, but its urban and postmodern mind-set has been unable to influence the PT's modernist left and Church sectors.[21] The Green Party is not driven by popular mobilization around environment but by a small postmodern academic and professional elite, mainly centered in Rio de Janeiro. It lost its registration because it was too focused on a single issue, which, in the minds of the poor who make up 80 percent of Brazil's population, is not immediately relevant. Its single deputy joined the congressional delegation of the PDT, Democratic Labor Party.

Environmental groups see congressional politics as artificial elite conflict, removed from their concerns, and strive to maintain distance from the fragmented parties, made of shifting coalitions of notables, none of them seriously embracing the environmental problematic. Because Brazil's party system enjoys little popular support or prestige, separating environmental issues from party politics is the best strategy for environmentalists. But the movement lacks resources to coordinate local resistance nationally, to lobby, conduct direct action, force its way into congressional dialog, or influence the mass media presentation of the issue. Environmentalists lack capacity to mobilize public pressure for comprehensive environmental transformation and must seek piecemeal issue-specific change using data and information as weapons, within a political game that does not include environmental issues in its means-ends equations.

Brazil's environmental sector is working to rebuild civil society within the constraints of a profound economic crisis and to animate the creation of a new postmodern politics that throws off both the left corporatist heritage and neoliberal "savage capitalism," neither of which is sustainable. Few elites and administrators understand the importance of these groups in reconstructing civil society and in preventing social deterioration.

5. Discovery of these four attitude types, types which overlap the leading sectors of Brazilian society, should assist the search for dialog between sectors. All opinion types are moderate and open to dialog with scientific input. Most are critical of Brazil's failed military experiment with "savage capitalism" and the lack of international program financing that would balance the constant barrage of foreign criticism of Brazil's handling of the Amazon.

The international community must begin large-scale, sustained funding of sustainable development and preservation programs for the

Amazon and for administrative capacitation of the Brazilian state. Debt restructuring tied to environmental performance targets and debt-for-nature swaps, and grants-in-aid, are the best mechanisms for financing Amazon conservation.[22]

The importance of this ecosystem transcends nationalistic interests; the Amazon, like the Antarctic, is the common heritage of humanity. But Brazil and the other five border nations cannot be expected to forgo exploitive development of this rich resource without full compensation by the international community in terms of debt relief and technical and developmental aid.

A coordinated program of international debt relief, restructuring, transfer, and side payments to Brazil must be utilized to compensate Brazil for forgoing exploitation of its environment, which Brazil's elites, especially the old industrialist, military, and security community, still falsely see as the road to wealth and national power. World consensus around sustainable development, as exemplified at Rio UNCED '92, must be translated into political and financial stimulation of Brazilian fiscal recovery, or the cause of Amazon preservation will surely be lost.

Mexico: Neoliberal Sustainable Development

The 1994 economic crisis made the conservation of Mexico's wonderfully rich and fragile environment into an international problem. Since the prior 1982 economic crisis, Mexico has followed a strict neoliberal adjustment package under international debt management, with "sustainable development" based on free trade and market-led regulation. Entry into the North American Free Trade Agreement in 1994 and the consequent liquidity crisis and deep recession demonstrated the limits of this model and put Mexico's environment at further risk. Mexico has recently made some strong moves toward a rational legal regime, but high debt, export-led development, and political fragmentation have shaken the state's capacity to perform its regulatory tasks.

In this chapter we examine Mexico's ecological crisis, its neoliberal environmental policy, and the attitudes of government, business, scientific, and environmentalist elites toward these questions.

Mexico's Environmental Problem

A nation of 1,958,200 sq km, Mexico ranks thirteenth in size and eleventh in population with 96,600,000 people, a 38.7 percent increase over 1980. Mexico has a dual economy, developed and impoverished. With GDP of U.S. $334 billion in 1996, the Mexican economy is the eleventh largest in the Organization for Economic Cooperation and Development (OECD), but per capita, its GDP of $8,149 was among the lowest in the OECD. GDP grew by 29 percent between 1980 and 1995; an impressive rate, but lower than population growth.

In 1995, Mexico underwent its worst recession in decades as GDP fell by 6.2 percent. Led by exports, growth resumed in 1996, reaching 5.1 percent. Inflation, which has been declining, was close to 20 percent in mid-1997. From January to July 1998 there was a 10 percent devaluation of the currency.

Mexico's production is 70 percent services, 24 percent industry and agriculture, 5.7 percent forestry and fishing. Exports are composed of 84 percent manufactures, 11 percent oil, and 5 percent agricultural goods. The United States takes 84 percent of Mexican exports by value, while 5 percent go to other Latin American countries.

Mexico's labor force was 36.6 million in 1996, or 55 percent of the working-age population (twelve years and older). About 55 percent of the work force is in services, 23 percent in industry, and 22 percent in agriculture. Maquiladoras employ 900,000 workers. One-third of the urban labor force is in the informal sector.

The ecosystem that sustains this industrializing economy is fragile and complex, with one of the world's highest percentages of endemic flora and fauna. Mexico is fourteenth in Greenhouse gas emissions, with 490 million tons per year of CO_2 about 1.6 percent of the world's emissions. Energy consumption is 53 million BTUs (British Thermal Units) per capita, placing Mexico in forty-seventh place.

Water is not scarce, but most settlements lie above 500 m in altitude while most water resources are found in the valleys below, so there are serious supply problems. About 625,000 ha/year are being deforested, and toxic waste levels along the border are some of the most critical in the world. Protected areas occupy 8.2 percent of the nation.[1]

There are four principal ecological zones in Mexico. The arid zone occupies 53 percent of the nation (1,027,051 km^2), and contains 966 ecogeographic systems. The dry tropics are 13 percent of the national territory (254,927 km^2) with 288 ecological systems and 12 hydrological regions. The temperate zone includes large mountain ranges, forests, and mountain valleys, with 20 percent of the territory (390,241 km^2), 369 ecological systems, and 16 hydrological regions, all seriously perturbed by development. The humid tropics comprise 15 percent of territory (285,983 km^2) with 190 ecogeographic systems and 11 hydrological regions. This area includes Mexico's most biodiverse and productive systems: rainforests, coral reefs, lagoons, mangrove wetlands, and the Gulf of Mexico.

Mexico has four major environmental problem areas: hydrological, soil and waste, air quality, and biodiversity.

Mexico's hydrological problem is unique. With a positive hydrological balance, the country nevertheless suffers water deficits in the main population centers, with serious draw down, salinization, and pollution of its groundwater resources. Mexico is well supplied with water; but the bulk of population and economic activity is located in the 52.7 percent of the territory with hydrological deficits. Dry urbanized areas are the most heavily polluted, while well-watered areas have problems of flooding and pollution from the petroleum industry. The government spends U.S. $1 billion subsidizing water delivery.

Water pollution has reached crisis proportions, with 77 percent of Mexico's rivers polluted and posing a risk to human health. For example, the Lerma River receives sewage from ninety-five cities and waste from 555 industrial plants as it crosses from Mexico City to Lake Chapala in Guadalajara. Lake Chapala suffers eutrophication and contamination with persistent chemicals; however, the Lerma–Chapala Basin Council has achieved a 65 percent reduction in pollution loading in the 1990s.

The total urban population uses 170 m^3/second of drinking water, 20 percent of which is lost to leaking pipes, and generates 115 m^3/second of waste water, of which only 15 percent receives any type of treatment. Industry generates 82 m^3/second of waste water, and agriculture 265 m^3/second, most of which is highly contaminated and discharged without treatment. Groundwater contamination with fecal matter causes extensive gastrointestinal diseases in about one-third of Mexico. The Clean Water Program established in 1991 aimed to disinfect tap water, regulate bottled water and ice, and build waste water treatment plants. The number of communities receiving disinfected tap water doubled between 1991 and 1997.[2]

But Mexico City still uses water much more rapidly than is sustainable. The aquifer has dropped more than 10 m in some areas. The ground is subsiding 45 cm per year in some locations, changing the gradient of the sewage, drainage, and water delivery systems and thus obstructing drainage and contaminating groundwater.

Industry channels 2,500 tons of toxic waste into Mexico City's water supply every day. The 1,407 billion cubic meters of water discharged annually into the Tula River through Emisor Central, the main drainage conduit for the valley of Mexico, contains 632,535 tons of organics. Only 8 percent of industrial waste water receives any sort of treatment, removing only 0.12 million tons of biochemical oxygen demand (BOD) out of 1.6 million. Some 92 percent of Mexican industry consists of small and micro companies, unable to comply with regulation or be regulated. Voluntary agreements recently signed with Pemex (Petroleos Mexicanos, the state oil company) and with coffee, alcohol, sugar, and textile industries set timetables for cleaning up discharges to water and air. Steel, pulp, paper, and sugar-refining industries have begun to conserve water as a result of enforced water fees and charges.[3]

Mexico's rich aquatic resources are also threatened by uncontrolled tourist development, ports for petroleum refining and transport, shipping pollution, and the introduction of exotic species. Urbanization of the coastal zone, with forty-four major ports, leads to oil and urban non-point-source pollution, particulate load from dredging and sea wall construction, and erosion of beach and dune structures.

Mexico's littoral is over 11,000 km in extent, with a 3 million km^2 exclusive economic zone created by the Law of the Sea (1985); 358,000 km^2 of continental shelf and 2.9 million ha of national waters give Mexico a territorial extension of 2,982,000 km^2. The Pacific upwelling zone, reefs, lagoons, and estuaries of the Gulf Coast are rich in nutrients and biologically highly productive. There are twenty-eight marine phyla (compared to only eleven on land) and over eight hundred species of fish. Freshwater ecosystems have forty-seven families and five hundred species of fish. Twenty-six species of marine animals are taken by artisanal (40 percent of fishing effort) and industrial fisheries, making Mexico the seventeenth fish-producing nation. With a catch of 1.45 million tons per annum, and a fleet of 75,757 fishing boats, about 10 percent of which operate in the pelagic province, Mexico is overfishing, with evident diminishing returns since 1981. Large parts of the catch are thrown back or wasted in transport and processing.

Lagoons, coral reefs, and wetlands are polluted and urbanized, seriously threatening the primary productivity of ocean species and hence Mexico's fishing industry. Mining of coastal phosphates, copper, molybdenum, calcium, and sand accelerates habitat destruction. Many programs were created in the last two presidential administrations, but marine biodiversity has only recently come to be considered a serious conservation issue.

Mexico has rules to reduce incidental dolphin kills by the tuna industry, and enforces MARPOL (International Convention for Prevention of Pollution from Ships, 1978) against shipping pollution, although no port has the infrastructure to comply fully with its provisions. Mexico signed the Declaration of Cancun 1992 on responsible fishing practices and belongs to the Caribbean Environmental Action Plan worked out as part of Agenda XXI at the UNCED conference at Rio de Janeiro in 1992. Thus, its concern for protection of oceanic resources stems mainly from the 1990s, and the required administrative, fiscal, and physical structures have yet to be created.[4]

Besides a serious water quality crisis, Mexico faces critical soil contamination and erosion. The country has twenty-three out of the twenty-five major world soil types and thus is rich in this precious resource. The uses of this soil are the following: 40.8 percent pastures, 13.9 percent agriculture, 15.6 percent scrub lands (*matorrales*), 12.3 percent tropical forests, and 13 percent temperate forests.

Mexico confronts rapid ongoing desertification—that is, the simplification of ecosystems and reduction of biological productivity. Some 66 percent of Mexico's soils are eroded, 13 percent are severely eroded, and declining crop yields cost Mexico U.S. $1 billion per year. Soils are intensively farmed, overtilled, and subject to erosion by wind and water. Ten percent of irrigated regions are too dry to flush salt loads out of the soils. Mexico loses a total of 535 thousand tons of soil per year, 69 percent of which is ultimately deposited in the oceans, thereby compounding another problem.

U.S. pesticide sales to Mexico are U.S. $300 million per annum, and thirty out of ninety pesticides banned in the United States are used south of the border. Pesticide poisoning kills 150 people per year, including at least fifty children in Sinaloa alone. The nationwide pesticide death toll is estimated at five hundred per year. Compare this chemical-intensive farming with pre-Columbian Indian agriculture, which sustained a population of 25.1 million in central Mexico with a mix of swidden, forest gardens, terraced and raised fields, and lacustrine hydroponics. Indian agriculture was, by all accounts, more environmentally responsible and sustainable than the European plough cultures that replaced it.[5]

About 45 percent of farmers are in the subsistence sector. Peasants comprise 88 percent of farmers and their parcels of under 4 ha utilize 57 percent of the land. Low income and lack of credit, technology, information, infrastructure, marketing, distribution, and storage facilities hinder development of self-sufficient agriculture. Commercial farmers are only 2 percent of the agricultural population, but control 21 percent of the land, in parcels over 12 ha, and 42 percent of irrigated lands.

Most of Mexico's agricultural reserve land is in humid tropical forest, so that further extension of the cultivated frontier directly threatens biodiversity. The other half of this reserve is cattle pasture, controlled by powerful political families who can effectively resist regulation. The agricultural frontier need not be extended, if intensive alley cropping, terracing, intercropping, organic soil and pest management, and simple irrigation were utilized, and if the peasants were given the security of tenure, control of land, social services, and extension technologies due them under the Constitution of 1917.

Maize, beans, sorghum, and wheat are major crops. Because of the Green Revolution—extensive monocultures of high-yield varietals requiring heavy irrigation, pesticide, and fertilizer use—Mexico experienced an agricultural boom, which however, rapidly reached diminishing returns. Now Mexico imports maize, wheat, and other foodstuffs.

The unstated policy in Mexico is to eliminate small producers in favor of corporate capital, and President Salinas's (1988–94) changes to the Constitution allowed the sale and mortgage of *ejidal* (communal) lands to attract transnational capital into farming. Not only does this policy disrupt and destroy remaining Indian cultures and their knowledge base, but it leads to increased urbanization and illegal emigration to the United States.

This negative image of peasant farming is based on racist attitudes toward Indians as well as corporatist one-party political control exercised by the Institutional Revolutionary Party (PRI), which uses the *ejidatarios* as an important base of support but shows little concern for improving productivity or implanting sustainable systems. Smallholder farming actually has great potential for both productivity and ecological balance, given proper inputs. Sixty percent of Mexico's coffee, 30 percent of export, is grown on parcels of 1–5 ha. In Tabasco, cacao farms averaging 3 ha profitably intercrop maize, bananas, coconuts, sugarcane, and cattle, depending on availability of family labor.

In the state of Chiapas, 667 individuals own 817,400 acres of productive coffee and cattle lands, much of it taken from Indian ejidos through violent invasion. The guerrilla movement that emerged on January 1, 1994, the Ejercito Zapatista de Liberación Nacional (EZLN), demands an end to NAFTA and PRI, effective democracy, indigenous rights, land reform, social services, and an end to state violence. Its sophisticated critique of neoliberalism on the Internet and clever liaison with nongovernmental organizations may make the EZLN the first "postmodern guerrilla movement." Subsequent negotiation and state repression have not prevented the movement's political influence, although they have cut its military potential.

Mexico could switch to sustainable agrosilvapastoral farming, instead of extensive corporate monoculture, which has the added advantage of maintaining biodiversity, a future economic resource of untold value. The government is already subsidizing some highly biodiverse Indian *chinampa* (floating gardens) and *milpa* (raised irrigated fields) agriculture as gene and knowledge banks.[6]

Another urgent aspect of Mexico's ecological crisis is solid waste disposal. Mexico City, with a population close to 24 million, produces one kilogram per capita of waste per day. Between 1950 and 1990, per capita waste increased 207 percent. Waste collection services cover only 70 percent of this output and only 17 percent of waste goes into controlled landfills, where recycling is done by communities of waste pickers who live in shacks on and around the dump.

Only in the 1990s has government begun the process of closing thirteen open waste dumps, reclaiming the land, and installing seven modern sanitary landfills. There are only four treatment or recycling plants in the nation, and the World Bank and U.N. Development Program have given loans to finance recycling. Thirty-four percent of solid wastes consist of packaging and bottles that could be recycled, and 47 percent are organic wastes, which could be used to generate compost or biogas for energy, so this industry is open to future development.

Hazardous industrial wastes are also a difficult problem for Mexico; estimates for 1997 are 8 million tons per year, not counting waste stored by industries, with only 25 percent recycled. Small and medium enterprises comprise 98 percent of transformation industry and half of its product and employment, even if they contribute only 10 percent of GDP. Such small and scattered enterprises are notoriously difficult to regulate. Mexico has only five operating toxic waste dumps, one public and two private incinerators (Bayer, Ciba-Geigy), fourteen treatment plants designed to recover heavy metals and oil, and four landfills. Some foreign companies are interested in investing in this area.

There are 2,042 maquiladoras (in-bond assembly industries, many of them sweatshops), 1,493 on the border. Some 821 of them generate hazardous wastes, but only 600, or 71 percent, comply with weak Mexican regulations. The Integral Frontier Environmental Plan should require controls over production and transport of toxic wastes, but there is heavy traffic across the borders in toxic wastes, and the Mexican border patrol lacks the resources, expertise, and political will to regulate this flow. There are at least 450 hazardous waste sites, legal and illegal, and serious pollution of aquifers and watercourses along the border. The International Boundary and Water Commission, a binational regulatory agency, meets in secret, and because of overlapping jurisdictions, hazardous wastes and chemicals are neither tracked nor regulated.

Mexico's Border Industrialization Program has created a shared ecological holocaust. The Tijuana River sends 12 million gallons of untreated sewage and discharge from 530 maquiladoras into the sea daily, costing San Diego $100 million in lost annual tourist revenue. The New River, flowing from Mexicali to the Salton Sea, carries several disease pathogens and ninety deadly chemical toxins. The seventy-five maquiladoras and sewage outfalls in Nogales have caused hepatitis rates twenty times higher than U.S. rates and require wells ten miles north of the border to be closed.

Ciudad Juarez sends 64 million gallons of raw sewage, industrial toxics, and irrigation waste water into its watershed daily, directly affecting El Paso's environment. Nuevo Laredo's 100 maquiladoras discharge 25 million gallons per day of toxics, and the fecal coliform count in the water column is a thousand times above U.S. safe standards. Water in the open canals of Matamoros gives children who play in them caustic burns, and the canals debouch into the Gulf of Mexico to complicate the situation there. One GM plant discharged xylene at six thousand times above safe limits, and Stepan Chemicals discharged 52,700 times above safe levels. A DuPont joint venture released hydrofluoric acid, the chemical that killed so many at Bhopal.

Government rule NOM-087-ECOL-1995 regulates infectious waste and controls landfills to protect aquifers. The government has signed agreements with cement, oil, lubricant, fertilizer, and pesticide industries to control discharges and transport.[7]

Air quality is Mexico's most striking problem. Mexico's annual SO_x and NO_x emissions, from energy, industry, transport, residential, and service sectors, are 3.7 million tons; a high level of emission per unit of GDP. Energy-related CO_2 emissions grow more than 3 percent per year. In 1995, the total was estimated at 327.6 million tons. Mexico's energy-related CO_2 emissions are 0.66 tons per U.S. $1,000 of GDP, close to the OECD average.

Mexico City is the world's largest, with its 24 million people. Its location at 2,240 m above sea level and surrounded with mountains up to 5,200 m in height produces frequent inversion layers, which stop the basin from airing out. A conurbation of some 2,110 sq km with 4 million motor vehicles and some 30,000 industries, Mexico uses 43 million liters of fossil fuel and emits 13,500 tons of contaminants into the atmosphere each day. Some 3.2 million private cars are owned by just 15 percent of the city's population, but the fleet is being upgraded. In 1996, the average Mexico City car was eight years old, down from fourteen years old in 1990.

Factories in Mexico City emit 105,721 tons of air pollutants annually, of which 25 percent are SO_x, 30 percent NO_x, 31 percent hydrocarbons, 6 percent suspended particles (PST) and 8 percent CO. Seventy percent of urban emissions come from transportation.

Ambient SO_2 in the city has declined since 1991 because of cleaner fuels and relocation of industry. Annual mean levels of NO_2 however, are still rising. Gasoline contributes 24 percent of hydrocarbon emissions in the city (70 percent from leaking storage tanks), and half of the emissions are from vehicles. Ozone remains a major problem. Ozone and suspended particulates exceeded maximum levels for 280 days in 1991. In 1992, 162 days required ozone "alerts." By 1998 ozone exceeded maxima 90 percent of the year. Suspended particulates, including fecal aerosols, pathogens, and lead, remain serious problems.

The General Law of 1988 set ambient standards and emission limits, improved permit enforcement, mandated agreements with industry to reduce emissions beyond legal requirements, improved fuel quality, adopted environmental audit procedures, and strengthened vehicle standards and emission requirements. The city must inspect 35,000 industries, 4,000 of which contribute some 15 percent of the pollution. Eighty industries were closed in the 1990s, including a major state refinery. The city contracted a U.S. company to build a hazardous waste incinerator to cope with the 2,500 tons per day of toxic wastes dumped into landfills and sewers.

Unleaded gasolines and the Hoy No Circula (No Driving Today) program, which was launched in 1989 and takes about 20 percent of private cars and taxis off the road on given days, should be aiding this problem. This program requires catalytic converters, periodic inspections, lead-free gasolines, and modernized taxi, bus, and *pesero* (routed taxi) fleets. Industries are to convert to low-sulfur fuels and natural gas. One-third of the U.S. $3.3 billion air pollution program is funded by Japanese grants. However, the program is circumvented by upper-middle-class Mexicans who can afford a second or third car; the total fleet increased 14 percent in the program's first year. Cars manufactured after 1993 circulate daily.

But the government encourages and subsidizes production and sales of older model cars like the Volkswagen Beetle, which is ten times more polluting than the Nissan Tsuru. An Automotive Emissions Verification Program begun in 1989 has become a racket for mechanics who "fix" the car to emit less but return to its original condition once it passes. Owners of cars made before 1993 pay biannual tribute to their mechanics.[8]

Respiratory disease, cancer, and hypertension rates remain high, and lead levels in the blood caused seriously high percentages of retardation; estimates ran to 20 percent or 4 million people. Fortunately, lead levels have dropped since 1990. Some 30,000 children die each year in the Federal District due to pollution-related diseases. Twenty-five percent of the population will develop respiratory problems. Health care costs and labor losses come to about U.S. $8,333,300 per day, about $3 billion per year.

Six hundred tons of fecal material are daily converted into dust and there are so many pathogens, like salmonella and streptococcus, per cubic meter that they are unassayable. Some progress is being made with foreign aid and aggressive emissions control and transport modernization, but the city's very size and growth rate counteract these gains and require ever higher expenditures and stronger regulations simply to achieve equilibrium.

Recent decentralization has given states and municipalities responsibility for air quality management, although many lack technical capacity and financial resources for monitoring, planning, and implementation. Developmental differences between the states could be worsened by large variations in standards of environmental management.

Air quality improvements in major urban centers will depend on integrated transport, urban, and environmental policies, such as the 1995–2000 Air Quality Improvement Program for the Mexico City basin. In 1997 Monterrey, Guadalajara, Toluca, Ciudad Juárez, and Mexicali (Baja California) implemented programs to improve air quality. Guadalajara has high rates of automobile ownership, accounting for 70 percent of the city's air pollution. The ozone standard is exceeded six days out of ten, but for NO_2, CO, and SO_2 the standards are exceeded only occasionally. Cement and chemical plants, glass factories, ceramic producers, and food processing are the main polluters.[9]

An important aspect of Mexico's environmental problem is the threat to biodiversity. Mexico is one of the most biodiverse nations in the world with one of the highest rates of endemism, or unique plants and animals. Mexico is among seven countries with the highest biodiversity in the world since it contains 60 percent of the world's species.

Its fauna is 52 percent endemic, a condition approached only by Brazil, Peru, India, and Australia, with the highest number of reptiles (393/707), and the second highest number of mammal species (505/4,170), being fourth in amphibians (176/293 endemic), and seventh in birds (1,150 species of the world's 9,198, with 85 endemic). Mexico has one-tenth of the world's 300,000 plant species.

However, 242 of these total species are in process of extinction, 435 are threatened, 244 are considered rare, and 84 require special protection. Of these endangered species, 411 are endemic and 73 percent are at serious risk. A high number of Mexican species are in "precarious condition," and 33.2 percent of mammals, 16.8 percent of birds, 18 percent of reptiles, 16.9 percent of amphibians, 4.5 percent of fish, and 2.5 percent of vascular plants are "threatened or under risk of extinction." Many of Mexico's endemic cacti, orchids, and bromeliads are threatened with extinction.

By 1996 there were 94 Protected Natural Areas, amounting to 11,171,000 ha., with a budget of U.S. $3 million, which has remained stable in the 1990s due to inflation and devaluation. A special reserve has been set up for the monarch butterfly. By 1999, 210,000 ha should be added to the protected areas. Nevertheless, actual protection of these areas has been relatively weak. Funds are limited, and local people are rarely consulted or involved with management. Protected areas are not representative in terms of habitat and biodiversity. The 1995–2000 Program of Natural Protected Areas stresses public participation, but the financial means are not forthcoming. Education, ranger patrols, and tourist and fire-control programs are being created. But Mexico has serious problems of poaching, contraband export of endangered species, and tourist impact on fragile wetlands, beaches, and coral reefs.

The Program of Wildlife Conservation and Diversification of Rural Production plans to preserve and protect biodiversity, ecosystems, wildlife habitat; to decrease species extinction; and to recover species at risk of extinction. From 141 units under the program in 1996, covering some 2.5 million ha, there was a jump in 1998 to 839 units covering more than 6 million ha.

Mexico suffers deforestation rates among the highest in the world. Between 1979 and 1990 there was a loss of 13 million ha. By 1996 Mexico had lost 44.2 million ha of forest out of a total of 98 million. Mexico has lost 95 percent of its rain forests, and over half of its temperate forests. The National Reforestation Program begun in 1995 replanted 148,457 ha, some 229 million trees. However, the survival rate is low.

Every hectare of Lacondon rainforest has more than a thousand plant species, but this genetic treasure trove has been reduced 75 percent from its original 1.5 million ha. Each year some 40,000 ha are cleared and army operations against the Zapatista guerrillas "required" construction of tank roads through the jungle. There are 200,000 squatters in the forest, cattle ranchers have illegally cleared large areas, and marijuana and opium poppies are illegally being grown under cover from remote sensing. Pemex is exploring the forest for oil. Some five hundred Lacandon Indians maintained a hunting and gathering lifestyle, but they are rapidly being absorbed into the tourist economy. The microclimate is changing and there are now torrential rains.

The Zedillo Administration has been moving to address these environmental crises. The new Secretariat of Environment, Natural Resources and Fisheries (SEMARNAP) took over the National Program of Reforestation in 1998. The 1998 General Law provides a framework for sustainable development, but only six specific plans were adopted by 1997. Ecological planning is new to Mexico, and the capacity of the National Institute of Ecology (INE) and of state and local authorities to plan and manage resources is limited.[10]

Mexico has a fragile and biologically rich ecology, which is stressed by urbanization, industrialization, heavy pollution, and overexploitation. It is attempting to regulate the use of resources within the neoliberal interpretation of sustainable development.

Mexico's Neoliberal Environmental Policy

Mexico passed its first environmental law in 1940, the Soil and Water Conservation Law. But the first comprehensive regulation was sparked by the 1972 U.N. Conference on the Human Environment in Stockholm. President Luis Echeverria (1970–76) added environmental contamination to the health clauses of the Constitution and passed a Federal Law for the Prevention and Control of Environmental Contamination in March 1971, giving regulatory power to the Secretariat of Health and Welfare. This law was implemented with administrative rules on air and water pollution and a new sanitary law. In January 1972, Echeverria created a Subsecretariat of Environmental Improvement (SMA), as part of the Ministry of Health and Public Assistance. Environmental initiatives came from the technobureaucracy, professionals, and researchers, not the president, and the emphasis was on public health rather than environmental regulation. With vague laws, diffuse responsibility, small budgets, and a lack of technicians, environmental law was applied in only a few cities.

In 1982 President José López Portillo (1977–82) implemented a Federal Law to Protect the Environment and modified the Mexican Constitution to allow state regulation of enterprises. Under president Miguel de la Madrid's administration, the Secretariat of Urban Development and Ecology (SEDUE) was created to regulate business, solid waste, and environmental impacts on human health. This activity was sparked by U.S. pressure, a World Bank loan, the Ixtoc 1 oil well blowout, and mass protests that led to closure of five polluting industries in Mexico City in 1981.

President Miguel de la Madrid (1982–88), although faced with national bankruptcy and debt crisis, included environment in the PRI platform, National Development Plan, and policy speeches. He initiated a series of national and state conferences, culminating in a national meeting during Ecology Week in June 1984, and announced a National Ecology Program. A 1984 law empowered SEDUE to coordinate other agencies and increased sanctions against polluters. A Nuclear Regulatory Law created higher standards in this area.

Plagued by legal uncertainty, overlapping jurisdiction, and a low budget (U.S. $7 million), SEDUE worked through compacts and understandings with industry rather than by direct monitoring and enforcement. Kimberly Clark was closed only two days for serious pollution, and only in 1991 did GM agree to begin sewage treatment in its thirty-five factories. The government was not prepared for major environmental crises; the massive explosion of a Pemex propane center in San Juanico in November 1984, the September 1985 earthquake, and dangerous mismanagement of the Laguna Verde nuclear power plant.[11]

The 1988 election was strongly contested and its results were controversial, but President Carlos Salinas de Gortari, a Harvard monetarist, conceived of environment as part of developmental policy. Manuel Camacho Solis became head of the troubled SEDUE, to be followed by Patricio Chirinos when the former became mayor of Mexico City. The U.S. Environmental Protection Agency promised technical assistance and the Japanese provided U.S. $1 billion in aid for Mexico City air pollution programs. The National Program for Ecological Conservation and Environmental Protection of January 19, 1989, strengthened regulations and technical norms. The administration began cleanup of the Lerma–Chapala River basin, protected the Lacandon rainforest with World Bank funds, began urban reforestation, and controlled vehicular and factory pollution in Mexico City. A U.S. $4 million debt-for-nature swap set up the Monte Azul Biosphere Reserve.

Mexico protects marine turtle breeding grounds, and although it won a judgment against U.S. efforts to embargo its tuna because of excessive dolphin kills (as a restraint of trade under GATT), Mexico later negotiated away this judgment to facilitate the signing of NAFTA. The United States gives aid and technical assistance, but demands economic adjustment, rigid debt payment scheduling, special treatment for its business, and foreign policy concessions, which has seriously reduced Mexico's fiscal capacity to help its environment recuperate.

In May 1992, SEDUE was disbanded because of inefficiency and corruption, and a new Secretariat of Social Development (SEDESOL) was created out of the housing and environment agencies, under the direction of the late presidential candidate Luis Colosio. SEDESOL included the National Institute of Ecology and the federal attorney general for environmental protection. The 1992 budget was U.S. $68 million, but a great deal was spent on the social assistance program Solidaridad, which some commentators saw as Salinas's patronage project.

In 1996 under President Ernesto Zedillo's administration (1994–2000), SEDESOL was replaced by the Secretariat of Environment, Natural Resources and Fisheries (SEMARNAP), a cabinet-level agency charged with regulation and interministerial coordination in air and water quality, forestry, soil, fisheries and aquaculture. Amendments in 1996 to the General Law of Ecological Equilibrium have provided a stable regulatory base, with environmental impact statements and national land use planning, and with emphasis on protecting biodiversity and natural areas and on control of air, soil, and water pollution. Legal sanctions were created under the "polluter pays" principle, and citizens can bring third-party lawsuits for enforcement and be compensated for damages by the polluter. There is no import tax on pollution control equipment, and industry may deduct 50 percent of equipment costs from taxable income.[12]

Mexican environmental policy is based on a neoliberal interpretation of sustainable development. The official theory argues that there is a positive relation between conservation and sustainable development, given proper use of market instruments. Most "deterioration of natural capital" has been caused by structural defects in the market, which cause distorted prices and inefficient use of natural resources. Market distortions—from public subsidies and protection under the old import substitution policy—create interest groups, monopolies, economically irrational government intervention, and extreme poverty, and these in turn distort economic calculations and limit growth and funds for conservation. The causes are economic and the solution is to "integrate costs and social benefits into the process of decision making; that is, to see that economic agents internalize all the social costs of their actions at the moment they decide as consumers or producers."[13]

The basic regulatory principle is to create property rights in natural resources so that actors conserve them out of self-interest. Natural goods will not be free inputs but social costs. The agricultural sector should be privatized so that peasants invest in their "natural capital" instead of drawing it down.

Government's role is to improve market operations, and the benefits of intervention must exceed the costs of planning, regulation, and distortions in other sectors. Command and control regulation is not the best option because "unfortunately, from the environmental viewpoint, on many occasions public policies introduce more market distortions instead of correcting existent ones."[14] Government regulation is subject to cost-benefit analysis, balancing the value of environmental services against the cost of regulation. Economic incentives are used in place of regulation whenever possible. An "open and multilateral economy" grounded in free trade will optimize use of natural resources. An open economy allows rapid growth and thus helps fund sustainable development. Environmental regulation should not be a hidden restraint on free trade, and foreign nations should not use unilateral trade sanctions to pressure Mexico into environmental action. This is the official interpretation of sustainable development.[15]

Mexico's environmental movement arose out of the mobilization campaign of Miguel de la Madrid and concern about the San Juan Ixhuatepec gas explosion, the Ixtoc well blowout, the Laguna Verde nuclear plant, and government incompetence during the 1985 earthquake. In the process of raising environmental issues to national priority status, the government co-opted many groups and constricted policymaking access to a few official channels, thus maintaining the tutelary structure of Mexican politics.

But with the 1988 presidential campaign and the emergence of strong right and left parties (the National Action Party or PAN and Democratic Revolutionary Party, PRD), the environmental movement aligned with the left, and President Salinas adopted a strategy of preemptive reform and dissent management. Thus, "the government—both Salinas and de la Madrid—have sought to recruit environmentalists into the government, on the one hand, and deflect environmental criticism into substantive policy channels rather than as a referendum on the PRI itself, or the political system in general."[16]

Out of 510 Mexican environmental groups, there are four major environmental movements. The Mexican Ecological Movement, MEM, founded in 1982 by Alfonso Cipres Villarreal, claims 52,000 members in various clubs. MEM has kept its autonomy by refusing funds from the PRI, industry, or the Catholic Church and has the support of prominent artists and scientists. MEM acts as a pressure group in favor of sustainable development, revolutionary nationalism, and indigenous people's causes but has no strong feminist or pacifist contingent.

The Grupo de Cien (Group of One Hundred) founded in 1984 is an association of prominent intellectuals and artists acting as an effective nonpartisan pressure group because of their international prominence, moral authority, and access to mass media. Their campaigns against Amazon clear-cutting, to control forest fires in Quintana Roo, and against low air pollution standards in the capital led the Salinas administration to exclude them from government fora and to limit their media access.

The Pacto de Grupos Ecologistas founded in 1986 is a network of autonomous movements that have resisted co-optation by the PRI, a network attempting to strengthen civil society by creating linkages among environmental, social, and international movements. Leaders of this group were recruited into the Salinas government, often into positions unrelated to environment.

The Partido Ecologista de Mexico (PEM) broke from the Alianza Ecologista in 1987 to seek party status under the leadership of Jorge Gonzalez Torres. The August 1991 elections found PEM seventh in a field of ten parties, with 330,799 votes and three representatives in the Mexico City assembly. As the party secretary told us, "Our function is to rescue the environment, respect all life, provide justice and liberty, to give political space to the Indians, and to receive their knowledge and traditions. We must complement technology with tradition. We have had contact with Indian movements for fifteen years, and we promote crafts, language, and culture. We are also in contact with Greens in the U.S. and Canada."

Critics charge that a large number of PEM leaders are ex-PRIistas, that the party is excessively personalist and designed to marginalize environmental issues. An environmental group director told us that "the presence of NGOs is politically important in pressuring government. Activists from MEM are very pro-government, and co-opted. The Grupo de Cien is internationally known and more honest. The Partido Ecologista Verde came from PRI, it has no clear platform and is very general, centralized; it represents one person's interests. But it opens political space and allows a vote on the issues. A weak party, with some indigenous connections, but too close to PRI, not dissident enough, and occupying a vital political space without a clear option."

As an official in the government's National Institute of Ecology said, "There are 510 NGOs in Mexico. The groups change too rapidly, they split a lot, so it is hard to relate to them officially. There are some old groups, but most are very local. Many disappear quickly, are too ideological. There are developmental organizations that raise environment as an important demand—they aren't ecological but incorporate the issues. They mainly want urban services, welfare, work. There is a lot of popular interest but a lack of funds. International organizations give money to big spectacular projects, but not to base workers or small local NGOs. This creates conflicts among NGOs; they fight over finances, dividing the movement instead of coordinating it."[17]

The North America Free Trade Agreement (NAFTA) raises serious environmental issues among its three parties signatory, the United States, Canada, and Mexico. In February 1990, the United States and Mexico agreed to negotiate a free trade treaty. Mexico had sought debt relief and investment in Europe and the Pacific Rim without much success, and bad trade balances and low foreign investment encouraged Mexico to open free trade relations with the United States. In June 1990, Presidents Bush and Salinas issued a joint communiqué, and in September President Bush obtained "fast-track" negotiating authority from Congress, renewed again in May of 1991, and in 1993 for President Clinton. Fast track, no doubt an unconstitutional authority, allows secret negotiations to create the treaty and a congressional vote on the whole without amendment. Negotiations began on June 12, 1991; NAFTA was ratified by the presidents of three nations on December 17, 1992, passed in Congress in November 1993 with majority Republican and minority conservative Democrat support, and entered into operation on January 1, 1994.

U.S. transnational corporations put enormous lobbying effort behind the passage of NAFTA. Mexico spent over U.S. $60 million hiring thirty-three Washington insiders, major law and lobbying firms, and giving expensive gifts and junkets to congressmen and their staff. In a notorious "power lunch" with twenty-nine Mexican business leaders, President Salinas extracted U.S. $25 million contributions from each, which were ultimately not delivered because the story was leaked to the press.

U.S. corporate contributions to seven major environmental groups— National Audubon Society, World Wildlife Fund ($2.5 million from Kodak), National Wildlife Federation (Dow, DuPont, Monsanto, Shell), National Resources Defense Council, Environmental Defense Fund, Defenders of Wildlife, and Nature Conservancy—induced them to join the pro-NAFTA coalition. Presidential candidate Ross Perot bought national television time to campaign against NAFTA and debated Vice President Albert Gore, but with little effect. The labor-environment-human rights coalition opposing NAFTA had only $200,000 and a full-time staff of one.

Congress was mesmerized by the notion of a combined North American market of 369 million people and GDP of U.S. $6.915 trillion, compared with the European Community's 340 million people and GDP of U.S. $4.9 trillion. However, 85 percent of that potential market is in the United States, while Mexico contributes only 4 percent of it, despite having 25 percent of the population. For those who were not mesmerized, President Clinton freely handed out exceptions to the treaty, satisfying swing-state congressmen and special interest groups with a pork barrel strategy that will ultimately cost consumers an estimated $50 billion.[18]

The environmental opposition was concerned that business would move south to "pollution havens" in Mexico, that the U.S. would wink at Mexico's weak regulatory system and exemption of maquiladoras, and that NAFTA as treaty law, with incomplete or merely symbolic environmental provisions, would supersede stricter U.S. federal and state law, in effect creating backdoor environmental deregulation in the United States and Canada. In the dophin-tuna case, a famous example of such deregulation, a secret panel of General Agreement on Trade and Tariffs (GATT) struck down U.S. boycotts of Mexican tuna imports due to high dolphin kills, as a restraint on free trade. In effect, a secret trade panel operating purely for business interests of the sort institutionalized under NAFTA nullified the U.S. Marine Mammal Protection Act.

A clause in NAFTA disallows the lowering of environmental standards to attract or maintain investment. But in reality, NAFTA utilizes weak U.N. Codex Alimentarius food standards and thus much U.S. regulation of pesticides, hormones, and antibiotics in food and meat imports could be nullified by Mexican challenges. Mexican agriculture uses banned agrotoxics like DDT and dieldrin in its food production, and 10 percent of Mexican exports are from highly polluting industries like cement, chemicals, pulp, paper, and petroleum. Polluting U.S. industries can move south to avoid high but necessary regulatory costs, which amount to 22 percent in copper production, 9 percent in oil, and 7 percent in steel.

It is not comforting that pro-NAFTA forces used the "maquiladora model" to sell the trade agreement. U.S. benefits and regulation add 28 percent to U.S. wages, while Mexican workers can be hired for less than the tax on U.S. salaries. An average 16 percent savings on production costs is enough to fund industry's removal south, and of course, U.S. tax revenues and jobs are thereby lost.

Under NAFTA, maquiladoras will no longer be limited to the borders but are encouraged to locate deeper in the nation, thus spreading the stain of pollution to new areas. Treaty provisions prohibiting pollution havens are not linked to concrete monitoring, compliance, or dispute settlement mechanisms. It is unclear who will pay for environmental regulation under NAFTA; there are no large funds for the border forthcoming from either the United States or Mexico.

President Clinton's supplemental agreement on environment set up a symbolic international commission, subsequently weakened by Republican pressure. Intergovernmental agreements involve a new area of law. Dispute resolution mechanisms under NAFTA are so weak, and member nations so touchy about sovereignty, that no firm intergovernmental action is likely to emerge. As NAFTA's corporate promoters intended, the North American environment will be left to the tender mercies of the marketplace.[19]

In January 1994, Mexico suffered devaluation of over 100 percent, a wage and price freeze, a negative balance of payments, and major capital flight, as investors refused to roll over Mexican Treasury bonds. Indeed half of the Clinton Administration's emergency U.S. $40 billion loan funded fleeing investors. The IMF and World Bank opened credit lines at the cost of increased austerity, direct U.S. control of Mexico's oil export revenues, strict adjustment targets, and a requirement of U.S. permission for new state expenditures. Mexico traded its sovereignty for short-term aid.

The Zedillo Administration, uncertain how to proceed and facing growing party opposition, is unable to come up with a viable policy to escape the crisis. The irony is apparent. Since 1982 Mexico has scrupulously followed neoliberal programs and was "rewarded" with the NAFTA treaty for its pains. But NAFTA led to a four-year depression, loss of major economic sectors to transnational competition, and foreign disinvestment.

Mexico faces serious environmental loss and globalization of its resources, without the funds, expertise, or political ability to regulate. Mexican environmental law suffers from being a "symbolic, prestige-oriented policy aimed at international recognition but lacking capacity and commitment to implementation."[20] The single-party government utilizes environmental issues for mobilization and patronage, and SEMARNAP, although a strengthened ministry, lacks significant mass or environmentalist backing. PRI corporativist tutelage extends to environmental parties and groups, and independent groups are denied significant media and policy access. Political demands take the form of supplication, and environmental issues are in danger of becoming another form of rhetoric for both petitioners and bureaucrats. President Zedillo is required by direct U.S. economic controls to deepen the very neoliberal policies that subordinate environment to development and free trade.

Given Mexico's critical environmental problems, the depression induced by free trade, and the ongoing fragmentation of the PRI, the Mexican state will have increasing difficulty with serious remediation or regulation. Let us examine the attitudes of decision makers in government, business, environmental groups, and the scientific community, to discover their perceptions of the environmental situation.

Mexican Decision Makers' Attitudes toward Environment

During May–June 1991 and December 1993–January 1994, the authors administered thirty-seven Q-sorts to nine high government officials, four prominent businessmen, eight NGO leaders, and sixteen environmental scientists, yielding four attitude types: Greens, Political Greens, Sustainable Developers, and Postmodern Managers.

All four types agreed with the following statements: "Biodiversity should be considered the common heritage of mankind to be classified, used, and above all, preserved. All living beings have the right to exist." "Economic development on a solid environmental basis is possible and cost beneficial." "The only alternative is a green economy with participatory democracy, voluntary simplicity, sustainable production, and recycling."

They disagreed with the following statements: "Development signifies that the rich redistribute natural resources in their own benefit." "Third world population will not decline naturally because of rising living standards. If it is not stopped, population growth will prevent even basic development." "The hidden ethical basis of biotechnology is human genetic engineering."

Mexican leaders favor a balanced green economy, yet support the economic status quo as socially just, and show a lack of concern with Mexico's high population growth rate, which strains the economy and infrastructure to the limit.

The *Greens* are an attitude composite of eight persons, including three women. One is a leader from the Grupo de Cien and two are from the

Grupo de Sobrevivientes; the other five are scientists in ecology, renewable resources, atmospheric biology, waste water treatment, and
biodigestion of wastes.

Greens invest their strongest feelings in a critique of Fordist development. Western modernism destroys nature and uses the Global South
as a waste dump and laboratory. International banks and development
agencies have promoted foolhardy programs, which have caused poverty, environmental damage, and even revolution. Greens do not believe that the West has any business enforcing environmental norms,
even if this involves side payments. The European Community environmental laws, Law of the Sea, Antarctic and Rio treaties do not, for
this type, prove any world consensus about environment.

Greens think that our radical humanism has led to cosmic vandalism and that violent conflict, stemming from environmental collapse,
has destroyed most civilizations and eventually will destroy the West.
The original economy of the human species was sustainable, but to
restore that economy now would require a revolution. Mexico's Greens
are neutral as to whether a fully green economy can ever be realized.
They refuse to criticize the system's unequal distribution of resources
but argue that environmental policy is fragmented and defensive rather
than global. They are neutral as to whether democracy can meet the
challenges of environmental crisis. They disagree about giving business incentives, instead of direct governmental regulation, and do not
believe that entrepreneurs and the market will protect the environment.

As a leader of the Grupo de Sobrevivientes said, "The green movement must work with popular consciousness. Parties defend partiali-
ties and don't listen to the people. Entrepreneurs are not the enemy;
they are simply ignorant, they believe hostile labels. Greens should be
a movement, not a party, open to all, not just the upper classes. We
have to overcome culture and old expectations. The mental mechanisms
of politics are greed, ambition, competition in reaction to other groups,
'great men,' leaders. We have a strong green movement in Mexico but
it is largely underground."

Greens believe that traditional farming imitates nature, is more sustainable than Green Revolution monocultures, and has the advantage
of utilizing indigenous knowledge. They think that poor nations should
develop without dependency on fossil fuel, and that nuclear power
costs so much in terms of risk, hazardous waste management, and potential for accidents that it is a devil's bargain. Although Greens do not
criticize biotechnology for leading to privatization of scientific knowl-

edge and corporate control, they strongly disagree with the idea that biotech is the next step in human evolution and that our destiny is to control nature.

Greens think that global warming can disrupt climate and food chains but do not think that it could lead to high human mortality. They strongly disagree with the complacent attitude that we should simply adapt to climate changes as they appear.

Greens have no consistent position on population. They strongly disagree with the linkage between overpopulation and environmental degradation, and disagree that population must be forced down to allow even the most basic development. Yet they are neutral on women's rights as the key to controlling population growth.

In summary, Mexican Greens oppose the Western model of hard-power development and are pessimistic about the future of Western civilization. They are concerned about global warming and nuclear power. They want sustainable development but are not sure that a green economy can be realized; are ambiguous about governmental policy and distrustful of business; and are unclear about population and women's rights issues. Mexican Greens are still attempting to create a program, distinct identity, and penetration into civil society.

Political Greens include seven decision makers, of whom five are women: an executive from SEDESOL, executives from the Verdes-Ecologistas-Pacifistas and Movimiento Ecologico Mexicano, a marine biologist, environmental engineer, environmental toxicologist, and hydraulic engineer.

Political Greens appear to be concerned with working within PRI's political system. They are politically astute but contradictory and vacillating Greens. For example, they weakly agree that the West has plundered Global South resources but refuse to blame international agencies for underdevelopment. They strongly disagree that environmental problems occasion social collapse. As a member of MEM said, "Not only capitalism destroyed the environment but precapitalist societies also. Regarding Mayan collapse there are two hypotheses, that they made sustainable use of their resources, and that they overpopulated a shifting cultivation system. But the Aztecs used chinampas and maintained a high population." They see no possibility of a social democratic and environmentally friendly model of development emerging on the world scene.

Political Greens believe that environmentally sound economic development is possible and back energy efficiency and recycling. They strongly oppose nuclear power, although fossil fuel will be necessary to future development. They think biotechnology is a strategic necessity for development and disagree that corporate control of this technique leads to scientific secrecy or that release of transgenic organisms is inherently risky. An environmental engineer said, "Biotechnology is an option, but in the Third World there are other simpler equivalent techniques. Biotechnology is a foreign import and impedes and obstructs our own development. The technique is useful but of questionable social utility."

They strongly oppose adjusting to the effects of global warming as they arise, but are only mildly concerned that warming will disrupt food chains and cause sea level rise. One environmental toxicologist was more pessimistic than the rest, saying, "The human species is a disaster and will destroy itself. It uses its intelligence for destruction and not construction."

Political Greens have no position on whether democracy is too fragmented by special interests to deal effectively with environment. As a leader of MEM said, "Humans are too complex to make either heaven or hell on earth, perhaps only purgatory. Our policy is a mess but we have to work with what we have. The big development project in Xochimilco cleaned up the canals but also is building big tourist hotels in the name of ecology."

Political Greens do not criticize the system in depth; development does not lead to unequal distribution. But they are moderately negative about giving business information and incentives instead of regulation. As a member of MEM said, "information and incentives are well and good, but you need sanctions also."

Political Greens respect women's rights as the key to birth control—not surprising since many are women. But they strongly deny linkage between poverty and population growth and oppose forcing Mexico's high population growth rates down through administrative measures.

In summary, Political Greens are difficult to characterize because of their moderation, excessive flexibility, and perhaps even conformism to official thought. They stand out only in their opposition to nuclear power and in their respect for women's rights; otherwise their positions on sustainable development and governmental policy are vacillating and rhetorical rather than substantial.

Sustainable Development is a model derived from six individuals: a PRI official, a government official in the arts, two members of the Grupo de Sobrevivientes, an ethnobotanist specializing in Mayan mil-pas, and an entomologist specializing in African bees.

Sustainable Developers take an anthropocentric and optimistic approach to environmental issues. Thus, they strongly disagree that humanity is doomed to extinction and that we must preserve nature to carry on after us. They strongly disagree with the Gaia hypothesis and do not believe that humans have vandalized the planet. They lend no credence to the notion that violent conflict over resources, occasioned by environmental collapse, ended most civilizations and that ours will end the same way.

They are only qualifiedly anti-Western. They believe that Western developmentalism has degraded and cynically used nature, but they do not believe that nature would be conserved if the West financed and enforced stricter regulation. Sustainable development is a clear option in this conjuncture. As the government official said, "The conception of development has been changing in Latin America. Because of the example of the East Asian countries there is a less radical point of view. Sustainable development now seems like a possibility. We are not discussing styles of development any more as an issue."

Sustainable Developers see no linkage between environmental degradation and excess population growth. But equally, they do not see women's rights as the key to population control. As the ethnobotanist said, "I'm not sure how we can slow population growth or if we should. The problem is complex, it has something to do with recognition of women's rights, but it is a small part. When you change social conditions the demographics fall."

Sustainable Developers do not believe that the original economy of the species was sustainable. Nor do they criticize the current economic system for unequal distribution of GNP. Sustainable Developers believe that environmental policy is piecemeal and defensive, but they also argue that government should give business information and economic incentives, instead of regulation, so that the market would take care of the environment. In this, they follow the PRI party line under Zedillo.

But there are differences in emphasis. Holders of this type make development a priority but are strongly interested in restoring sustainable traditional farming practices, energy efficiency, and recycling to reduce demand for fossil fuel. As the ethnobotanist said, "Some Indian settlements have not destroyed nature but have preserved it through traditional production methods. Traditional producers conserve biodiversity, for which service the government should pay them something. But there are also some old settlements in indigenous communities which have been forced to overexploit their lands, violating their own traditional values."

Sustainable Developers think nuclear power risky but are not as concerned about it as are the Greens. Like Greens, they believe that biotechnology converts bioscience into corporate trade secrets, but they do not believe that biotechnology represents the next step in evolution or that our destiny is to control nature. The difference is that these beliefs are held with less than half the intensity found among the Greens. Similarly, they reject, but more weakly than Greens, the wait-and-see attitude on global warming, but they do think that sea levels and food chains will be seriously disrupted and human lives threatened by the phenomenon.

In summary, Sustainable Developers believe in the priority of human needs and are not pessimistic about our collective future. They do not profess a Green model of the economy, are not critical of government regulation, and are more pro-business than Greens. They believe in adopting traditional farming, energy efficiency, and recycling, are mildly antinuclear, and do not oppose biotechnology, though they do not expect it will be a panacea. They believe in prudent measures to lessen impacts of global warming but do not believe these impacts will be as dramatic as projected.

Postmodern Managers represent the voice of officialdom. The strongest type with sixteen individuals (one female), this type includes the attitudes of high-level officials in SEDESOL (Secretariat of Development and Solidarity) and INE (Instituto Nacional de Ecologia); a Department of the Federal District (DDF) official in charge of urban pollution control and a DDF advisor to the mayor; the head of the environmental commission of CANACINTRA (Chamber of Commerce); the presidents of a chemical firm and an important environmental think tank; a transnational corporate executive in charge of environmental issues; a chemist in a private laboratory; the secretary of the Partido Ecologista, the Latin American coordinator for the U.N. Environment Program, a chair of atmospheric sciences, and a veterinary microbiologist working in SARH (Secretariat of Agriculture and Hydraulic Resources); and a meteorologist, limnologist, and environmental engineer.

This type is firmly anthropocentric, strongly denying that humanity is doomed or that ecological collapse ended most prior civilizations. They deny that human egoism has vandalized the planet and argue that sustainability was the original economy of the species but that to restore it now would require a revolution.

Postmodern Managers admit that environmental policy is piecemeal and defensive but think democracy can meet the challenge of ecological crisis, even though it works slowly and through compromise. They see a growing international consensus about environmental issues emerging in EC legislation, the Law of the Sea, and the Rio treaties.

Postmodern Managers are neutral about favoring entrepreneurs so that the market will protect the environment. However, entrepreneurs within this type complain about the regulatory system. The CANACINTRA official said:

> Business participates in several consultation groups which seek the consensus of impacted groups. Last year there were heavy meetings about environmental norms. But there are bottlenecks in paperwork; the bureaucracy gives written opinions that are full of ambiguities. The administrative regulations are generic rules—inspectors can say you are violating them and fine you, but they are unsure of the norms and don't do scientific measurements, they lack equipment, and are pretty arbitrary. Under the General Law of Ecological Equilibrium and Environmental Protection, if there is a risk to health they can close the factory temporarily or permanently, but without scientific basis. There are many temporary closings, and this leads to corruption. Industry has an interest in helping regulation and has the expertise but can only propose or comment. They know no one will follow their suggestions; there is a reverse ratchet effect.
>
> Regulators are very purist and strict without considering the economic problem. Industry sends lawyers to the bureaucracy to fight back, so the issues never get resolved. Entrepreneurs need more consciousness. Small industries don't know the norms, and inspection is catastrophic for them. Government treats industry like delinquents.

A university limnologist said, "Many industries won't comply because they lack information, but would collaborate if regulated and forced to comply. They think only about production and need incentives to spend money on their own garbage, an idea which seems strange to them. We can give education and incentives, build their consciousness or force them, but control cannot be free."

A president of a chemical firm admitted that "the market doesn't always work for the environment. Business requires sanctions or it won't care for the environment. Palmolive, for example, only changed after a threat from the government; they only stopped heavy water contamination after three inspection visits and a threat of closure. It doesn't matter if they are foreign or national companies. NAFTA will send some polluters here; Mexico wants foreign investment at any cost. We need inspectors that are less corrupt, stricter."

An environmental group director disagrees regarding NAFTA's effects: "NAFTA will change production technology and create more investment. Dirty industries probably cannot come down here—they are not profitable in an open economy. New industries must compete with cutting-edge technology."

The limnologist said, "The Third World merits the same respect for environment as the First World. We must have the same standards and regulation of environment because we have less means to clean up here. Mexico has high environmental standards, higher than the country can support. It is good to try to enforce them; it forces technology and education, but they are expensive. Environmental equality will have positive social effects. But with NAFTA some sectors will win, others will lose."

Postmodern Managers strongly support recycling and energy efficiency and are sure that fossil fuel cycles will be necessary to future development in Mexico. They mildly oppose nuclear power. Maximizing GNP is a legitimate goal that does not lead to damaging externalities. As a chemist in a private laboratory said, "Public opinion is alarmist. It is costly to control pollution so we must balance regulation against economic costs."

Biotechnology is a strategic necessity for Mexican development, of this they are sure, and they do not worry about corporate secrecy in this industry; nor do they think that biotech represents the next step in human evolution. The CANACINTRA official said, "Biotechnology can maximize production, but you can also maximize with other technologies which produce with a lower cost, better equality of distribution, and less waste. Biotechnology may be very useful in agriculture, but it is only another technical weapon if it is used right. No generalization is possible about the whole science."

Their view of global warming is moderate. Postmodern Managers do not believe that its effects will be catastrophic, but they advocate preventing further damage. As the DDF official said, "The Greenhouse effect may occur, but it is not going to destroy us."

Postmodern Managers are mildly in favor of women's rights as a key to population control but do not think that economic improvement will automatically bring about decline in population growth rates.

Postmodern Managers are less favorable to market mechanisms than are Sustainable Developers, more interested in rational regulation, and less impressed by the Asian model of development. They share a common humanism. Postmodern Managers have stronger faith in democracy and, like Sustainable Developers, are conservationists, believing in rational use of limited resources.

Postmodern Managers are more interested in a rational regulatory regime involving business inputs to standards and technology development than in streamlining the state so that market mechanisms can come to the fore. Managers are postmodern in their recognition of market failure and incorporation of environment into governmental planning, and in recognizing the international attitude shift toward the centrality of environmental issues.

On environmental policy, Mexican elites seem to have reached an incipient consensus that transcends the left-right politics of PRD-PRI-PAN.

Figure 7.1 graphs Mexican environmentalism on post-Fordist/ postmodern economic/cultural axes. In the postmodern/post-Fordist quadrant, Political Greens and Greens lie in close conjunction. Greens are moderate critics of the system, working to open political space for mass action and pressure, largely from outside the party system, but they face co-optation of issues and leading personalities in bargaining. Greens are not radical preservationists or grassroots bioregionalists. They seem more concerned to fight defensive actions and gain a hearing from the administration and big business. Political Greens are more advanced along the postmodern/post-Fordist political trajectory than Greens, but their adaptation to the political game as defined by the PRI party-state prevents them from developing a complete green ideology or program. Political Greens take no firm position on the issues but are open to pressure, and so they may comprise a large shifting bloc of well-placed decision makers capable of supporting environmental consensus as it becomes politically viable and expedient.

Postmodern Managers and Sustainable Developers occupy the Fordist/postmodern quadrant, indicating their interest in promoting green capitalism rather than ecotopia. Sustainable Developers represent a slightly greener version of President Zedillo's neoliberal market-driven approach to environment, in which market rationality is central to conservation. Postmodern Managers are executives in business, government, and environmental groups, who are willing to modernize the regulatory system to emphasize environment, although their view of Green, Greenhouse, and energy issues is moderate. Postmodern Managers believe that administrative rationality is the key to environmental conservation.

This moderate elite consensus in these types is more advanced than the party-state's official neoliberal encouragement of market solutions

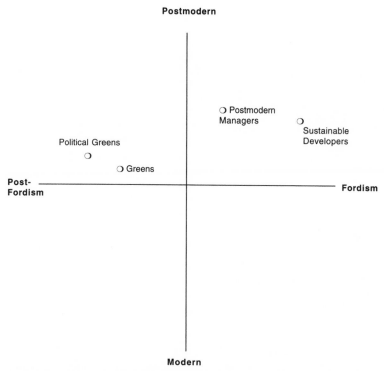

Postmodern

○ Postmodern
Managers

○
Sustainable
Developers

Political Greens

○

○ Greens

**Post-
Fordism**

Fordism

Modern

7.1. Mexican Attitude types on Postmodern and Post-Fordist Indicators
Postmodern indicator is a positive score on statement 18. The only alternative
is a green economy, with grassroots democracy, voluntary simplicity, sustainable production, and recycling.
Post-Fordist indicator is a negative score on statement 13. If government gave
business information and incentives, not command and sanction, the market
and entrepreneurs would protect the environment.

and conservationist "wise use" of nature as a renewable resource base.
Neoliberal environmental policy constrains regulation with market limits and narrow economic definitions of rational state action. Proposals
by Postmodern Managers, Political Greens, and Sustainable Developers to modernize the regulatory system promise stronger and more
immediate effects.

But NAFTA and GATT work in the direction of deregulation to lowest common denominator international standards, and Mexico may
sacrifice its environment on the altar of free trade, only to find that the
benefits accrue to its rich partners and its own tiny political elite. The
majority of Mexicans may be left to deal with overpopulation and socio-
ecological breakdown on their own.

Conclusions

1. Mexico's complex and fragile environment and high numbers of endemic species are in danger of rapidly intensified destruction. The neoliberal regulatory system evolved since the 1982 economic crisis combined with NAFTA and GATT, the 1995 depression, guerrilla challenges from the EZLN, and an ongoing succession crisis in PRI all work to assign environmental issues low national priority. Because Mexico has surrendered sovereignty over economic decisions to the United States, this neoliberal state has seen so many assets stripped away that it has lost much of its capacity to defend national resources or health.

2. Mexican decision makers manifest four different attitude types: Greens, Political Greens, Sustainable Developers, and Postmodern Managers. All four types are postmodern, but a central division separates the post-Fordist Greens and Political Greens—who have an ecotopian vision, however underdeveloped it may be—and the Fordist Sustainable Developers and Postmodern Managers, who want green capitalism.

3. All four types manifest an interelite, intersectoral consensus, which elevates environment out of the left-right political struggle of the PRD, PRI, and PAN. The official parties do not capture this new politics dimension. All four attitude types are "greener" than PRI's neoliberal definition of "sustainable development," so that if future mass mobilization comes to include environmental justice demands, as it logically should, these elites could shift policy in a more positive direction. Enlarged democracy, decentralization, increased party competition, and international pressure may all work to open up Mexico's corporativist civil society, allowing popular environmental concern to drive policy. Elites, who are less conservative than official neoliberal doctrine, may prove responsive.

Rationalization of the ministry and strong recent legislation are steps in the right direction. Free trade accelerates production, makes the hazardous waste stream more complex, and increases the health effects of pollution, urbanization, and overpopulation. Installation of a consumer society, with utilitarian attitudes toward nature, will not help preserve Mexico's bounteous but fragile ecosphere. Mexico has traded much of its sovereignty for the dubious gains of free trade and international debt management, and the strong state necessary for environmental regulation is being fragmented by international pressure, debt, and partisan competition. The prognosis for Mexican nature is rather grim.

8

Puerto Rico: From "Operation Bootstrap" to Ecodisaster

Rafael Albarrán and N. Patrick Peritore

In this chapter, we will consider the small islands of Puerto Rico, where an anomalous "commonwealth" relationship with the United States and decades of predatory peripheral Fordist industrialization have lead to environmental tragedy. The island follows U.S. federal environmental regulation under the Environmental Protection Agency (EPA) but also has its own local regulatory bodies. Environmental groups have mobilized a number of successful actions around industrial siting and other local issues but have yet to develop an alternative program or political identity. Puerto Rican elites are belatedly converting to sustainable development, because of pressure from Green movements and local mobilizations and the international consensus that emerged after UNCED in Rio de Janeiro in 1992 and as a result of U.S. pressure.

I examine here Puerto Rico's "economic miracle" and subsequent environmental crisis, the anomalous layered regulatory system, and the attitudes of elites toward this postmodern complex of issues.

Puerto Rico's Environmental Crisis

The Spanish-American War of 1898 announced the beginning of U.S. hegemony in the Caribbean. Puerto Rico, an island one hundred by thirty-five miles in size, fell under U.S. dominion in 1899 with the Treaty of Paris. In 1917, the Jones Act made all Puerto Ricans U.S. citizens, and Public Law 600 of 1952 allowed the island to choose the commonwealth form, becoming thereby an unincorporated territory of the United States with an elected government and constitution. This legal framework was created in part to satisfy the U.N. Trusteeship Council that the island was no longer a colony at international law and thereby legally free to liberate itself "by any means necessary."[1]

The first elected governor, Luis Muñoz Marin, launched "Operation Bootstrap," an economic strategy designed to attract U.S. corporate investment through subsidized infrastructure, cheap labor, and tax exemptions.[2] This peripheral Fordist strategy brought in large amounts of foreign capital and technology. The period 1948 to 1950 saw U.S. $14 million growth in investment, and by 1953 there were eighty-three firms operating on the island. From 1948 through 1968, the foreign share of manufacturing increased from 22 percent to 77 percent. In the 1960s industrial composition shifted from light industry to mechanized, energy-intensive chemicals, petrochemicals, oil refining, and pharmaceuticals.[3]

However, these investments did not lead to autonomous Puerto Rican development. As noted in the *Industrial Newsletter*, "Almost every firm elected to accumulate its profits until the end of the tax exemption grant and then liquidate its subsidiary company into the parent corporation and send home all the profits free of any taxes in Puerto Rico or the United States." In 1976 the Internal Revenue Service of the United States changed the tax code so that firms not reinvesting in the island were forced to pay a 10 percent tax on profits, but this dropped to only 4 percent if it were reinvested or banked in Puerto Rico. Eighty-five pharmaceutical firms then operating in Puerto Rico show 246 percent profits, over $2 billion dollars, and the top twenty industries on the island show 15 percent profits—compared to the 3.2 percent profit rate of five hundred principal companies in the continental United States.[4]

Operation Bootstrap proved successful, in Fordist terms, in installing an industrial base in Puerto Rico, but the environmental costs of this process are only now becoming apparent. Puerto Rican policy makers lacked both environmental consciousness and a regulatory structure to address the issue. The key enabling legislation, Public Law 9, was passed only in 1970, and soon afterward the U.S. Environmental Protection Agency, founded in 1971, set up a branch on the island.

Puerto Rican legislation is fully compatible with U.S. laws because the island has a complex federal relation with the United States, based on the U.S. and Puerto Rican constitutions, several codes, the U.S.–Puerto Rico Law of Federal Relations, and Public Law 600. During the environmental revolution of the 1970s, U.S. federal environmental laws came to apply to Puerto Rico and to be enforced by branches of U.S. departments and agencies.

Public Law 9, the Puerto Rico Environmental Public Policy Act of

1970, set up an Environmental Quality Board (EQB) as the main regulatory and enforcement agency for all environmental laws. The EQB can offer "initiatives, resolutions and programs" when they "harmonize with the foreign policy of the United States" and are compatible with U.S. law. Puerto Rican law and policy may be stricter than U.S. equivalents, but not more lax, and the EPA enforces compliance by controlling the EQB's $4 million annual budget.[5]

The U.S. EPA has authority to enforce all environmental statutes and regulations in Puerto Rico, and delegates to "sister agencies" with capacity and expertise the safe drinking water act, deep well disposal control programs, construction grant programs, municipal dumps, and landfill regulation. Other programs, such as the National Pollutant Discharge Elimination System, were not delegated because of local incapacity. EPA consults with EQB, which has veto power, as do local governments.

Local government reports to the EQB, which is backed by EPA. In 1992, the EPA regional administrator threatened to cut infrastructure and development project funds if the governor did not make compliance with the Clean Air Act a priority and seriously enforce other environmental measures. The warning said that EPA "would intervene and set up its own permit program and small business assistance program in 1995 if the government failed to do so, with proceeds going to the U.S. Treasury."[6]

According to a recent survey of eight hundred Puerto Ricans, the most important environmental problems were perceived to be water quality, 44.6 percent; air quality, 27 percent; waste, 25.7 percent; urban development, 14.9 percent; energy, 13.5 percent; coastal zone management, 10.8 percent; population growth, 9.5 percent; and historic site preservation, 8.1 percent.[7] This popular concern is not misplaced. Puerto Rico's environmental situation is serious and deteriorating. In September 1993, the governor declared a "state of emergency" due to shortages of drinking water caused by overpopulation of San Juan, polluting non-point-source runoff into the aquifer, inadequate sewage and water systems, lack of soil conservation, and, as one administrator put it, "the abusive behavior of industries." In the summer of 1998, more than 740,000 out of a total of 3.5 million people were left without drinking water as a result of inadequate infrastructure and excess demand due to overpopulation.[8]

Solid and hazardous wastes are serious problems in Puerto Rico, which takes all of its water from easily contaminated aquifers. The developmentalist thinking of the 1950s distributed industry among the various municipalities. In the late 1960s, industry was concentrated in "industrial parks," especially in Barceloneta, Arecibo, and Manati, which had the wellhead access to groundwater needed by the pharmaceutical industry.

The following cases should indicate the depth of Puerto Rico's environmental problem. Barceloneta is the site of a 20 sq mi landfill, which has no artificial barriers to prevent wastes from percolating into groundwater. Three hundred tons of hazardous waste were poured into sinkholes, direct conduits into the aquifer for rainwater. Numerous heavy metals and volatile organic compounds were identified by Superfund (Comprehensive Environmental Response, Compensation, Liability Act of 1980) inspection teams. In the mid-1980s RCA Del Caribe (purchased by General Electric in 1986), poured a million gallons of chloride into sinkholes, and the pharmaceutical giant Upjohn contaminated four wells with chemical wastes.[9]

The municipality of Manati, three miles from Barceloneta, is home to the bulk of pharmaceutical wastes on the island. The city of Cataño, located near San Juan, is considered one of the most contaminated on the island, with the highest cancer rate and the most negative health indicators, according to studies done by the Puerto Rico Medical Association. In 1972 Pittsburgh Plate Glass Industries periodically emitted toxic gas, poisoning its own workers and the adjacent community of Guayanilla, and was accused of dumping large amounts of neurotoxic mercury into the soil. Two large electric plants and a Gulf Oil refinery emit high levels of sulfuric oxides. Maximum visual opacity of air is set at 20 percent, but these plants' emissions regularly exceed 70 percent opacity levels. The Commonwealth Oil Refining Company in Peñuelas has contaminated large tracts of land, Beckton Dickenson in Guanajibo has been accused of mercury discharges affecting more than a thousand people, and workers have collapsed on the job because of toxic pollution.[10]

At the other end of the island, the city of Juncos was forced to close its landfill when mercury thermometers were dumped into it by a U.S. firm. The municipality of Guayama closed four wells due to contamination by chlorine, bromide, and polychlorinated biphenyls (PCBs), dumped by the American Home Products, Anaquest, Phillips Petroleum, and Synthetic factories. Puerto Rico, only the size of Massachusetts, has seven Superfund toxic waste priority cleanup sites.

Since the 1940s, Puerto Rico has disposed of waste in open landfills, but due to its small territory and inadequate management, many of these dumps are inoperative and new ones are increasingly difficult to site. Municipal San Juan dumps waste thirty miles away. Municipal waste is calculated at 5,700 tons daily, and the annual industrial waste load is 92,418 tons. Agriculture generates 7,850,550 tons of waste annually.

In 1989, an Authority for Management of Solid Wastes investigation revealed that of sixty-two municipal waste dumps, forty-two needed rehabilitation because of serious violations of local and federal regulations, seventeen needed to be closed, and only two operated adequately. The study found that 75 percent of dumps were open-air facilities, with an average life of less than five years because of mismanagement. Fifteen major dumps were contaminating the groundwater. Most dumps are located in the lagoons and are not adequately drained to avoid percolation into aquifers.[11]

Of course, "adequate drainage" signifies that the toxics are instead routed into the sea, where they poison coral reefs and the aquatic biome that is the basis of island's tourism. Puerto Rico is simply running out of land for waste and is endangering both the fresh water supply without which it cannot live and the surrounding ocean on which much of its economy depends.

Only recently have local governments mobilized to address these problems, aided by a nascent environmental movement. Following the "not-in-my-backyard" (NIMBY) model of the new politics, these groups were local, single-issue bodies, intense but short-lived, and they fail to coordinate into a national movement, although the level of public awareness has increased greatly.

The new environmental movement resisted installation of the Cogentrix Carbon Industry in the town of Mayaguez. Nationwide opposition to this polluting industry forced all three mayoral candidates to campaign against the company or face angry voters. National candidates in the New Progressive and Independence parties took stands against Cogentrix. The Popular Democratic Party candidate declined to take a position, but local candidates openly denounced the project. Similarly, residents of the badly contaminated municipality of Cataño, angry at the sluggish response of local government to environmental violations and citizen petitions, began organizing demonstrations and ultimately forced EPA to override local jurisdiction and investigate the problem.[12]

Rapid industrial development has been a priority for fifty years, and now the staggering environmental costs of unbridled industrial and urban development have become apparent and are sparking a strong popular movement. Government is actively responding to popular pressure, but business resists, its representatives arguing the importance of their contribution to the island's economy. For decades, pharmaceutical firms have benefited from the income tax code, which allowed them to claim exemptions for reinvestment in research and development. President Clinton revoked the IRS 936 tax exemption, 38 percent of which business claimed, without much credibility, to reinvest in research and development.[13]

Pharmaceutical firms attributed their world competitiveness to this tax write-off. But it is hard to ascertain how much of this research and development benefits Puerto Rico and what percentages of profits are subsidized by environmental destruction. Business has a great deal of leverage in Puerto Rico, but with 17 percent unemployment, and 40 percent of the population receiving food stamps, it is evident that fifty years of unbridled capitalist development has not benefited the island's people or environment.

Although there has been a growing environmental consciousness in Puerto Rico, it has lacked effectiveness. It took a $6 million dollar lawsuit by the EPA against the Puerto Rico Electrical Power Authority, which is responsible for power and water, to end some obvious abuses. However, the local Congress will probably pass Bill 1581, which restricts public access to developmental project hearings until after approval. The bill limits public access to environmental impact statements, evidence, and hearings concerning either government or corporate developmental projects.

Puerto Rican Elite Environmental Ideologies

Professor Rafael Albarrán of the University of Puerto Rico–Rio Piedras performed the environmental Q-sort with forty-three decision makers, including fourteen in government, ten in business, seven in environmental groups, fourteen academic scientists, and two environmental journalists. Individuals overlap within these categories, as is usual in environmental issues. Eight of the sample are women. I then ran and analyzed the data, comparing it to the other six countries' factorial attitude types.

Let us look at these factorial attitude types before mapping them in postmodern/post-Fordist policy space.

Greens are a composite of the attitudes of four government officials in natural resource administration, two business lobbyists, and six academics and administrators. Greens are neither as postmodern as the Political Greens nor as post-Fordist as the Postmodern Managers.

Greens think that sound ecological development makes economic sense and that recycling and energy efficiency can cut fossil fuel use. Sustainability was the original economy of the species, and a simple participatory green economy is the only viable option, an option increasingly favored by the international community.

They reject the Fordist development model and believe that environmental collapse will ultimately destroy the West. Yet Greens do not believe that humanity is doomed to extinction or that the ideology of technocratic humanism is responsible for vandalizing nature. As a regional environmental health director said, "That which is human creation is not stupid, unless there are bad intentions." As a senatorial candidate said, "They say that we don't have adequate natural resources, but we use up our land as if it were a continent." Greens do not believe that rich Western nations can conserve nature by financing enforcement of high environmental standards.

Greens strongly believe in the capacity of democracy to provide environmental solutions. As the senatorial candidate said, "We don't talk politics and argue ideology on these issues—that is doing the same thing as always. You only advance through struggle, but the solutions have to come from the people, from the base of an organized struggle." Yet a forest guide from the Department of Natural Resources expressed a certain cynicism about the concept: "What kind of democracy are you talking about? Almost all governments nowadays define themselves as democracies."

Greens believe that GNP growth is a legitimate goal and do not think that development mainly benefits the rich. Yet they oppose giving business incentives, instead of regulation, so that the market can protect the environment. As a leading environmentalist in the Industrial Mission, an environmental group, said, "There is a problem in this environmentalist boom; the industries have taken advantage of it to open up new ways of gaining money. The distribution of wealth won't change, the industrial sectors are just using the movement."

When it comes to concrete policy, Puerto Rican Greens are neutral on key issues. Thus, Greens think it important to avert global warming instead of adjusting to its effects as they appear, but they are ambiguous as to what those effects are. On the one hand they think radical climate change and food chain disruption is in the offing, but they do not believe that massive flooding and famine will result. As a scientist argued, "It could be that we will extinguish ourselves as a result of the Greenhouse effect or the ozone layer, but this is a very fatalistic viewpoint." They are neutral about women's rights, population control, and about using administrative measures to force population down. Yet they do not believe that population will drop automatically with rising prosperity.

They believe in energy efficiency to reduce fossil fuel use but are neutral about future resource exhaustion and about the Global South's need to avoid fossil fuel dependency. They are also neutral as to whether the risks of nuclear power outweigh its benefits. Greens are unclear regarding biotechnology. They disagree that the human genome project's goal is the genetic engineering of human beings, but they also disagree that our destiny is to control evolution using biotechnology. They are neutral as to whether biotech is a strategic necessity for the Global South or of real benefit to agriculture.

In summary, Puerto Rico's Greens are strong on ideology but lack concrete policy on population, women's rights, and risks associated with global warming, fuel cycles, nuclear power, and biotechnology. They support GNP growth but distrust business. Puerto Rican Greens have not matured into a consistent ideological and programmatic force.

The *Political Greens* are an attitude composite including a former governor, the president of the Puerto Rican Independence Party, a mayor, a department director, an environmental manager in a large firm, an executive for Abbot Pharmaceuticals, an environmental engineer, a biologist, and psychologist. Their position on environmental issues is vacillating and contradictory—"political" in the sense of trimming their sails to the wind. Political Greens fall within the postmodern value set and weakly embrace post-Fordism. They are closest to the Greens in factor space and show the same immaturity in terms of defining issues and policy alternatives. This type could become a major Green ally and share the Green characteristic of postmodern value-based rhetoric without realization of its post-Fordist economic implications or of the large-scale industrial conversion required by their position.

Political Greens believe in environmentally sound development and energy efficiency and recycling and even subscribe to a green economy with participatory democracy, sustainability, and voluntary simplicity. But they do not think that sustainability was the original economy of the species; nor do they agree that maximizing GNP creates environmental problems.

They do not believe that humanity is doomed to extinction or that environmental collapse will lead to social collapse. Averting global warming is worthwhile, but Political Greens are negative about dire predictions regarding its effects. Women's rights are the key to population control, but Political Greens see no link between environmental decline and population growth and do not believe in forcing population down with administrative measures.

Political Greens are neutral about democracy being unable to meet the challenge of environmental issues and neutral about the piecemeal and defensive outcomes of democratic decision making. They are neutral about giving business incentives to protect the environment and neutral as to whether development aids the rich most.

Political Greens strongly support international development programs and do not agree that the Western model has led to environmental vandalism. As an executive of Bristol Myers Corporation said, "Those programs are not stupid; they are run by countries that know what they are doing. It is just that they lack education in Third World realities."

Political Greens are unconcerned with fossil fuels running out in the next century, although they believe in recycling and increased energy efficiency. They are neutral about the risks of nuclear power. Their strongest hope lies with biotechnology, which they see as a strategic basis for development, an improvement over chemical farming, and the next step in human evolution, our destiny being total control over nature. However, Puerto Rico is not a major agricultural exporter, so that agricultural biotech is not economically feasible. Medical biotechnology is the intellectual property of the seven pharmaceutical giants that manufacture on the island, but their in-house research is unlikely to create local forward and backward linkages.

On environmental issues Political Greens take rhetorical positions that are contradicted by their neutrality toward concrete policies needed to implement them. They mirror changing public opinion in Puerto Rico, which is just beginning to recognize the issues, and show that mobilized environmentalists could influence such undecided policy makers in the parties, agencies, transnational corporations, and universities, with political pressure, information, and mass mobilization.

Sustainable Developers are a composite of the opinions of government executives in environmental quality, urban development, and solid waste disposal administrations, the director of fisheries, a corporate executive, and a journalist.

Holders of this attitude type subscribe to many aspects of Green philosophy but ultimately are concerned with sound environmental management of capitalist development using conventional fuel cycles. They believe that maximizing GNP will not lead to waste, pollution, or inequality and thus are willing to envision a business-government partnership in which information and incentives replace regulation and sanctions so that entrepreneurs are led by the market to protect the environment.

Philosophically, Sustainable Developers believe in the Gaia hypothesis that "Life on earth is a single organism which modifies the atmosphere to serve its own needs." Although incorrect in evolutionary terms, Gaia is popular with greens of various types. They strongly support a green economy with democracy, voluntary simplicity, and sustainability and believe that the international system is converging toward consensus on this model, as seen in EC legislation and international treaties. But creating a sustainable economy may require a revolution as great as the industrial revolution. Continuing economic development on a sound ecological basis is both feasible and cost effective.

Sustainable Developers are ambiguous about population issues. On the one hand, they believe that women's rights are the key to population control; but on the other, they believe that the Global South's population will not decline with rising affluence, the famous demographic transition, but must be forced down so that development can proceed at all. Because they strongly deny linkages between population growth and environmental degradation, Sustainable Developers do not see the population question as a policy imperative.

Sustainable Developers are also ambiguous regarding the future of humanity and nature. They believe that humanity is doomed to extinction but do not believe that environmental collapse will destroy the West. They are neutral regarding the critique of Western Fordist development or international aid programs. They strongly reject the scenario under which global warming could cause flooding and famine, not agreeing that global warming and acid rain could disrupt oceanic and land food webs and alter the climate, but they firmly believe that policy must adjust to global warming instead of waiting for its effects.

Sustainable Developers are primarily interested in managed development that includes environmental considerations. Thus, they believe that democracy can meet the challenge of ecocatastrophe even though it works slowly through compromise.

Sustainable Developers believe that poor countries must avoid fossil fuel dependency and the cost, pollution, and alienation that accompany it. But they also believe that the next century's economy must be powered by coal, gas, oil, and uranium, and that far from being a devil's bargain, nuclear power has benefits outweighing its environmental costs. Regarding that other high-tech item in the developmental repertoire, biotechnology, Sustainable Developers are ambiguous. They strongly disagree that the next step in human evolution is to control nature through biotechnology, but they also think that its commercial potential outweighs the environmental risks associated with release of engineered organisms. They are neutral about biotech being a strategic necessity for development or an improvement over chemical farming.

Puerto Rico's Sustainable Developers believe in a variant of clean, green capitalism. They accord with postmodern green values but are the most pro-business and least democratic and believe sustainable development to be a key managerial value. They fall within the postmodern and Fordist axis, the telos of which is green capitalism.

Postmodern Managers are an attitude composite of two government executives in forestry and zoology; four transnational pharmaceutical executives (including one woman); four academics, of whom one is a woman and two are department heads; and one journalist. Seven out of eleven in this type are corporate, government, or academic executives.

Postmodern Managers believe that economic development on a sound environmental basis is feasible and that sustainability was the original economy of the species. They weakly accord with the Green model, enough to place them in the postmodernist camp, and are the strongest of all types in their distrust of business and markets; this puts them strongly at odds with Sustainable Developers.

Postmodern Managers support democratic decision making but think that current environmental policy is piecemeal and defensive instead of global, as the issue warrants. They oppose giving business incentives and information so that entrepreneurs can protect the environment by responding to market signals. They do not believe that development will solely benefit the rich and they are neutral about problems associated with GNP growth.

Postmodern Managers are strongly critical of Western Fordist development, which has plundered and polluted the Global South, and blame foolish international development programs for much of the environmental and social damage seen in poor countries. They believe that our mastery of nature has led to technological pillage but do not believe that we have doomed ourselves through environmental destruction. Civilizations will not collapse because of environmental problems; somehow we will adjust. As an anthropologist said, "Humanity is going to survive; it is our mission as a species and we will succeed. But there will have to be changes to preserve nature, along with ourselves."

Postmodern Managers are the most concerned of all the types to avert global warming but are largely neutral about its projected effects. As an anthropologist said, "There are conflicting data on acid rain and its effects, and in relation to the Greenhouse effect, they haven't been able to prove if it's true or not."

They believe, as a practical matter, that fossil fuels are necessary for development, but recycling and energy efficiency should be used to lessen dependency on these fuels. They are neutral about the risks of nuclear power, and although they oppose the idea that biotechnology is the next step in human evolution, they are neutral regarding its potential benefits and risks. Managers are neutral about women's rights being the key to population control and strongly negative about stopping environmental degradation in order to cut population growth.

Postmodern Managers do not believe that humanity is doomed, thinking that somehow we will muddle through, but are critical about government, business, and international development programs. They subscribe to sustainable development, but are skeptical and pragmatic regarding the means to that end. Postmodern Managers wish to pursue sustainable growth through recycling and industrial conversion; they believe that fossil fuel cycles must eventually be replaced, but until then it is possible to manage the risks even of nuclear power. They are anxious to control the consequences of global warming but will wait for more conclusive scientific information. They are moderate in their support of democracy and think that environmental issues require global policy making.

An attitude type discovered in Puerto Rico but also found in Iran is *Cultural Traditionalists,* in this case representing a composite including a biology professor, a mayor involved in fighting a major coal corporation, and the vice president of the Senate. Holders of this attitude type have a certain respect for nature but no real interest in green ideology, and they tend to separate environmental and economic issues when considering policy. Although Traditionalists lie in modernist value and post-Fordist economic space, it is most likely that they represent an organic conservative and Hispanic cultural mind-set; a premodern view of postmodern issues, which does not really fit within the political space of postmodern transition. Cultural Traditionalists are best compared with the antimodern, anticapitalist Religious Conservatives of Iran, for which see chapter 10.

Traditionalists agree with the Gaia hypothesis, that the film of life on the earth's surface regulates the climate, and believe that sustainability was the original economy of the species, although its restoration will require a revolution equal to the industrial revolution. They strongly believe that our technological hubris has led to the pillage of nature; they think that energy efficiency and recycling can cut fuel use and that traditional farming practices are more sustainable than chemical farming. But they do not believe in human extinction because of environmental degradation and are simply neutral about global warming, although showing a minor interest in averting such effects if possible.

Cultural Traditionalists strongly believe in democratic decision making in environmental questions, even though democratically generated environmental policy ultimately ends up being piecemeal and defensive. In the view of a mayor who successfully resisted a campaign to eradicate cocaine plants by aerial spraying of agrotoxics, "The basis for success of a campaign or movement to conserve the environment is educating the people." Traditionalists do not blame international development programs or the Western model of high-tech industrialization for environmental problems.

Traditionalists distrust business and do not believe that information and incentives will allow the market to protect Puerto Rico's environment. They do not believe sustainable development is cost beneficial, nor do they subscribe to a participatory green economy with voluntary simplicity. They believe that GNP growth is a legitimate policy goal, though they acknowledge that it will allow the rich disproportionate benefits. Thus, Cultural Traditionalists could provide strong opposition to Sustainable Developers and, unlike the Postmodern Managers, they believe that capitalist development is not convertible to intensive sustainable forms.

Traditionalists show little interest in environmental issues or policy, so they are bound to be in conflict with Greens and Political Greens. As the vice president of the Senate said, "In many cases environmental problems result from having more interest in resolving economic problems, and in some cases responding to political interests. I personally think that environment should have more priority than economic results."

Conventional fossil fuels are necessary to development, and Traditionalists are neutral regarding the risks of nuclear power. They are worried about the risks of biotechnological releases but neutral as to its agricultural benefits or strategic necessity. They believe that respect for women is linked to population control and strongly oppose administrative measures to force population down.

Environmental Policy Cleavages in Puerto Rico

By aggregating typal array z-scores on combinations of statements, issue indicators can be constructed to show affinities and cleavages among these types on major issues. Environmental politics is grounded on consensus regarding sustainable development but pulls in different directions on the definition.

Table 8.1 suggests that on specific issues, the new environmental politics creates alliances traducing normal left-right distinctions. Thus, Green values—which mix a biocentric worldview, a dislike of technology and maximizing economic growth, and the ideal of a sustainable, balanced economy stressing community over growth—are values that appeal to Cultural Traditionalists whose elitism and Catholicism was upset by neoliberal ideas of an "economic miracle," such as Operation Bootstrap.

Sustainable Developers adhere more to green values than do Greens, the latter disagreeing that the technological pillage of the world stems from Western technocratic humanist ideology. Sustainable Developers more strongly oppose fossil and nuclear fuel cycles than do Greens, who are largely neutral about these issues. Sustainable Developers appear to constitute the dominant type of postmodern thinking in Puerto Rico.

Postmodern Managers are also positive on green values, although they support the necessity of fossil fuels and are neutral on nuclear energy. Political Greens largely oppose green values and believe in technological solutions, but they are neutral regarding nuclear power. Popu-

Table 8.1. Issue Indicators

Issues	SD	Gr	CT	PM	PG
Green values	3.5	2.9	4.6	1.2	-1.1
Greenhouse danger	-1.5	0.7	-0.7	0	-0.7
Pessimism	0.1	1.1	0	-2.7	-2.3
Critique policy	1.1	0.3	-0.7	0.4	0.1
Pro-business	0.6	1.1	-0.7	-1.5	-0.2
Biotechnology	-4.9	-0.1	0.4	-1.9	1.9

Green values includes statements 1, 2, 3, 4, 5, 18, 21, 26, 27; Greenhouse danger items 29, 30; Pessimism 6, 11; Critique of policy 14, 15; Pro-business item 13; Biotechnology items 31 through 36.

lar initiatives for sustainability and slower, controlled growth may find unsuspected political allies among Traditional Conservatives and the Managers.

On the six biotechnology items (three negative, three positive), Sustainable Developers are strongly against this new science, as are Postmodern Managers, while the Greens and Cultural Traditionalists are neutral and the Political Greens are quite positive about its potentialities. This suggests another set of alignments regarding technology policy.

Regarding the dangers of global warming and pessimism about the human prospect, Sustainable Developers oppose negative prognoses but are neutral about a catastrophic end for the human race. Greens are worried by both possibilities. Traditionalists are not afraid of global warming and are not pessimists, while Postmodern Managers have such fears and are pessimistic. Only Political Greens resist catastrophic prognoses and are optimistic about the human future.

The critique that environmental policy is piecemeal and defensive because democracy works through compromise is advanced by Sustainable Developers and denied by Cultural Traditionalists. The other types are neutral about democracy. The pro-business policy of giving incentives and information and allowing entrepreneurs and the market to take care of environmental problems is surprisingly supported by Greens and Sustainable Developers, the Managers and Traditionalists being most negative about business, and the Political Greens neutral on the issue.

Greens and Sustainable Developers in general appear ready to reach accommodations with business, while the other three types, largely representing the political and governing classes, are anti-business and favor command and control regulation. Thus, Puerto Rico's environmental movement can find allies among Cultural Traditionalists and Postmodern Managers for values or programs that accord with traditional values or that advance regulatory power over business.

Figure 8.1 places Puerto Rican elite attitudes on the postmodern/ post-Fordist spectrum. Sustainable Developers, the principal type to emerge, are Fordist and postmodern, thus moving in the direction of green capitalism. Political Greens and Greens, for all their ideological and policy immaturity, cluster together as postmodern and post-Fordist. Postmodern Managers are the farthest along the post-Fordist dimension but only weakly advanced in postmodern values. Postmodern Managers and Sustainable Developers have similar approaches on many issues and could work in coalition to promote intensive development and environmental responsibility, but they differ significantly on the role of markets and high-technology risk aversion.

The Green/Political Green cluster opposes Sustainable Developer green capitalism but suffers from ideological immaturity and lack of clarity regarding concrete alternatives to the dominant business-generated definition of sustainable development. On concrete issues of social harmony and biorestoration, this cluster can find support from Cultural Traditionalists, who adhere to older elite and religious conservatism, but Greens will find Traditionalists opposing postmodern

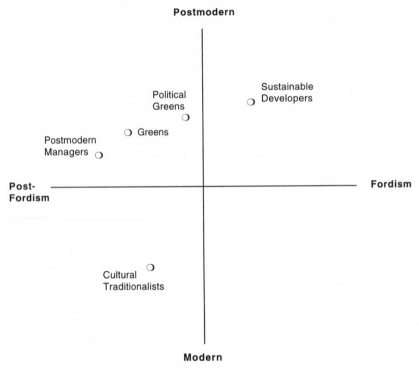

8.1. Puerto Rican Attitude Types on Postmodern and Post-Fordist Indicators
Postmodern indicator is positive score on statement 18. The only alternative is a Green economy, with grassroots democracy, voluntary simplicity, sustainable production, and recycling.
Post-Fordist indicator is a negative score on statement 13. If government gave business information and incentives, not command and sanction, the market and entrepreneurs would protect the environment.

social issues. Their strongest allies could be Postmodern Managers, and Puerto Rican Greens would do well to develop the mass political base necessary to push Political Greens in a favorable policy direction and to establish the technical and concrete policy positions necessary to influence Postmodern Managers, if they are to build a coalition against the Sustainable Developers' green capitalist program and create a definition of "sustainable development" more in concert with their values.

A glance at table 8.1 shows that the main cleavage in Puerto Rican environmentalist attitudes is between the postmodern yet Fordist Sustainable Developers and the postmodern/post-Fordist Postmodern Managers. Political Greens and Greens lie close together in postmodern/post-Fordist factor space between these two forces, but their lack of developed ideological or policy positions and of clear political identity makes it difficult for these forces to find issue-specific coalition partners across this cleavage.

The other cleavage lies between Postmodern Managers and Cultural Traditionalists, who have premodern, organic, conservative views and a non-Fordist vision of the economy. Traditionalists may provide Greens with important coalition partners on issues like biorestoration, organic farming, and community maintenance, but postmodern value issues will prove strongly divisive.

Conclusions

1. Puerto Rican environmental issues are so serious that they create the possibility of consensus cross-cutting left-right ideology and sectoral and class interests, which could allow concrete issue-driven change to occur. The depth of the crisis fuels a shift to a "new politics" of environment.

2. Green ideology and policy are poorly developed in Puerto Rico. The mass mobilization needed to resist the predatory industrialization manifesting such serious health and environmental hazards is in its early stages, preventing environmental issues from being raised in island and U.S. political fora.

3. Sustainable Developers and Postmodern Managers are the commanding attitude types among Puerto Rican elites and represent an attitude transition from predatory developmentalism to industrial conversion and green capitalism. This in itself is a gain, but both the strength of this condominium and the fact that it provides the major

issue cleavages, combined with the weakness of Green movements, mean that elites will be able to contain and redirect the NIMBY mobilizations that are increasingly frequent in Puerto Rico. Cultural Traditionalists, many in leadership positions in government, may support specific proposals for biorestoration and community development but will oppose postmodern lifestyle issues.

4. The Greens' wisest strategic move would be to embrace environmental justice ideologies, asking for redistribution of the gains and risks of development and making urban crime, social breakdown, and the island's ambiguous status into environmental issues—which they are, when considered globally. Greens must articulate a detailed set of policies for sustainable development, while at the same time incorporating the rich set of social justice and cultural nationalism issues as the basis for popular mobilization. Puerto Rico's environmental problem is so serious that it must be brought forcibly to the attention of island and U.S. publics, international agencies, and environmental groups as a crisis situation that can no longer safely be ignored.

Romania: Candidate Democracy, Vulnerable Environment

Steven D. Roper and N. Patrick Peritore

The 1996 parliamentary and presidential elections marked a turning point in Romanian politics. President Ion Iliescu, the longest-serving post-1989 East European president, and his ruling Romanian Social Democratic Party (PDSR) were defeated by an opposition coalition, the Democratic Convention of Romania (CDR). The CDR includes a number of centrist and right-of-center parties and the Romanian Ecological Party (PER). Since 1991, coalition infighting and the lack of a clear message had undermined the CDR's electoral showing.

Taking office in 1996, the new government coalition faced a number of pressing issues, including NATO expansion, European Union membership, economic restructuring, and sustainable development. Given the unstable economic situation, there was a great deal of speculation as to how the government would balance business and environmental concerns (e.g., privatization versus enforcement of existing environmental legislation).

How do the ideological values of government officials, business elites, party functionaries, and scientists influence Romanian environmental policy? A Q-method study of Romanian environmental elites was performed in spring of 1994 and the resultant field data indicate that a new ideological spectrum is emerging in the environmental area. In this chapter we examine the development of environmental policy before and after Romania's communist regime and analyze the factorial attitude types that emerged from the field data.

Romanian Political History and Environmental Policy

During the late nineteenth century and early years of the twentieth, Romania was largely an agricultural country. Despite a nascent petroleum industry, agriculture and forestry accounted for most export earnings. Drives for industrialization during the period of "Greater Romania" (1918–40) were only partially successful. The post-1948 communist government made industrial development the top priority. As a Stalinist, the general secretary of the Romanian Communist Party (PCR), Gheorghe Gheorghiu-Dej, believed in rapid, priority development of heavy industry, hoping that industrialization would provide both legitimacy and political-economic autonomy from the Soviet Union. Thus Gheorghiu-Dej stressed industrialization and ignored other parts of the Stalinist program, like forced collectivization.

Industry suffered from a lack of skilled manpower, so the PCR shifted agricultural labor resources into industry. Between 1948 and 1953, an industrial proletariat was created, with a net increase of approximately eight hundred thousand nonagricultural laborers.[1] Most of these workers were assigned to chemical and petrochemical facilities.

The first five-year plan was generally unsuccessful. By developing heavy industry, Romanian economic policy was denying some basic principles of comparative advantage. Romanian workers were much less skilled than their European counterparts, and technical training never reached the level of that in other communist countries such as East Germany or Czechoslovakia.

As among its communist neighbors, during the 1940s and 1950s, Romanian industrialization policy ignored the environmental impact of the petrochemical sector. Development, autonomy, and legitimacy were primary. During the 1950s and 1960s, the Council for Mutual Economic Assistance (Comecon) attempted to rationalize the development of heavy industry in communist Europe. Comecon included every communist European country except Albania and Yugoslavia. Industrialized members of Comecon, East Germany and Czechoslovakia, wanted countries to specialize in areas of comparative advantage, which for Romania meant the export of foodstuffs and raw material. While this might have been the best economic policy from a comparative advantage perspective, and even an environmental one, Gheorghiu-Dej and party leadership resisted attempts to limit Romanian industrialization. Even when other countries were de-Stalinizing policy and leadership after 1956, Romania continued to pursue heavy industrialization.

Following Gheorghiu-Dej's death in 1964, a four-year succession struggle saw the emergence of Nicolae Ceausescu as PCR general secretary. While Ceausescu's foreign policy was based on autonomy from the Soviet Union (for example, he refused to participate in the Soviet invasion of Czechoslovakia in 1968 and hosted President Nixon in Bucharest), he continued the policy of industrialization inherited from his predecessor. A 1971 visit to North Korea led him not only to copy

Kim Il-Song's cult of personality but to promote further the growth of heavy and extractive industry at the expense of agriculture.

During the 1973–74 oil crisis, Romanian exports of refined petroleum products increased the hard currency earnings that Ceausescu levered to obtain developmental loans from private Western banks. However by the late 1970s, export earnings from refined products slowed compared to the price of crude oil imports, and by 1981, the Romanian economy was facing productivity losses and a mounting debt service ratio; that is, the country was using more export earnings to pay its debt.[2] To counter a growing structural crisis, Ceausescu utilized tough austerity measures to repay U.S. $10 billion of foreign debt. The rationing of heat, gas, food, and medical care was begun in 1981 and continued throughout the 1980s, leading to dramatic declines in Romanian living standards, health, and welfare, and massive increases in malnutrition and infant mortality. By the late 1980s, Romania had the highest infant mortality in Europe. Ceausescu had sacrificed an entire generation to his economic program.

The environmental impact of these austerity measures was equally disastrous. In order to continue industrial production, brown coal was used in many factories and pollutants were indiscriminately emitted into the air and water supply. Between 1972 and 1982, Romania experienced the largest increase in per capita emissions of sulfur dioxide in Europe. Brown coal and lignite production increased 160 percent in the late 1980s, and sulfur dioxide emissions rose over 100 percent. Water contamination exceeded purification plant capacity. Of the 2,767 pretreatment and treatment plants, 844 were operating below standard, and sixty-eight plants were inoperable. In addition, 1,364 miles of Romanian rivers were polluted and less than 20 percent of the main waterways provided drinkable water.

The Romanian Environmental Protection Law passed in 1973 was never enforced.[3] To increase industrial capacity, Ceausescu began building a nuclear facility at Cernavoda in 1978, but ultimately Ceausescu's Canadian partners blocked his attempts to place the reactor on-line.

Perhaps the most infamous environmental legacy of the Ceausescu period was the carbon processing plant at Copsa Mica. With the assistance of a British company, the processing capacity of the plant was expanded so that it dumped thousands of tons of soot and exotic metals into the air. This Transylvanian city was encased in black carbon. Rady notes that "no animal life could survive in the immediate area except for wildfowl, the flesh of which was sufficiently noxious to be inedible."[4] Copsa Mica was emblematic of Romania's communist legacy of heedless industrialization.

The economic, political, and environmental situation in Romania had severely deteriorated by the time the communist leaderships in East Germany, Hungary, and Czechoslovakia were repudiated and forced to relinquish power in November and December of 1989. Unlike Honecker in East Germany or Husak in Czechoslovakia, Ceausescu refused to step down. A prisoner of his own cult of personality, he could not recognize the illegitimacy of his regime, leadership, and familial dynasty.[5] The "Romanian revolution" would be the most violent transition in Eastern Europe.

There were visible signs in early 1989 that Ceausescu's regime was creating a growing feeling of despair and disgust among the public and within the party, the military, and the secret police. In March, six party veterans had circulated an open letter criticizing Ceausescu's economic policies. Two of the signatories, Gheorghe Apostol and Constantin Parvulescu, had been general secretaries of the PCR, indicating the level of frustration felt even among the nomenklatura.

In November 1989, the Fourteenth PCR Congress reelected Ceausescu General Secretary, and he took this opportunity to denounce the events in other Eastern European countries and to proclaim Romania's adherence to traditional Marxist-Leninist principles. During this time, the Romanian public knew that changes were occurring in neighboring Hungary, Bulgaria, and Czechoslovakia. As Tismaneanu argues, the Fourteenth Congress "only showed how much Ceausescu and his clique had lost touch with reality. They could not grasp the magnitude of the social crisis in Romania and failed to realize the effect on the Romanians of the revolutionary events in the other Eastern European countries."[6]

The social crisis became manifest on December 17 when thousands of Romanians entered the streets of Timisoara to protest the police eviction from his parish house of Pastor Laszlo Tokes, who had attempted to mobilize the population against the government. Many have argued that the brutal clashes between unarmed civilians and the security forces in Timisoara constituted the "threshold of violent conflict" in the Romanian revolution. The revolution spread rapidly from city to city. In order to bolster support, Ceausescu organized a government rally on December 21 in Bucharest; however, his own rally turned into an anti-Ceausescu protest.

Protesters soon seized the state television station and formed the National Salvation Front (FSN), which initially was composed of old communist cadres, students, and human rights activists. After their capture, Ceausescu and his wife were tried and executed on national television.

Romanian Politics and Environmental Policy: 1990–1996

Immediately following the revolution, the National Salvation Front began the process of transforming itself from a political movement to a political party. The FSN was formed on December 22, 1989, as a "spontaneous" reaction to events in Romania, and because of its role in the revolution of 1989, the party tried to control the new institutions emerging in the vacuum left by the fall of Ceausescu.[7] The FSN proclaimed a provisional government with Petru Roman as prime minister and Ion Iliescu, the head of the FSN Council, as interim president of the country. Iliescu had been a prominent member of the PCR before his demotion in 1971. The original members of the FSN Council included intellectuals, army officers, and students, but the most prominent members were former communist officials. In fact, within just a few weeks, many of the important opposition intellectuals quit the organization.

On December 27, the FSN Council issued a ten-point program abolishing the Communist Party—the PCR—and guaranteeing future free elections. The FSN was not so much a political party as a catch-all political movement, but it enjoyed widespread support. Although several interwar parties, such as the National Peasant Christian Democratic Party (PNTCD) and the National Liberal Party (PNL), were refounded within a month of the events of December 1989, these parties were in no organizational position to challenge the FSN.

Not surprisingly, the FSN did very well in the May 1990 parliamentary and presidential elections, receiving an overwhelming 66 percent of the popular vote and 72 percent of the parliamentary seats. Petru Roman was named prime minister. Presidential candidate Ion Iliescu received over 85 percent of the vote. The FSN was more successful than any East European party in the first postcommunist election, due to the lack of any real opposition and the violent nature of Romania's transition.

The FSN inherited Romania's disastrous environmental situation. According to some estimates, there were at least 625 centers of serious pollution.[8] Almost every city contained at least one industry that was severely polluting the environment. The environmental problem coupled with the large number of reported AIDS cases and orphans focused Western attention on the public policy failures of the Ceausescu regime.

There was a feeling among many Romanian environmentalists that economic issues would once again dominate public policy. Therefore, several environmental parties were formed in 1990 to give environmental issues more prominence. Romania developed a significant en-

vironmental political movement, with six of the first 159 formally registered political parties being green parties.[9] The Romanian Ecological
Movement (MER), the first environmental party to register, claimed to
have over 60,000 members. The MER received almost 3 percent of the
1990 parliamentary vote.

The Romanian Environmental Party (PER) has a substantially smaller
membership than the MER, with which it cooperates politically. PER
is a center-right party permanently affiliated with the aforementioned
National Peasant Christian Democratic Party (PNTCD), which stresses
the harmony between environmental and political and social interests.
The PER has publicly supported Greenpeace and has called for a reduction in fossil fuel use. The platform of the MER does not differ substantially from that of the PER; one member of the MER has said that
"the differences between these two political parties are political not
policy related."[10] After the forced resignation of the Petru Roman government, the MER participated in the formation of the Theodor Stolojan
government in October 1991, and member of MER held the Ministry
of Environment portfolio.

There was a feeling among environmental parties that the MER minister of the environment did not address the worst environmental lega-
cies of the Ceausescu regime; for example, Romania continued to use
soft brown coal for industrial production. Parties such as the PER and
the Environmental Foundation of Romania (FER) felt that the ruling
FSN was simply continuing the economic and environmental policies
of the old regime. The FER, registered in 1990, argued that environmental problems required national solutions, and in 1992 the PER and
the FER joined the newly formed opposition coalition, the Democratic
Convention of Romania (CDR).

The CDR was formed in November 1991 to contest local elections
scheduled for March 1992. While coalition members have changed
through the years, certain parties have continued their affiliation with
the CDR. The PNTCD is the leading party in this coalition, which
includes the Hungarian Democratic Union of Romania (UDMR), the
National Liberal Party (PNL), the National Liberal Party–Democratic
Convention (PNL-CD), the PER, and the FER. Several associations
are also affiliated with the CDR.

The local elections of February and March 1992 indicated a shift in
the preferences of the Romanian electorate. While in 1990 the FSN had
won an overwhelming majority of votes in both the parliamentary and
presidential elections, it received far fewer votes in mayoral and county
council elections. While single parties had participated in the 1990 elec-

tions, the 1992 local elections marked the first time that the CDR as a coalition participated in Romanian elections. The CDR won almost 65 percent of the mayoral contests in municipalities with populations of more than two hundred thousand, including a hundred mayoralties and Romania's largest cities—Bucharest, Timisoara, Constanta, and Brasov.

Shafir concludes that while the "electoral preferences in Romania had changed radically since 1990," the ability of the CDR to capitalize on this shift in the 1992 national elections was dependent on "whether the Democratic Convention [would] be able to maintain unity in the run-up to the forthcoming general elections."[11]

By early 1992 the political landscape in Romania had changed substantially. The 1990 elections had been conducted under provisional decree, but the 1992 parliamentary and presidential elections were conducted under the newly approved Romanian Constitution (adopted on December 8, 1991). President Iliescu stated that he was uncomfortable with the rapid pace of economic reform proposed by the Petru Roman government, and Roman was replaced in September 1991 by former Minister of Finance Stolojan. In March 1992, those FSN members loyal to Iliescu left the party to form the Democratic National Salvation Front (FDSN). This split within FSN reflected the animosity between Iliescu and Roman. Because of the local election results and the obvious rift within FSN, the CDR leadership felt that the coalition would be able to capture a significant portion of the September 1992 vote.

The changes in Romania's electoral law for the 1992 national elections had a significant impact on the composition of the parties that entered parliament. Because of the 3 percent threshold instituted for the 1992 parliamentary elections, the number of parties that entered parliament declined dramatically. While eighteen parties and coalitions entered the parliament after the 1990 elections, only seven parties and coalitions entered the House of Deputies (the lower house) after the 1992 parliamentary elections, and the CDR did far worse than many of the preelection surveys had predicted. Instead of capturing the 30–35 percent of the vote that had been predicted, the CDR received just over 20 percent of the vote. The FDSN still garnered a plurality in the election, although, the party failed to receive the absolute majority that it had enjoyed following the 1990 elections. Ultimately, the FDSN had to form a coalition government with several extremist parties, including the Party of Romanian National Unity (PUNR) and the Greater Romanian Party (PRM), and nominated Nicolae Vacariou as prime minister. Although the FDSN formed a coalition with nationalist and leftist parties, its members held almost all the government portfolios, including the renamed Ministry of Waters, Forests and Environmental Protection.

While Romanian public opinion polls accurately predicted a second-round presidential run-off election between Iliescu and Constantinescu, the polls had underestimated voter support for Iliescu. Although the margin of victory for Iliescu declined in the 1992 presidential election, he still received over 61 percent of the second-round vote. FDSN opponents argued that the sharp decline indicated a lack of confidence; the FDSN argued that these returns reflected a more moderate and realistic view of Romanian politics. The FDSN changed its name to the Romanian Social Democratic Party (PDSR) in 1995.

Because of the schism between Iliescu and former Prime Minister Roman, the Vacaroiu government inherited several unresolved economic, social, and environmental questions. For example, a December 1990 law proposed the return of state property to Romanian citizens, but this required land surveys and titling. This was a major issue because while 25 percent of peasants had prerevolutionary land claims that were settled, the rest of the land titles were unclear.

Because of the unstable economic situation, the International Monetary Fund promised credits of U.S. $1 billion to Romania conditional upon opening the economy to foreign capital and privatizing farming, housing, and state enterprises. By 1994, only twenty-five out of four thousand medium-sized state enterprises had been privatized, and inflation was over 300 percent. Unemployment and underemployment were chronic. Large segments of the population were falling into poverty and the health care system remained in dreadful condition. A decline in agricultural production led to the import of several basic foodstuffs, including grain. Because necessary market reforms were not enacted, the IMF in 1994 refused to release additional tranches (payments).

The Vacariou government's environmental policy was hampered by a lack of financial resources and by developmentalist thinking. The two major sources of environmental investments in Romania have been private investments and allocations from the state budget. According to the National Center for Statistics, total annual environmental expenditures remained constant at approximately 0.6 percent of GDP between 1993 and 1996. By 1995, government environmental expenditures accounted for 2.7 percent of the state budget. State funds accounted for approximately 57 percent of total environmental spending.

The Romanian Environmental Protection Law was passed in December 1995, creating an environmental fund but also disallowing the Ministry of Waters, Forests and Environmental Protection from managing its own budget. In 1996, the ministry issued its strategies and priorities for the next ten years. The short-term objectives (prior to 2000) included reducing sulfur dioxide and nitrogen emissions by 20 percent and chlorine and H_2Cl by 40 percent, increasing the reuse of solid wastes by 20 percent, irrigating 1.5 million hectares, and planting 50,000 hectares of forest.

The ministry's ambitious medium-term objectives (to be attained prior to 2005) included reducing the existing water shortage by 50 percent; improving the quality of surface waters by raising the length of clean rivers to 60–65 percent of the total and reducing the length of degraded rivers by 10–15 percent; reducing air pollution by 20–30 percent of 1989 levels for SO2, CO, NH3, CH4; reducing heavy metal pollution by 80 percent; and recovering 70–80 percent of the Danube Delta.

While the short- and the medium-term goals of the ministry were supported by several Romanian environmental activists and parties, funding these projects proved extremely difficult. Indeed, the 1996 state budget devoted less to environment than any previous budget, and most funding came from the private sector and municipalities. Because of the poor state of Romanian air and water quality, significantly larger public investment is required to meet the ministry's goals.

Reduction in sulfur dioxide and other emissions requires the cooperation of Romanian state industry. Factory managers view inflation and increasing wages as inimical to environmental protection. Six years after the revolution, the Romanian environmental situation had changed little.

However, the 1996 national elections represent a turning point in Romanian political history. Several political factors have changed since 1992. First, the PDSR could not control the electronic media as it had in 1992. The independent and very popular station Pro-TV ensured that the opposition received equal and fair news coverage in urban centers. This was important because the PDSR still dominated state television.

Second, the opposition CDR has matured, and rather than relying on anticommunist themes, it adopted a "contract with Romania," which described the problems a CDR government would solve. The 1996 campaign demonstrated that CDR presidential candidate Constantinescu had also matured as a leader.

Third, there was a change in the Romanian electorate itself. The new entrepreneurial class distrusted the PDSR's economic policy, and the public shifted their party allegiances due to the Vacaroiu government's poor economic performance.

Polls conducted by the Romanian Public Opinion Survey Institute (IRSOP) indicated that many voters approved of the "contract," 68 percent of respondents expressing a "very good" or "good" opinion of it. While the opposition focused on a positive, substantive message, the PDSR presented its same negative 1992 message, that the CDR would restore the monarchy and punish former communist members.

This message, however, did not resonate with the Romanian electorate in 1996. The CDR received a plurality of votes in both houses (30 percent) and formed a coalition government with the Social Democracy Union and the Hungarian Democratic Union of Romania; Victor Ciorbea was named prime minister. In the second round of the 1996 presidential election, Constantinescu received 54.4 percent of the vote while Iliescu received 45.6 percent.

While the contract with Romania focused primarily on economic reform, environmentalists hoped that the new Ciorbea government would address the country's environmental problems. By 1996, total environmental investment amounted to more than U.S. $200 million, high by Romanian standards but low compared to the European Union. Romania will require massive environmental investment by both the government and industry to attain EU standards, but the speculation is that government spending on environment will continue to decline over the next five to ten years.

The Ciorbea government stated that environmental funding from the state budget would be significantly reduced through the introduction of economic reforms such as price liberalization and privatization. The government announced an environmental fund as a basic instrument to implement policy. User fees, disposal charges, and noncompliance fines would generate income for the fund, and therefore, environmental protection would not compete with other social programs for funding.

The government's priorities include the development of an extensive monitoring system, management plans for highly polluted areas, professional accreditation, and efficient enforcement. There are numerous environmental laws, and some success stories. For example, the government has successfully cleaned up Copsa Mica. However, compliance is generally poor because of the country's depressed economy, poor management, and lack of information.

Environmental administration is coordinated on the national, regional, and local levels by the Ministry of Waters, Forests and Environmental Protection, which maintains offices in every Romanian county. There are also several research institutes that focus on environmental protection (e.g., the Institute for Research for Environmental Engineering, the Institute for Maritime Waters, and the Institute for Forestry Research and Planning). However, coordination among these various agencies and institutions has been lacking.

Ciorbea was recently replaced by current Prime Minister Radu Vasile, and while the new government has continued much of the environmental policy of its predecessor, it is not clear that the new government will be any more successful in finding the necessary funding to solve Romania's environmental problems.

Romania's Environmental Ideological Spectrum

Between March and May 1994, a Q-protocol was administered to a sample of sixteen Romanian political, academic, and business elites in the Transylvanian town of Sibiu and in the capital, Bucharest. The political elites included leaders of the following parties: PDSR, PUNR, MER, PER, UDMR, and the Civic Alliance Party (PAC). The sample included two governmental officials, three business persons, and seven academics, for a total of thirteen men and three women. The functional overlap and relatively small size of Romania's emerging environmental elite is not unusual among the countries studied in this book. With so many movements and parties, and with international—especially European—standards to be met, environmental issues have penetrated public discourse and become an important part of national policy.

Two ideological types emerged from the data: Developmentalists and Bureaucratic Nationalists, demonstrating that environmentalism is still subordinate to capitalist developmentalism and to a nationalist variant of the prior socialist project of import substitution industrialization. These types also show that the self-characterization of the MER and the PER as center-right parties was accurate.

Developmentalists are a composite of the attitudes of seven academics who are members of the MER, PSDR, and UDMR, and a government health inspector. Holders of this attitude type believe that global warming could have catastrophic effects but that Romania cannot spend scarce resources to prevent its major effects. Instead, the government must react defensively as global warming becomes manifest. They believe that environmental collapse extinguished former civilizations, but they do not think humanity is doomed in the long run. Philosophically, this type strongly rejects the idea that all living things have the right to exist and that biodiversity is a common heritage of mankind to be preserved.

Developmentalists are mildly disillusioned about democracy's ability to meet the environmental crisis, reflecting dislike of government environmental policies and low funding. One member of the MER commented that "the limited money that the government has goes into social rather than environmental projects." Even with these reservations, this type thinks that democracy can ultimately rise to meet the challenge. However, they believe that environmentally balanced economic development is not really possible, and a green economy with voluntary simplicity and participatory management is utopian. Romanian urbanites are not far from village life, and their frugality, recycling, and husbandry of resources are natural. However, these characteristics appear to elites as signs of underdevelopment (compared to Western European consumerism).

These Developmentalists agree that Western models plunder and destroy nature but reject the argument that international programs have produced more poverty than development. The impetus for environmental protection must come from outside (i.e., elites look to the EU for funding and technology). An ecologist argued that "the government wants the West to help with environment. There is no political leader pushing ecology. Specialists are not involved in politics." An agronomist stated that "academics have little influence in the process. Ecological departments are new and reflect good intentions, but none of the political parties, including the greens, really know how to solve these environmental problems." Economic development can be accomplished on a sound environmental basis, but development should not lead to unequal distribution of resources. For this reason, Developmentalists favor incentives and information for business instead of governmental regulation, so that market mechanisms can take care of the environment.

This reflects a lack of confidence in the government and identification with capitalism as efficient and self-regulating. As a UDMR senator stated, "I believe that the biggest problem involves money and education of the government as well as the people. I believe that the government is not acting fast enough, but the opposition is not unified either on the environment. Environmental policy is not a large concern of parliament; there are too many problems currently facing the government. No one party or group has the answers. The economy is placed above the environment for now."

A county health inspector was not as pro-business as the others in this type. She argued that "businesses will not follow environmental guidelines without enforcement. My experience shows that you must regulate business. The current government is concerned about environment, but the problems are large and the laws really do not give as much power to civil servants as is necessary. With increasing numbers of businesses, it is going to be more difficult to police them."

Holders of this attitude type believe that poor countries could potentially develop without fossil fuel but that energy efficiency will not cut the pollution costs of industrialization. They are neutral about the problems of fossil fuel and neutral about the dangers of nuclear energy. This may reflect concern that Romania's oil industry cannot sustain a rapid pace of development and that nuclear power may be a future necessity. As the UDMR senator stated, "energy policy overrides all environmental concerns."

Romanian environmental parties are debating the Cernavoda nuclear reactor, which was to be operational in 1985 and complete in 1990. Financial and political difficulties with Canada prevented it from coming on-line, but in 1991, Canada provided U.S. $277 million to complete construction. An executive and former member of Romoil (Romanian International Oil Company) stated that "I am against nuclear power and believe that gas and oil can be used without its problems. But oil companies need to be regulated too. I distrust big business and think that government must regulate business more; the West is a good model for Romania."

Their stance toward biotechnology is anomalous. The purpose of biotechnology is eugenic (i.e., to engineer the human gene pool), and this strong agreement reflects the older generation's respect for technology. There are risks of collusion in the biotechnology industry, but this type rejects the idea that the risks of biotechnology outweigh the gains. Population growth is not a problem in Romania, which has achieved zero growth, so that population growth need not be forced down for development to proceed. This type does not consider women's rights important to population control.

Developmentalists reflect the transitional nature of Romanian environmental thinking. They look to the West for developmental aid and do not give priority to sustainable development or green thinking. They are open to using any energy source and new technology, although they are ambiguous about the ecological effects. They also support democratic business-oriented solutions to environmental problems.

The second type, *Bureaucratic Nationalists*, is a composite of two businessmen, a senator in the PUNR, and two officers in the FER. Holders of this attitude type are strongly critical of human arrogance toward nature and think that environmental collapse caused destruction of prior civilizations and may bring down the West. Ecologically responsible development is not really a possibility. The green economic alternative requires a revolution as great as the industrial revolution and is unlikely in Romania's economy. A PUNR businessman explained that "economic development is more important than the environment. Environmental regulation could damage economic development and put people out of work. Environmental issues are secondary." A PUNR senator agreed that "environmental laws should assist business, not harm it. Our biggest need is balancing the needs of environment with the needs of social and economic protection. The problem of environment must be studied for the future."

Sustainable development is not a necessity for this type—they strongly reject the notion that all life has value and do not believe biodiversity to be an important common heritage. Bureaucratic Nationalists strongly assert the West's responsibility for funding and enforcing environmental regulations on a world scale, and they see a growing international consensus supporting such action. They reject the notions that international developmental programs have caused poverty and dislocation and that the West has plundered the environment and utilized poor countries for experimentation.

At the same time, this type is culturally and economically nationalistic. A PUNR businessman said that "the West must provide financial assistance," but a PUNR senator stated that "I don't believe that the West wants to help. The West wants to use environmental policy to dictate economic policy." As a member of the FER argued, "the role of nongovernmental organizations like the FER is to assist Romania. The FER believes in self-help. Romania must solve its own problems, and international organizations can provide a framework, but Romanians must solve their own problems. The biggest problem with Romanian nongovernmental organizations is their lack of funding." A functionary in the MER stated that "these are Romanian problems. We cannot wait for outside help but must solve the problems by ourselves. People do think of environmental problems, but as the economy grows the level of social and environmental protection declines. Our biggest problem is money."

Nationalists strongly support democracy as a tool for environmental management even though they believe that environmental policy is piecemeal and defensive. Development does not cause unfair distribution of national income, but environmentally sound development is not possible. Giving businesses incentives and allowing the market free rein will not benefit the environment as much as would government regulation.

Since Romania has large natural gas reserves, it has an opportunity to pursue cleaner forms of energy than exclusively oil-based economies. A PUNR senator explained that he believes "that coal and gas need to be used; the future, and the Romanian economy, are dependent on these resources for economic growth."

Bureaucratic Nationalists believe that fossil fuels and nuclear power will be necessary in the future and are only mildly concerned about the risks of nuclear power. A member of the FER stated that he "believes that nuclear power is all right, the problem is having advanced technology like in France." This type believes that biotechnology must be developed as a strategic necessity in the future economy but that it is clearly not cheaper than chemical and mechanical farming.

Holders of this attitude type are only mildly concerned that global warming will disrupt world climate and economies, leading to mass migrations and famine. They weakly agree that Romania should wait and see what effects emerge before making adjustments. Given their fiscal crisis, there is probably little alternative to this policy.

Figure 9.1 indicates the relative placement of Romanian elites on postmodern/post-Fordist indicators. Bureaucratic Nationalists are dislocated into postmodern space because they represent the old left, with their strong distrust of business and agreement with elements of a green economy. Realization of such an advanced program is not, in their thinking, possible in the recurrent economic downturn.

Developmentalists are Fordist modernists with a stronger belief in market mechanisms and a willingness to subordinate the environment to extensive growth. These two types capture the division between Westernizing liberal capitalists and the bureaucratic authoritarian left.

Both types occur in Romania's Green parties, but there is little political space for a green or sustainable development paradigm to emerge until basic political conflicts between new and old systems are resolved. Neither of these "old politics" alternatives—state socialism or neo-liberalism—has had much success in Romania, so that a green alternative may eventually prove attractive if linked to agrarian, national, religious and cultural values.

In conclusion, the two factorial types that emerged from this study indicate that environmental concerns are not being addressed by the government and that the environmental parties are organized along the old Fordist left-right dimensions. The left wants a gradual transi-

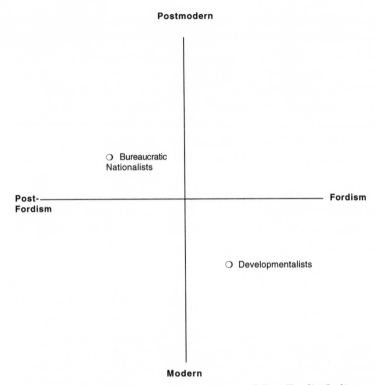

9.1. Romanian Attitude Types on Postmodern and Post-Fordist Indicators

Postmodern indicator is positive score on statement 18. The only alternative is a Green economy, with grassroots democracy, voluntary simplicity, sustainable production, and recycling.

Post-Fordist indicator is a negative score on statement 13. If government gave business information and incentives, not command and sanction, the market and entrepreneurs would protect the environment.

tion, with state intervention balancing economic changes and environmental protection, while the right supports rapid change to a market system, with minimum state intervention.

Both Bureaucratic Nationalists and Developmentalists exclude environmental regulation from current consideration. Both groups identify the need for development, foreign aid, and growth to counteract growing social problems. Given the environmental problems currently facing Romania, there is an urgent need for elites, both Developmentalist and Bureaucratic Nationalist, to arrive at an environmental policy consensus. Unfortunately, neither the West nor Romanian elites have seen the evident economic advantages of integrating environmental regulation into development.

✺ 10

Iran: From Revolution to Ecological Collapse

The environmental posture of Iranian government, business, scientific, and environmentalist elites are explored in this chapter, based on a Q-method protocol run in Teheran in 1991. The Iranian environmental situation is critical, with rapid overpopulation, desertification, and the endangerment of virtually all species in the country. But debate on environmental issues, values, and policy occurs among government intellectuals and technicians, without extensive pressure, input, or support by grassroots or public voluntary organizations.

Four attitude models emerged from our field survey of elites: two of them, Cultural Traditionalists (Religious Conservatives) and Developmentalists, represent the major policy split within Iranian government, while Sustainable Developers and Bureaucratic Nationalists bring out divisions within the bureaucratic elite. Sustainable development is the only environmental option available within Iran, but is possible only if the country attains some economic security and a measure of international recognition. These four attitude types correspond closely to the factional structure that emerged during the revolution. I here review Iran's environmental situation and policy, the Islamic revolution and its factions, and the attitude types discovered among business, government, and scientific elites.

Iran's Environmental Crisis

An arid, overpopulated country, Iran faces desertification, soil erosion, biodiversity loss, major oil and industrial pollution, uncontrolled urbanization, and exponential overpopulation. Iran's environmental problem is among the most critical in the world.

Iran is 1,648,000 sq km in extent, with a population of 67 million in 1995, growing at a rapid 3.15 percent per year. Almost half the population (48.5 percent) is under fifteen years or over sixty-five years old. Population density is already 34.5 persons per square kilometer and the country is 54 percent urban. Iran's population could reach an impossible 100 million soon after 2000, if this trend continues. Population growth is rapidly eroding any gains from economic growth or environmental regulation. However, the government is considering family planning measures to cut the growth rate to 2.3 percent by 2010, simply because infrastructure, food production, and education must otherwise increase an impossible 33 percent by that date to accommodate so many people.

Iran's Palearctic territory is 80 percent arid, with 50 million ha of desert. Only 10 percent of Iran's 18 million ha of forests are commercially productive, and arable land comprises only 15 percent of the 18.5 million ha of semi-arid prairie. Despite its policy of self-sufficiency, Iran will be permanently dependent on imports of food, fodder, and wood, which it must purchase with oil, gas, copper, and lead exports.

Iran averages only 256 mm of rain per year and its surface water is regulated by nineteen reservoirs. Groundwater totals 45 billion m^3, of which most goes to drinking and sanitation. Some 390 cities have yet to construct sewer systems.

Iran emits 39,700,000 tons of carbon per year, a figure similar to that for Indonesia, another major oil economy. Air pollution is serious because Iranian cities rely on private cars rather than modern mass transit. Cars in Teheran are, on average, 15–20 years old and consume 40 percent of the domestic gasoline supply. Traffic jams create heavy photochemical smog, lead, and dust loads, but all imported cars, taxis, and buses are now being switched to LPG.

In two decades Iran's industry has grown 100 percent. Five large cities have some six hundred industries, and there are twenty-three new industrial cities. The main industrial polluters are petrochemical complexes, cement factories, copper and aluminum smelters, a steel mill, pulp and paper plants, and large chemical firms. Numerous brick furnaces and small foundries are serious polluters, but new regulations will eventually require them to fuel-inject their furnaces and ultimately to convert to LPG.

The outfall from these industries is carelessly disposed of without treatment or control. Hospital, industrial, and radioactive wastes, along with raw sewage, are dumped into the watershed. Throughout the country hospital wastes are illegally scavenged by humans and animals, and pathological or radioactive wastes are not separated or specially treated. Maharloo Salt Lake near Shiraz contains high fecal coliform counts, cadmium, lead, nickel, arsenic, and copper, which chemicals are found in table salt and in vegetables grown with lake water. The Korr River, a major water source for the city of Fars, receives wastes from animal processing plants (organics), from petrochemical complexes (ammonium and mercury), and from electronics manufacturing plants (heavy metals, especially cadmium, chromium, and arsenic). The Black River discharges agrotoxic runoff, sewage, and heavy metals into the Caspian Sea.

The February 1991 Gulf War cut fish catches in the Persian Gulf by half. Oil fires caused acid rain, smog, and soot deposition over the whole country. Soil and water lead counts increased 600 percent and carcinogen loads increased 200 percent. Some 12.5 million persons suffered health problems, and 5 million ha of cultivated land were degraded, along with 8 million ha of forests and an equal amount of pasture lands.

Agriculture is a strategic sector in a country that must export oil to buy food, but lack of water allows only 8.5 million ha to be irrigated. Dry farming, which accounts for 66 percent of cereal production, leads to rapid wind erosion. Water erosion removes 1.5 billion tons of topsoil annually, about 1 mm of topsoil per year. A quarter of the 400 billion m^3 of surface water is lost through runoff, causing nutrient loss and rapid siltation of dams. Pests and diseases damage 30 percent of each year's crop, and pesticide use is a dangerous 300 g per capita per year. In 1992, 605,000 kg of herbicides were applied; seepage into groundwater and rivers caused serious health problems and fish kills. Iran uses toxins banned in the West, such as DDT, DDE, DDD, 2,4-d,a, and 2,4,S-d, which bioaccumulate and biomagnify in tissues. The food supply contains a heavy toxin load, and agrotoxins have been losing their effect as natural selection produces resistant strains.

Heavy fertilizer use has burned Iran's thin topsoil and contaminated the groundwater. From 1949 to the present, fertilizer use has increased from 5,000 to 1.7 million tons per annum, but there has been no expansion in the extent of agricultural land during this period. Iran imports 5.5 million tons of food annually.

Total forest cover is 18 million ha, of which only 3.8 million ha are under forest proper, the rest being scrublands and heath. Most forest lies in the wet north near the Caspian Sea. The government is reforesting at a rate of 54,000 ha per year, although many of the trees do not take. Some 90 million ha of range lands are grazed by 60 million animals; that is, grazing is four times over carrying capacity (15 million animals). Not surprisingly, 1.5 million ha per year of pasture are subject to desertification. Programs to fix sand dunes, restore range lands, and manage watersheds are in place.

Iran degraded some 50 percent of its wildlife refuges and 70 percent of protected areas during the Iran-Iraq War; and 80 percent of wildlife populations are claimed to have been lost. Some 7.5 million ha are now set aside as parks or refuges, but all mammals are considered threatened, and migratory waterfowl have declined. There is no clear policy on biodiversity protection, and the local populations lack consciousness of the long-term impact of their overexploitation.[1]

An oil economy, heavily dependent on chemical agriculture, and seeking economic independence from a hostile international community, Iran has proven surprisingly receptive to environmental concerns, if unable administratively or financially to rectify the situation. In 1972 Iran founded a Department of the Environment, which received a legal mandate in Article 50 of the postrevolutionary constitution, making environmental conservation a public duty and forbidding economic activity leading to irreversible harm. The UNCED Rio 1992 principle of sustainable development is the framework for Iranian legislation, and environmental impact statements are a major consideration in all projects. Thus, "preparing integrated plans for all natural resources of the country and applying proper exploitation systems based on modern technology suitable for the sustainability of natural resources" is basic policy.[2]

In 1986 the Department of Environment was reorganized and charged with research on appropriate technology, a national biological survey, public education, and national regulation of air, water, urban development, biodiversity, waste disposal, noise pollution, and agrotoxics. National family planning and population limitation programs, incorporation of women into conservation (the present minister of environment is a woman), and encouragement of grassroots environmental movements are priorities. The department responds to the Environmental High Council chaired by the president of the republic and consisting of most important ministries. Several ambitious programs—including national birth control, conversion to agrosilvapastoral systems, change to LPG, reclamation of oil wastes, urban decentralization, construction of forty-five dams, reforestation, wetland and river reclamation, and industrial restructuring—are on the books. Iran plans to allocate 0.1 percent of industrial revenues to environmental rehabilitation.

But there are serious constraints operating against these policies. International prices for raw materials are declining, and agricultural and textile products face continued protectionism from rich nations. Damage from the Iran-Iraq War (1980–88), the Gulf War (February 1991), a heavy flow of refugees, overpopulation, rapid unplanned urbanization, and the depressing effect of international trade sanctions all make the Iranian situation difficult. Seid Zekavat notes that "none of the . . . projects presented in Rio has been implemented, although . . . Iran . . . has adopted a comprehensive environmental protection program." Zekavat continues: "The inability of Iranian officials to control the environment is due to (1) poor enforcement programs; (2) lack of public awareness and noncompliance of firms and individuals with policies and regulations; and (3) budget appropriation priorities in areas other than the environment."[3]

On the positive side, Iran has nine biosphere preserves, with 2.2 percent of its land under protection regimes. It is signatory to a number of important environmental treaties: the Nuclear Test Ban Treaty and the Biological and Toxic Weapons Ban; Wetlands, World Heritage, and CITES (endangered species trade protection) treaties; the Law of the Sea, the UNEP Regional Seas program, and the Paris Convention on water bird habitats; Montreal and Vienna protocols on ozone layer protection; and the Rio UNCED treaties. Iran is a member in good standing of 140 U.N. organizations. However, there are indications that Iran may be developing chemical and biological weapons, and its attempts to join the nuclear powers have so far been blocked by strong diplomatic pressures.

It is instructive to review the policy changes and factional structure that emerged from the Iranian revolution of 1979.

Iranian Politics and Policy

Iran was invaded by Britain and the U.S.S.R. in 1941 and Reza Shah Palavi took the throne from his father. Mohammad Mossadeq became prime minister, set up a national plan, and pushed for nationalization of oil in the face of British and Soviet demands for concessions. In 1953 the United States and Britain overthrew the government and firmly established the Shah as their agent in Middle East politics. Using harsh repression and censorship, and abolishing political parties, the Shah set up a "developmental dictatorship," which organized land reform, a literacy campaign, profit sharing for workers, and investment of oil revenues in industrial growth. Forests and pastures were nationalized.

The Islamic clergy opposed these programs, especially women's suffrage and cultural Westernization, and in June 1963 Ayatollah Sayyid Ruhollah Musavi Khomeini was arrested for attacks on the Shah, sparking riots and his eventual exile as leader of the opposition. The National Front provided secular opposition, and Mehdi Bazargan worked to coordinate with the clergy. Guerrilla movements—the Mujahedin, Fedayin, and Peykar—emerged, as did various nationalist movements.

By 1976, the Shah's overly ambitious developmental scheme was in economic trouble, with military waste, general corruption, rapid inflation, and social dislocation. The old social classes—landed and trading dynasties from which government officials were recruited, the wealthy middle strata of bazaar merchants and artisans, the senior clergy, and rural poor—turned to Islamic fundamentalism in opposition to modernization and Westernization. The new Westernized professional middle class, a repressed working class of some 2.5 million, and the bureaucratic and military elites supported pragmatic modernization. A growing urban underclass of the unemployed, casual workers, squatters, and beggars was marginalized from the political process. They originated in the near-feudal countryside, where half of the agricultural land was owned by two hundred thousand absentee landowners, and sharecropping and low-wage labor prevailed. Islamic religious ideology was used by the traditional classes and the urban and rural poor to protest against the power and prerogatives of the Shah's modernizing elites, the presence of sixty thousand resident foreigners, and against Western culture.

In 1978, under pressure from President Carter, the Shah released political prisoners, unmuzzled the press, and attempted to control inflation with adjustment programs. This effort sparked powerful opposition movements, supported by the clergy, bazaar, and workers, who clashed with the police and army in a downward spiral of violence. Following an unsuccessful policy of conciliation, the Shah declared martial law in September 1978, and eighty-seven protesters were shot on September 9. June and August saw strikes by industrial and public sector workers, and the Shah began negotiating with the opposition, finally allowing Shapour Bakhtiar of the National Front to form a government. The Shah left Iran on January 16, 1979.

Specialists argue that Iranian elite factionalism has gone through three periods since the 1979 revolution. The mass uprising against the Shah, royal court, and small body of industrialists, bureaucrats, and technocrats left the shape of the successor regime open to struggle among the various social classes that participated in the rising: the middle class, including intelligentsia, bazaari merchants, and privileged industrial workers; and marginal urbanites or ex-peasants working in the informal sector, led by the mullahs or religious leaders. Imam Khomeini's Shiite Islam claimed to unify all social strata in an Islamic Republic that represented a return to the traditional culture displaced by years of dependent development and Westernization under the Shah. There followed a period of dual power in which the modern opposition was gradually displaced by religious elites. However, religious elites subsequently split over policy issues, and pragmatic technocrats have emerged as important players in the government.

Because of his ties to the Shah, Bakhtiar was rapidly deposed by Khomeini, who returned to Iran on February 1, 1979. The intelligentsia organized a liberal front under Mehdi Bazargan, who was nominated by Khomeini to run the provisional government. The mullahs accepted Bazargan because of their admitted lack of political experience, but five of them constituted a Revolutionary Council to act as a legislature. Bazargan saved the old regime's state machinery and armed forces and brought together a secular left-center Cabinet, which pursued Keynesian policies and tried to demobilize the enthusiastic masses.

Between the Cabinet and Revolutionary Council, there was a clear secular-religious divide, and the mullahs began creating a parallel government through "Islamization." In February 1979, the Islamic Republican Party was founded by clerics, backed by two paramilitary groups, the Hizbollah (Army of God, formerly the Black Shirts Storm Troopers), and the Mujahedin. Clerics set up the revolutionary guards (*pasdaran*)—political bureaus in every military establishment—and began purging the armed forces. Clerics also set up revolutionary courts, foundations, and local security committees (*komitehs*), purged the schools and universities, took control of the mass media, and used Friday communal prayers as socialization and communication mechanisms.

A new constitution written by clerics was ratified in December 2, 1979, enshrining *velayat-e-faqih*, or the Shiite notion of the imam as personification of the state and sovereign, and thereby merging political and religious rule. Khomeini kept his authority by holding the balance of power between factions, and the parliament or Majlis is overseen by a Council of Guardians, who can veto law on religious grounds.

Seizure of the U.S. Embassy on November 4, 1979, led to a diplomatic crisis that undermined Bazargan and the secular wing of the government, leading to his resignation. With Khomeini's backing, the secular politician Abdolhasan Bani-Sadr was elected president in January 1980 but was forced to accept a clerical prime minister and Cabinet.

The Iran-Iraq War (1980–88) allowed Bani-Sadr to canvass top military leaders for political support, but the clerics had already penetrated the bottom ranks and held most of the military in their faction. The clerics, with strong institutional support and unified ideology, faced a secular modernist intelligentsia with governing ability but badly divided on policy and unified only in its opposition to clerical rule. In May 1980 the revolutionary courts began massive executions and widespread purges of the government and military. In June 1981, Bani-Sadr went into hiding, and the clerical victory was complete.

Iran faced serious problems: an Iraqi invasion, left guerrillas (Fedayin, Peykar, Mujahedin), and Turkoman and Kurdish insurgencies as well as U.S. hostility over the hostage issue. The regime used brutal repression, executing up to six thousand leftists and an undisclosed number of ethnic minorities. The compliant communist party (Tudeh) was outlawed, and a number of its cadres were executed. Religious thugs suppressed basic civil liberties and the right to assemble, and there were widespread allegations of police torture.

Having eliminated secular liberals and the left from the revolution, the dominant clerical faction split over economic policy. Clerics backed by war-wealthy bazaari merchants—the Rissalat group, including President Ali Khameneh'i—argued for neoliberalism, a minimal state, absolute private property rights, and an end to taxation. Clerics representing lower-middle-class interests, including future president Ali Akbar Hashemi-Rafsanjani, argued for state capitalism, property as a public trust, and Keynesian fiscal and monetary policy.

Prime Minister Mir-Hosain Moussavi's government, under attack by neoliberals, appealed to Khomeini, who intervened in favor of state capitalism. Pressing their advantage, the Keynesians pushed bills for cooperatives, agrarian reform, public housing, and a state industrial sector and against profiteering. These bills were held up in the Council of Guardians, but in January 1988, Khomeini intervened in favor of Rafsanjani's faction, saying that community rights are superior to private property, that the state has absolute economic authority and should regulate the economy and provide welfare services. In 1987, the Islamic Revolutionary Party, paralyzed by factional disputes and lacking purpose, had been abolished. Khomeini issued decrees strengthening state control over religion and assisting the poor and working classes.

The reformists' victory over neoliberalism seemed complete, but reformists then split into two factions. The pragmatists (Rafsanjani, Velayati) represented the modern professional middle class and private industrial sector, with Khomeini's support. They wanted normalized relations with other countries, responded to the Reagan administration's arms-for-hostages trade in the "Irangate" scandal, and negotiated a ceasefire with Iraq. They believed in reconstructing Iran's economy with state control but including foreign investment. The nationalists advocated an isolationist import substitution regime.

The economic situation has not improved under the revolution. The government initially spent its foreign exchange reserves to provide basic services. Extensive government regulation and nationalization accompanied the growth of a large informal economy and of inflation. Ideological purges of government workers greatly reduced efficiency and managerial capacity. Public sector managers became a class of new rich. By 1984, the state controlled almost all large industry, employed four-fifths of the industrial work force, and produced 73.5 percent of value added. Between 1988 and 1997 real GDP fell 15 percent and population rose 52 percent. By 1988, per capita GDP was slightly over half of the 1977 level. Agriculture improved somewhat, so that real non-oil GDP rose 12 percent. But with the population increase factored in, there was a 26 percent drop in per capita terms. Private consumption in 1988 was 80 percent of its 1977 level. The government drastically curtailed public spending to less than two-thirds of the 1972 level. Elite squabbling, the incompetence of religious leaders and the low administrative capacity of government, massive repression, and wars and embargo have combined to make wretched both the plight of the poor and the state of the environment.

Ayatollah Khomeini died on June 3, 1989, and Ali Khamenei emerged as successor, with Rafsanjani as president, the prime ministry having been abolished. A Cabinet of Western-educated technocrats controls the government, while conservatives control the weakened Council of Guardians and the Imamate. The nationalists are weakened but hold positions in the bureaucracy and Majlis. The election in May 1997 of Ali Khamenei, by a 70 percent vote, brings a liberal cleric to the presidency. Although he faces a Majlis dominated by conservatives, Khamenei has made diplomatic overtures to the United States and appointed a woman to head a new Ministry of Environment.[4]

Iranian Elite Environmental Attitudes

The twenty-eight Iranian subjects were carefully chosen decision makers in academia (12), government (7), business (6), the environmental movement (2), and journalism (4). There was some sectoral overlap, with three academics also having governmental positions, and with a total of nine women and nineteen men. The attitude types that emerged from the data are the following.

Cultural Traditionalists (Religious Conservatives) represent a composite of the opinions of ten individuals. Two are female journalists, two managers of an environmental organization, and two female scientists. Three of these persons also serve in the Ministries of Health and of Environment. Also represented are businessmen from technology and architectural firms.

This attitudinal type represents the Shiite Islamic politico-religious viewpoint. Metaphysical pessimism places this type outside the international debate on environment; Religious Conservatives lie outside the postmodern and post-Fordist dimensions of our model. Like the Cultural Traditionalists in Puerto Rico, they are premodern organic conservatives.

Cultural Traditionalists reject both technocratic and Green viewpoints and see the environmental problematic within a religious framework that leaves small latitude for human intervention. Pessimistic about government, business, and international policies, this type sees the destruction of nature and the end of humanity as inevitable.

The religious belief in apocalypse, after which the hidden Mahdi (savior) will emerge to judge the world, is shown in fatalism regarding nature and mankind. Nature is a providential process beyond human control. The three classical Iranian literary images of nature as a garden (Paradise), as a sown field wrested from nature by human effort, and as a hostile desert show a contemplative attitude toward a nature over which humans have little control but which may be only fleetingly enjoyed.

Pessimists who believe in living the immediate moment to the fullest, Iranians reject both otherworldly and (Western) future orientations. Individual life represents a unique opportunity to snatch enjoyment from a cosmic context of universal entropy; humans are without power or choice, given an all-powerful but opaque providence. Striving for future success, or regret over the passing of traditional values, are both useless to this pessimistic realism. As Seid Zekavat said, "The value placed on life is very low in Iran. Iranians hold a fatalistic view of life. That is, whatever happens to a person is his or her fate; this life is not meant to be happy. For the religiously virtuous, a happy life begins after death."[5]

Western materialist definitions of progress conflict with the Iranian religious worldview, which treats nature as beginning in perfection and gradually declining. As one subject said, "Industrial countries need religion and without this, they permit themselves to damage the Third World for their own profits." Cultural Traditionalists are strongly pessimistic about business or the market promoting environmental protection and equally pessimistic about the usefulness of Western modernist development programs or international treaty regimes and policies.

Toward all statements about technical solutions to environmental problems and about Green values, holders of this attitude type are neutral. In fact, this type has an unusually large area of neutral responses to statements; only nineteen out of thirty-six statement items had strong responses. Cultural Traditionalists, like Puerto Rico's Hispanic traditionalists, stand outside of postmodern/post-Fordist dimensions, remaining resolutely premodern.

Cultural Traditionalists show a strong predilection for authoritarian solutions to the population problem. Population will not decline by itself and needs be forced down. The Koranic ideology of respect for women and the political necessity of family planning lead them to agree that women's rights are the key to population control.

Pessimistic organic conservatives, Cultural Traditionalists are hostile to modernism and postmodernism alike. Their metaphysics lead them to stand outside the international debate on development and environment (as is underscored by the unusually high number of neutral statement items in their collective Q-sort), but Religious Conservatives represent a strong, hitherto predominant, current of thought within the Islamic Republic.

The *Developmentalist* type comprises nine persons: one female journalist, two male and two female academicians, one of whom also works in the Ministry of Health, one researcher in the Ministry of Mining and Industry, and three businessmen in the chemical and banking industries.

Developmentalists are rising to predominance within the Iranian state and form a major alternative to religious programs of government. This type also manifests neutrality on the international environmental debate, with only nineteen out of thirty-six statements being significant for them.

The goal of this type seems to be independence of the West through a government-regulated market economy, a stance that may reflect current government policy. Developmentalists show short-term confidence in human control of the environment. But in the long term, their view of the human prospect is pessimistic, more on technical-scientific than on religious grounds. This type tends to be anti-Western but on pragmatic grounds accepts market and technological solutions for development.

Development does not lead to unfair distribution of resources. GNP growth is a necessary policy goal and can be attained through nuclear power and chemical farming. As one subject noted, "There must be more emphasis on energy, industry, and research." With proper government regulation and stimulus, the market will protect the environment with practical recycling and conservation measures. Government must take the threat of global warming seriously and not delay adjustments to prevent it.

Cultural Traditionalists and Developmentalists represent the main competing emphases among Iranian policy elites. Religious Conservatives are authoritarian traditionalists, hostile to Western materialism, and submissive to nature as a realm governed by an unseen divine will. Developmentalists are pessimistic about the future as a matter of scientific judgment, but this does not stop the drive for development and self-sufficiency, using a regulated market and mixed economy.

Developmentalists pragmatically accept technological and market solutions, along with government economic stimulation and regulation, as means to national autonomy. Although aware of the environmental dangers of rapid development, they are willing to sacrifice environment to economic growth. Hence their neutrality on sustainability and other Green values. Their neutrality on biotechnology probably indicates that this science is not currently available in Iran.

Sustainable Developers are a type represented by four academics (one female), a newspaper editor, and a high-level member of the Ministry of Health and another important agency (not specified to preserve anonymity).

Sustainable Developers are optimistic positivists, who approach environmental conservation as part of state-led development. Rather than being pessimistic about the future of humanity and the environment, holders of this attitude type are neutral about the idea of humanity and civilization being doomed by environmental collapse and neutral regarding many Green items. But they strongly believe that biodiversity is a common heritage of humanity that must be preserved and that all living things have a right to exist.

They believe that economic development on a sound environmental basis is possible and that recycling and energy efficiency can be built into governmental planning. They believe that democracy can meet the environmental challenge but are skeptical about government giving incentives to business.

Sustainable Developers give GNP growth high priority and think fossil and nuclear fuel necessary but requiring replacement in the long term. Nuclear power is a necessary risk. Iran has no major reactors on-line but is building two commercial reactors and has one for research. Thus Iranians have yet to confront the risks and costs of nuclear waste disposal, safety, and security. The United States has diplomatically blocked Chinese and French sales of nuclear technology to Iran, but it is thought that the country is developing biological weapons.

Biotechnology, at least in principle, is considered a strategic necessity for developing nations like Iran, and a legitimate tool of development, its benefits outweighing the environmental risks involved. Sustainable Developers are concerned about global warming and believe that planners must take it seriously into account.

Sustainable Developers are not necessarily anti-Western, although they oppose the ethos of Promethean individualism propagated in Western developmental models. They do not blame international development programs for poverty in the Global South and are neutral on anti-Western statements. They are neutral about evolving international environmental treaties. If the West enforced environmental standards and paid developing nations to adopt them, then perhaps international treaty regimes would be more important for this type.

Sustainable Developers address environmental issues from a bureaucratic scientific viewpoint, with optimism regarding planned development. Fossil and nuclear fuels and biotechnology can all be used in development. GNP growth can lead to fair income distribution and can include environmental goals and democratic means. Non-ideological, and not really anti-Western, Sustainable Developers believe in government-led import substitution over market forces and believe that the dangers of fossil fuels and global warming can be factored into developmental planning.

Bureaucratic Nationalists. This type is an opinion composite of a governmental marine scientist, a banker, and a female academic environmental engineer.

This type is technocratic, anti-Western, pessimistic, and autocratic. Pessimistic about global warming, they believe environmental and social collapse to be inevitable but are neutral about whether humanity will become extinct as a result. They do not believe that demographic transition is inevitable—that is, that population will decline as living standards rise—but believe that population must be forced down with government measures.

This type is not as strongly anti-Western as Cultural Traditionalists. Western international development programs have caused most Global South poverty, in their view, and the West has plundered the natural endowment of poor nations. The Western individualist ethos will inevitably result in ecological crash and the collapse of Western civilization. Bureaucratic Nationalists perceive no real international consensus around environmental issues, so it is unlikely that the West will pay for environmental repair in the Global South.

Bureaucratic Nationalists believe GNP maximization an important goal and that wealth should be fairly distributed by the system. But truly sustainable development is not possible. Bureaucratic Nationalists are willing to sacrifice environment to economic growth. Government planning should dominate the market in their view, but they are critical of the way in which planning has been executed so far. Environmental policy is piecemeal and defensive, and governmental incentives to business will only weakly affect the environment.

Thus, Bureaucratic Nationalists are anti-Western and pessimistic about the environmental future, which they are willing to sacrifice to GNP growth. They are as critical about governmental planning for sustainability as they are about the market. Their underlying ethos is bureaucratic and autocratic, framed within a certain pessimism.

One way to compare these types and clarify their differences is to construct indicators of the major issues in their universe of discourse. Table 10.1 illustrates these attitude differences by adding Z-scores on the important statement items in each subject area and converting them, for clarity of exposition, to standard scores [(Z x 10) + 50], which range from 1 to 100, with 50 being the median.

None of the four types is strong on Green items. Cultural Traditionalists (Religious Conservatives) score highest, probably because of the anti-materialistic premodern flavor of some of the statements. The Sustainable Developers follow in concern simply because of their conservationist perspective. The other two types are below the mean in this respect.

Cultural Traditionalists and Bureaucratic Nationalists score highest on concern for global warming, probably because of their pessimist worldviews rather than out of interest in the problem; the individual

Table 10.1. Major Issue Indicators

Attitudes	Green values	Greenhouse danger	Anti-Western Programs	Critique of Gov't Policy	Pessimism
Cultural Traditionalists	68	64	77	36	69
Developmentalists	<46	57	73	58	49
Sustainable Developers	55	58	45	65	56
Bureaucratic Nationalists	43	60	81	50	67

The chart below illustrates these attitude differences by adding Z-scores on the salient statement items in each subject area, and converting them, for clarity of exposition, to standard scores $[(Z \times 10) + 50]$, which range from 1 to 100, with 50 being the median.

Green ideology indicator = statements 5, 7, 18, 21, 25, 26, 27; Greenhouse concern = 29, 30; Anti-Western development model = 8, 10, 11, 12; Government Policy efficacy = 13, 14, 15, 19; Pessimism = 3, 6, 11.

statement scores are weak. Thus, Cultural Traditionalists and Bureaucratic Nationalists maintain the darkest view of human and natural prospects, one on religious and the other on scientific grounds. Sustainable Developers and Developmentalists are less given to apocalyptic visions of the future.

Sustainable Developers, followed by Developmentalists, have the highest regard for government planning to balance development and environment. Bureaucratic Nationalists show strong opposition to the Western developmental model and modernist culture and pessimism regarding the human and natural prospect. Neutral about government efficacy, they show some concern for global warming but manifest little interest in Green thinking.

Cultural Traditionalist attitudes are markedly anti-Western, pessimistic, and concerned with global warming as part of an apocalyptic vision of the world's end. They share only the anti-industrialism of Green values, not the constructive vision of an alternative future. Cultural Traditionalists have a low regard for government's ability to impact the Iranian situation.

Sustainable Developers and Developmentalists are not as anti-Western, due to their pragmatic emphasis on national autonomy and the mix of plan and market. Developmentalists are anti-Western but believe in governmental planning for high-priority "national reconstruction." They show technical concern for global warming, with little interest in Green positions, but are free of the pessimism of the other types. Sustainable Developers most strongly believe in inserting environmental concerns into governmental measures but are neutral about Green issues and global warming. They are not strongly pessimistic.

Figure 10.1 provides a speculative factional model combining the expert factional analysis reported in the first section of this chapter with the factorial attitude types discovered in this study. In the first stage of the revolution the religious forces defeated the seculars, but the latter reemerged under the protection of pragmatist reformers and are seen in the Developmentalist and Sustainable Developer types. The latter are anthropocentric, relatively more optimistic, and they believe in a mix of planning and markets and are aware of the future importance environmental issues.

The "nationalist reformers" emerge in the factorial types as Bureaucratic Nationalists, showing apocalyptic, anti-Western, anti-government, anti-business thinking. They appear to be authoritarian bureaucratic nationalists. Religious Conservatives are the original type of metaphysical premodern apocalyptic pessimists; their affiliation/ fission with neoliberals (socioeconomic conservatives) is speculative; they could divide into further types, but the Q-method instrument was not designed to capture these differences.

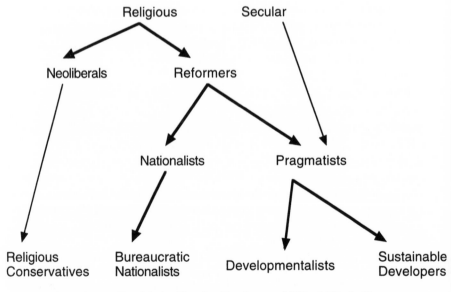

10.1. Speculative Graphing of Iranian Factions and Elite Attitude Types

Figure 10.2 maps Iranian elite types on postmodern/post-Fordist indicators, revealing that no Iranian elites are culturally postmodern. Only the Sustainable Developers are truly post-Fordist; the Cultural Traditionalists are premodern, as seen in their large number of neutral responses to the protocol. Again, the Q-method instrument was not designed to include premodern types such as Cultural Traditionalists and Hispanic Cultural Traditionalists.

All Iranian types are modernists, and only Sustainable Developers respond to the environmental concerns of the post-Fordist economy. Iranian informants suggest that the current policy spectrum is shifting

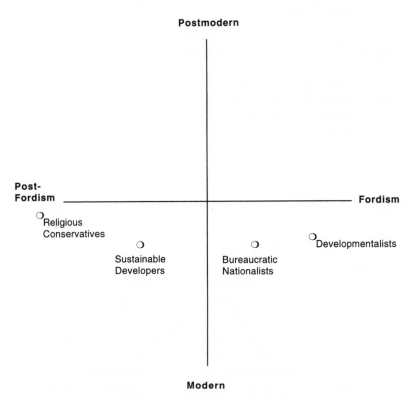

10.2. Iranian Attitude Types on Postmodern and Post-Fordist Indicators
Postmodern indicator is positive score on statement 18. The only alternative is a Green economy, with grassroots democracy, voluntary simplicity, sustainable production, and recycling.
Post-Fordist indicator is a negative score on statement 13. If government gave business information and incentives, not command and sanction, the market and entrepreneurs would protect the environment.

from religious to pragmatic-technocracy, and thus ideological arguments for a Green perspective may not find the same favorable response as does the hard economic reasoning behind sustainable development. The current emphasis in public life and media is on national reconstruction, growth, and recuperation after a decade of war. While not insensitive to environmental concerns, as borne out by new legislation and adherence to many international treaties, Iranian elites place absolute priority on rebuilding lost productive capacity. Environmental remediation is considered a luxury even though there is awareness of its growing urgency

Iqtidar Zadeh argues that Shiite Islam could be interpreted to include environmentalist concerns: "According to the Islamic world view man is ecologically dominant, but unlike materialist schools of thought he is not permitted to misuse the bounties of God on Earth and engage in excesses. . . . This world is only a temporary abode for man.

"As faithful adherents of Islam, [governments] must . . . set aside the idea of maximization of benefits without any regard for the maintenance of environmental balance. Our approach should be optimization of resources, and the alteration and modification of environmental features needed to be properly managed in accordance with Islamic principles."[6]

Some Tentative Conclusions

1. In Iran, we found four types of elite attitudes toward environment: Cultural Traditionalists, Developmentalists, Sustainable Developers, and Bureaucratic Nationalists. Environment remains a policy issue within the technobureaucracy. There is no apparent grassroots movement, political pressure, or public debate on environment. National reconstruction is paramount. Diffusion of environmental values may become possible only when production is restored and Iran is reintegrated with the community of nations.

2. The four types correspond well with expert analyses of factional structure in Iran, as seen in figure 10.1, and suggest a factional split between "Nationalists" (Cultural Traditionalists and Bureaucratic Nationalists) and "Pragmatists" (Developmentalists and Sustainable Developers).

3. In Iran, there is no apparent transition to a postmodern social paradigm. Modernist elites seem to be divided between metaphysical pessimism and pragmatic technocracy, with the latter apparently coming

to the fore as a new generation takes office. All types give priority to development and national independence, but they differ in the degree to which they think control over nature and incorporation of environmental concerns into technical planning are feasible. Iran is closed upon itself in its drive for autarchy, made urgent by marginalization from the world market and by strategic considerations.

4. Iran has a good record in ratifying international environmental treaties. Environmentalism could emerge at the intersection of religious and scientific worldviews and sustainable development. Sustainable development may be as far as Iran moves toward postmodern environmental concerns in the near future. However, the dangerous imbalance between population and carrying capacity, combined with high levels of pollution and unregulated environmental depredation, are acknowledged by the government to be major concerns for both Iran and the world community. It can only be hoped that Iranian moderates will open to the world community in order to find remediation for a tragic situation that verges on environmental collapse.

The New Environmentalism in the Global South

We have here modeled environmental politics in seven countries on postmodern value and post-Fordist economic coordinates and developed seven factorial attitude types from the comparative data. In this chapter we will review and summarize the argument to see what conclusions and future directions can fairly be drawn from this fieldwork.

1. Postmodern philosophy, primarily the works of Derrida, Foucault, and Baudrillard, tends to be dramatic, schematic, and extreme in its claims to absolute historical novelty. Postmodernism sees the "world as text" and therefore has a warrant to deconstruct, supplement, and evert the texts of Western modernism (Enlightenment liberalism), freeing the signs in these texts to spill out endlessly and to refer to other texts and signs. All subjectivity, origins, telos, linear narrative, means-ends relations, political practice, and hope for social change are dissolved in scholastic textual analysis.

Postmodernism claims to be absolutely new, a rupture with Western culture, but offers no real political hope because it deals with texts and not with opening political space. Its fashionable nihilism is unwarranted, because postmodernism is the decay product of avant-garde leftist modernism and continues some of its delusions: that human nature is purely a cultural product constructed in discourse, and that biology plays no role because language and culture set us apart from the animal kingdom. Changing discourses, textual criticism, and sign manipulation will not lead to liberation in a world of stubborn facts. Human nature cannot be changed by talking about it differently.

The claims of postmodernism cannot be defended in the face of massive biological evidence to the contrary and in the face of concrete history and political economy. Our epoch seems to be one of transitional modernism and globalization of corporate capitalism. Claims to a "rupture" with modernism, and the world as text, are premature, unprovable, metaphysical, and they deny scientific and historical facts that deconstructive methods cannot touch.

If there is at least one fact in the universe of discourse, then, all the claims of postmodernism to a world of signs and texts are false. If there is at least one fact (for example, the incontrovertible and massive data on evolution by natural and sexual selection, or the dynamics unearthed by quantum physics), then all signs (signifiers) necessarily point to, and are verified in, realities. Texts are then anchored in reality, and the relation between text and reality becomes a matter of evidence and testing. Deconstruction is confined to textual criticism, which ultimately must prove its truth or relevance against tangible evidences.

This result is elegant, because it restores the hope that science, theory, reason, philosophy can be used to change the world. It allows for liberation from reification and alienation and cancels the fashionable nihilism that ultimately reduces us to stupid uncomprehending silence. (As was said in Latin America under the dictatorships, "Hemos guardado un silencio bastante parecido a la estupidez"—"We have kept a silence which appears to be no more than utter stupidity.")

2. This is not to say that postmodernism does not express some of the attitudes of the new service- and knowledge-sector bourgeoisie, because it certainly is characteristic of their libertarianism, lifestyle engineering, hyperconsumerism of positional goods (status indicators), public deployment of the self (emotional work, feminization of culture, confessional subjectivity), multiculturalism (tempered with hip indifference), feminism, cynicism and apoliticism, risk aversion, and—this is the good part—environmental concern. Postmodernism also reflects their cynicism bordering on nihilism, detachment, "coolness," and utter egocentrism. This service/knowledge-sector bourgeoisie reflects the shift to a global post-Fordist economy grounded in the quaternary economic sector (information science, telecommunication, artificial intelligence, robotics, remote sensing, biotechnology, fine chemistry and engineering, new material sciences, nonlinear dynamics, complexity). And postmodernism reflects restructured transnational corporate production and distribution chains, built around global out-sourcing, dematerialization of material transformation into production of signs/symbols/events, automated small-batch production for niche markets, and deregulation of physical, ethical, legal, welfare, or moral constraints on free trade. Post-Fordism is a model of transition to global corporate hypercapitalism.

3. Poll data from the Global North indicate a shift to postmaterialism (the polling proxy of postmodernism). As the theory goes, prosperity drives postmaterial values, which can fluctuate with economic swings (period effects), to advance in a population. The inevitable march of generations (cohort replacement) overwhelms period effects in the long term and leads to the growing dominance of postmaterialist values. This survey literature fails to argue whether this shift is socially beneficial or not. The postmaterial transition seems clearest in large-batch data but tends to become muddier in the detail of fine-grained national studies, when different methods are used (rating versus ranking, multivariate analysis), or when different statistical controls are used for social class, education, employment status, ethnicity, and so forth.

This methodological debate about postmaterialism is not a central question in this book. Environmental values, however framed or manifested, are central to postmodernism and will outlive it, because they do not depend on affluence, cohort socialization, Maslow's hierarchy of needs, or statistical measurements. Environmental concern is grounded in hard objective reality, which urgently intrudes itself into all national and international political debate. Air and water pollution, global warming, ultraviolet radiation, overpopulation, massive extinctions, the death of the oceans, desertification, the loss of relict biomes—all these immediately threaten our continued existence without reference to our ideologies, attitudes, feelings, wishes, wants, or desires.

4. One of our most important findings is that Global South elites already have largely "postmodern" attitudes toward environmental issues. These attitudes are based on objective environmental threats to national security, economy, and elite survival. Poll data show that environment is also an urgent and growing issue among Global South mass publics, who are critical of government passivity and corporate corruption and are mobilizing themselves in thousands of local movements.

One can conjecture that Global South elites are driven only partly by this mass pressure because the message is distorted and weakened by fragmented unrepresentative party systems and dishonest mass media. However, the elites in our sample show a strong proclivity toward postmodern ideas, international viewpoints on environment, foreign education, and a general cosmopolitanism, which lead them to deal with environment on a non-ideological, pragmatic, data-driven, dialogal, and moderate basis.

5. In the Global North, environmental politics are transmitted through party and electoral systems. Proportional representation opens

political space for articulation of new parties, while "first past the post" electoral systems lead to co-optation of environmental rhetoric by standing parties and require Greens to become more contestatory and antisystem. Northern Greens uniformly suffer from their single-issue focus, internal faction, and distrust of parliamentary politics and must eventually broaden their program to deal with issues such as welfare state versus neoliberal deregulation, unemployment, international relations, immigration, and labor relations, in order to tap their extensive latent electorates. If they do not acquire this political maturity and flexibility, their green banner risks being seized by agile left and right parties, which are already realigning their ideologies to capture new electorates. While this effect would be beneficial in the sense of "greening" the political spectrum, and skewing the left-right spectrum upward into postmodern issue space, Greens also risk seeing their platform dissolve into rhetoric and official inaction.

In contrast, Global South Greens are not effectively organized as national parties but form networks of grassroots environmental groups led by elites and having direct access to decision makers in leading sectors. Local struggles around single issues are often skillfully leveraged into international grant money and national government access. Global South Greens benefit from being antipolitical because the standing parties are often coalitions of notables with low public credibility, with no consistent ideology or program, and whose decisions are filtered through semiautonomous bureaucratic, military, and police apparatuses. Thus, Greens work to prevent co-optation by parties. They avoid polarizing ideological discourses in favor of data-driven negotiation, skillful international pressure tactics, and personal compromises with the effective power brokers in government and business.

Global South Green discourse is not highly developed in terms of ideological or theoretical consistency. But it has the advantage of substituting the apocalyptic quasi-religious style of its Northern counterpart for a scientific discourse that is easier for elites to digest. The muted discourse of Global South Greens makes good sense when elite media sensationalize and politicize an essentially consensual and apolitical issue, and where media can rarely be used for public mobilization or pressure. Greens, who are in reality sophisticated insiders, benefit from appearing to be outsiders. Green movements and mini-parties include important scientific, academic, and government elites, and their deliberations and negotiations with networks of power brokers often result in concrete policy.

Grassroots movements and Green parties are already bricked into

Global South governments (in my sample), which are taking active measures to avert environmental risks to their own political and national security. Green movements seem to have much better government access than the old left and labor movements, because the situation is so serious, data are readily available, elites are concerned, and the leaders of government, business, and environment groups share international education and postmodern attitudes toward the issues. Speaking a common language, and driven by objective circumstances, elites and movement leaders are bound to come to more agreement than labor could with capital (simply because their economic interests and worldviews were always at loggerheads).

6. Neither postmaterialism based on rising affluence nor the sociology of new social movements—nor rational choice economics—can explain the surge of environmental movements in the Global South. Neoliberal theories of sustainable development, based on the idea that export capitalism and free trade must first create the affluence necessary to purchase a clean environment, simply ignore the facts. Global South majorities are already environmentalist and mobilizing around the issue. Elites are already aware and concerned, all in the absence of affluence. These theories share the fault of ignoring the complex motivations and lifeways of primary producers in favor of simple marginalist models that see politics as a business, not a question of survival. These models and abstractions dissolve the moment one steps into the field. It is a shame that global policy makers take them so seriously and that social scientists keep propagating them.

7. The findings of field research in seven nations of the Global South can be related to the hypotheses developed in chapter 1.

Regarding *culturalism*, we expected each country to have a unique "political culture" and each to deal with environmental politics in a different way. This proved simply to be wrong. Some of the seven factorial attitude types consistently recurred in all countries studied, despite their diversity of languages, cultures, religions, and political and economic systems. These seven countries include Catholic, Orthodox, Protestant, Confucian, Muslim, Hindu, Buddhist, and Animist religions, and the political systems include capitalist democracy, democratic transitions from military or bureaucratic socialist regimes, controlled corporativist democracy, religious autocracy, and a neocolonial "commonwealth." The languages and cultures in this sample can be counted in the hundreds. Yet the elites, Western educated, internationally networked, and cosmopolitan, reflect postmodern environmentalism and articulate their platforms in terms of the international debate.

As regards *sectoral cleavages,* we assumed that environmental attitudes are organized along sectoral (occupational) lines and that the main conflict would be between big business (polluters), government (regulators), and environmentalists (pressure groups). The data showed this to be a wrong assumption. There was strong consensus among elites in all sectors in the seven countries studied; the seven factorial attitude types all contain strong sectoral mixing. Occupation does not necessarily determine environmental attitudes. Because there is strong interlocking among the small elites in these countries, the environmental issue is not as ideologically or politically conflictual as it could be.

In terms of the *left-right dimension,* we expected environmental attitudes to line up along this dimension, with environmentalists on the left, business on the right, and government regulators in the middle. But this was too simple. The left-right spectrum of Fordist modernism is being superseded by attitude sets that slew obliquely upward into postmodern/post-Fordist dimensions.

8. The transitions from modernism to postmodernism, and Fordism to post-Fordism, provide axes on which the shift from old to new politics may be mapped. This hypothesis was strongly confirmed in the cross-national data but requires some explanation.

Figure 11.1 represents a speculative mapping of attitudinal transition in the developed West, focusing on environmental movements. The vertical axis shows the transition from modern to postmodern worldviews, and the horizontal axis reflects the change from Fordist to post-Fordist political economy. The old politics occupies the bottom right quadrant and its spectrum spans liberal capitalism, social democracy, Eurocommunism, and the New Left. The new politics lies on the slant, between the upper left and lower right quadrants.

The corners of the diagram express the historical tendency, or telos, of each quadrant. The modernist worldview combined with Fordist production tends toward the liberal capitalism of quadrant three—the hegemonic quasi-corporatist welfare state created after World War II, which came into crisis in the 1970s. The combination of modernism and post-Fordism leads to the "disorganized capitalism" of quadrant four, in which the disintegrative effects of post-Fordist global economy on the state, social classes, civil society, and economy lead to a recrudescence of modernist values in the core, a reaction against post-modernity on the part of social strata displaced by it. The reassertion of modernist values in peripheral Fordist world regions, or in the post-Fordist core, creates misalignment between ideology, the structures of civil society, and the world economy. These contradictions lead to in-

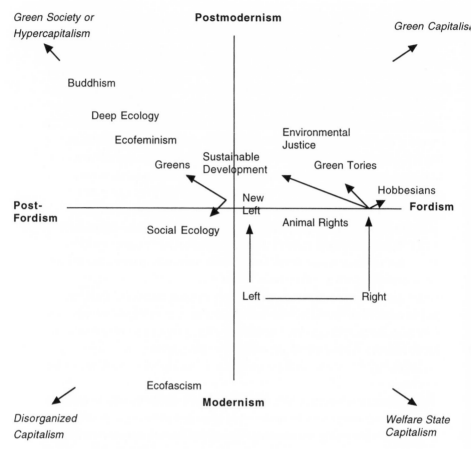

Green Society or   **Postmodernism**
Hypercapitalism   *Green Capitalis*

Buddhism

Deep Ecology
                                                   Environmental
            Ecofeminism   Justice
                        Sustainable
            Greens   Development   Green Tories
                                                              Hobbesians
Post-   New   **Fordism**
Fordism   Left
                        Social Ecology   Animal Rights

                        Left ———————— Right

                        Ecofascism
                        Modernism
Disorganized   *Welfare State*
Capitalism   *Capitalism*

11.1. Speculative Model of Western Attitude Shift

creasing frustration and violence, because no policy generates anticipated consequences.

For example, the U.S. reactionary right, with its use of religious,
coded racist and sexist, and anti–new politics rhetoric, is attempting to
restore the lost social idyll of liberal capitalism, while at the same time
supporting such institutions as WTO, NAFTA, and the Asian Pacific
Economic Cooperation network (APEC), which represent the very post-
Fordist globalization that creates the postmodern culture they reject.
Reactionary authoritarian social regulation uses pseudolibertarian and
post-Fordist appeals against the postmodern multiculturalism, feminism, and environmentalism that these engender.

But reactive nationalism and increasingly violent cultural exclusivity work against the grain of the transnational corporate economy that the right promotes in the name of neoliberal "free trade." Repetition of ideological-religious-cultural formulas perceived to have brought the United States to hegemony in the old Fordist economy is counterproductive in post-Fordism. Global South equivalents of disorganized capitalism involve nationalist, nativist, xenophobic, tribal, and fundamentalist reactions, and these can take quite complex and baffling forms—as in the breakdown of Yugoslavia in tribal wars, or the Iranian revolution of 1979, in which leftist economic/cultural nationalism was captured by the religious right and used to purge the radical/modernizing middle-class movements that brought about the downfall of the Shah.

The combination of postmodernist values and Fordist production in quadrant two tends toward a social program of "green capitalism"; that is, technological conversion of production and distribution to conserve resources and wilderness for economic values (tourism, gene banking), to create cost savings through recycling and energy efficiency, and to capitalize on a green corporate image. Green capitalism avoids state regulation by corporate environmental programs, which, it is argued, are more cost effective, industry specific, and technologically advanced than government command and control and do not restrain free trade.

Corporate stockholders are broadened, at least in theory, to include investors, customers, and the local community. Recycling, energy efficiency, and technological substitution of polluting processes enhance a company's creditworthiness and public image and diffuse pressure from environmental groups. But companies cannot move too far in advance of regulatory standards without suffering declining profitability, problems of intellectual property rights in technologies which ethically should be diffused to other companies, and rising Global South demands for technology transfer.[1]

Green capitalism does not reassess and restructure production, transportation, and commodities in terms of social and environmental need and feasibility but does so only in terms of market demand and profitability. Thus, pollution control and process conversion will always occupy that small portion of corporate investment which can be paid back in advertising gains and market shares.

Also, at the international level, the World Trade Organization, the world's predominant treaty regime, uses a "product over process rule," which allows only the end product, not the process by which it is elaborated, to be considered when regulating potential environmental damage. Import restrictions directed against the process of production are "in restraint of trade" and may be struck down by a secret treaty tribunal. This rule represents a strong disincentive for industry to substitute polluting technologies and a positive incentive to site smokestacks in the Global South.

Driven by fear of government regulation and public pressure, green capitalism wants to give economic incentives to make business self-regulating. However, without the negative incentive of command and control regulation, the small positive incentive of marginal profitability will not ensure continued environmental performance. Post-Fordist niche markets drive intensive industrial conversion, a side-effect of which may be lowered environmental impacts, but this benefit will decline as clean technologies age, leading to a new round of regulation and struggle over standards. Green capitalism weakens public regulatory pressure and co-opts "responsible" environmentalists and regulators, so that business can lapse back into profit taking while gradually slowing the pace of environmental investment.

The combination of post-Fordist economy and postmodern worldviews in quadrant one points toward an ambiguous social outcome. The optimal outcome is a green economy with sustainable production, maximized throughput, minimized input and output, knowledge-intensive production, a radically reduced human population, bioregional lifestyles, participatory democracy, and diversity maintenance for both natural and cultural species. The worst outcome is a descent into hypercapitalism, the production of virtual reality—signs, symbols, events—for a small elite of superconsumers and marginalization of the majority of humanity, and nature, into an criminalized global underground economy.

Green capitalism represents a short- to medium-term extension of capitalism's lease, until social and ecological externalities constrict the system to a few affluent regions and a limited elite. Disorganized capitalism and hypercapitalism, unsustainable, catastrophic, hypercomplex productive and regulatory relations, can only crash into chaos and recover at much lower levels of organization and comity. The positive alternative, a green economy, has yet to be articulated in consistent political theory and social policy, although there are many candidate ideologies along the curve of the new politics.

9. Postmodern/post-Fordist new politics could potentially create a wide range of new environmentalist ideologies, which could structure more coherent social movements in twenty-first-century civil society.

Ascending the scale from Fordist modernism (quadrant three) to post-Fordist postmodernism (quadrant one), we find a range of ideologies-in-waiting. Inscribed on figure 11.1 we find the following ideological tendencies.

The *animal rights* movement, which lies in the modernist/Fordist (liberal capitalist) quadrant, argues, on either utilitarian grounds (suffering) or liberal grounds (natural right), that the social contract should be extended to include other sentient beings, which have a natural interest in their own life and suffer from humans using them for food or raw material. The burden of proof is placed on humans who would destroy these animals to prove that there is no alternative and that an important interest is being served. Despite their apparently progressive extension of contract theory, animal rights activists tend in practice to be reactionary, caring more for specific animals than for ecological balance, which must sometimes be remediated by moving or eliminating animals.[2]

In the postmodern Fordist (green capitalist) quadrant we find *Green Toryism*, proponents of which reject Thatcherite neoliberalism and want to use state regulation of the economy (to protect markets from predators), aiming to preserve the environment, local communities, and cultural traditions; to enlarge public goods and services; and to rebuild cities in socially and environmentally friendly ways. Population control is needed to reach a steady state or social equilibrium at more sustainable levels.[3]

Hobbesians argue that individual rational choice leads to destruction of the commons, or market failure, and privatization leads to creation of free riders. Earth is a spaceship with limited resources. Thus, the state must create a social contract that enables it to make drastic cuts in population, to curtail individual liberties, and to regulate the environment strongly. Peoples in the Global South who overpopulate or draw down their resources are subject to triage; that is, they must suffer the natural consequences of their improvidence.[4]

The *environmental justice* movement emerged in minority communities disproportionately burdened with the pollution, toxic waste, occupational, and health hazards of industrial society. The beneficiaries of this waste disposal subsidy, white upper-middle-class elites, share out little of their wealth generated through such pollution. These movements in minority communities are multicultural, often led by women, and nationally networked. They argue that environment is a natural right and involves questions of social and economic justice.[5]

Proponents of *sustainable development*, spanning the postmodern-

Fordist/post-Fordist quadrant (i.e., conflicted between green capitalism and hypercapitalism), argue that the ecological problem comes from the true costs of using nature not being reflected in the market because of price distortions, government subsidies, and regulations that do not answer a cost-benefit test. Rational pricing and property rights in resources allow the market to align the economy with natural limits. Governments should regulate only when benefits outweigh administrative costs and do not distort the market. Free trade maximizes rational global resource use, promotes export of environmentally friendly technologies, and should not be constrained by domestic regulation.[6]

Crossing over into the post-Fordist/postmodernist political space, we find the *Greens*, complex political parties held together by an uneasy consensus on ecological values, alternative lifestyles, feminism, grassroots democracy, disarmament, and nonviolence. Greens work within the dominant system to open political space for groups and movements normally excluded. They are highly critical of centralized decision making and seek to restore local communities and grassroots participatory democracy.[7]

Deep ecology is most representative of the postmodern/post-Fordist quadrant. Rather than social revolution, deep ecology seeks self-realization, consciousness of unity with nature, and expansion of empathy to include other peoples, species, and nature. Humans must admit our ignorance and inability to control nature, history, and technology. Progress, growth, and development are no longer viable goals.

We must instead evolve toward soft energy, low-impact alternative technologies, preserving remaining wilderness, defending native cultures from Westernization, and encouraging a plurality of philosophies and responsible lifestyles. The human population must be drastically reduced, at the same time preserving its ethnic and cultural diversity, and our standard of living must be radically simplified to open space for spiritual self-realization. Direct nonviolent action is required for change, "acts beautiful in themselves" that transform the actor.[8]

Ecofeminism proceeds on a number of fronts, attacking patriarchy, racism, classism, speciesism; critiquing the logic of modern science; reworking language to create "gender-sensitive" concepts and theories; and attempting to change media and daily language in order to socialize a new generation into androgyny.[9]

The *social ecology* movement, which is post-Fordist/materialist, argues that environmental problems ultimately derive from ethnic, class, and gender conflicts. A social movement to overthrow class, gender domination, and hierarchy would allow humans to take moral responsibility for their own evolution. Anarcho-syndicalist communitarian social organization, direct democracy and common property, and a return to the "original matriarchy" constitute their political goals.[10]

These then, are the main trends in environmentalist ideology and new politics in the Global North. Quite unfortunately, the new politics also includes cartoonlike new age religions, infantile libertarianism, fanatical religions, xenophobic nationalisms, know-nothing reaction, criminal subcultures, perverts, racists, and fascists, which barely reach the margins of any possible conceptual map and are best approached through psychopathology.

The cultural transitions from modernism to postmodernism and economic transition from Fordism to post-Fordism provide axes on which the transverse shift from old to new politics may be mapped and allow the speculative mapping of emergent political ideologies of the new environmentalism in figure 11.1.

Note that a new left and the new right are forming within postmodernism, around the different social goals of a green society versus green capitalism. The postmodern and post-Fordist axes of our model provide a conceptual map on which Global South elite attitudes toward environment can be arrayed.

10. The trend away from modernist Fordism toward postmodern post-Fordist new politics is as clear in the Global South as in the Global North. The mapping of elite attitudes in India, Brazil, Korea, Puerto Rico, Mexico, Romania, and Iran on these same axes clearly shows this shift into a new political space. Figure 11.2 summarizes the seven factorial attitude types found in field data from seven nations, by arraying them in postmodern and post-Fordist attitude space. The factorial attitude types found in our fieldwork are the following.

Greens are both postmodern and post-Fordist. They value life and biodiversity and want a green economy with energy efficiency and soft power, recycling, democratic popular management, regulation of business, and adherence to treaty regimes. They are mildly critical of modernist developmentalism. Greens are technology averse and want a redefinition of basic human "needs." They are concerned about global warming but do not share an apocalyptic vision of the world's future. They do not see population as a problem and only mildly support women's rights. Greens are moderate, non-ideological, and open to data-driven dialog with other types. They do not promote formation of Green parties, but want to "green" the political spectrum through mass mobilization and interelite dialog.

Political Greens are elites who have absorbed environmentalist rheto-

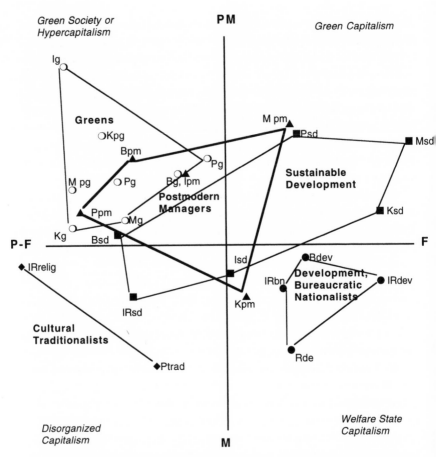

11.2. Third World Elite Environmental Attitudes Mapped on Postmodern/
Modern and Post-Fordist/Fordist Axes
Key: Country Names—B = Brazil, I = India, IR = Iran, K = Korea, M = Mexico,
P = Puerto Rico, R = Romania.
Types—g = Greens, pg = Political Greens, sd = Sustainable Developers, pm =
Postmodern Managers, bn = Bureaucratic Nationalists, dev = Developmen-
talists, trad = Cultural Traditionalists.

ric but have not formulated concrete policy positions. They have not
integrated theory and practice. They blame Fordism for plundering
the Global South but do not blame international aid agencies for concrete programs. They would like to mix economic growth with conservation, recycling, and energy efficiency but will also countenance hard
fuel cycles and high technologies. They are not pessimistic about glo-

bal warming or overpopulation and are neutral about democracy and state versus market issues.

Political Greens represent leaders with environmental awareness but whose positions do not allow them to develop concrete programs implementing such ideas. Given the right mass mobilization and political conjuncture, Political Greens could play a positive role in environmental preservation. Lacking this, they will not take the initiative. They are just as postmodern and post-Fordist as Greens, or more so, but are constrained by their executive jobs from developing their ideas beyond what is politically feasible or prudent.

Sustainable Developers span the Fordism/post-Fordism spectrum within postmodern attitude space. They form a broad band of attitudes but tend toward green capitalism. They correspond to the neoliberal free trade "sustainable development" concept elaborated at UNCED in Rio de Janeiro in 1992. Sustainable Developers are anthropocentric rationalists who reject apocalyptic visions and critiques of Western Fordist developmentalism. Reason, technology, regulated markets, and democracy all can conserve nature. Future development must proceed around technological transformation of industry, but Sustainable Developers distrust business and believe that regulation as well as incentives are needed for conservation. Sustainable Developers are not as risk averse as Greens and are willing to consider using fossil and nuclear fuels and biotechnology.

Postmodern Managers occupy postmodern factorial space with their main concentration in post-Fordism. This type overlaps Greens and Sustainable Developers and mediates between their differing social projects: a green society versus green capitalism. Managers are concerned to develop environmentally sound economies and technologies and are risk averse regarding fossil and nuclear fuel cycles and biotechnology. They are quite worried about global warming and plan to counter its effects. Managers are key decision makers in all of the three sectors who see capitalism evolving away from its obsessive extensive growth. But they distrust business and are neutral about using economic incentives versus direct regulation. Managers are pro-democratic, and look to international treaty regimes and aid to create environmentally responsible development.

Developmentalists are modernist Fordists who believe in rational management, technology, growth, and the primacy of markets. Markets can blend development and conservation and can control the effects of global warming, hard fuels, biotechnology, and population growth.

Developmentalists reject green and sustainable development notions as utopian and intend to maintain market-driven economies. But they are aware of environmental problems and, of all types, are the most democratic and most favorable to women's rights, probably in the economic sense of allowing them to enter the work force, rather than supporting feminist ideas. This type may be evolving away from the modernist/Fordist quadrant toward the postmodern/Fordist space of sustainable development.

Bureaucratic Nationalists are Global South Hobbesians, modernist Fordists who take a technocratic, bureaucratic, authoritarian perspective on environment and development. They are not democrats and distrust both business and markets. But they are quite critical of government's capacity for regulation and see the need for large-scale government modernization to improve both ecological and economic situations.

They consider Greens utopian and range from skeptical to pessimistic about the human future. Hard fuels and high technology are necessary for development, and Bureaucrats see little risk in them. They are neutral to hostile on women's rights. Bureaucratic Nationalists strongly criticize Western Fordist development models and think the West will collapse. No treaty regimes or side payments are acceptable to them, as they want purely national solutions to environmental and developmental issues—import substitution and autarchy—but are pessimistic about their being realized.

Cultural Traditionalists are premodern organic conservatives who stand entirely outside the postmodern/post-Fordist model. These types emerged in Iran and Puerto Rico and consist of Iranian Shiite religious conservatives and Hispanic Catholic traditionalists. Traditionalists are strongly critical of Western modernist culture and economy for destroying traditional values and community, pillaging nature, and dooming the human race to extinction. They are neutral about technology, energy, population, and women's issues. Such organic conservatives (like Grey's Green Tories) can provide Greens with issue-specific coalition partners in the fight against corporate power and neoliberal ideology and in restoring communities, organic farming, and reurbanization of lost public spaces. But this type will not assist in postmodern lifestyle issues, nor will they have a strong brief for social justice issues.

These seven types comprise a spectrum of environmental attitudes among Global South elites, and a compact model of potential policy directions and forms of regulation that could emerge as the post-Fordist economy matures and transcends its neoliberal origins toward novel systems of economy and governance.

11. Global South elites, because of international education, interests, and contacts, mirror many postmodern values of the North. This is manifest in figure 11.2, which maps the seven types in postmodern/post-Fordist space, in effect summarizing the diagrams in the national studies. In the lower right quadrant, the liberal capitalist mode, lie the Developmentalists and Bureaucratic Nationalists. Cultural Traditionalists lie in post-Fordist/modernist space: note that the Q-method protocol was not designed to measure their premodern concerns. Thus, a third premodern dimension emerged that was not anticipated and therefore not measured in the field space of our model.

Greens and Political Greens inhabit postmodern/post-Fordist space and tend toward a green society. Sustainable Developers lie in all four quadrants, but the bulk of them lie in Fordist/postmodern space, showing that they largely advocate the green capitalist model that emerged at the Rio UNCED conference. The surprising finding is that Postmodern Managers, the executives in business, environmental groups, and government, are largely postmodern and post-Fordist. Their political project, forestalled by their dependent economies, would likely be hypercapitalism rather than the green model, which they tend to criticize.

Note that the trend line is from modernist/Fordism to postmodern/post-Fordism, as predicted in the figure 11.1 model of ideological and attitude shifts.

This is perhaps the major finding of this book: a postmodern/post-Fordist value shift in the area of environmental concern is occurring among Global South elites, and this shift gives priority to regulatory concerns and industrial conversion to intensive sustainable development. Whether or not these countries have the capacity to realize environmental regulation, conservation, preservation, or repair will depend, in most instances, on side payments and technical assistance from the international community.

12. The trajectories of Global North environmental ideologies, and of Global South elite attitudinal types, both move together from the old liberal capitalist welfare state toward a bifurcation. The ideological choice is now between modern/post-Fordist green capitalism and a leap into something new, a postmodern/post-Fordist environmental ethos that can either result in a truly green society (bioregional, sustainable, participatory) or slide into an unsustainable and rather night-

marish hypercapitalism—which is not the main goal of any type but which could emerge as the unwanted product of their conflict or of ecological chaos and social breakdown.

Another possible vector is the fall downward into disorganized capitalism due to the irresolvable contradictions between post-Fordist and Fordist productive systems and between old modernist left-right ideologies and postmodern ideas and social strata. This is less likely, but it represents a scenario of socioeconomic breakdown. Western environmental ideologies, although largely postmodern, are strongly divided between post-Fordist and Fordist economic visions; they strain toward either green society or green capitalism as their telos.

This tension does not seem so evident among Global South elites because there is so much overlap among Greens, Postmodern Managers, and Sustainable Developers, indicating a large area of consensus. The overlap also indicates the crucial mediating role of Postmodern Managers between distinct social programs and socioeconomic trajectories, between Greens and Sustainable Developers. Thus, the options are narrower, more easily mediated, and less ideologized than in the Global North. The environmental new politics could, paradoxically, come more easily in the Global South than in the North, where there are more sunk costs in the old productive system and relations, where politics are more entrenched and ideologically developed, and where there is a broader range of interests composing the elite bloc.

Global South countries may reap the advantage of the novelty and flexibility of their democracies, just as they face all the disadvantages of dependent insertion into the new global economy. But they will face governmental incapacity, augmented by debt and neoliberal deregulation, to create the technostructures needed to regulate ecosystems. Often the government's writ does not run beyond the boundaries of the capital city. Local elites and mafias have understandings with the army and security services and wreak their will without hindrance. Global South governments are usually coalitions of local elite powerbrokers rather than rational bureaucracies, and thus environmental regulation, however well drafted and designed, is often vetoed on the ground.

Global South state structures require modernization, technological streamlining, and the centralization of regulatory processes, in order to become more democratic and effective. But, of course, this runs counter to neoliberal international aid agencies and banks, which use debt leverage to force an economic model based on possessive individualism and atomistic contractarianism (combined with heavy-handed moralism) on societies with lineage coalitional structures as the principal actors. Post-Fordist liberalism is as blind as Fordist developmentalism to cultural differences in power relations and insists in applying "one-size-fits-all" neoliberal economics (based on a brutally egoistic utilitarian "rational choice") to all nations. Such policy cannot but yield contradictory results; at their most successful, hypercapitalism and ecological breakdown; at their least successful, disorganized capitalism and social breakdown.

Global South Greens have evolved a moderate, consensual, information-driven politics, from which we may learn. We may yet outgrow our destructive adolescence and gain the maturity to comprehend what Daoists, Buddhists, and native peoples have been saying for millenia: the world is not a juxtaposition of things but a complex network of interrelations. Our actions affect the whole and return to reward and punish us with their feedback. All knowledge is positional and limited by this network, and there is no outside standpoint. Our best rule of action is "do no harm." If we do not relearn these basic truths, and reconstruct our future society, economy, and technologies around them, then we will deserve the extinction that is our probable future.

The new postmodern green politics is complex and sophisticated. It is not based on corporativist party building but on international and national networking, local mobilizations, and tactical alliances between parties, government, business, and environmentalists to get access and apply maximum pressure where crucial decisions are being made. This new politics will require large informational and emotional inputs, and the players will constantly turn over, requiring aggressive recruitment and training. But it is no small victory when a species or ecosystem is preserved intact. The game is worth the candle.

As the Buddha said in the Sutta-Nipata,

> let all embracing thoughts for all that lives be thine,
> an all-embracing love for all the universe
> in all its heights and depths and breadth,
> unstinted love unmarred by hate within,
> not arousing enmity.

This would, indeed, be a New Politics.

Appendix: National Q-Sort Data

India

Person Sample

Person	Organization	City	Factor Weight
SUSTAINABLE DEVELOPERS			
4, f	Center for Cultural Research	New Delhi (N.D.)	0.62
6, f	INTACH (Indian National Trust)	N.D.	0.80
9, f	Center for Policy Research	N.D.	1.22
14	INFAR, Concern for Calcutta	Calcutta	1.29
17	Bombay Natural History Society	Bombay	2.37
19	Bombay Natural History Society	Bombay	1.1
30	Development Alternatives	N.D.	1.17
GREENS			
1	Center for Study of Developing Societies	N.D.	1.17
2	Lokanyan (environmental NGO)	N.D.	2.18
3, f	Institute of Economic Growth	N.D.	0.41
5, f	INTACH (environmental NGO)	N.D.	0.36
7, f	INTACH	N.D.	0.77
16	Sanctuary (environmental NGO)	Bombay	1.79
21, f	Environmental Education	Calcutta	0.67
22	Environmental Education	Calcutta	0.57
23, f	Seva Mandir (private development agency)	Udaipur	0.83
25, f	Indira Gandhi Center for Env. Science	Jaipur	0.52
27	Indian Institute of Public Administration	N.D.	1.02
31, f	Development Alternatives (environmental NGO)	N.D.	1.49
32	Development Alternatives	N.D.	0.79

Person	Organization	City	Factor Weight
33, f	Center for Science and Environment	N.D.	1.32
34	Save Bombay Committee (environmental NGO)	Bombay	2.13

POSTMODERN MANAGERS

Person	Organization	City	Factor Weight
8	U.N. Environmental Program	N.D.	0.61
10	World Wildlife Fund	N.D.	0.55
11	World Bank	N.D.	1.36
12	Minister, Planning Commission	N.D.	1.84
13	2d Minister, Ministry of Environment	N.D.	1.18
15	INFAR, biotechnologist	N.D.	0.90
18	Save Bombay Committee	Bombay	0.64
20	Bombay Natural History Society	Bombay	0.65
24	Seva Mandir	Udaipur	0.27
26	World Wildlife Fund	N.D.	0.67
28, f	Multiple Action Research Group (env. NGO)	N.D.	0.73
29	Development Alternatives	N.D.	0.51

Statement Scores

	SD	G	PM
1. All living things have a right to exist.	1.3	1.4	1.5
2. Sustainability was the original economy of the species. To restore it now will require a revolution as great as the industrial revolution.	.7	1.2	.4
3. The view of man as the infallible creator, whose salvation lies in his own technology, is the origin of cosmic vandalism.	1.6	.8	–0.1
4. Biological diversity must be treated as a common heritage of mankind, to be indexed, used, and above all preserved.	1.5	1.4	1.8
5. Life on earth is a single organism which modifies the atmosphere to serve its own needs.	0	–.6	.2

6. Humanity is doomed to extinction. Our main effort
   must be to preserve maximum diversity so nature can carry
   on after us.   .2   −.6 −1.0

7. Traditional farming mimics nature and is more
   sustainable than Western monoculture. But we kill natives
   and their knowledge.   −.3   1.1   .8

8. Development means the rich redistributing natural
   resources in their own favor.   −1.1   −1.6 −.6

9. Foolish international development programs caused most
   Third World poverty, revolution, and environmental damage.   −1.6   .6 −.6

10. Poor countries must develop without fossil fuel dependency,
    thus avoiding the cost, pollution, and alienation of the West. −1.2   −.2 −.5

11. Environmental collapse and violent conflict over
    resources destroyed most ancient civilizations, and will
    surely destroy the West.   −.7   −.3 −1.1

12. Western development plunders and destroys nature, uses
    the Third World as a dumpsite and laboratory.   −.3   1.3 −.1

13. If government gave business information and
    incentives, not command and sanction, the market and
    entrepreneurs would protect the environment.   0   −1.6 −.5

14. Environmental policy is piecemeal and defensive,
    not global as required by the urgency of the problem.   1.6   .3   1.2

15. Democracy cannot meet the challenge of imminent
    ecocatastrophe, because it acts slowly and through   −.6   −.6 −1.2
    compromise.

16. East and West are converging toward a social democratic
    model with a mixed economy, equity, and control of
    environmental damage.   .8   −1.6   .3

17. European Community legislation, Law of the Sea,
    and Antarctic treaties show growing international
    consensus about environment.   .7   −.8   .7

	SD	G	PM
18. The only alternative is a Green economy, with grassroots democracy, voluntary simplicity, sustainable production, and recycling.	−.3	1.7	.7
19. Economic development on a sound environmental basis is possible and cost effective.	1.4	.6	1.6
20. If the West enforces and pays for high environmental standards, then the world's nature will be conserved.	.5	−.9	−1.1
21. Maximizing GNP means maximizing cost, resource waste, pollution, and inequality.	−1.9	.6	−1.0
22. Third World population will not decline naturally due to rising affluence; if not forced down it will prevent even basic development.	.3	−.5	−.6
23. Respect for women should not be based on having children. Women's rights are the key to population control.	−.7	1.2	1.7
24. Stop environmental degradation and population growth will decline by itself.	−1.4	−.1	−1.6
25. Investment in energy efficiency and recycling can reduce fossil fuel demand without sacrificing growth.	1.2	.7	1.2
26. The world economy of the next century will not be powered by coal, oil, gas, or uranium.	−.1	−.3	.1
27. Nuclear power's long-term costs in waste disposal, accidents, and terrorist threats far outweigh its benefits.	1.2	1.4	−1.2
28. Why spend large sums to avert Greenhouse effects that may not happen? Better to adjust if climate changes appear.	−1.1	−1.9	−2.3
29. Greenhouse radiation and acid rain will disrupt oceanic and land food chains, and dramatically change the climate.	.7	.6	−.3
30. Greenhouse warming will lead to death by flooding, famine, of up to a billion people.	−.3	.1	−.6
31. Biotechnology is the next step in human evolution. Our destiny is to control evolutionary change on this planet.	−1.8	−1.6	.5

32. The hidden ethical basis of biotechnology is eugenics.   −.8   −.4   −.3

33. Biotechnology replaces free scientific information with secrecy, collusion, and research geared toward corporate needs.   −.8   0   −.2

34. Biotechnology offers cheaper, quicker ways to improve Third World diet than costly mechanical-chemical technologies.   0   −1.0   1.2

35. The risks posed by release of engineered microbes or plants into the environment far outweigh commercial gains.   1.1   .5   −.1

36. Biotechnology R&D is not a luxury for the Third World but a strategic necessity for avoiding permanent underdevelopment.   .4   −.8   1.4

Typal Q-Sorts

−5	−4	−3	−2	−1	0	+1	+2	+3	+4	+5

SUSTAINABLE DEVELOPERS

−5	−4	−3	−2	−1	0	+1	+2	+3	+4	+5
21	31	24	8	23	6	17	27	19	3	14
	9	10	33	15	13	29	35	1	4	
		28	32	7	5	20	16	25		
			11	18	34	36	2			
				12	26	22				
					30					

GREENS

−5	−4	−3	−2	−1	0	+1	+2	+3	+4	+5
28	8	13	20	5	14	9	2	1	27	18
	31	16	17	15	30	21	7	12	4	
		34	36	22	33	29	3	23		
			6	32	24	19	25			
				11	10	35				
					26					

POSTMODERN MANAGERS

−5	−4	−3	−2	−1	0	+1	+2	+3	+4	+5
28	24	15	21	9	26	18	34	1	23	4
	27	11	6	22	3	31	25	36	19	
		20	30	10	35	2	7	14		
			8	13	12	16	17			
				29	33	5				
					32					

Korea

Korean Subjects' Demographics and Factor Loadings

		Demographics			Factor Loadings		
Person	Age	Organization	Title	G	PM	SD	PG
11, f	23	NGO7	Executive officer	*.682*	.098	.146	.038
66, m	30	NGO3	Member	*.760*	.220	.064	.063
25, m	19	Yonsei Univ.	Science student	*.637*	.068	.060	.206
61, m	29	NGO2	High executive	*.569*	.069	.191	.039
72, m	35	NGO6	Member	*.669*	.209	.115	.216
58, f	30	NGO1	Secretary	*.672*	.039	−.065	.374
57, f	28	NGO1	Secretary	*.584*	−.005	.014	.335
59, f	29	NGO1	Member (housewife)	*.721*	.222	.174	.353
60, m		NGO1		*.611*	.219	.150	.318
41,* m	34	Bus 1	Employee	.436	.347	−.027	.025
20, m	25	Yonsei Univ.	Researcher	*.587*	.419	−.015	.257
26, m	20	Yonsei Univ.	Student	*.605*	.275	.022	.429
74, m	34	NGO3	Manager (PR dept.)	*.467*	.230	.255	.274
9,* m	29	NGO8	Member	.555	−.039	.216	.527
63,* m	28	NGO2	Researcher	.513	−.043	.190	.500
64,* m	31	NGO2	Researcher	.520	−.140	.514	.112
69,* m	27	NGO4	Researcher	.534	.176	.456	.318
28,* m	28	NGO11	Researcher	.472	.028	.282	.442
21, f	24	Yonsei Univ.	Researcher	*.521*	.311	.400	.334
36,* m	27	Bus 1	Employee	.390	.025	.366	.276
56, m	30	Bus 2	Employee	−.151	*.736*	−.008	.100
8, m	30	Environmental Administration		.158	*.699*	−.009	.177
52, m	36	Bus 2	Manager (advertising)	.144	*.644*	.140	.140
2, m	38	Environmental Administration		.045	*.437*	−.027	.161
6, m	36	Environmental Administration		.087	*.391*	.108	−.093
34, m	29	Bus 3	Asst. manager	−.002	*.604*	.092	−.262
51, m	35	Bus 2	Manager (marketing)	.128	*.808*	.304	.172
7, m	35	Environmental Administration		.124	*.404*	−.052	.141
40, m	34	Bus 1	Manager	.085	*.648*	.316	.095
27, m	28	Seoul Nat'l Univ.	Researcher	.344	*.660*	.126	.233
55, m	32	Bus 2	Manager (advertising)	.257	*.586*	.324	.047
3		Environmental Administration		.333	*.577*	.165	.182
50		Bus 2	Manager (marketing)	−.077	*.679*	.270	.406
4		Environmental Administration		−.075	*.550*	.364	.224
48, m	34	Bus 2	Manager (advertising)	.127	*.462*	.128	.365
5, m	54	Environmental Administration		.168	*.333*	.170	.185
54,* m	33	Bus 3	Manager	.014	.445	.384	.135
39,* m	29	Bus 1	Employee	−.067	.452	.408	−.063

35,* m	25	Bus 3	Engineer	.428	.504	−.162	.117
19,* m	25	Yonsei Univ.	Researcher	.267	.426	.324	.053
62,* m	29	NGO2	Member	.265	.483	.360	.181
44,* m	34	NGO10	Manager	.050	.408	.407	.128
67,* m	34	NGO4	Researcher	.035	.410	.400	.291
32,* m	32	Bus 4	Engineer	.212	.353	.307	.226
65,* f	25	NGO10	Employee	.002	.463	.459	.394
22,* f	23	Yonsei Univ.	Researcher	.394	.428	.365	.186
23, m	31	NGO5	Prof. (Yonsei Univ.)	.156	.066	.369	.108
7, m	30	NGO6	Member	.178	.303	.680	.131
37, m	34	Bus 1	Manager	.193	.234	.587	.118
49, m	34	Bus 2	Employee	−.237	.033	.515	.173
31, m	29	Bus 4	Manager	−.128	.199	−.412	.084
14, f	36	NGO9	Manager	.206	.250	.464	.117
24, m	42	Seoul Nat'l Univ.	Prof.	−.091	.402	.606	.243
38, m	31	Bus 1	Employee	.054	.241	.513	.369
15,* f	30	NGO9	Manager	.401	.080	.464	.077
33, f	28	Bus 4	Manager	−.256	.148	.319	−.011
71,* f	30	NGO6	Member	.531	.113	.585	.001
30,* m	34	Bus 4	Manager	.186	.079	.425	.384
17,* f	32	NGO9	Manager (PR dept.)	.336	.009	.369	−.178
45,* m	32	NGO10	Manager	.135	.366	.392	.179
42, m	23	Bus 4	Employee	.141	.136	.034	.654
13, m	25	NGO7	Member	.204	.055	.115	.709
68, f	24	NGO4	Member	.279	.142	−.036	.691
46, m	29	NGO10	Employee	.124	.303	.068	.630
10, m	29	NGO8	High executive	.268	.112	.239	.699
70, m	25	NGO5	Secretary	.426	.020	−.080	.700
53, m	28	Bus 2	Employee	.219	.217	.279	.635
1, m	39	Environmental Administration		.314	.188	.276	.656
12, m	31	NGO7	High executive	.421	.196	.408	.709
43, m	57	NGO10	High executive	−.130	.247	.180	.379
47,* m	36	Bus 2	Manager (advertising)	.112	.249	.299	.322
16,* f	40	NGO9	Manager	.286	.281	.328	.400
18,* f	47	NGO9	High executive	.286	.343	.219	.352
29,* m	26	Seoul Nat'l Univ.	Student	.273	.404	.414	.449

Eigenvalues	22.709	5.981	3.244	3.166
Total Variance	13.10	13.12	9.99	11.34 (Total 47.43%)
Variance Within	27.61%	27.66%	20.83%	23.91%

*Variables that were either confounded or statistically not significant. These 26 respondents were not used for the interpretation of the factors, and the remaining factor loadings were used as input for the item descriptions of the four types. Organizations are as follows:

Korean Organizations

NGO1   National Alliance of Movements for the Expulsion of Pollution
NGO2   Korea Peace Research Institute
NGO3   Environmental Conservation Association
NGO4   Korea Anti-Nuclear, Anti-Pollution, and Peace Research Institute
NGO5   The Friends of Nature
NGO6   Society for the Study of Environment and Pollution
NGO7   Kwanju Environmental Pollution Research Institute
NGO8   Catholic Farmers' Federation (Kwangju)
NGO9   YWCA (Kwangju)
NGO10   Hankook Environmental Technology Corporation
NGO11   Environmental Planning Institute
Bus 1   Ssangyong Engineering
Bus 2   Lucky Goldstar and L.G. Advertising Agency
Bus 3   Korea Incinerator Manufactory
Bus 4   Seorim Environmental Development Corporation

Statement Scores

	G	PM	SD	PG
1. All living things have a right to exist.	1.4	2.1	2.5	2.3
2. Sustainability was the original economy of the species. To restore it now will require a revolution as great as the industrial revolution.	–0.9	0.4	1.3	1.2
3. The view of man as the infallible creator, whose salvation lies his own technology, is the origin of cosmic vandalism.	0.4	–0.0	1.0	1.3
4. Biological diversity must be treated as a common heritage of mankind, to be indexed, used, and above all preserved.	1.1	2.0	1.6	1.5
5. Life on earth is a single organism which modifies the atmosphere to serve its own needs.	–0.0	–0.8	–0.3	–2.0
6. Humanity is doomed to extinction. Our main effort must be to preserve maximum diversity so nature can carry on after us.	0.3	0.9	–0.3	1.4
7. Traditional farming mimics nature and is more sustainable than Western monoculture. But we kill natives and their knowledge.	–0.7	–1.1	–1.0	0.7
8. Development means redistributing natural resources according to natural order.	–0.4	–0.3	1.2	–0.4

9. Foolish international development programs caused most
Third World poverty, revolution, and environmental damage. 1.2   0.2   0.6   0.2

10. Poor countries must develop without fossil fuel dependency,
avoiding the cost, pollution, and alienation of the West.   −0.4   −1.5   −0.8   0.4

11. Environmental collapse and violent conflict over resources
destroyed most ancient civilizations, and will surely destroy
the West.   −0.3   −1.1   −0.6   0.8

12. Western development plunders and destroys and nature,
uses the Third World as a dumpsite and laboratory.   1.4   0.4   0.3   1.0

13. If government gave business information and incentives, not
command and sanction, the market and entrepreneurs would
protect the environment.   −1.6   0.1   1.4   −1.3

14. Environmental policy is piecemeal and defensive, not global
as required by the urgency of the problem.   1.3   0.6   0.8   0.9

15. Democracy cannot meet the challenge of imminent
ecocatastrophe, because it act as slowly and through
compromise.   −1.4   −1.2   −1.7   −1.0

16. East and West are converging toward a social democratic
model with a mixed economy, equity, and control of
environmental damage.   −0.9   −1.2   −0.0   −1.2

17. European Community legislation, Law of the Sea and Antarctic
treaties show growing international consensus about
environment.   −0.5   0.6   −0.2   −1.1

18. The only alternative is a Green economy, with grassroots
democracy, voluntary simplicity, sustainable production, and
recycling.   0.1   −0.4   0.2   1.0

19. Economic development on a sound environmental basis is
possible and cost effective.   1.4   1.1   1.3   0.7

20. If the West enforces and pays for high environmental
standards, then the world's nature will be conserved.   −1.0   −0.4   1.0   −1.4

21. Maximizing GNP means maximizing cost, resource waste,
pollution, and inequality.   0.9   −1.1   −0.2   0.2

	G	PM	SD	PG

22. Third World population will not decline naturally due to rising affluence; if not forced down it will prevent even basic development.   −1.1 −0.1 −0.6 −0.5

23. Respect for women should not be based on having children. Women's rights are the key to population control.   0.5 0.4 −1.1 −0.3

24. Stop environmental degradation and population growth will decline by itself.   −1.2 −1.0 −1.6 −1.1

25. Investment in energy efficiency and recycling can reduce fossil fuel demand without sacrificing growth.   0.7 1.4 1.1 0.1

26. The world economy of the next century will not be powered by coal, oil, gas, or uranium.   1.2 0.2 −0.6 0.5

27. Nuclear power's long-term costs in waste disposal, accidents, and terrorist threats far outweigh its benefits.   1.7 −1.0 −0.1 0.5

28. Why spend large sums to avert Greenhouse effects that may not happen? Better to adjust if climate changes appear.   −2.1 −2.2 −0.9 −1.8

29. Greenhouse radiation and acid rain will disrupt oceanic and land food chains, and dramatically change the climate.   1.3 1.4 0.6 0.3

30. Greenhouse warming will lead to death by flooding, famine, of up to one billion people.   0.4 0.8 −1.6 0

31. Biotechnology offers cheaper, quicker ways to improve Third World than costly mechanical-chemical technologies.   −0.9 0.7 −0.3 −0.4

32. The hidden ethical basis of biotechnology is eugenics.   −0.7 0.9 −0.3 −0.8

33. Biotechnology replaces free scientific information with secrecy, collusion, and research geared toward corporate needs.   0.3 −1.0 −0.7 −0.5

34. Biotechnology offers cheaper, quicker ways to improve Third World diet than costly mechanical-chemical technologies.   −0.7 0.2 −0.1 −0.6

35. The risks posed by release of engineered microbes or plants into the environment far outweigh commercial gains.   0.5 −0.6 −1.4 −0.2

36. Biotechnology R&D is not a luxury for the Third World but
a strategic necessity for avoiding permanent under-
development.   −1.0   0.5 −0.3 −0.2

Typal Q-Sorts

+5	+4	+3	+2	+1	0	−1	−2	−3	−4	−5

GREENS

+5	+4	+3	+2	+1	0	−1	−2	−3	−4	−5
27	1	19	9	25	6	34	36	24	13	28
	12	29	26	35	33	32	16	22	15	
		14	4	23	18	7	31	20		
			21	30	5	17	2			
				3	11	10				
					8					

POSTMODERN MANAGERS

+5	+4	+3	+2	+1	0	−1	−2	−3	−4	−5
1	4	25	6	17	9	5	21	15	10	28
	29	19	30	36	26	35	33	11	16	
		32	31	12	34	20	24	7		
			14	23	13	18	27			
				2	3	8				
					22					

SUSTAINABLE DEVELOPERS

+5	+4	+3	+2	+1	0	−1	−2	−3	−4	−5
1	4	19	25	29	34	22	28	35	24	15
	13	2	20	9	27	26	10	23	30	
		8	3	12	17	5	33	7		
			14	18	21	36	11			
				16	32	31				
					6					

POLITICAL GREENS

+5	+4	+3	+2	+1	0	−1	−2	−3	−4	−5
1	4	3	18	7	9	22	24	13	28	5
	6	2	14	26	21	33	15	16	20	
		12	11	27	25	31	32	17		
			19	10	36	8	34			
				29	35	23				
					30					

Brazil

Person Sample with Loadings on Factors

Person	Role	G	MD	PM	SD
GREENS					
27	CIMI exec.	.81	.15	.06	.05
19	PDT/PV deputy	.75	−.07	.20	.09
5	IPSN (NGO)	.59	.02	.04	.24
12	PSDB deputy	.58	.16	.10	.17
26	Embrapa (scientist)	.67	.28	.13	.13
4	IPSN (NGO)	.71	−.03	.20	.45
28	CIMI exec.	.54	−.19	.01	.49
35, f	Envir. journalist	.52	.111	.22	.45
11	PMDB deputy	.45	.22	.38	.30
32	Ministry of the Environment exec.	.46	.43	.23	.33
MODERATE DEVELOPMENTALISTS					
10	PFL deputy	.15	.77	−.08	.21
30	PPR deputy	−.21	.74	.16	−.12
9	Min. Envir. exec.	.33	.62	.03	−.02
2	IPSN exec. (NGO)	−.08	.69	.23	.34
25	Embrapa scientist	.22	.46	.20	.23
18, f	Ibama exec.	.15	.41	.32	.03
33	Embrapa CEO	.15	.41	.32	.03
POSTMODERN MANAGERS					
31	Fed. of Commerce CEO	.15	.18	.63	−.03
24	Embrapa administrator	.21	−.10	.76	.29
15	Ibama exec.	.39	.07	.79	.02
13, f	PMDB deputy	−.04	−.02	.61	.32
16	Ibama exec.	−.10	.56	.60	.05
23	Funatura (NGO)	.44	.30	.50	.24
7	Envir. businessman	.35	.33	.44	.28
SUSTAINABLE DEVELOPERS					
1, f	Bioscientist	.16	.16	−.13	.74
20	Biotechnologist	.16	−.01	.33	.72
22	Funatura CEO (NGO)	.43	.02	.11	.76
21, f	Bioscientist	.26	.02	.39	.69
29	Wld. Wildlife Fund (NGO) sci.	.13	.29	.34	.65
6	Envir. lawyer	.30	.40	.14	.56

17, f	Ibama exec.	−.19	.13	.45	.53
3	IPSN scientist (NGO)	.21	.52	.23	.59
34, f	IEAA (NGO)	.45	.33	.09	.47
14, f	Ibama exec.	.42	.44	.36	.49
8, f	Min. of Envir. exec.	.36	.30	.40	.41

Statement Scores

	G	MD	PM	SD
1. All living things have a right to exist.	2.0	.8	−.4	1.6
2. Sustainability was the original economy of the species. To restore it now will require a revolution as great as the industrial revolution.	.9	1.1	−.5	.5
3. The view of man as the infallible creator, whose salvation lies in his own technology, is the origin of cosmic vandalism.	.1	−.1	−.7	.5
4. Biological diversity must be treated as a common heritage of mankind, to be indexed, used, and above all preserved.	1.3	1.3	1.2	1.6
5. Life on earth is a single organism which modifies the atmosphere to serve its own needs.	−.1	−.3	.7	0
6. Humanity is doomed to extinction. Our main effort must be to preserve maximum diversity so nature can carry on after us.	−2.1	−.6	−1.5	−.1
7. Traditional farming mimics nature and is more sustainable than Western monoculture. But we kill natives and their knowledge.	.3	−.7	−1.8	.7
8. Development means the rich redistributing natural resources in their own favor.	−.4	−.2	−2.3	−2.6
9. Foolish international development programs caused most Third World poverty, revolution, and environmental damage.	1.0	−1.2	1.0	.5
10. Poor countries must develop without fossil fuel dependency, thus avoiding the cost, pollution, and alienation of the West.	.6	−.1	−1.5	−.2

	G	MD	PM	SD
11. Environmental collapse and violent conflict over resources destroyed most ancient civilizations, and will surely destroy the West.	–.6	–1.4	.2	–.1
12. Western development plunders and destroys nature, uses the Third World as a dumpsite and laboratory.	1.3	.3	.9	.7
13. If government gave business information and incentives, not command and sanction, the market and entrepreneurs would protect the environment.	–.5	.6	–1.0	–1.1
14. Environmental policy is piecemeal and defensive, not global as required by the urgency of the problem.	1.1	1.2	.6	1.1
15. Democracy cannot meet the challenge of imminent ecocatastrophe, because it acts slowly and through compromise.	–1.6	–1.0	–.7	–.1
16. East and West are converging toward a social democratic model with a mixed economy, equity, and control of environmental damage.	–.7	.4	.1	–.4
17. European Community legislation, Law of the Sea, Antarctic treaties, and Rio '92 show growing international consensus about environment.	–.3	1.4	1.1	.5
18. The only alternative is a Green economy, with grassroots democracy, voluntary simplicity, sustainable production and recycling.	.7	–.1	.8	.1
19. Economic development on a sound environmental basis is possible and cost effective.	.9	1.2	1.4	1.2
20. If the West enforces and pays for high environmental standards, then the world's nature will be conserved.	.3	.5	.6	–1.0
21. Maximizing GNP means maximizing cost, resource waste, pollution, and inequality.	–.1	–.9	.4	–.5
22. Third World population will not decline naturally due to rising affluence; if not forced down it will prevent even basic development.	–1.5	1.5	.2	.9

23. Respect for women should not be based on having children.
Women's rights are the key to population control.   0   1.3   −.8   1.0

24. Stop environmental degradation and population growth
will decline by itself.   −1.3 −1.5 −.2 −1.6

25. Investment in energy efficiency and recycling can reduce
fossil fuel demand without sacrificing growth.   1.1   1.7   1.4   1.2

26. The world economy of the next century will not be
powered by coal, oil, gas, or uranium.   0   −.8   0   −.7

27. Nuclear power's long-term costs in waste disposal,
accidents, and terrorist threats, far outweigh its benefits. 1.4 −1.1   1.0   .9

28. Why spend large sums to avert Greenhouse effects that may
not happen? Better to adjust if climate changes appear.   −2.5   −.4 −1.8 −2.2

29. Greenhouse radiation and acid rain will disrupt oceanic and
land food chains, and dramatically change the climate.   −.1   −.1   .2   .5

30. Greenhouse warming will lead to death by flooding,
famine, of up to a billion people.   −.2   −.9   .9   0

31. Biotechnology is the next step in human evolution. Our
destiny is to control evolutionary advance on this planet. −.3   .3   −.3   −.8

32. The hidden ethical basis of biotechnology is eugenics.   −1.2 −1.5 −1.5 −1.8

33. Biotechnology replaces free scientific information with secrecy,
collusion, and research geared toward corporate needs.   .8   1.4   1.1   .7

34. Biotechnology offers cheaper, quicker ways to improve Third
World diet than costly mechanical-chemical technologies.   .1 −1.7   −.2   −.3

35. The risks posed by release of engineered microbes or plants
into the environment far outweigh commercial gains.   −.2   .6   .9   −.5

36. Biotechnology R&D is not a luxury for the Third World but
but a strategic necessity for avoiding permanent under-
development.   −.3   −.9   .4   −.2

Typal Q-Sorts

−5	−4	−3	−2	−1	0	+1	+2	+3	+4	+5

GREENS

−5	−4	−3	−2	−1	0	+1	+2	+3	+4	+5
28	6	22	16	17	3	18	9	4	27	1
	15	24	11	36	26	10	2	25	12	
		32	13	31	23	20	19	14		
			8	35	29	7	33			
				30	5	34				
					21					

MODERATE DEVELOPMENTALISTS

−5	−4	−3	−2	−1	0	+1	+2	+3	+4	+5
34	32	11	35	26	12	13	14	33	22	25
	24	9	30	7	18	35	19	4	17	
		27	21	6	10	20	2	23		
			36	28	29	16	1			
				5	3	31				
					8					

POSTMODERN MANAGERS

−5	−4	−3	−2	−1	0	+1	+2	+3	+4	+5
8	7	32	13	2	36	18	9	33	19	25
	28	6	23	1	22	5	12	17	4	
		10	15	31	29	14	35	27		
			3	24	11	20	30			
				34	16	21				
					28					

SUSTAINABLE DEVELOPERS

−5	−4	−3	−2	−1	0	+1	+2	+3	+4	+5
8	28	24	31	16	2	7	27	19	1	4
	32	13	26	34	18	3	22	14	25	
		20	35	36	30	29	12	23		
			21	10	5	17	33			
				6	15	9				
					11					

Mexico

Person Sample, Factor Weights by Type

Person	Job	Factor Weight
POSTMODERN MANAGERS (N = 16)		
2, m	Sedesol exec. (Gov.)	.708
3, m	INE exec.	.589
4, m	DDF Metro planner	2.52
5, m	DDF exec.	.888
7, m	Canacintra exec. (Business)	1.293
8, m	Inorquim pres. (Business)	.981
9, m	Lanfi exec. (Business)	1.34
10, m	IBM exec. (Business)	.678
12, m	Inane NGO	2.214
13, f	Partido Ecologista exec.	.65
16, m	U.N./UNEP exec.	.667
22, m	SARH biotechnologist	1.02
26, m	UNAM scientist	.818
32, m	UNAM limnologist	.615
34, m	Unam geographer	1.04
35, m	UNAM environmental engineer	.883
GREENS (N = 8)		
17, m	Grupo de Cien executive (NGO)	1.895
18, m	Grupo de Sobrevivientes (NGO)	.630
20, m	Grupo de Sobrevivientes pres.	2.34
23, m	UA Chapingo ecologist	1.3
25, f	UNAM meteorologist	1.11
28, m	UNAM hydrologist	.74
29, f	UNAM ecological engineer	.942
36, f	UNAM botanist	.400
POLITICAL GREENS (N = 7)		
1, m	Sedesol exec.	.765
14, m	Ptdo. Verdes Ecologistas VP	.571
15, f	M.E.M. exec. (NGO)	.57
27, f	AUM-marine biologist	.62
30, f	UNAM ecol. engineer	.574
31, f	UNAM toxicologist	.44
33, f	UNAM hydrographer	.982

Mexico

Person Sample, Factor Weights by Type

Person	Job	Factor Weight
SUSTAINABLE DEVELOPERS (N = 6)		
6, m	PRI executive	.775
11, m	INCINE exec.	.766
19, m	Grupo de Sobrevivientes	.8857
21, m	Pacto de grupos ecologistas NGO	.392
24, m	UA-Chapingo ethnobotonist	.962
37, m	UNAM entomologist	.763

Statement Scores

	PM	G	PG	SD
1. All living things have a right to exist.	2.0	.8	−.4	1.6
2. Sustainability was the original economy of the species. To restore it now will require a revolution as great as the industrial revolution.	1.3	1.4	1.6	2.3
3. The view of man as the infallible creator, whose salvation lies in his own technology, is the origin of cosmic vandalism.	−0.5	.5	−0.4	−0.8
4. Biological diversity must be treated as a common heritage of mankind, to be indexed, used, and above all preserved.	2.1	1.5	1.8	1.6
5. Life on earth is a single organism which modifies the atmosphere to serve its own needs.	.4	−.5	−.1	−1.6
6. Humanity is doomed to extinction. Our main effort must be to preserve maximum diversity so nature can carry on after us.	−2.0	−.3	−.4	−2.1
7. Traditional farming mimics nature and is more sustainable than Western monoculture. But we kill natives and their knowledge.	.0	1.4	.4	1.3
8. Development means the rich redistributing natural resources in their own favor.	−1.9	−1.2	−1.1	−1.0
9. Foolish international development programs caused most Third World poverty, revolution, and environmental damage.	0	.9	−.7	.2

10. Poor countries must develop without fossil fuel dependency, thus avoiding the cost, pollution, and alienation of the West.   −1.0 1.1 −.5 −.2

11. Environmental collapse and violent conflict over resources destroyed most ancient civilizations, and will surely destroy the West.   −.7 −.7 −1.6 −.7

12. Western development plunders and destroys nature, uses the Third World as a dumpsite and laboratory.   −.2 1.5 .7 .6

13. If government gave business information and incentives, not command and sanction, the market and entrepreneurs would protect the environment.   .3 −.7 −1.3 .7

14. Environmental policy is piecemeal and defensive, not global as required by the urgency of the problem.   .9 1.5 −.2 1.2

15. Democracy cannot meet the challenge of imminent ecocatastrophe, because it acts slowly and through compromise.   −1.2 .1 .4 −.2

16. East and West are converging toward a social democratic model with a mixed economy, equity, and control of environmental damage.   .4 −1.3 −.6 −.2

17. European Cmmunity legislation, Law of the Sea, Antarctic treaties, and Rio '92 show growing international consensus about environment.   .6 −.5 .2 .2

18. The only alternative is a Green economy, with grassroots democracy, voluntary simplicity, sustainable production, and recycling. 1.2 .3 .7 .9

19. Economic development on a sound environmental basis is possible and cost effective.   1.7 1.2 1.2 1.6

20. If the West enforces and pays for high environmental standards, then the world's nature will be conserved.   .2 −.7 0 −1.2

21. Maximizing GNP means maximizing cost, resource waste, pollution, and inequality.   −1.2 −.4 .3 −.3

22. Third World population will not decline naturally due to rising affluence; if not forced down it will prevent even basic development.   −.1 −.9 −1.0 −.3

	PM	G	PG	SD
23. Respect for women should not be based on having children. Women's rights are the key to population control.	1.1	–.2	1.3	–.6
24. Stop environmental degradation and population growth will decline by itself.	–.5	–1.6	–2.1	–1.7
25. Investment in energy efficiency and recycling can reduce fossil fuel demand without sacrificing growth.	1.3	.3	1.3	.7
26. The world economy of the next century will not be powered by coal, oil, gas, or uranium.	–.7	.3	.2	0
27. Nuclear power's long-term costs in waste disposal, accidents, and terrorist threats far outweigh its benefits.	.5	1.1	1.8	.6
28. Why spend large sums to avert Greenhouse effects that may not happen? Better to adjust if climate changes appear.	–1.5	–1.7	–2.3	–1.3
29. Greenhouse radiation and acid rain will disrupt oceanic and land food chains, and dramatically change the climate.	.2	.7	.9	1.5
30. Greenhouse warming will lead to death by flooding, famine, of up to a billion people.	–.7	–.5	–.4	0
31. Biotechnology is the next step in human evolution. Our destiny is to control evolutionary advance on this planet.	–.6	–2.2	–.2	–.7
32. The hidden ethical basis of biotechnology is eugenics.	–.8	–.8	0	–.6
33. Biotechnology replaces free scientific information with secrecy, collusion, and research geared toward corporate needs.	–.7	–1.2	–1.1	.6
34. Biotechnology offers cheaper, quicker ways to improve Third World diet than costly mechanical-chemical technologies.	0	–.4	.5	–.1
35. The risks posed by release of engineered microbes or plants into the environment far outweigh commercial gains.	–.2	0	–.6	0
36. Biotechnology R&D is not a luxury for the Third World but is strategic necessity for avoiding permanent underdevelopment.	1.5	0	.9	.4

Typal Q-Sorts

–5	–4	–3	–2	–1	0	+1	+2	+3	+4	+5

GREENS

–5	–4	–3	–2	–1	0	+1	+2	+3	+4	+5
31	28	16	22	30	18	11	10	7	12	4
	24	33	32	5	15	2	27	1	14	
		8	20	17	35	3	9	19		
			35	30	20	2	18			
				31	5	21				
					14					

POLITICAL GREENS

–5	–4	–3	–2	–1	0	+1	+2	+3	+4	+5
28	24	13	22	10	17	34	36	23	4	27
	11	33	9	26	15	29	25	1		
		8	16	3	32	7	12	19		
			35	30	20	2	18			
				31	5	21				
					14					

POSTMODERN MANAGERS

–5	–4	–3	–2	–1	0	+1	+2	+3	+4	+5
6	8	21	32	33	29	27	23	1	19	4
	28	15	30	31	7	16	14	25	36	
		10	26	24	9	5	2	18		
			11	3	34	13	17			
				12	22	20				
					35					

SUSTAINABLE DEVELOPERS

–5	–4	–3	–2	–1	0	+1	+2	+3	+4	+5
6	24	28	2	23	26	33	18	29	4	1
	5	20	3	32	35	27	13	7	19	
		8	31	22	30	36	25	14		
			11	21	10	9	12			
				15	34	17				
					16					

Puerto Rico

Person Sample

Person	Job	Factor Weight
SUSTAINABLE DEVELOPERS (N = 6)		
2, m	Environmental Quality Council	.72
5, m	Solid waste manager	.36
10, m	Corp. executive	1.46
14, m	Director, Fish and Wildlife Service	.94
27, m	Director, Urban Env. Health	1.08
34, m	Environmental journalist	.83
POLITICAL GREENS (N = 10)		
8, m	Director Regional Agronomy Office	.63
12, m	Env. manager, Bristol Laboratories	.81
13, m	Toxicology professor, writes EIS for govt.	.78
20, f	Env. engineer DEC Corp.	.68
22, f	Psychology student, environmentalist	1.15
23, m	Ex-governor, President, P.R. Nationalist Party	.96
25, m	Mayor, env. activist	.54
30, m	Abbott Pharmaceuticals executive	1.05
32, m	Biologist	.47
40, m	President, P.R. Independence Party	.87
POSTMODERN MANAGERS (N = 11)		
6, m	Executive, Warner-Lambert Pharmaceuticals	.65
7, m	Executive, Smith-Kline Pharmaceuticals	1.14
16, f	Professor, chemistry	.57
18, f	Pharmaceutical executive	1.12
21, m	Anthropologist, envir. activist	1.02
31, m	Exec., Dept. Forest Mgt.	.65
33, f	Environmental journalist	.46
35, m	Professor; director, Federal Sea Grant Program	2.07
37, m	Director, Dept. of Zoology	.54
39, m	Zoologist	.39
42, m	Executive, Baxter Pharmaceuticals	1.02
GREENS (N = 13)		
1, m	Executive in EPA	.70
3, m	Prominent Environmentalist, Industrial Mission	.81
4, f	Science Services Office	.71

m	University administrator	1.01
, m	Director, Regional Env. Health Dept.; envir. activist	.82
), m	University president, microbiologist	.68
', f	Professor, biology	1.04
), m	Env. director, Abbott Laboratories	.53
), f	Director, Dept. of Natural Resources	.41
), m	Economic anthropologist	.57
), m	Natural Resources forest guide	.73
, m	Biologist	.59
), m	V.P., Assn. of Industrialists of P.R.	.96

ULTURAL TRADITIONALISTS (N = 3)

', m	Professor of biology	.80
, m	Senator; Vice President, Senate	1.05
, m	Mayor of town, active in local envir. struggle	1.11

mple N = 43, including 10 business, 14 government, 14 academics, 2 journalists, 7 environ-
ental activists; 8 women; some overlap in categories.

atement Scores

	SD	PG	PM	G	CT
All living things have a right to exist.	1.8	1.6	2.0	2.0	2.0
Sustainability was the original economy of the species. To restore it now will require a revolution as great as the industrial revolution.	1.2	−0.9	.8	1.0	.9
The view of man as the infallible creator, whose salvation lies in his own technology, is the origin of cosmic vandalism.	.4	−.6	.6	−.9	1.8
Biological diversity must be treated as a common heritage of mankind, to be indexed, used, and above all preserved.	1.6	.8	1.6	1.6	1.7
Life on earth is a single organism which modifies the atmosphere to serve its own needs.	1.2	−1.3	−1.0	−0.1	1.1
Humanity is doomed to extinction. Our main effort must be to preserve maximum diversity so nature can carry on after us.	.8	−1.7	−2.2	.4	.3

	SD	PG	PM	G	CT
7. Traditional farming mimics nature and is more sustainable than Western monoculture. But we kill natives and their knowledge.	.3	.1	.4	−.4	.6
8. Development means the rich redistributing natural resources in their own favor.	−.1	.5	−1.0	−1.2	1.7
9. Foolish international development programs caused most Third World poverty, revolution, and environmental damage.	−.1	−1.8	1.4	−.8	−1.1
10. Poor countries must develop without fossil fuel dependency, thus avoiding the cost, pollution, and alienation of the West.	1.1	.3	.9	−.2	−1.2
11. Environmental collapse and violent conflict over resources destroyed most ancient civilizations, and will surely destroy the West.	−.7	−.6	−.5	.7	−.3
12. Western development plunders and destroys nature, uses the Third World as a dumpsite and laboratory.	−.2	−1.0	1.0	.8	−.8
13. If government gave business information and incentives, not command and sanction, the market and entrepreneurs would protect the environment.	.6	−.2	−1.5	−1.1	−.7
14. Environmental policy is piecemeal and defensive, not global as required by the urgency of the problem.	.4	.1	.9	1.5	1.8
15. Democracy cannot meet the challenge of imminent ecocatastrophe, because it acts slowly and through compromise.	.7	0	−.5	−1.2	−2.2
16. East and West are converging toward a social democratic model with a mixed economy, equity, and control of environmental damage.	.9	1.4	.1	−.6	
17. European Community legislation, Law of the Sea, and Antarctic treaties show growing international consensus about environment.	1.2	1.4	0	1.2	−.2

18. The only alternative is a Green economy, with grassroots
    democracy, voluntary simplicity, sustainable production,
    and recycling.   1.0   1.0   .4   .8 –1.2

19. Economic development on a sound environmental basis
    is possible and cost effective.   .6   1.8   1.5   1.7 –.9

20. If the West enforces and pays for high environmental
    standards, then the world's nature will be conserved.   .1   .6   .4   –.6 –1.3

21. Maximizing GNP means maximizing cost, resource
    waste, pollution, and inequality.   –1.1 –1.5 –.2 –1.5 –.6

22. Third World population will not decline naturally due to
    rising affluence; if not forced down it will prevent even
    basic development.   –.6   .6   –.2   –.3 –1.4

23. Respect for women should not be based on having
    children. Women's rights are the key to population
    control.   .8   1.0   .5   –.2 1.1

24. Stop environmental degradation and population
    growth will decline by itself.   –1.3 –1.7 –1.6 –.9   .1

25. Investment in energy efficiency and recycling can
    reduce fossil fuel demand without sacrificing growth.   .7   1.5   1.1   1.8   .9

26. The world economy of the next century will not be
    powered by coal, oil, gas, or uranium.   –1.4 –.6   –.6   0 –.3

27. Nuclear power's long-term costs in waste disposal,
    accidents, and terrorist threats far outweigh its
    benefits.   –1.2   .4   –.2   .2   .1

28. Why spend large sums to avert Greenhouse effects that
    may not happen? Better to adjust if climate changes
    appear.   –1.5 –1.3 –2.0 –1.6 –.6

29. Greenhouse radiation and acid rain will disrupt oceanic
    and land food chains, and dramatically change the
    climate.   –.7   .2   .3   1.2 –.2

	SD	PG	PM	G	CT
30. Greenhouse warming will lead to death by flooding, famine, of up to a billion people.	−1.8	−.9	−.3	−.5	−.5
31. Biotechnology is the next step in human evolution. Our destiny is to control evolutionary advance on this planet.	−1.8	.6	−1.0	−1.0	−.3
32. The hidden ethical basis of biotechnology is eugenics.	−1.1	−.4	−.9	−1.2	−.2
33. Biotechnology replaces free scientific information with secrecy, collusion, and research geared toward corporate needs.	−.8	−.2	−.6	−.4	−.2
34. Biotechnology offers cheaper, quicker ways to improve Third World diet than costly mechanical-chemical technologies.	−.2	−.8	0	.1	.5
35. The risks posed by release of engineered microbes or plants into the environment far outweigh commercial gains.	−1.2	.1	.2	−.5	1.0
36. Biotechnology R&D is not a luxury for the Third World but a strategic necessity for avoiding permanent under-development.	.2	1.0	.4	.3	−.1

Typal Q-Sorts

−5	−4	−3	−2	−1	0	+1	+2	+3	+4	+5

SUSTAINABLE DEVELOPMENT

30	31	26	35	11	14	25	18	2	4	1
	28	24	32	29	7	15	16	5	7	
		27	21	22	36	19	23	10		
			33	34	20	13	6			
				12	8	3				
					9					

POLITICAL GREENS

9	24	21	12	3	29	31	36	16	1	19
	6	5	2	22	35	20	18	17	25	
		28	30	26	7	8	34	23		
			11	32	14	27	4			
				13	15	10				
					31					

POSTMODERN MANAGERS

6	28	13	5	15	29	23	14	9	4	1
	24	8	32	11	35	36	10	25	19	
		31	26	30	16	20	2	12		
			33	22	34	18	3			
				21	17	7				
					27					

GREENS

28	21	8	31	16	26	11	17	4	25	1
	32	15	24	20	5	6	2	14	19	
		13	3	30	23	36	12	29		
			9	35	10	27	18			
				33	22	34				
					7					

CULTURAL TRADITIONALISTS

15	22	10	19	12	36	7	5	8	3	1
	20	18	13	34	23	6	35	14	4	
		9	28	30	32	24	2	23		
			21	31	33	27	25			
				26	17	16				
					11					

Romania

Person Sample, Factor Weights by Type

Person	Job	Factor Weight
DEVELOPMENTALISTS		
3, m	President, MER	1.37
5, m	UDMR deputy	1.00
6, f	State Government, Health Dept.	0.87
7, m	Businessman, PSDR	0.86
10, m	Scientist, Member of PAC	1.49
11, m	Scientist, REP VP	2.15
12, m	Scientist, MER	1.75
13, m	Scientist, Bucharest	1.44
14, m	Scientist, Sibiu	3.56
15, f	Scientist, Sibiu	4.00
16, f	Scientist, Bucharest	3.05
BUREAUCRATIC NATIONALISTS		
1, m	Vice President, MER	1.11
2, m	Member, MER	0.90
4, m	PUNR deputy	4.49
8, m	Businessman; PUNR member	7.66
9, m	Businessman; PUNR member	8.00

Statement Scores

	D	BN
1. All living things have a right to exist.	–1.3	–1.3
2. Sustainability was the original economy of the species. To restore it now will require a revolution as great as the industrial revolution.	0.4	1.0
3. The view of man as the infallible creator, whose salvation lies in his own technology, is the origin of cosmic vandalism.	–0.4	1.2
4. Biological diversity must be treated as a common heritage of mankind, to be indexed, used, and above all preserved.	–1.3	–0.7

5. Life on earth is a single organism which modifies the atmosphere
to serve its own needs.   −0.4   0

6. Humanity is doomed to extinction. Our main effort must be to
preserve maximum diversity so nature can carry on after us.   −0.6   0

7. Traditional farming mimics nature and is more sustainable than
Western monoculture. But we kill natives and their knowledge.   −0.8   −1.3

8. Development means the rich redistributing natural resources in
their own favor.   −1.0   −1.3

9. Foolish international development programs caused most Third
World poverty, revolution, and environmental damage.   −1.0   −1.3

10. Poor countries must develop without fossil fuel dependency,
thus avoiding the cost, pollution, and alienation of the West.   1.7   1.6

11. Environmental collapse and violent conflict over resources destroyed
most ancient civilizations, and will surely destroy the West.   0.6   1.0

12. Western development plunders and destroys nature, uses the
Third World as a dumpsite and laboratory.   1.1   −1.0

13. If government gave business information and incentives, not
command and sanction, the market and entrepreneurs would
protect the environment.   0.7   −1.2

14. Environmental policy is piecemeal and defensive, not global
as required by the urgency of the problem.   −0.1   1.5

15. Democracy cannot meet the challenge of imminent
ecocatastrophe, because it acts slowly and through compromise.   −0.9   −1.3

16. East and West are converging toward a social democratic model with
a mixed economy, equity, and control of environmental damage.   −0.2   −1.1

17. European Community legislation, Law of the Sea, and Antarctic
treaties show growing international consensus about environment.   −0.9   1.7

18. The only alternative is a Green economy, with grassroots democracy,
voluntary simplicity, sustainable production, and recycling.   −1   0.5

	D	BN
19. Economic development on a sound environmental basis is possible possible and cost effective.	–0.8	–1.2
20. If the West enforces and pays for high environmental standards, then the world's nature will be conserved.	1.0	1.8
21. Maximizing GNP means maximizing cost, resource waste, pollution, and inequality.	–0.3	–0.3
22. Third World population will not decline naturally due to rising affluence; if not forced down it will prevent even basic development.	–0.6	0.9
23. Respect for women should not be based on having children. Women's rights are the key to population control.	–0.1	1.1
24. Stop environmental degradation and population growth will decline by itself.	1.4	1.5
25. Investment in energy efficiency and recycling can reduce fossil fuel demand without sacrificing growth.	–1.0	0.3
26. The world economy of the next century will not be powered by coal, oil, gas, or uranium.	0.2	–1.1
27. Nuclear power's long-term costs in waste disposal, accidents, and terrorist threats far outweigh its benefits.	0	–0.6
28. Why spend large sums to avert Greenhouse effects that may not happen? Better to adjust if climate changes appear.	2.4	–0.6
29. Greenhouse radiation and acid rain will disrupt oceanic and land food chains, and dramatically change the climate.	–0.6	–0.4
30. Greenhouse warming will lead to death by flooding, famine, of up to a billion people.	1.4	–0.6
31. Biotechnology is the next step in human evolution. Our destiny is to control evolutionary advance on this planet.	0	–1.2

32. The hidden ethical basis of biotechnology is eugenics.   2.7   0.3

33. Biotechnology replaces free scientific information with secrecy,
    collusion, and research geared toward corporate needs.   0.7   –0.2

34. Biotechnology offers cheaper, quicker ways to improve Third
    World diet than costly mechanical-chemical technologies.   0.2   0.1

35. The risks posed by release of engineered microbes or plants into
    the environment far outweigh commercial gains.   –0.5   0.3

36. Biotechnology R&D is not a luxury for the Third World but a
    strategic necessity for avoiding permanent underdevelopment.   –0.4   0.9

Typal Q-Sorts

–5	–4	–3	–2	–1	0	+1	+2	+3	+4	+5

DEVELOPMENTALISTS

–5	–4	–3	–2	–1	0	+1	+2	+3	+4	+5
1	4	25	15	29	23	2	20	30	28	32
	6	9	17	22	14	26	13	24	10	
		18	8	7	16	34	33	12		
			19	35	21	27	11			
				3	5	31				
					36					

BUREAUCRATIC NATIONALISTS

–5	–4	–3	–2	–1	0	+1	+2	+3	+4	+5
1	15	8	19	4	34	22	23	14	17	20
	9	13	16	27	5	18	2	24	10	
		31	26	28	7	25	11	3		
			12	30	33	35	36			
				29	21	37				
					6					

Iran

Person Sample

Person	Role	Loadings on Factors			

CULTURAL TRADITIONALISTS (RELIGIOUS CONSERVATIVES)

Person	Role				
1, f	Journalist	.74	.03	.06	.13
3, m	Manager, environmental NGO	.69	.05	.46	.03
4, m	Exec., Dept Nat'l Resources	.5	.01	.30	.03
5, m	Manager, environmental NGO	.54	.16	.30	.30
13, f	Chem. engineer, university	.56	.14	.43	−.42
14, f	Nuclear engineer, Health Ministry	.6	.19	.14	−.48
18, m	Govt. engineer	.92	.17	−.06	.09
22, m	Business manager	.54	.38	.36	.19
23, f	Reporter	.76	.33	.1	.06
24, m	Bus., architect	.65	.08	.22	.08

DEVELOPMENTALISTS

Person	Role				
2, f	Journalist	.06	.21	−.03	.07
7, m	Oceanographic chemist, university	.01	.48	.38	.04
12, f	Sanitary engineering, university	.14	.63	.25	.25
15, f	Family health, university, Health Ministry	.49	.50	.15	.15
19, m	Agricultural engineer, university	.43	.54	.38	−.16
25, m	Engineer, Mining, and Industrial Ministry	.47	.53	.34	.1
26, m	Business manager	.02	.84	.19	.06
27, m	Business, chemical industry	.18	.76	.15	.15
28, m	Banker	.23	.88	−.01	.22

SUSTAINABLE DEVELOPERS

Person	Role				
8, m	Hydrologist, university	.16	.21	.63	−.11
9, m	Environmental planner, university	.22	−.09	.68	.26
10, f	Archaeologist, university	.33	−.01	.49	.11
16, m	Newspaper editor	.17	.37	.56	.05
17, m	Environmental Health Dept., univ., govt.	−.04	.32	.68	.11
21, m	Economist, university	.20	.08	.60	.33

BUREAUCRATIC NATIONALISTS

Person	Role				
6, m	Govt. marine geologist	.18	.2	.06	.66
11, f	Environmental engineer, university	.5	.06	.12	.54
20, m	Banker	−.07	.15	.24	.68

Statement Scores

	CT	D	SD	BN
1. All living things have a right to exist.	1.3	1.7	0.7	–0.1
2. Sustainability was the original economy of the species. To restore it now will require a revolution as great as the industrial revolution.	–0.2	0.2	–0.8	–1.5
3. The view of man as the infallible creator, whose salvation lies in his own technology, is the origin of cosmic vandalism.	0.4	–1.4	0.6	1.5
4. Biological diversity must be treated as a common heritage of mankind, to be indexed, used, and above all preserved.	0	–0.1	1.8	0.4
5. Life on earth is a single organism which modifies the atmosphere to serve its own needs.	0.8	1.2	–0.3	0.4
6. Humanity is doomed to extinction. Our main effort must be to preserve maximum diversity so nature can carry on after us.	0.7	0.6	0	–0.4
7. Traditional farming mimics nature and is more sustainable than Western monoculture. But we kill natives and their knowledge.	–0.2	–1.4	–0.9	–1.8
8. Development means the rich redistributing natural resources in their own favor.	–2.4	–0.7	–1.5	–2.0
9. Foolish international development programs caused most Third World poverty, revolution, and environmental damage.	0.2	–0.2	–0.6	1.2
10. Poor countries must develop without fossil fuel dependency, thus avoiding the cost, pollution, and alienation of the West.	0.6	0.8	–0.2	0.6
11. Environmental collapse and violent conflict over resources destroyed most ancient civilizations, and will surely destroy the West.	0.8	0.7	0	0.6
12. Western development plunders and destroys nature, uses the Third World as a dumpsite and laboratory.	1.1	1.0	0.3	0.7

	CT	D	SD	BN

13. If government gave business information and incentives, not
command and sanction, the market and entrepreneurs would
protect the environment.   −2.4   1.5 −1.0   0.6

14. Environmental policy is piecemeal and defensive, not global
as required by the urgency of the problem.   −0.5   −0.5   1.7   1.3

15. Democracy cannot meet the challenge of imminent
ecocatastrophe, because it acts slowly and through
compromise.   0.4   −0.5 −0.9   0.1

16. East and West are converging toward a social democratic model
with a mixed economy, equity, and control of environmental
damage.   −0.9   −0.4 −0.1 −0.7

17. European Community legislation, Law of the Sea, and
Antarctic treaties show growing international consensus
about environment.   −0.9   −0.4 −0.1 −0.7

18. The only alternative is a Green economy, with grassroots
democracy, voluntary simplicity, sustainable production,
and recycling.   0   −0.4 −0.4 −0.5

19. Economic development on a sound environmental basis is
possible and cost effective.   1.1   0.3   1.7 −0.6

20. If the West enforces and pays for high environmental
standards, then the world's nature will be conserved.   −1.3   1.2   1.4   1.1

21. Maximizing GNP means maximizing cost, resource waste,
pollution, and inequality.   −0.4   −2.0 −1.9 −0.7

22. Third World population will not decline naturally due to rising
affluence; if not forced down it will prevent even basic
development.   1.1   1.3   0.2   1.8

23. Respect for women should not be based on having children.
Women's rights are the key to population control.   1.0   1.4   1.7   1.5

24. Stop environmental degradation and population growth
will decline by itself.   –2.4   –1.8 0.4 –1.8

25. Investment in energy efficiency and recycling can reduce
fossil fuel demand without sacrificing growth.   0.4   0.6 1.1 0.2

26. The world economy of the next century will not be powered
by coal, oil, gas, or uranium.   0.7   0.4 0.5 –1.9

27. Nuclear power's long-term costs in waste disposal, accidents,
and terrorist threats far outweigh its benefits.   0.5   –1.6 –1.0 0.8

28. Why spend large sums to avert Greenhouse effects that may
not happen? Better to adjust if climate changes appear.   –2.1   –2.2 –1.8 –0.7

29. Greenhouse radiation and acid rain will disrupt oceanic and
land food chains, and dramatically change the climate.   0.8   0.4 0.8 0.7

30. Greenhouse warming will lead to death by flooding, famine,
of up to a billion people.   0.6   0.3   0 0.3

31. Biotechnology is the next step in human evolution. Our
destiny is to control evolutionary advance on this planet.   –0.1   –0.2 –0.1 –0.4

32. The hidden ethical basis of biotechnology is eugenics.   –0.5   –0.1 –0.5 –0.4

33. Biotechnology replaces free scientific information with secrecy,
collusion, and research geared toward corporate needs.   0.1   –0.3 –1.5   0

34. Biotechnology offers cheaper, quicker ways to improve Third
World diet than costly mechanical-chemical technologies.   0.4   –0.4 0.4 –0.1

35. The risks posed by release of engineered microbes or plants
into the environment far outweigh commercial gains.   –0.3   –0.2 –1.0 –0.7

36. Biotechnology R&D is not a luxury for the Third World but a
strategic necessity for avoiding permanent underdevelopment. 0.4   0.1 0.9 1.0

Typal Q-Sorts

–5	–4	–3	–2	–1	0	+1	+2	+3	+4	+5

CULTURAL TRADITIONALISTS

–5	–4	–3	–2	–1	0	+1	+2	+3	+4	+5
8	13	28	32	7	36	10	29	19	22	1
	24	20	14	2	3	30	5	23	12	
		17	21	31	35	27	6	11		
			34	4	16	25	26			
				18	9	15				
					33					

DEVELOPMENTALISTS

–5	–4	–3	–2	–1	0	+1	+2	+3	+4	+5
28	29	27	8	34	19	6	12	22	13	1
	24	3	14	17	2	25	10	5	23	
		7	15	33	36	29	11	20		
			18	9	4	36	16			
				31	32	30				
					35					

SUSTAINABLE DEVELOPERS

–5	–4	–3	–2	–1	0	+1	+2	+3	+4	+5
21	28	8	13	9	22	26	36	19	14	4
	33	27	7	32	6	16	29	20	23	
		32	15	18	11	24	1	25		
			2	5	30	34	3			
				10	31	12				
					17					

BUREAUCRATIC NATIONALISTS

–5	–4	–3	–2	–1	0	+1	+2	+3	+4	+5
8	26	24	28	18	30	11	36	14	23	22
	7	2	17	31	25	13	27	9	3	
		35	21	32	15	10	12	20		
			19	6	33	4	29			
				16	34	5				
					1					

Glossary

Acid rain. Rain, vapor, or snow with a pH lower than 5.6, resulting from precipitation of pollutants from the atmosphere. Acid deposition poisons aquatic systems, forests, farmlands, and wetlands, lowering their biological productivity. It also damages human artifacts.

Adaptation. Evolutionary process by which organisms are suited to their environment by selection of individuals with characteristics enhancing their ability to cope with the environment or with competition from other organisms.

Anthropocentrism. Humanist doctrine that considers human interests over those of nature in ethics, economics, policy, or industry.

APEC. Asian Pacific Economic Cooperation. A free trade area in the Pacific Basin emerging through complex ongoing negotiations.

Aquaculture. Farming of aquatic animals in a fixed area for commercial ends.

Biochemical oxygen demand (BOD). The amount of oxygen needed by organic material in a water column; a measure of pollution by organic wastes over enrichment by mineral nutrients, both of which lead to overproduction of biota, depletion of oxygen, and subsequent population crash.

Biocentrism. The ethical doctrine that locates humans within their ecology, and gives ecological equilibrium priority over immediate human needs.

Biodiversity. Measure of the heterogeneity and complexity of relations among organisms and species in a fixed area.

Bureaucratic Nationalists. A factorial attitude type. Global South Hobbesians and modernist Fordists who take a technocratic, bureaucratic, authoritarian perspective on environment and development. They are undemocratic and distrust both business and markets. But they are quite critical of government's capacity for regulation and see the need for large-scale system change to improve both ecological and economic situations.

They consider Greens utopian and range from skeptical to pessimistic about the human future. Bureaucrats see hard fuels and high technology as necessary for development and see little risk in them. They are neutral to hostile on womens rights. Bureaucratic Nationalists strongly criticize Western Fordist development models and think the West will collapse. No treaty regimes or side payments are acceptable to them, as they want purely national solutions to environmental and developmental issues—import substitution and autarchy—but are pessimistic about these being realized.

Carrying capacity. K, in the Lotka-Volterra equation. A model of the number of individuals that a habitat can support; also, organisms which live at carrying capacity with high biological efficiency.

Conservation. Rational use of natural resources for maximum sustained yield of products of interest to humans; usually "rational" means economically optimal.

Corporativism. A political system in underdeveloped civil societies, in which the state organizes civil society from the top down in hierarchical, exclusive, and officially sanctioned interest groups, usually based on an organized interest category: union, student, women, business, military, church groups. A means of interest representation and mobilization and of social control found in both leftist and rightist governments and in some welfare states.

Cultural Traditionalists are premodern organic conservatives who stand entirely outside the postmodern/post-Fordist model. These factorial attitude types emerged in Iran and Puerto Rico, and consist of Iranian Shiite religious conservatives and Hispanic Catholic traditionalists. Cultural Traditionalists are strongly critical of Western modernist culture and economy for destroying traditional values and community, pillaging nature, and dooming the human race to extinction. They are neutral about technology, energy, population, and women's issues. Such organic conservatives (like Grey's Green Tories) can provide Greens with issue-specific coalition partners in the fight against corporate power and neoliberal ideology, in restoring communities, in organic farming, and in reurbanization of lost public spaces. But this type will not assist in postmodern lifestyle issues, nor will they have a strong brief for social justice issues.

Developmentalists. A factorial attitude type which is modernist and Fordist. Developmentalists believe in rational management, technology, growth, and the primacy of markets. Markets can blend development and conservation and can control the effects of global warming, hard fuels, biotechnology, and population growth. Developmentalists reject green and sustainable development notions as utopian and intend to maintain market-driven economies. But they are aware of environmental problems, and of all types are the most democratic and most favorable to women's rights; probably in the economic sense of allowing them to enter the work force, rather than in supporting feminism. This type may be evolving, in its thinking, away from the modernist/Fordist quadrant toward the postmodern/Fordist space of Sustainable Development.

Disorganized capitalism, wherein the disintegrative effects of post-Fordist global economy on the state, social class relations, civil society, and economy lead to a recrudescence of modernist values in the core, a reaction against postmodernity on the part of social strata displaced by it.

Ecofeminism criticizes patriarchy, racism, classism, speciesism, critiquing the logic of modern science, reworking language to create gender-sensitive concepts and theories, and attempting to change media and daily language in order to socialize a new generation into androgyny.

The *Environmental justice* movement emerged in minority communities disproportionately burdened with the pollution, toxic waste, occupational, and health hazards of industrial society. The beneficiaries of this waste disposal subsidy, white upper-middle-class elites, share out little of their wealth generated through such pollution. These movements in minority communities are multicultural, often led by women, and nationally networked. They argue that environment is a natural right and involves questions of social and economic justice.

Ecology. The study of the nature of the relations of organisms to one another and the natural environment; also this concrete stratified set of relationships.

El Niño. ENSO or El Niño/Southern Oscillation. Occasional shift in ocean currents and temperatures in the South Pacific, which modifies worldwide climate and ecologies.

Environment. The sum of structured relations with other organisms and physiochemical conditions of life in a specific region.

Extensive growth. Multiplication of the basic modules of economic growth; for example, drilling for oil, mining coal throughout the country, etc. An early stage of economic development when the basic infrastructure and heavy industry is replicated, usually under state promotion, without regard to economic efficiency or ecological costs.

Four sectors of the economy. The first sector is capital goods—heavy and extractive industry, infrastructure. The second sector is consumer durables—cars, housing, appliances. The third is services, such as education, health, welfare, personal services, transport, and so forth. The fourth is research and development, reproduction and application of knowledge and the extension of the technostructure to information intensification of production.

GATT. See WTO, General Agreement on Tariffs and Trade.

Global South. Another term for the Third World, countries lagging behind the Global North, or wealthy countries, in terms of technology, indebtedness, and transnational corporate penetration of their leading economic sectors. Often these countries have dual economies with small upper and middle classes living in a relatively modern consumer society and a majority of urban slum dwellers, poor peasants, landless workers, and native peoples living in a subsistence economy.

GNaP. Gross Natural Product, GNP with an environmental deflator; that is, a measure subtracted from productivity indicating the present and future values of ecological damage occasioned by that productivity.

GNP. Gross National Product, a measure of domestic production plus the difference between exports and imports. The measure does not include any consideration of the present or future value of ecological costs of production. Thus, for example, the Exxon Valdez oil spill cleanup added U.S. $4 billion to our GNP in jobs and services, but the cost to fisheries, tourism, and ecosystem production is not subtracted from this figure.

Green parties are complex political parties held together by an uneasy consensus on ecological values, alternative lifestyles, feminism, grassroots democracy, disarmament, and nonviolence. Greens work within the dominant system to open political space for groups and movements normally excluded. They are highly critical of centralized decision making and seek to restore local communities and grassroots participatory democracy.

Greens. A factorial attitude type that emerged from our field data and is both postmodern and post-Fordist. Greens value life and biodiversity and want a green economy with energy efficiency and soft power, recycling, democratic popular management, regulation of business, and adherence to treaty regimes. They are mildly critical of modernist developmentalism. Greens are technology averse and want a redefinition of basic human needs. They are concerned about global warming but do not share an apocalyptic vision of the world's future. They do not see population as a problem and only mildly support women's rights. Greens are moderate, non-ideological, and open to data-driven dialog with holders of other attitude types. They do not promote formation of Green parties but want to "green" the political spectrum through mass mobilization and interelite dialog.

Green capitalism is the technological conversion of production and distribution to conserving resources and wilderness for economic values (tourism, gene banking); creating cost savings in business through recycling and energy efficiency; and capitalizing on a green corporate image.

Green economy features sustainable production, maximized throughput, minimized input and output, knowledge-intensive production, a radically reduced human population, bioregional lifestyles, participatory democracy, and diversity maintenance for both natural and cultural species.

The *Green Revolution* involved extensive monocultures of high-yield dwarfed varietals of rice, wheat, corn, and potatoes, requiring heavy irrigation and heavy pesticide and fertilizer use.

Green Tories reject Thatcherite neoliberalism and want to use state regulation of the economy to protect markets from predators; to preserve the environment, local communities, and cultural traditions; to enlarge public goods and services; and to rebuild cities in socially and environmentally friendly ways. Population control is needed to reach a steady state or social equilibrium at more sustainable levels.

Hileia. Closed-canopy tropical rain forest circulating nutrients through a constant evapotranspirative cycle and creating its own microclimate.

Hypercapitalism is the production of virtual reality—signs, symbols, and events—for a small elite of superconsumers, involving marginalization of the majority of humanity, and nature, into a criminalized global underground economy.

Import substitution industrialization. A developmental strategy used in the Global South from the end of World War II to the 1970s. It involves state promotion and programming of industrial development, high protective barriers for infant industry, imported technologies paid for with foreign debt, and some corporate penetration into key sectors. But this kind of industrialization leads to debt, fosters strong interest groups that do not allow eventual planned opening to international competition, and cannot finance technological intensification.

Intensive growth. Reorganization of production around computerization and robotics, with just-in-time stocking, driven by considerations of efficiency and sometimes by ecological concern. In the latter case it could involve energy efficiency or alternative sources, cogeneration, recycling, etc. An economy based on information and control rather than on gross material productivity.

Laterite. Hard soil resulting from leaching of minerals through rain and heat, often found in rain forests. Usually alkaline, rich in iron and aluminum oxides, and poor in productivity.

Legume. Species of plants in the pea family, which fix nitrogen through symbiotic association with the *Rhizobium* bacteria in root nodules. Legumes are, in effect, self-fertilizing plants.

Liberal capitalism is the hegemonic quasi-corporatist welfare state created after World War II, which came into crisis in the 1970s. Involving production of heavy industry and infrastructure, and consumer durables, liberal capitalism was based on a triangular relationship among big labor, big business, and big government, fed by a consensus on Cold War ideology. The state regulated the economy using fiscal and monetary policy, to provide full employment and thus full consumption. It repressed groups marginal to the system and purchased social peace with welfare.

MAI. Multilateral Accord on Investments, a secret treaty system now in negotiation and comprising a bill of rights for transnational corporations. Some provisions allow corporations to sue nation-states on par of equality and to demand full compensation for any nationalizations; others allow corporations to shift management and labor around the globe freely. Such a treaty system almost totally deregulates the world environment. Since treaties override domestic law, it would in effect cancel most environmental law and administration within nations signatory. President Clinton tried to "fast-track" MAI through Congress, which has so far resisted it. To date the public has been little aware of this treaty and its impacts.

Maquiladoras. There are 2,042 in-bond assembly industries in Mexico, many of them sweatshops, 1,493 on the border; some 821 of them generate hazardous wastes. These assembly plants use imported raw material and cheap wage labor, usually with no health or environmental controls, and immediately reexport the finished product.

NAFTA. North American Free Trade Agreement, set up by treaty between the United States, Canada, and Mexico.

New politics is not based on corporativist party building but on international and national networking, local mobilizations, and tactical alliances among parties, government, business, and environmentalists, to get access and apply maximum pressure where crucial decisions are being made. Usually based on networks of evanescent local movements mobilized to resist some form of corporate or governmental imposition on the environment. Such groups are usually led by women, are multicultural, and mobilize all local voluntary associations.

Old politics is based on the left-right ideological spectrum, which hinges upon conflicts between working and managerial classes over who controls the surpluses, social benefits, and social wage generated by capitalist technology and production. This kind of politics is organized by national political parties, unions, and other organizations in a pyramidal or corporatist manner.

NGO. Nongovernmental organization, a voluntary association or interest group in civil society.

pH. Positive hydrogen, a measure of concentration of hydrogen ions. A logarithmic scale of acidity or alkalinity.

Political Greens. A factorial attitude type that emerged from our field data: elites who have absorbed environmentalist rhetoric but have not formulated concrete policy positions; they have not integrated theory and practice. They blame Western Fordism for plundering the Global South but do not blame international aid agencies for concrete programs. They would like to mix economic growth with conservation, recycling, and energy efficiency but will also continence hard fuel cycles and high technologies. They are not pessimistic about global warming or overpopulation and are neutral about democracy and state versus market issues.

Political Greens represent leaders with environmental awareness but whose positions do not allow them to develop concrete programs implementing such ideas. Given the right mass mobilization and political conjuncture, Political Greens could play a positive role in environmental preservation. Lacking this, they will not take the initiative. They are just as postmodern and post-Fordist as Greens, or more so, but are constrained by their executive jobs from developing their ideas beyond what is politically feasible or prudent.

Pollution. Emission of material or energy that prejudices the biological productivity of water, air, or soil.

Post-Fordism is a socioeconomic model of transition to global corporate hypercapitalism and can be defined as restructuring transnational corporate production and distribution chains around global outsourcing, dematerialization of material transformation into production of signs/symbols/events, automated small-batch production for niche markets, and deregulation of physical, ethical, legal, welfare, or moral constraints on free trade.

Postmaterialism. Prosperity drives postmaterialist values, which can fluctuate with economic swings (period effects), to advance in a population. The inevitable march of generations (cohort replacement) overwhelms period effects in the long term and leads to the growing dominance of postmaterialist values. The survey literature fails to argue whether this shift is socially beneficial or not. The postmaterialist transition seems clearest in large-batch data but tends to become muddier in the detail of fine-grained national studies, when different methods are used (rating versus ranking, multivariate analysis), or when different statistical controls are used for social class, education, employment status, ethnicity, etc.

Postmodern Managers. A factorial attitude type occupying postmodern factorial space with the main concentration in post-Fordism. This type overlaps Greens and Sustainable Developers and provides crucial mediation between their differing social projects: a green society versus green capitalism. Postmodern Managers are concerned to develop environmentally sound economies and technologies and are risk averse regarding fossil and nuclear fuel cycles and biotechnology. They are quite worried about global warming and plan to counter its effects. Postmodern Managers are key decision makers in all three sectors who see capitalism evolving away from its obsessive extensive growth. But they distrust business and are neutral about using economic incentives versus direct regulation. Managers are pro-democratic and look to international treaty regimes and aid to create environmentally responsible development.

Postmodern philosophy sees the world as text and therefore has a warrant to deconstruct, supplement, and evert the texts of Western modernism (Enlightenment liberalism), freeing the signs in these texts to spill out endlessly and refer to other texts and signs. All subjectivity, origins, telos, linear narrative, means-ends relations, political practice, and hope for social change are dissolved in scholastic textual analysis.

Postmodern values. Libertarianism, lifestyle engineering, hyperconsumerism of positional goods (status indicators), public deployment of the self (emotional work, feminization of culture, confessional subjectivity), multiculturalism (tempered with hip indifference), feminism, cynicism and apoliticism, risk aversion, and environmental concern. Also cynicism bordering on nihilism, detachment, coolness, and utter egocentrism. Refers to art forms that involve copy and pastiche of symbols taken out of context and juxtaposed arbitrarily; an example is MTV.

Preservation. Maintenance of whole ecosystems or areas of same in the original state, without human interference, as a park, or biological reserve for future study, utilization, or for its intrinsic value.

Quaternary economic sector. The fourth sector of the economy, involving information science, artificial intelligence, telecommunication, robotics, remote sensing and global information systems, biotechnology, fine chemistry and engineering, new material sciences, nonlinear dynamics, complexity. The leading sector of the new global post-Fordist economy.

Sustainable development. An economic theory based on the idea that the ecological problem comes from the true costs of using nature not being reflected in the market because of price distortions, government subsidies, and regulations that do not answer a cost-benefit test. Rational pricing and property rights in resources allow the market to align the economy with natural limits. Governments should regulate only when benefits outweigh administrative costs and do not distort the market. Free trade maximizes rational global resource use, promotes export of environmentally friendly technologies, and should not be constrained by domestic regulation.

Sustainable Developers. A factorial attitude type spanning the Fordism/post-Fordism spectrum within postmodern attitude space. Holders of this factorial type form a broad band of attitudes but tend toward green capitalism. They correspond to the neoliberal free trade sustainable development concept elaborated at UNCED in Rio de Janeiro in 1992. Sustainable Developers are anthropocentric rationalists who reject apocalyptic visions and critiques of Western Fordist developmentalism. Reason, technology, regulated markets, and democracy can all conserve nature. Future development must proceed around technological transformation of industry, but Sustainable Developers distrust business and believe that regulation as well as incentives are needed for conservation. They are not as risk averse as Greens and are willing to consider using fossil and nuclear fuels and biotechnology.

Taylorism. Friedrich Taylor, Henry Ford's efficiency expert, invented the microscopic division of labor and time and motion studies that deskilled, routinized, and idiotized manual labor. The term implies routine, unskilled, low paid, alienated, and often dangerous or unhealthy work.

Varzea. Alluvial plain with nutrient-rich waters and with high productivity on land and in the water.

WTO. The World Trade Organization, administrative apparatus based on the General Agreement on Tariffs and Trade treaty system, the world's largest treaty, which tends to override the more than two hundred environmental treaties in place because of its total lack of provision for the issue. GATT mandates product over process (a nation cannot question the origin or ecological costs of a product imported into its territory), which conflicts with the precautionary principle (do no environmental harm) and the "polluter pays" principle, both of which have emerged as international common law. WTO has national committees in each signatory country to find solutions to the problem of conflicts of law, but free trade is the paramount principle, and countries are not allowed to use protection or trade sanctions to enforce environmental treaty provisions. This leaves, of course, few other mechanisms short of war to do so.

Notes

Chapter 1

1. Environics Ltd., *Environmental Monitor.*
2. Brown, *Political Subjectivity.* Stephenson, *The Study of Behavior; The Play Theory;* "The Quantimization of Psychological Events," 1–25; "Quantum Theory," 180–95; "William James," parts 1–4. Comrey, *A First Course.* Cornwell, *Nature's Vision.* D'Abro, *The Rise of the New Physics.* Heisenberg, *Physics and Philosophy.* Folse, *The Philosophy.* Herbert, *Quantum Reality.*
3. The studies are found in Peritore, "Liberation Theology"; *Socialism;* "Brazilian Communist Opinion"; "Brazilian Party Left Opinion." Peritore and Galve-Peritore, "Brazilian Attitudes toward Agrarian Reform." See also Peritore and Galve-Peritore, "Cleavage and Polarization in Mexico's Ruling Party," and Peritore, "Environmental Attitudes of Indian Elites," and "India's Environmental Crisis."
4. Brown, *Political Subjectivity,* 68, 250, 251.
5. Brown, *Political Subjectivity,* 247.
6. Brown, *Political Subjectivity,* 191.
7. Brown, *Political Subjectivity,* 67.
8. Peritore, "Reflections on Dangerous Fieldwork."
9. Brown, *Political Subjectivity,* 70.
10. Brown, *Political Subjectivity,* 68.
11. Brown, *Political Subjectivity,* 166.

Chapter 2

1. Gitlin, "Postmodernism." Harland, *Superstructuralism.* Jameson, *The Prison-House; Postmodernism.* Kristeva, *Language the Unknown.* Bakhtin, *Marxismo e filosofia.* Ryan, *Marxism.* Lyotard, *The Postmodern Condition.* Lacan, *The Language.* Deleuze and Guattari, *Anti-Oedipus.* Bataille, *The Accursed Share.* Marcus and Fischer, *Anthropology.* Geertz, *The Interpretation.* Shweder and LeVine, eds., *Culture Theory.* Lutz, *Unnatural Emotions.* Kitzinger, *The Social Construction.* Horkheimer and Adorno, *The Dialectic of Enlightenment.* Adorno, *Negative Dialectics.* Habermas, *The Philosophical Discourse.*
2. Derrida, *Of Grammatology; Writing and Difference; Dissemination.* Foucault, *The Archaeology of Knowledge; The Order of Things; Discipline and Punish; Madness*

and Civilization; The History of Sexuality. Rabinow, ed., *The Foucault Reader*. Dreyfus and Rabinow, *Foucault*. Baudrillard, *For a Critique of the Political Economy; Le Miroir de Production; A Sociedade de Consumo*. Poster, ed., *Jean Baudrillard: Selected Writings*. Phillips, "Is Nature Necessary?" Larrain, "The Postmodern Critique." Castells, *End of Millenium*.

3. Bourdieu, *Distinction*, 56, 55; *Language*.

4. Castells, *End of Millenium*, chap. 3. Robb, *Midnight in Sicily*. Sterling, *Octopus*. McConnaughey and Zottoli, *Introduction to Marine Biology*, 483. Gibson, *Neuromancer; Count Zero; Mona Lisa Overdrive*.

5. R. Roy, "India in 1993," 205–6.

6. Inglehart, *Culture Shift*, 83–99, 103. Inglehart and Abramson, "Economic Security." Milbrath, *Environmentalists; Envisioning a Sustainable Society*.

7. Inglehart, *The Silent Revolution; Culture Shift*, 151–52, 155–57. Abramson and Inglehart, "Generational Replacement." Pelletier and Guerin, "Postmaterialisme." Gibson and Duch, "Postmaterialism." Dryzek and Lester, "Alternative Views." Milbrath, *Environmentalists*, chap. 3. Steger, Pierce, Steel, and Loverich, "Political Culture." Van Liere and Dunlap, "The Social Bases." Pierce, Tsurutani, and Loverich, "Vanguards and Rearguards in Environmental Politics." Gill, Crosby, and Taylor, "Ecological Concern." Gilroy and Shapiro, "The Polls." Hall, "Soviet Perceptions." Pierce, Loverich, Tsuratani, and Abe, "Environmental Belief Systems." McKean, *Environmental Protest*. Brooks and Manza, "Do Changing Values Explain the New Politics?" Hofrichter and Reif, "Evolution of Environmental Attitudes." Knutsen, "The Priorities of Materialist and Post-Materialist Values." Steger, Pierce, Steel, and Loverich, "Political Culture."

8. Knutsen, "The Priorities of Materialist and Post-Materialist Values," 233, 231. Andersen, "'Environmentalism'." Finger and Sciarini, "Integrating 'New Politics'." Weale, "The Greening of the European Polity?" Kitschelt and Hellemans, *Ideological and Political Action*, 67.

9. Reimer, "No Values—New Values?" Knutsen, "The Priorities of Materialist and Post-Materialist Values," 235, 239. Uusitalo, "Are Environmental Attitudes and Behaviour Inconsistent?" 221–25. Bean and Papadakis, "Polarized Priorities?" Inglehart "Polarized Priorities." Granato, Inglehart, and Leblanc, "Effects of Cultural Values." Braithwaite, Makkai, and Pittelkow, "Inglehart's Materialism." Evans, Heath, and Lalljee, "Measuring Left-Right." DeGraaf and Evans, "Why Are the Young More Postmaterialist?" Duch and Taylor, "Postmaterialism," 747, and "A Reply to Abramson." Abramson and Inglehart, "Education, Security, and Postmaterialism," 797.

10. Andersen, "Denmark." Inglehart, "From Class-Based to Value-Based Politics." Aardal, "Green Politics." Rule, "Green Politics," 21–23. Joppke and Markovits. "Green Politics," 235.

11. Kreuzer, "New Politics?" Hofrichter and Reif, "Evolution of Environmental Attitudes," 122–23.

12. Burckhardt, *The Civilization*. Huizinga, *The Waning of the Middle Ages*. Huyssen, *After the Great Divide*.

13. Buttel and Taylor, "Environmental Sociology." Dunlap and Mertig, "Glo-

bal Concern." World Commission on Environment and Development, *Our Common Future*. Garrett, *Living within Limits*. Ophuls, *Requiem for Modern Politics*. Poll data in *Scientific American*, 120.

14. Environics Ltd., *Environmental Monitor*.

15. Dunlap and Mertig, "Global Concern for the Environment," 135. Disease statistics in Inglehart, "Public Support."

16. Broad, "The Poor."

17. Kay, "Aboriginal Overkill." Kirch, *The Evolution*; "Man's Role," 26–31. McGlone, "Polynesian Deforestation." Alvard, "Conservation." Vickers, "From Opportunism to Nascent Conservation." Stearman, "Only Slaves Climb Trees." Bayliss-Smith, "Constraints on Population Growth." Meggers, "Environmental Limitation."

18. Inglehart "Public Support," 66, 70.

19. Dunlap and Mertig, "Global Concern," 27. Steven and Kempton, "Global Environmentalism." Kidd and Lee, "Postmaterialist Values." Brechin and Kempton, "Beyond Postmaterialist Values." Dunlap and Mertig, "Global Environmental Concern." Pierce, "The Hidden Layer of Political Culture."

20. Inglehart, "Public Support," 64.

21. Lash and Urry, *The End of Organized Capitalism*. Harvey, *The Condition of Postmodernity*. Lipietz, *Towards a New Economic Order*. Vallas and Beck, "Transformation of Work Revisited." Polanyi, *The Great Transformation*. Polanyi, Arensberg, and Pearson, eds., *Trade and Market*. O'Connor, *The Fiscal Crisis of the State*. Habermas, *Legitimation Crisis*. P. Kennedy, *The Rise and Fall of the Great Powers*. Dryzek, *Democracy in Capitalist Times*.

For world systems theory see Braudel, *The Mediterranean; Capitalism; The Wheels of Commerce*. Wallerstein, *The Modern World System; The Politics of the World Economy; The Capitalist World Economy*. Beaud, *A History of Capitalism*. Tainter, *The Collapse of Complex Societies*. Conrad and Demarest, *Religion and Empire*.

For hypercapitalism see Poster, ed., *Jean Baudrillard*; Baudrillard, *The Mirror of Production, For A Critique of the Political Economy of the Sign*, and *A Sociedade de Consumo*; Henwood, "Post What?"; Carter and Rayner, "The Curious Case of Post-Fordism."

22. Scott and Storper, *Production, Work, Territory*, chap. 2. Tavares and David, *A economia política*. Singer, *Economia política*. Marcussen and Torp, *Internationalization of Capital*. R. Lee, "Modernization." Pollard and Storper, "A Tale of 12 Cities."

23. Lipietz in Scott and Storper, *Production*. 28.

24. Lipietz in Scott and Storper, *Production*. 28–29.

25. Scott and Storper, *Production*. 28–29.

26. Van Parijs, "A Revolution." Holmes, "The Organization."

27. Castells, *End of Millenium*.

28. Peritore, "High-Tech Import Substitution." Hollerman, *Japan's Economic Strategy*. J. Halliday, *A Political History*. Halliday and McCormack, *Japanese Imperialism Today*.

29. Bergson, *The Economics of Soviet Planning*. Nove, *An Economic History*. Gregory and Stuart, *Soviet Economic Structure*. Dyker, *The Soviet Economy*. Lane, *The Socialist*. Bettleheim, *Class Struggles*. D'Encausse, *Le pouvoir confisqué*. Ziegler, *Environmental Policy*. Habermas, *Legitimation Crisis*.

Andors, *China's Industrial Revolution*. Wheelwright and McFarlane, *The Chinese Road*. Gurley, *China's Economy*. Eckstein, *China's Economic Revolution*. Silverman, ed., *Man and Socialism*.

Chapter 3

1. Quotes from Kellner and Heuberger, eds., *Hidden Technocrats*, 126. See also Milbrath, *Environmentalists*, chaps. 2, 3.

2. Kellner and Heuberger, eds., *Hidden Technocrats*, chaps. 1, 2. Essays in this book indicate the conservative ideological tone and data-poor nature of the new-class literature. Martin, "Symbolic Knowledge," chap. 5. Bourdieu, *Distinction*, 402, 405.

3. Esping-Anderson, "Postmodern Cleavage Structures." Van Parijs, "A Revolution." Argentina data from Brasnet, an e-mail listserve.

4. Brint, "'New Class'." Lamont, "Cultural Capital."

5. Savage, "Postmaterialism of the Left and Right."

6. Martin, "Symbolic Knowledge," 125.

7. Andersen, "Denmark," 114.

8. Vedung, "The Formation of Green Parties," 264, 272. Kitschelt, "La Gauche Libertaire." Faucher and Doherty, "The Decline of Green Politics." Szarka, "Green Politics in France." Inglehart, *Culture Shift*, 89.

9. Finger and Sciarini, "Integrating 'New Politics'," 110. Kreuzer, "New Politics." Christoff, "The 1993 Australian Elections," 130 ff. Doern, "Sectoral Green Politics."

10. Kreuzer, "New Politics," 10–29. Vedung, "The Formation of Green Parties." Bennulf and Holmberg, "The Green Breakthrough." Micheletti, "Swedish Corporatism."

11. Aardal, "Green Politics." Brundtland Commission, *Our Common Future*. Lester and Loftsson, "The Ecological Movement."

12. Andersen, "Denmark," 203–4.

13. Kitschelt and Hellemans, *Beyond the European Left*, 91–92, and see chaps. 3 and 4. Kitschelt, *The Logics of Party Formation;* "Left-Libertarian Parties." Kitschelt and Hellemans, "The Left-Right Semantics."

14. Müller-Rommel, "New Political Movements," chap. 11. Dalton, *Citizen Politics*. Müller-Rommel, ed. *New Politics*. Franklin and Rudig, "On the Durability of Green Politics." Rudig, "Green Party Politics," 25–31. Dryzek, *Democracy*.

15. Müller-Rommel and Pridham, eds. *Small Parties*, chaps. 1–3, 6, 9. Burklin, "Governing Left Parties."

16. On France see Hoffmann-Martinot, "Grüne and Verts," and Sainteny, "Les dirigeants écologistes." Kitschelt, "The Green Phenomenon."

17. Peritore, *Socialism;* "Brazilian Party Left Opinion"; "Brazilian Communist Opinion"; "Liberation Theology."

18. Peritore and Galve-Peritore, "Cleavage and Polarization in Mexico's Ruling Party."

Chapter 4

1. Fox, *Gandhian Utopia,* chap. 3. Gandhi, *My Autobiography.*

2. Bhattacharya, "Growth and Distribution." Roy et al., eds., *Economic Development.* Echeverri-Gent, *Economic Reform,* chap. 3.

3. Roy et al., eds., *Economic Development,* chap. 2.

4. Centre for Science and Environment, *The State of India's Environment,* 206. Center for Science and Environment, *The Wrath of Nature.*

5. Data in Singh, ed., *Environmental Regeneration,* passim. Ahmad, "Bangladesh." Bandyopadhyay, "The Ecology of Drought." Guha, *The Unquiet Woods,* chap. 3. Lal, *India's Forests,* chap. 2. *Illustrated Weekly of India.* Alvares and Billorey, "Damning the Narmada." Paranjpye, *Evaluating the Tehri Dam.* Dhawan, *Big Dams.* INTACH, *The Tehri Dam.* D'Monte, *Temples or Tombs?* Swain, *Environmental Trap.*

6. Guha, *The Unquiet Woods.* Vohra, *The Greening of India,* 4–5. Lal, *India's Forests,* 30–32. Centre for Science and Environment, *The State of India's Environment,* 49.

7. Guha, *The Unquiet Woods,* 89–95, 129, 159, 179–84, and chap. 7 for history. Bandyopadhyay and Shiva, "Chipko," 26–34; "Development," 111–17, 217–26; *Chipko.* Shiva, *Staying Alive,* chap. 4. D'Monte "India's Environment," chap. 4. *Cultural Survival Quarterly,* special edition on India's environment and movements. Bhatt, "The Chipko," 43–56; "Green the People," 1–4. Berreman, "Chipko." Hegde, "The Appiko Movement," 29–30. Callicott and Ames, *Nature in Asian Traditions.*

8. The account of Uttaranchal is based on Khator, *Environment,* chap. 6; Guha, *The Unquiet Woods,* 177; and Peet and Watts, *Liberation Ecologies,* chap. 10.

9. Developmental Alternatives, *To Choose a Future,* 3. Government of India, *Approach to the 8th Five Year Plan,* 2–3; *Ministry of Environment Annual Report.* Author interviews with NGOs, high officials in Ministries of Environment and Planning, UNEP, UNDP, and the World Bank, July–Aug. 1990.

10. Agarwal, *Towards Green Villages,* 22, 23, 28, 40–41, chaps. 4–5. Jayal, *Eliminating Poverty.* Government of India, *Approach to the 8th Plan,* 12–13, passim. Bhatt, "The Chipko." Bandyopadhyay, "Deforestation," 28–36. Gupta, "How Common Is Commons?," 101–9.

11. Kothari, *Illustrated Weekly of India.* Shiva, *The Violence.* Karlekar, *Indian Express.*

12. Khator, *Environment,* 100. Government of India, *Ministry of Environment Annual Report.*

13. Khator, *Environment,* 26, chap. 3.

14. Environics Ltd., *Environmental Monitor.*

15. Khator, *Environment*, 104–14; this account of bureaucratic politics based on Khator's fieldwork reported in chap. 4.

16. Khator, *Environment*, 194, chap. 6.

Chapter 5

1. Bennett, "Trade: The Key," 11–17. Amsden, "Third Industrialization," 5–31. Hart-Landsberg, "South Korea." Sunoo, *The South Korean Economy*. Kim and Kihl, eds., *Political Change*. Rhee, "The Economic Problems," chap. 10. Steinberg, *The Republic of Korea*, 140. Chang, "Korean Students and Anti-American Attitudes." Shinn, "Education and Quality of Life." Macdonald, *The Koreans*. Yoon, "National Interest and the Press in Korea." Young-Khee, "Mass Media and Environmental Issues." *World Almanac*, 1994. Griffin, *Korea*. Ministry of Environment, *Environmental White Paper*, 4. *Korea Newsreview,* June 22, 1991. Kuznets, *Korean Economic Development*. Burmeister, "South Korea's Rural Development Dilemma."

2. Kuznets, *Korean Economic Development*, 2. *Korea Newsreview,* June 22, May 4, March 23, 1991. Bennett, "Korea Adopts Seventh Five-Year Plan," 1–7. Steinberg, *The Republic of Korea*. *Jung-ang Daily News*, various issues. Ministry of Environment, *Environmental White Paper*, 4.

3. Koo, ed. *State and Society*, especially chap. 3 by Carter Eckert. Macdonald, *The Koreans*. Cho and Kim, eds., *Korea's Political Economy*. Lee and Sohn, "South Korea in 1993," 1–9. Amirahmadi, "Development Paradigms," 167–85. Environics Ltd., *Environmental Monitor*, 1998.

4. The following analysis is based on data from OECD, *Environmental Performance Reviews: Korea* and from *National Action Plan for Agenda 21*. In Seoul the figure is over 60.8% of total air pollutants in 1993. *Korea Newsreview,* June 22, 1991. *Jung-ang Daily News*, March 16, August 19, 1991. Chun, "All-Out War Proposed for Preserving Environment," 52–56. Barker and Barker, eds., *Clean Air*, 91–98. *The Environmental White Paper*, 1990, i–iii, 34, 197–212. *Korea Newsreview,* April 6, 1991. Macdonald, *The Koreans*, 238.

5. Macdonald, *The Koreans*, 237.

6. Taeruik Research Institute, *National Poll on Environmental Preservation*, 7–27. Lee and Sohn, "South Korea in 1993," 1–9. In 1993, Professor Kim Young-Khee applied the Q-method protocol to a sample of environmentalists, scientists, governmental officials, businessmen, and journalists in Korea with the aid and advice of the research team at Lucky Goldstar Advertising Agency (L.G. Ad). The 74 Q-sorts, which Dr. Kim and L.G. Ad interviewers ran in January 1991—representing nine life scientists and students, thirty-four environmentalists, eight government officials in the Ministry of Environment, and twenty-three businessmen—were found to be reducible to four different factorial attitude types, which were named Greens (N = 13), Postmodern Managers (N = 16), Sustainable Developers (N = 9), and Political Greens (N = 10).

Chapter 6

1. National Resources Council, *Sustainable Agriculture*, 285, passim. Myers, *The Primary Source*.

2. Butts and Bogue, *International Amazonia*. Cardoso, *Amazônia*. Martins, *Os camponeses;* "Impasses políticos dos movimentos sociais," 131–48.

3. Funatura, *Custo da Implantação de Unidades de Conservação na Amazônia Legal*, 14–17. Funatura, *Alternativas ao desmatamento na Amazônia*.

4. National Resources Council, *Sustainable Agriculture*, 283.

5. Bradford and Glock, *The Last Frontier*. Cota, *A Invasão Desarmada. Cultural Survival: Special Report—Brazil*. Fearnside, "Deforestation and International Economic Development." Foresta, *Amazon Conservation*. Hecht and Cockburn, *The Fate of the Forest*. Hildyard, "Adios Amazonia?" 53–63. Lutzenburger, "Who Is Destroying the Amazon Rainforest?" 155–60. Warford and Warford, eds., *Environmental Management*. Sioli, *Amazônia. Veja*, "Sinais de vida e morte." "A morte ronda os indios." Fernandes, *Quém é quém*.

For the impact of deforestation on global warming see Fletcher, "Tropical Deforestation"; Hensen-Sellers, Dickinson, and Wilson, "Tropical Deforestation"; Hekstra, "Global Warming"; Kellogg, "Mankind's Impact on Climate"; Lave, "The Greenhouse Effect"; MacDonald, "Scientific Basis for the Greenhouse Effect"; and Schneider and Londer, *The Coevolution of Climate and Life*.

6. Serrão and Homma, "Brazil," 265–351.

7. Feldman, ed., *Guía da Ecología*. Interview with Deputy Fabio Feldman, who became minister of environment under the presidency of Fernando Henrique Cardoso.

8. Serrão and Homma, "Brazil," 265.

9. Martins, "Impasses políticos."

10. Eden, *Ecology and Land Management in Amazonia*, chaps. 4, 7. Clusener-Godt and Sacik, eds., *Brazilian Perspectives*. Ng, "Ecological Principles." Dahlberg, "Redefining Development Priorities." Dias, *Alternatívas de Desenvolvimento. EcoAmazônia*, photocopy. "Our Nature," President Sarney's speech, commission reports. Encontro dos Empresarios da Amazônia, *Carta da Amazônia*. Wilson, ed., *Biodiversity*. Prance, Balee, Boom, and Carneiro, "Quantitative Ethnobotany," 296–310. Ricklefs, *Ecology*. Seger, "Native Americans," in Hallsworth, ed., *Socio-Economic Effects*. "War in the Amazon," 12–38. Nations and Komer, "Rainforests," 161–67.

11. Serrão and Homma, "Brazil," 330–33.

12. Eden, *Ecology*, chap. 7. Hanan and Batalha, *Amazônia*, chap. 4. Author interviews in Embrapa, Ibama, Congress. Serrão and Homma, "Brazil," 336.

13. Feldman, ed., *Guía da Ecología*, 210–11. Hanan and Batalha, *Amazônia*. Secretaria do Meio-Ambiente, *Curso de Direito Ambiental*.

14. Guimaraes, *Ecopolitics*, chap. 7.

15. Hall, *Sustaining Amazonia*, 55–78.

16. Guimaraes, *Ecopolitics,* 193–94. CIMA, *The Challenge,* 150. Inglehart, "Public Support," 57–71. Environics Ltd., *Environmental Monitor,* 1998.

17. Hall, *Sustaining Amazonia,* 70–71.

18. Hochstetler, "The Evolution," 192–216.

19. Schmink and Wood, *Contested Frontiers,* chap. 4. Zirker and Henberg, "Amazonia," 259–81.

20. Hewitt, "The Roman Catholic Church," 239–58. Peritore, "Liberation Theology," 59–92; *Socialism.* Peritore and Galve-Peritore, "Brazilian Agrarian Reform."

21. Peritore, *Socialism.* Peritore and Peritore, "Brazilian Agrarian Reform."

22. Winthrop, "Debt for Nature Swaps?" 129–49.

Chapter 7

1. OECD, *Environmental Performance Reviews: Mexico,* 41–43. World Resources Institute, *World Resources 1990–1991; 1992 Information,* 544–45.

2. OECD, *Environmental Performance Reviews: Mexico,* 58, 60, 73. Russell, *Mexico under Salinas.*

3. Russell, *Mexico under Salinas.* Sedesol, *México: Informe de la Situación General,* chap. 5. OECD, *Environmental Performance Reviews: Mexico,* 58.

4. Solis-Weiss and Mendez Ubach, "Los Recursos naturales," 381–420. Solis Weiss, "Edenes productivos," 421–52. Sedesol, *México: Informe de la Situación General,* chaps. 5, 8.

5. Sedesol, *México: Informe de la Situación General,* 76–85. Russell, *Mexico under Salinas.* Gomez-Pompa, Kaus, Jimenez-Osornio, Bainbridge, and Rorive, "Mexico," 484–548.

6. National Resources Council (NRC), *Sustainable Agriculture,* 491–93, 488, 495–96. Peritore and Galve-Peritore, eds., *Biotechnology in Latin America,* chap. 4. The EZLN as a "postmodern guerrilla movement" was taken from a paper by Barry Carr at AILASA (Australasian Ibero-American Studies Association) in Brisbane, Australia, 1996.

7. SEMARNAP, *Programa de Trabajo 1998,* 41.

8. Sedesol, *México: Informe de la Situación General,* 181–92, 197, 202. Russell, *Mexico under Salinas,* 257–60.

9. Sedesol, *México: Informe de la Situación General,* chap. 12. Mumme, "System Maintenance and Environmental Reform," 123–43. SEMARNAP, *México hacia el Desarrollo Sustentable,* 33. OECD, *Environmental Performance Reviews: Mexico,* 80, 82, 88.

10. Russell, *Mexico under Salinas.* Finkleman, "Medio ambiente," 547–81. Puente and Legorreta, *Medio ambiente.* Leff, "Cultura democrática." Menendez-Garza, "Comisión Metropolitana." OECD, *Environmental Performance Reviews: Mexico,* 84. SEMARNAP, *Programa de Trabajo 1998,* 37, 91–93.

11. Sedesol, *México: Informe de la Situación General,* 84–85, 97–99. SEMARNAP, *Informe de Labores 1995–1996,* 20, 23, 49–50; *Programa de Trabajo 1998,* 19; *Mexico*

hacia el Desarrollo Sustentable, 27. OECD, *Environmental Performance Reviews: Mexico,* 111–13.

12. SEMARNAP, *México hacia el Desarrollo Sustentable,* 11–13. Sedesol, *México: Informe de la Situación General,* 92. Russell, *Mexico under Salinas. NACLA Report on the Americas* 28, no. 1, July 1994.

13. SEMARNAP, *México hacia el Desarrollo Sustentable,* 11–13. Russell, *Mexico under Salinas.* Goldrich, "Sustainable Development," 97–122.

14. Sedesol, *México: Informe de la Situación General,* xxvii, our translation. Mumme and Sanchez, "Mexico's Environment." SEMARNAP, *México hacia el Desarrollo Sustentable,* 11–13; *Ley General.*

15. Sedesol, *México: Informe de la Situación General,* xxviii, xxv–xxxvi, our translation.

16. Mumme, Bath, and Asseto, "Political Development," 7–33.

17. Redclift, "Environmental Conflict?"; "Mexico's Green Movements," 44–46. Mumme and Sanchez, "Mexico's Environment." Mumme, Bath, and Asseto, "Political Development," 7–33. "Pacto de Grupos Ecologistas." Authors' interviews with NGO leaders. Partido Ecologista Mexicano Documents, photocopy. "Partido Verde Ecologista," offprint.

18. Russell, *Mexico under Salinas,* 348. Perot and Choate, *Save Your Job,* 70.

19. Beyers, "The U.S./Mexico Tuna Embargo." Russell, *Mexico under Salinas,* 369. Perot and Choate, *Save Your Job,* 47, 68–69. Morici, *Trade Talks with Mexico; Canada-United States.*

20. Mumme, Bath, and Asseto, "Political Development."

Chapter 8

1. Puerto Rico has a population of 3.5 million, of whom 1 million reside in metropolitan San Juan.

2. USDC, *Economic Study #1,* 73–74, in Dietz, *An Economic History of Puerto Rico,* 209–10. Hogner, *Enchanted Toxics 1990.*

3. Ross, *The Long Uphill Path,* 126. NACLA *Report on the Americas, Puerto Rico.* Pierce, *Under the Eagle,* 50.

4. PREDA, *Industrial Newsletter,* 1. Dietz, *An Economic History of Puerto Rico,* 253. Ramos de Santiago, *E1 Desarrollo Constitucional,* 172.

5. Puerto Rico, *Environmental Public Policy Act,* 4. Prof. Albarrán interview with Carl Solderberg, regional director, Environmental Protection Agency.

6. *San Juan Star,* June 6, 1992, 5.

7. *E1 Nuevo Dia,* Dec. 26, 1992, 8.

8. *E1 Nuevo Dia.* Sept. 14, 1993, 14.

9. Hogner, *Enchanted Toxics 1990.*

10. Prof. Albarrán interviews with municipal government officials, NGOs.

11. Prof. Albarrán interviews with EPA.

12. Prof. Albarrán field interviews in municipalities.

13. Puerto Rico USA Foundation document, offprint, 1992, 5.

14. *Verde Luz,* 1–2. *San Juan Star,* 6.

Chapter 9

1. King, *A History,* 72. Mungiu and Pippidi, "Letter from Romania," 356. Calinescu and Tismaneanu, "The 1989 Revolution," 42–59. Sislin, "Revolution Betrayed?" 395–411. Gallagher, "Romania's Communist Dystopia," 552–57. *Romania: Encyclopedic Survey,* 1994.

2. Fischer, *Nicolae Ceausescu,* 250.

3. Zvosec, "Environmental Deterioration," 101–2. Maitland, "Romania's Environmental Crisis." 235. Waller, "The Ecology Issue," 303–27.

4. Rady, *Romania in Turmoil,* 79.

5. Tismaneanu, "The Revival of Politics," 89. Radio Free Europe, *Situation Report,* 18. *Anuarul Statistic al Romaniei.* Frausum, Gehman, and Gross, "Market Economy," 735–56.

6. Rady, *Romania in Turmoil,* 78.

7. *Partide politice.*

8. Interview with Romanian Ecological Movement (MER) party activist in Bucharest in April 1994.

9. Shafir, "Romanian Local Elections," 30–31.

10. Mihut, "The Emergence of Political Pluralism," 421.

11. Shafir, "Romanian Local Elections."

Chapter 10

1. Bill and Leiden, *The Middle East.* Halliday, *Iran.* Keddie, *Roots of Revolution.* Readman et al., "Oil and combustion product," 662–65. Williams, Heckman, and Schneeberger, *Environmental Consequences.* Dept. of the Environment, Islamic Republic of Iran, *National Report.* Zekavat, "The State of the Environment," 49–72. Wolfson, "The Caspian Sea," 14–21.

2. Dept. of the Environment, Islamic Republic of Iran, *National Report,* 34. World Resources Institute, *World Resources 1990–1991.* World Resources Institute, *1992 Information.*

3. Zekavat, "The State of the Environment," 56, 70. Dept. of the Environment, Islamic Republic of Iran, *National Report,* passim.

4. Malek, "Elite Factionalism." Behrooz, "Factionalism in Iran," 597–614. This was the political situation when the Q-method survey was run in Tehran. Bakhash "Perils of an Iranian Moderate," 3–4. Metz, ed., *Iran.* Bayat, *Street Politics.* Nowshirvani and Patrick, "The State."

5. Zekavat, "The State of the Environment," 68. Hillmann, *Iranian Culture.* Hunter, "Iran." Szalay, Moftakhar, and Mir-Djalali, "The Iranian Self-Image," 1–23. Mir-Djalali, "The Failure of Language."

6. Zadeh, "On the Ethics of Man's Interaction," 43, 47.

Chapter 11

1. Wyburd, "Case Study: Industry," 204–21.

2. Zimmerman et al., eds. *Environmental Philosophy*. McCormick, *Reclaiming Paradise*. Miller, *Gaia Connections*. Paehlke, *Environmentalism*. Wenz, *Environmental Justice*. Marshall, *Nature's Web*. Steiguer, *Age of Environmentalism*. Kennedy, *The New Anthropomorphism*. Vauclair, *Animal Cognition*.

3. Grey, *Beyond the New Right*, chap. 4.

4. Hobbes, *Leviathan; De Cive or The Citizen*. Heilbroner, *Inquiry into the Human Prospect*, 124, 134. Hardin, "The Tragedy"; *The Limits of Altruism*. A biological critique of utilitarian ethics is found in Alexander, *The Biology*; Masters, *The Nature of Politics*, and Masters and Gruter, *The Sense of Justice*.

5. Bryant and Mohai, eds., *Race*. Taylor, "Blacks and the Environment," 175–205.

6. Schmidheiny, *Changing Course*. Buchholz, *Principles of Environmental Management*. Peritore and Galve-Peritore, eds., *Biotechnology in Latin America*. Reid, *Sustainable Development*. Lind, *Up from Conservatism*. Chatterjee and Finger, *The Earth Brokers*.

7. Hoffmann-Martinot, "Grüne and Verts," 70, 78. Capra and Spretnak, *Green Politics*. Dobson, *Green Political Thought*. Switzler, *Green Backlash*. Princen and Finger, *Environmental NGOs*. Papadakis, *The Green Movement*. Dalton and Kuechler, eds., *Challenging the Political Order*. Parkin, *Green Parties*. Richardson and Rootes, eds., *The Green Challenge*. Rainbow, *Green Politics*. For the Green Party in Brazil see Peritore, *Socialism*. Barry, "The Limits of the Shallow."

8. Zimmerman et al., eds., *Environmental Philosophy*. Deval and Sessions, *Deep Ecology*. Reed and Rothenberg, *Wisdom in the Open Air*. Rothenberg, *Is It Painful to Think?* Murti, *The Central Philosophy*.

9. Zimmerman et al., eds., *Environmental Philosophy*, 184. Shiva, *Staying Alive; The Violence*. Evans, "Ecofeminism," 181. Buss, *The Evolution*, 47. Short and Balaban, eds., *The Differences between the Sexes*. Fisher, *Anatomy of Love*, 283. Hrdy, *The Woman That Never Evolved*, 189–91, passim. Fluehr-Lobban, "Marxist Reappraisal," 341–59. Baker and Bellis, *Human Sperm Competition*, 7. Trivers, *Social Evolution*; "The evolution," 35–57. Hamilton, "The Evolution of Social Behavior," 427–37. Gould and Gould, *Sexual Selection*. Andersson, *Sexual Selection*. Van der Dennen, ed., *The Nature*, chaps. 1–3, 5, 6. Daly and Wilson, *Homicide*, 15, chaps. 3–4. Palmer, ed., *Shining Path of Peru*.

10. Zimmerman et al., eds., *Environmental Philosophy*. Shiva, Staying Alive.

Bibliography

Aardal, Bernt. "Green Politics: A Norwegian Experience." *Scandinavian Political Studies* 13, no. 2 (1990): 147–63.

Abramson, Paul R., and Ronald Inglehart. "Education, Security, and Postmaterialism." *American Journal of Political Science* 38, no. 3 (1994): 797–814.

————. "Generational Replacement and the Future of Post-Materialist Values." *Journal of Politics* 49 (1987): 131–41.

Adorno, Theodor. *Negative Dialectics*. New York: Seabury, 1973.

Agarwal, Anil. *Towards Green Villages*. New Delhi, India: Centre for Science and Environment, 1989.

Agarwal, Anil, et al., eds. *The Fight for Survival*. New Delhi, India: Centre for Science and Environment, 1987.

Ahmad, M. "Bangladesh: How Forest Exploitation Is Leading to Disaster." *Ecologist* 17, no. 4 (1987): 168–69.

Alexander, Richard D. *The Biology of Moral Systems*. New York: Aldine de Gruyter, 1987.

Alvard, Michael. "Conservation by Native Peoples: Prey Choice in a Depleted Habitat." *Human Nature* 5, no. 2 (1994): 127–354.

Alvares, Claude, and Ramesh Billorey. "Damning the Narmada: The Politics behind the Destruction." *Ecologist* 17, no. 2 (1987): 62–74.

Amirahmadi, Hoosang. "Development Paradigms at a Crossroad and the South Korean Experience." *Journal of Contemporary Asia* 19, no. 2 (1989): 167–85.

Amsden, Alice H. "Third Industrialization: 'Global Fordism' or a New Model?" *New Left Review* 182 (July-Aug. 1990): 5–31.

Andersen, Jorgen Goul. "Denmark: Environmental Conflict and the 'Greening' of the Labour Movement." *Scandinavian Political Studies* 13, no. 2 (1990): 185–209.

————. "'Environmentalism,' 'New Politics' and Industrialism: Some Theoretical Perspectives." *Scandinavian Political Studies* 13, no. 2 (1990): 101–17.

Andersson, Malte. *Sexual Selection*. Princeton, N.J.: Princeton University Press, 1994.

Andors, Stephen. *China's Industrial Revolution*. New York: Pantheon, 1977.

Anuarul Statistic al Romaniei (Annual statistics of Romania). Bucharest: Comisia Nationala pentru Statistica, 1993.

Bahaguna, Sunderlal. "People's Response to Ecological Crisis in the Hill Area." In Bandyopadhyay, ed., 1985.

Bakhash, Shaul. "Perils of an Iranian Moderate." *New Leader* (July 14, 1997): 3–4.

Baker, R. Robin, and Mark Bellis. *Human Sperm Competition.* London: Chapman and Hall, 1995.

Bakhtin, Mikhail. *Marxismo e filosofía da linguagem* (Marxism and philosophy of language). São Paulo: Hucitec, 1971.

Bandyopadhyay, Jayanto. "Deforestation in Himalaya and the Way to Survival." In Jayal, 1989.

———. "The Ecology of Drought and Water Scarcity." *Ecologist* 18, no. 2 (1988): 88–95.

———, ed. *India's Environment.* Dehra Dun, India: Natraj, 1985.

Bandyopadhyay, Jayanto, and Vandana Shiva. *Chipko.* New Delhi, India: INTACH, 1986.

———. "Chipko: Rekindling India's Forest Culture." *Ecologist* 17, no. 1 (1987): 26–34.

———. "Development, Poverty, and the Growth of the Green Movement in India." *Ecologist* 19, no. 3 (1989): 111–17.

Barker, Ivor, and Joan Barker, eds. *Clean Air around the World: The Law and Practices of Air Pollution Control in 14 Countries in 5 Continents.* Brighton, U.K.: International. Union of Air Pollution Prevention Associations, 1988.

Barry, John. "The Limits of the Shallow and the Deep: Green Politics, Philosophy, and Praxis." *Environmental Politics* 3, no. 3 (autumn 1994): 369.

Bataille, Georges. *The Accursed Share.* 2 vols. New York: Zone Books, 1991.

Baudrillard, Jean. *For a Critique of the Political Economy of the Sign.* St. Louis: Telos Press, 1981.

———. *Le Miroir de Production* (The mirror of production). Paris: Galileo, 1985.

———. *The Mirror of Production.* St. Louis: Telos Press, 1975.

———. *A Sociedade de Consumo* (Consumer society). Lisbon: Edicoes 70, n.d.

Bayat, Asef. *Street Politics: Poor People's Movements in Iran.* New York: Columbia University Press, 1997.

Bayliss-Smith, Tim. "Constraints on Population Growth: The Case of the Polynesian Outlier Atolls in the Precontact Period." *Human Ecology* 2, no. 4 (1974): 259–95.

Bean, Clive, and Elim Papadakis. "Polarized Priorities or Flexible Alternatives? Dimensionality in Inglehart's Materialism-Postmaterialism scale." *International Journal of Public Opinion Research* 6, no. 3 (fall 1994): 264–89.

Beaud, Michel. *A History of Capitalism. 1500–1980.* New York: Monthly Review Press, 1983.

Behrooz, Maziar. "Factionalism in Iran under Khomeini." *Middle Eastern Studies* 27, no. 4 (Oct. 1991): 597–614.

Bennett, John T. "Korea Adopts Seventh Five-Year Plan." *Korea's Economy.* Washington, D.C.: Korea Economic Institute of America, 1992.

———. "Trade: The Key to Korea's Growth." *Korea's Economy.* Washington, D.C.: Korea Economic Institute of America, 1990.

Bennulf, Martin, and Soren Holmberg. "The Green Breakthrough in Sweden." *Scandinavian Political Studies* 13, no. 2 (1990): 165–83.

Bergson, Abram. *The Economics of Soviet Planning.* New Haven: Yale, 1964.

Berreman, Gerald. "Chipko: A Movement to Save the Himalayan Environment and People." In Borden, ed., 1989.

Berry, R. J., ed. *Environmental Dilemmas.* London: Chapman and Hill, 1993.

Bettleheim, Charles. *Class Struggles in the U.S.S.R.* Vols. 1, 2. New York: Monthly Review Press, 1976, 1978.

Beyers, Carol. "The U.S./Mexico Tuna Embargo Dispute: A Case Study of the GATT Environmental Progress." *Maryland Journal of International Law and Trade* 16 (1992): 229–53.

Bhagvati, Jagdish. *India in Transition: Freeing the Economy.* Oxford: Clarendon Press, 1993.

Bhatt, P. "The Chipko Andolan: Forest Conservation Based on People's Power." In Agarwal et al., eds., 1987.

———. "Green the People." In Agarwal et al., eds., 1987.

Bhattacharya, Debesh. "Growth and Distribution in India." *Journal of Contemporary Asia* 19, no. 2 (1989): 150–66.

Bill, James, and Carl Leiden. *The Middle East: Politics and Power.* Boston: Allen and Bacon, 1974.

Borden, Carla, ed. *Contemporary Indian Tradition: Voices on Nature and the Challenge of Change.* Washington, D.C.: Smithsonian Institution Press, 1989.

Bourdieu, Pierre. *Distinction.* Cambridge, Mass.: Harvard University Press, 1984.

———. *Language and Symbolic Power.* Cambridge, Mass.: Harvard University Press, 1991.

Bouton, M., and P. Oldenburg. *India Briefing 1989.* Boulder, Colo.: Westview Press, 1989.

Bradford, Sue, and Oriel Glock. *The Last Frontier.* London: Zed Books, 1985.

Braithwaite, Valerie, Toni Makkai, and Yvonne Pittelkow. "Inglehart's Materialism-Postmaterialism Concept: Clarifying the Dimensionality Debate through Rokeach's Model of Social Values." *Journal of Applied Social Research* 26, no. 17 (Sept. 1996): 1536–56.

Braudel, Fernand. *Capitalism and Material Life 1400–1800.* New York: Harper, 1973.

———. *The Mediterranean and the Mediterranean World in the Age of Philip II.* 2 vols. New York: Harper, 1976.

———. *The Wheels of Commerce.* New York: Harper and Row, 1979.

Brechin, Steven, and Willett Kempton. "Beyond Postmaterialist Values: National versus Individual Explanations of Global Environmentalism." *Social Science Quarterly* 78, no. 1 (Mar. 1997): 16–23.

———. "Global Environmentalism: A Challenge to the Postmaterialism Thesis?" *Social Science Quarterly* 75, no. 2 (1994): 245–69.

Brint, Steven. "'New Class' and Cumulative Trend Explanations of the Liberal Political Attitudes of Professionals." *American Journal of Sociology* 90, no. 1 (1984): 30–71.

Broad, Robin. "The Poor and the Environment: Friends or Foes?" *World Development* 22, no. 6 (1994): 811–22.

Brooks, Clem, and Jeff Manza. "Do Changing Values Explain the New Politics? A Critical Assessment of the Postmaterialist Thesis." *Sociological Quarterly* 35, no. 4 (Nov. 1994): 541–71.

Brown, Stephen R. *Political Subjectivity.* New Haven: Yale University Press, 1985.

Brundtland Commission. *Our Common Future.* New York: United Nations, 1987.

Bryant, Bunyan, and Paul Mohai, eds. *Race and the Incidence of Environmental Hazards.* Boulder, Colo.: Westview Press, 1992.

Buchholz, Rogene. *Principles of Environmental Management: The Greening of Business.* Englewood Cliffs, N.J.: Prentice-Hall, 1993.

Burckhardt, Jacob. *The Civilization of the Renaissance in Italy* London: Phaidon Press, 1965.

Burklin, Wilhelm. "Governing Left Parties Frustrating the Radical Non-Established Left: The Rise and Inevitable Decline of the Greens." *European Sociological Review* 3, no. 2 (1987): 109–26.

Burmeister, Larry L. "South Korea's Rural Development Dilemma." *Asian Survey* 7 (1990): 711–23.

Burnside, Craig, and David Dollar. "Aid Spurs Growth in a Sound Policy Environment." *Finance and Development* 34, no. 4 (Dec. 1997): 4–7.

Buss, David. *The Evolution of Desire.* New York: Basic Books, 1994.

Buttel, Fredrick, and Peter Taylor. "Environmental Sociology and Global Environmental Change: A Critical Assessment." *Society and Natural Resources* 5 (1992): 211–30.

Butts, Yolanda, and Donald Bogue. *International Amazonia: Its Human Side.* Chicago: Social Development Center, 1989.

Calinescu, Matei, and Vladimir Tismaneanu. "The 1989 Revolution and Romania's Future." *Problems of Communism* (Jan.–Apr. 1991): 42–59.

Callicott, Baird, and Roger Ames. *Nature in Asian Traditions of Thought.* Albany, N.Y.: SUNY Press, 1989.

Capra, Fritjof, and Charlene Spretnak. *Green Politics.* New York: E. P. Dutton, 1984.

Cardoso, Fernando Henrique. *Amazônia: Expansão do Capitalismo.* São Paulo: Brasiliense, 1977.

Carter, John, and Mary Rayner. "The Curious Case of Post-Fordism and Welfare." *Journal of Social Policy* 25, no. 3 (July 1996): 347–68.

Castells, Manuel. *End of Millenium.* Cambridge: Blackwell, 1998.

Centre for Science and Environment. *The State of India's Environment 1984–1985.* New Delhi, India: Centre for Science and Environment, 1985.

Centre for Science and Environment. *The Wrath of Nature*. New Delhi, India: Centre for Science and Environment, 1987.

Chalmers, Douglas A., et al., eds. *The New Politics of Inequality in Latin America*. Oxford: Oxford University Press, 1997.

Chang, Won Ho. "Korean Students and Anti-American Attitudes: A Q-Methodological Study." *Journal of Social Science and Humanities* 67 (1989): 49–66.

Chatterjee, Pratap, and Matthias Finger. *The Earth Brokers* London: Routledge, 1994.

Cho, Lee-Jay, and Yoon Hyung Kim, eds. *Korea's Political Economy* Boulder, Colo.: Westview Press, 1994.

Christoff, Peter. "The 1993 Australian Elections: A Fading Green Politics?" *Environmental Politics* 3, no. 1 (spring 1994): 130–39.

Chun, Yong. "All-Out War Proposed for Preserving Environment." *Koreana* 5, no. 1 (1991): 52–56.

CIMA. *The Challenge of Sustainable Devlopment: The Brazilian Report for U.N.C.E.D.* Brasilia, D.F. Offprint, Mar. 1992.

Clusener-Godt, M., and I. Sacik, eds. *Brazilian Perspectives on Sustainable Development of the Amazon Region*. London: Parthenon Publishing Group, 1995.

Comrey, Andrew. *A First Course in Factor Analysis*. New York; Academic Press, 1973.

Conrad, Geoffrey, and Arthur Demarest. *Religion and Empire*. Cambridge: Cambridge University Press, 1984.

Cornwell, John. *Nature's Vision: The Frontiers of Scientific Vision*. Oxford: Oxford University Press, 1995.

Cota, Raymundo Carajas. *A Invasão Desarmada* (The invasion disarmed). Petropolis, Brazil: Editora Vozes, 1984.

Cultural Survival Quarterly 13, no. 2 (1989).

Cultural Survival: Special Report—Brazil. Dec. 1979.

D'Abro, A. *The Rise of the New Physics*. 2 vols. New York: Dover, 1952.

Dahlberg, Kenneth. "Redefining Development Priorities: Genetic Diversity and Agroecodevelopment." *Conservation Biology* 1, no. 4 (Dec. 1987).

Dalton, Russell. *Citizen Politics in Western Democracies*. Chatham, N.J.: Chatham House, 1988.

Dalton, Russell, and Manfred Kuechler, eds. *Challenging the Political Order*. Cambridge: Polity Press, 1990.

Daly, Martin, and Margot Wilson. *Homicide*. New York: Aldine de Gruyter, 1988.

DeBardeleben, Joan, ed. *To Breathe Free*. Washington, D.C.: Woodrow Wilson Center, 1991.

DeGraaf, Nan Dirk, and Geoffrey Evans. "Why Are the Young More Postmaterialist? A Cross-National Analysis of Individual and Contextual Influences on Postmaterial Values." *Comparative Political Studies* 27, no. 4 (Jan. 1995): 608–36.

Deleuze, Gilles, and Felix Guattari. *Anti-Oedipus: Capitalism and Schizophrenia*. Minneapolis: University of Minnesota Press, 1983.

D'Encausse, Hélène Carrère. *Le pouvoir confisqué* (Confiscated power). Paris: Flammarion, 1978.

Dept. of the Environment, Islamic Republic of Iran. *National Environmental Almanac*. Boston: Houghton Mifflin, 1992.

Dept. of the Environment, Islamic Republic of Iran. *National Report to the UNCED*. Rio de Janeiro, Brazil, June 1–12, 1992.

Derrida, Jacques. *Dissemination*. Chicago: University of Chicago Press, 1981.

———. *Of Grammatology*. Baltimore: Johns Hopkins University Press, 1976.

———. *Writing and Difference*. Chicago: University of Chicago Press, 1978.

Deval, Bill, and George Sessions. *Deep Ecology*. Salt Lake City: Gibbs Smith, 1985.

Developmental Alternatives. *To Choose a Future*. New Delhi, India: Developmental Alternatives, n.d.

Dhawan, B. D. *Big Dams: Claims, Counterclaims*. New Delhi, India: Commonwealth Publication, 1990.

Dias, Braulio de Souza. *Alternativas de Desenvolvimento dos Cerrados*, (Alternatives to prairie development). Brasilia: Funatura, 1992.

Dietz, James. *An Economic History of Puerto Rico*. Princeton, N.J.: Princeton University Press, 1986.

D'Monte, Darryl. "India's Environment: More Diversity than Unity." In Bouton and Oldenburg, 1989.

———. *Temples or Tombs? Industry Versus Environment*. New Delhi, India: Centre for Science and Environment, 1985.

Dobson, Andrew. *Green Political Thought*. London: Routledge, 1992.

Dobson, Andrew, and Paul Lucardie, eds. *The Politics of Nature* London: Routledge, 1993.

Doern, G. Bruce. "Sectoral Green Politics: Environmental Regulation and the Canadian Pulp and Paper Industry." *Environmental Politics* 4, no. 2 (summer 1995): 219–44.

Dreyfus, Herbert, and Paul Rabinow. *Foucault: Beyond Structuralism and Hermeneutics*. Chicago: University of Chicago Press, 1983.

Dryzek, John. *Democracy in Capitalist Times*. New York: Oxford University Press, 1996.

Dryzek, John, and James Lester. "Alternative Views of the Environmental Problematic." In Lester, ed., 1989.

Duch, Raymond, and Michael Taylor. "Postmaterialism and the Economic Condition." *American Journal of Political Science* 37, no. 3 (1993): 747–79.

———. "A Reply to Abramson and Inglehart." *American Journal of Political Science* 38, no. 3 (Aug. 1994): 815–24.

Dunlap, Riley, and Angela Mertig. "Global Concern for the Environment: Is Affluence a Prerequisite?" *Journal of Social Issues* 51, no. 4 (1995): 121–37.

———. "Global Environmental Concern: An Anomaly for Postmaterialism." *Social Science Quarterly* 78, no. 1 (Mar. 1997): 24–35.

Dyker, David. *The Soviet Economy*. New York: St. Martin's Press, 1976.

Eckstein, Alexander. *China's Economic Revolution*. London: Cambridge University Press, 1977.

Echeverri-Gent, John. *Economic Reform in Three Giants.* New Brunswick: Transaction Books, 1990.

EcoAmazônia: Carta Para O Desenvolvimento Sustentavel da Amazônia (Ecoamazonia: a letter about sustainable development of Amazonia). Manaus. Photocopy, 1991.

Eden, Michel. *Ecology and Land Management in Amazonia.* London: Belhaven Press, 1990.

El Nuevo Día. San Juan, P.R. Dec. 26, 1992.

El Nuevo Día. Sept. 14, 1993.

Encontro dos Empresarios da Amazônia (Meeting of Amazonian entrepreneurs). *Carta da Amazônia* (Letter from the Amazon), Manaus 1989, n.p.

Environics Ltd. *Environmental Monitor 1998,* on line at <www.environics.net/eil>.

Esping-Anderson, Gosta. "Postmodern Cleavage Structures: A Comparison of Evolving Patterns of Social Stratification in Germany, Sweden, and the United States." In Piven, 1991.

Evans, Geoffrey, Anthony Heath, and Mansur Lalljee. "Measuring Left-Right and Libertarian-Authoritarian Values in the British Electorate." *British Journal of Sociology* 47, no. 1 (Mar. 1996): 93–113.

Evans, Judy. "Ecofeminism and the Politics of the Gendered Self." In Dobson and Lucardie, eds., 1993.

Faucher, Florence, and Brian Doherty. "The Decline of Green Politics in France." *Environmental Politics* 5, no.1 (spring 1996): 108–14.

Fearnside, Philip. "Deforestation and International Economic Development Projects in Brazilian Amazonia." *Conservation Biology* 1, no. 3 (Oct. 1987): 214–21.

Feldman, Fabio, ed. *Guía da Ecología.* São Paulo: Ed. Abril, 1992.

Fernandes, Francisco. *Quém é quém no subsolo Brasileiro?* (Who's who in Brazilian land tenure). Brasilia, D.F.: C.N.Pq., 1987.

Finger, Matthias, and Pascal Sciarini. "Integrating 'New Politics' into 'Old Politics': The Swiss Party Elite." *West European Politics* 14, no. 1 (1991): 98–111.

Finkleman, Jacobo. "Medio ambiente y salud en México." In Leff, ed., 1990.

Fischer, Mary Ellen. *Nicolae Ceausescu: A Study in Political Leadership.* Boulder, Colo.: Lynne Reiner Publishers, 1989.

Fisher, Helen. *Anatomy of Love.* New York: Fawcett, 1992.

Fletcher, Susan. "Tropical Deforestation: International Implications." Washington, D.C.: Congressional Research Service. Offprint, 1989.

Fluehr-Lobban, Carolyn. "Marxist Reappraisal of the Matriarchate." *Current Anthropology* 20, no. 2 (1979): 341–59.

Folse, Henry. *The Philosophy of Neils Bohr.* Netherlands: Elsevier, 1985.

Foresta, Ronald. *Amazon Conservation.* Gainesville: University Press of Florida, 1991.

Foucault, Michel. *The Archaeology of Knowledge.* New York: Pantheon, 1972.

———. *Discipline and Punish.* New York: Vintage, 1971.

———. *The History of Sexuality.* Vol. 1. New York: Pantheon, 1986.

———. *Madness and Civilization*. London: Tavistock, 1971.

———. *The Order of Things*. New York: Pantheon, 1971.

Fox, Richard G. *Gandhian Utopia*. Boston: Beacon Press, 1989.

Franklin, Mark, and Wolfgang Rudig. "On the Durability of Green Politics." *Comparative Political Studies* 28, no. 3 (Oct. 1995): 409–39.

Frausum, Yves, Ulrich Gehman, and Jurgen Gross. "Market Economy and Economic Reform in Romania: Macroeconomic and Microeconomic Perspectives." *Europe-Asia Studies* 46, no. 5 (1994): 735–56.

Funatura. *Alternativas ao desmatamento na Amazônia* (Alternatives to deforestation in the Amazon). Brasilia: Funatura, 1990.

———. *Custo da implantação de unidades de conservação na Amazônia legal* (Setup costs for conservation units in the legal Amazon). Brasilia: Funatura, 1991.

Gadgil, Madhav, and Ramachandra Guha. *Ecology and Equity*. London: Routledge, 1995.

Gallagher, Tom. "Romania's Communist Dystopia." *Journal of Communist Studies* 7, no. 4 (Dec. 1991): 552–57.

Gandhi, M. K. *My Autobiography*. Ahmedabad, India: Navajivan Publishing House, 1996.

Ganguly, Sumit. "India in 1997: Another Year of Turmoil." *Asian Survey* 38, no. 2 (Feb. 1998): 126–34.

Geertz, Clifford. *The Interpretation of Cultures*. New York: Basic Books, 1973.

Gibson, James, and Raymond Duch. "Postmaterialism and the Emerging Soviet Democracy." *Political Reserch Quarterly* 47, no. 1 (Mar. 1994): 5–40.

Gibson, William. *Count Zero*. New York: Ace Books, 1986.

———. *Mona Lisa Overdrive*. New York: Bantam, 1988.

———. *Neuromancer*. New York: Ace Books, 1984.

Gill, James, Lawrence Crosby, and James Taylor. "Ecological Concern, Attitudes and Social Norms in Voting Behavior." *Public Opinion Quarterly* 50 (1986): 537–54.

Gilroy, John, and Rob Shapiro. "The Polls: Environmental Protection." *Public Opinion Quarterly* 50 (1986): 270–79.

Gitlin, Todd. "Postmodernism: Roots and Politics." *Dissent* (winter 1989): 100–8.

Goldrich, Daniel, and David Carruthers. "Sustainable Development in Mexico?" *Latin American Perspectives* 19, no. 1 (winter 1992): 97–122.

Gomez-Pompa, Arturo, Andrea Kaus, Juan Jimenez-Osornio, David Bainbridge, and Veronique Rorive. "Mexico." In National Resources Council (NRC) *Sustainable Agriculture*, 1993.

Gould, James, and Carol Gould. *Sexual Selection*. New York: W. H. Freeman, 1989.

Government of India. *Approach to the 8th Five Year Plan: 1990–1995*. India: Government of India, Planning Commission, 1990.

Government of India. *Ministry of Environment Annual Report*. India: Government of India, 1990.

Granato, Jim, Ronald Inglehart, and David Leblanc. "Effects of Cultural Values on Economic Development: Theories, Hypotheses, and Some Explicit Empirical Tests." *American Journal of Political Science* 40, no. 3 (Aug. 1996): 607–32.

Gregory, Paul, and Robert Stuart. *Soviet Economic Structure and Performance.* New York: Harper and Row, 1981.

Grey, John. *Beyond the New Right: Markets, Government, and the Common Environment.* London: Routledge, 1993.

Griffin, Trenholme J . *Korea: The Tiger Economy.* London: Euromoney Publications, 1988.

Grimshaw, Jean. *Philosophy and Feminist Thinking.* Minneapolis: University of Minnesota Press, 1986.

Guha, Ramachandra. *The Unquiet Woods.* New Delhi, India: Oxford University Press, 1989.

Guimaraes, Roberto. *The Ecopolitics of Development in the Third World.* Boulder, Colo.: Lynne Reiner Publishers, 1991.

Gupta, Anil. "How Common Is Commons?" In Jayal, *Deforestation*, 1989.

Gurley, John. *China's Economy and the Maoist Strategy.* New York: Monthly Review Press, 1976.

Habermas, Jurgen. *Legitimation Crisis.* Boston: Beacon Press, 1973.

———. *The Philosophical Discourse of Modernity.* Cambridge, Mass.: MIT Press, 1991.

Hall, Anthony. *Sustaining Amazonia: Grassroots Action for Productive Conservation.* Manchester, England: Manchester University Press, 1997.

Hall, Barbara. "Soviet Perceptions of Global Ecological Problems: An Analysis of Three Patterns." *Political Psychology* 2, no. 4 (1990): 653–80.

Halliday, Fred. *Iran: Dictatorship and Development.* London: Penguin, 1979.

Halliday, Jon. *A Political History of Japanese Capitalism.* New York: Monthly Review Press, 1975.

Halliday, Jon, and Gavan McCormack. *Japanese Imperialism Today.* London: Penguin Books, 1973.

Hallsworth, E. G., ed. *Socio-Economic Effects and Constraints in Tropical Forest Management.* New York: John Wiley and Sons, 1982.

Hamilton, W. D. "The Evolution of Social Behavior." *Journal of Theoretical Biology* 7 (1964): 427–37.

Hanan, Samuel, and Beh Hur Batalha. *Amazônia: Contradições no Paraiso ecológico* (Contradiction of an ecological paradise). São Paulo: Cultura Editores Associados, 1995.

Hansen, J. A., ed. *Environmental Concerns.* London: Elsevier, 1991.

Hardin, Garrett. *The Limits of Altruism.* Bloomington: Indiana University Press, 1977.

———. *Living within Limits: Ecology, Economics, and Population Taboos.* New York: Oxford University Press, 1993.

————. *Promethian Ethics.* Seattle: University of Washington Press, 1980.

————. "The Tragedy of the Commons." *Science* 162 (1968): 1243–60.

Harland, Richard. *Superstructuralism.* London: Methuen, 1987.

Harvey, David. *The Condition of Postmodernity.* Cambridge: Blackwell, 1989.

Hart-Landsberg, Martin. "South Korea: The 'Miracle' Rejected." *Critical Sociology* 15, no. 3 (1988): 29–51.

Hecht, Susanna, and Alexander Cockburn. *The Fate of the Forest.* New York: Harper, 1990.

Hegde, Pandurang. "The Appiko Movement: Forest Conservation in Southern India." *Cultural Survival Quarterly* 13, no. 2, (1989): 29–30.

Heginbotham, Stanley J. *Cultures in Conflict.* New York: Columbia University Press, 1975.

Heilbroner, Robert. *Inquiry into the Human Prospect.* New York: Norton, 1991.

Heisenberg, Werner. *Physics and Philosophy.* New York: Harper, 1958.

Hekstra, G. P. "Global Warming and Rising Sea Levels: The Policy Implications." *Ecologist* 19, no. 1 (1989): 5–14.

Hensen-Sellers, A., R. E. Dickinson, and M. F. Wilson. "Tropical Deforestation: Important Processes for Climate Models." *Climatic Change* 13 (1988): 43–67.

Henwood, Doug. "Post What? (Economics in the Postmodern Era)." *Monthly Review* 48, no.4 (Sept. 1996): 1–12.

Herbert, Nick. *Quantum Reality.* New York: Anchor Books, 1987.

Hewitt, W. E. "The Roman Catholic Church and Environmental Politics in Brazil." *Journal of Developing Areas* 26 (Jan. 1992): 239–58.

Hildyard, March. "Adios Amazonia? A Report from the Altamira Gathering." *Ecologist* 19, no. 2 (1989): 53–63.

Hillmann, Michael. *Iranian Culture.* New York: Lanham Publishers, 1990.

Hobbes, Thomas. *De Cive or The Citizen.* New York: Appleton Century Crofts, 1949.

————. *Leviathan.* New York: E. P. Dutton, n.d.

Hochstetler, Kathryn. "The Evolution of the Brazilian Environmental Movement and Its Political Roles." In Chalmers et al., eds., 1997.

Hoffmann-Martinot, Vincent. "Grüne and Verts: Two Faces of European Ecologism." *West European Politics* 14, no. 4 (Oct. 1991): 70–95.

Hofrichter, Jurgen, and Karlheinz Reif. "Evolution of Environmental Attitudes in the European Community." *Scandinavian Political Studies* 13, no. 2 (1990): 119–45.

Hogner, Robert, H. *Enchanted Toxics 1990: Puerto Rico 1990 Toxics Release Inventory.* Florida: Florida International University, 1992.

Hollerman, Leon. *Japan's Economic Strategy in Brazil.* Boston, Mass.: Lexington Books, 1988.

Holmes, John. "The Organization and Locational Structure of Production Subcontracting." In Scott and Storper, 1986.

Horkheimer, Max, and Theodor Adorno. *The Dialectic of Enlightenment.* London: Allen Lane, 1972.

Hrdy, Sarah Blaffer. *The Woman That Never Evolved.* Cambridge, Mass.: Harvard University Press, 1981.

Huizinga, Johan. *The Waning of the Middle Ages.* Garden City, N.Y.: Anchorbooks, 1954.

Hunter, Shireen. "Iran and the Spread of Revolutionary Islam." *Third World Quarterly* 10, no. 2 (Apr. 1988): 730–49.

Huyssen, Andreas. *After the Great Divide.* Bloomington: Indiana University Press, 1986.

Illustrated Weekly of India. May 6, 1990.

Inglehart, Ronald. *Culture Shift.* Princeton, N.J.: Princeton University Press, 1990.

———. "From Class-Based to Value-Based Politics." In Mair, ed., 1990.

———. "Polarized Priorities . . . A Comment." *International Journal of Public Opinion Research* 6, no. 3 (fall 1994): 289–93.

———. "Public Support for Environmental Protection: The Impact of Objective Problems and Subjective Values in 43 Societies." *PS: Political Science and Politics* (Mar. 1995): 57–71.

———. *The Silent Revolution.* Princeton, N.J.: Princeton University Press, 1977.

Inglehart, Ronald, and Paul R. Abramson. "Economic Security and Value Change." *American Political Science Review* 88, no. 2 (June 1994): 336–55.

———. "Generational Replacement and the Future of Post-Materialist Values." *Journal of Politics* 49 (1987): 131–41.

INTACH. *The Tehri Dam.* New Delhi, India: INTACH, 1987.

Jameson, Fredrick. *Postmodernism.* Durham: North Carolina University Press, 1991.

———. *The Prison-House of Language.* Princeton, N.J.: Princeton University Press, 1972.

Jayal, N. D. *Deforestation. Drought and Desertification.* New Delhi, India: INTACH, 1989.

———. *Eliminating Poverty.* New Delhi, India: INTACH, 1986.

Joppke, Christian, and Andrei Markovits. "Green Politics in New Germany." *Dissent* 41, no. 2 (spring 1994): 235.

Joshi, Vijay, and J. M. D. Little. *India's Economic Reforms: 1991–2001.* Oxford: Clarendon Press, 1996.

Jung-ang Daily News [Jung-ang Ilbo]. Various issues. Mar. 16, Aug. 19, 1991.

Kamieniecki, Sheldon, ed. *Environmental Politics in the International Arena.* Albany, N.Y.: SUNY Press, 1993.

Karlekar, H. *Indian Express.* July 2, 1990.

Kay, Charles. "Aboriginal Overkill: The Role of Native Americans in Structuring Western Ecosystems." *Human Nature* 5, no. 4 (1994): 359–98.

Keddie, Nikki. *Roots of Revolution.* New Haven: Yale University Press, 1981.

Kellner, Hansfried, and Frank Heuberger, eds. *Hidden Technocrats: The New Class and New Capitalism.* New Brunswick, N.J.: Transaction Publishers, 1992.

Kellogg, William. "Mankind's Impact on Climate: The Evolution of an Awareness." *Climatic Change* 10 (1987): 113–36.

Kennedy, J.S. *The New Anthropomorphism*. Cambridge: Cambridge University Press, 1992.

Kennedy, Paul. *The Rise and Fall of the Great Powers*. New York: Vintage Books, 1987.

Khator, Renu. *Environment, Development and Politics in India*. Lanham, Mass.: University Press of America, 1991.

Kidd, Quentin, and Aie-Rie Lee. "Postmaterialist Values and the Environment: A Critique and Reappraisal." *Social Science Quarterly* 78, no. 1 (1997): 1–15.

Kim, Ilpyong J., and Young Whan Kihl, eds. *Political Change in South Korea*. New York: Korean PWPA, 1988.

Kim, Young-Khee. "Mass Media and Environmental Issues." *Sungkok Journalism Review* 3 (1992): 55–87.

King, Robert R. *A History of the Romanian Communist Party*. Stanford, Calif.: Hoover Press, 1980.

Kirch, Patrick Vinton. *The Evolution of the Polynesian Chiefdoms*. New York: Cambridge University Press, 1989.

———. "Man's Role in Modifying Tropical and Subtropical Polynesian Ecosystems." *Archaeology in Oceania* 18 (1983): 26–31.

Kitschelt, Herbert. "La Gauche Libertaire et les écologistes français" (The Libertarian Left and the French ecologists). *Revue Français de Science Politique* 40, no. 3 (June 1990): 339–65.

———. "The Green Phenomenon in Western Party Systems." In Kamieniecki, 1993.

———. "Left-Libertarian Parties: Explaining Innovation in Competitive Party Systems." *World Politics* 40, no. 2 (Jan. 1988): 194–234.

———. *The Logics of Party Formation*. Ithaca, N.Y.: Cornell University Press, 1989.

Kitschelt, Herbert, and Staf Hellemans. *Beyond the European Left*. Durham: Duke University Press, 1990.

———. *Ideological and Political Action in the Belgian Ecology Parties*. Durham: Duke University Press, 1990.

———. "The Left-Right Semantics and the New Politics Cleavage." *Comparative Political Studies* 23, no. 2 (1990): 210–38.

Kitzinger, Celia. *The Social Construction of Lesbianism*. London: Sage, 1987.

Knutsen, Oddbjorn. "The Priorities of Materialist and Post-Materialist Values in the Nordic Countries: A Five Nation Comparison." *Scandinavian Political Studies* 12, no. 3 (1989): 221–43.

Koo, Hagen, ed. *State and Society in Contemporary Korea*. Ithaca, N.Y.: Cornell University Press, 1993.

Korea Newsreview. June 22, May 4, Apr. 6, Mar. 23, 1991.

Kothari, Rajni. *Illustrated Weekly of India*. May 6, 1990.

Kreuzer, Markus. "New Politics: Just Post-Materialist? The Case of Austrian and Swiss Greens." *West European Politics* 13, no. 1 (Jan. 1990): 10–29.

Kreuzer, Markus, and John Kurien. "Ruining the Commons: Coastal Overfishing and Fishworkers' Actions in South India." *Ecologist* 23, no. 1 (Jan. 1993): 5–11.

Kristeva, Julia. *Language the Unknown.* New York: Columbia University Press, 1989.

Kuznets, Paul W. *Korean Economic Development: An Interpretative Model.* Westport, Conn.: Praeger, 1994.

Lacan, Jacques. *The Language of the Self.* New York: Delta, 1968.

Lal, J. B. *India's Forests: Myth and Reality.* Dehra Dun, India: Natraz Publication, 1989.

Lamont, Michele. "Cultural Capital and the Liberal Political Attitudes of Professionals: Comment on Brint." *American Journal of Sociology* 92, no. 6 (1987): 1501–5.

Lane, David. *The Socialist Industrial State.* London: Allen and Unwin, 1978.

Larrain, Jorge. "The Postmodern Critique of Ideology." *Sociological Review* 42, no. 2 (May 1994): 289–314.

Lash, Scott, and John Urry. *The End of Organized Capitalism.* Madison: University of Wisconsin Press, 1987.

Lave, Lester. "The Greenhouse Effect: What Government Actions Are Needed?" *Journal of Policy Analysis and Management* 7, no. 3 (1988): 460–70.

Lee, Aie-Rie, and Quentin Kidd. "More on Postmaterialist Values and the Environment." *Social Science Quarterly* 78, no.1 (Mar. 1997): 36–43.

Lee, Chong-Sik, and Hyuk-Sang Sohn. "South Korea in 1993: The Year of the Great Reform." *Asian Survey* 34, no. 1 (Jan. 1994): 1–9.

Lee, Raymond. "Modernization, Postmodernism and the Third World." *Current Sociology* 42, no. 2 (summer 1994): 1–66.

Leff, Enrique. "Cultura democrática, gestión ambiental y desarrollo sostenido en América Latina." Paper delivered in Conferencia Internacional sobre Cultura democrática y desarrollo, Montevideo, Uruguay, Nov. 1990.

———, ed. *Medio Ambiente y desarrollo en México.* Mexico: Universidad Nacional Autónoma de México, 1990.

Lester, James P., ed. *Environmental Politics and Policy.* Durham: Duke University Press, 1989.

Lester, James, and Elfar Loftsson. "The Ecological Movement and Green Parties in Scandinavia: Problems and Prospects." In Kamieniecki, ed., 1991.

Lind, Michael. *Up from Conservatism.* New York: Free Press, 1996.

Lipietz, Alain. *Towards a New Economic Order.* Cambridge: Polity Press, 1992.

Lutz, Catherine. *Unnatural Emotions.* Chicago: University of Chicago Press, 1988.

Lutzenburger, Jose. "Who Is Destroying the Amazon Rainforest?" *Ecologist* 17, no. 4 (1987): 155–60.

Lyon, David. *Postmodernity.* Minneapolis: University of Minnesota Press, 1994.

Lyotard, Jean-François. *The Postmodern Condition.* Minneapolis: University of Minnesota Press, 1989.

Macdonald, Donald Stone. *The Koreans: Contemporary Politics and Society.* Boulder, Colo.: Westview Press, 1988 (2d ed., 1990).

MacDonald, Gordon. "Scientific Basis for the Greenhouse Effect." *Journal of Policy Analysis and Management* 7, no. 3 (1988): 425–44.

Mair, Peter, ed. *The West European Party System.* London: Oxford University Press, 1990.

Maitland, Edward. "Romania's Environmental Crisis." In DeBardeleben, ed., 1991.

Malek, Mohammed H. "Elite Factionalism in the Post-Revolutionary Iran." *Journal of Contemporary Asia* 19, no. 4 (1989): 435–60.

Marcus, George, and Michael Fischer. *Anthropology as Cultural Critique.* Chicago: University of Chicago Press, 1986.

Marcussen, Henrik, and Jens Torp. *Internationalization of Capital.* London: Zed Books, 1982.

Marshall, Peter. *Nature's Web.* London: Simon and Schuster, 1992.

Martin, Bernice. "Symbolic Knowledge and Market Forces at the Frontiers of Postmodernism: Qualitative Market Researchers." In Kellner and Heuberger, eds., 1992.

Martins, Jose de Souza. "Impasses políticos dos movimentos sociais na Amazônia." *Tempo Social* 1, no. 1 (1989): 131–48.

———. *Os camponeses e a política no Brasil* (Peasants and politics in Brazil). Petropolis: Editora Vozes, 1983.

Masters, Roger D. *The Nature of Politics.* New Haven: Yale University Press, 1989.

Masters, Roger, and Margaret Gruter. *The Sense of Justice: Biological Foundations of Law.* Newbury Park, Calif.: Sage, 1992.

McConnaughey, Bayard, and Robert Zottoli. *Introduction to Marine Biology.* St. Louis: C. V. Mosby, 1983.

McCormick, John. *Reclaiming Paradise.* Bloomington: Indiana University Press, 1991.

McGlone, M. S. "Polynesian Deforestation in New Zealand: A Preliminary Synthesis." *Archaeology in Oceania* 18 (1983): 11–25.

McKean, Mary. *Environmental Protest and Citizen Politics in Japan.* Berkeley: University of California Press, 1981.

Meggers, Betty. "Environmental Limitation on the Development of Culture." *American Anthropologist* 56 (1954): 801–24.

Menéndez-Garza, Fernando. "Comisión Metropolitana para la prevención y control de la contaminación ambiental en el Valle de México." Offprint internal document, Dec. 1993.

Metz, Helen Chapin, ed. *Iran: A Country Study.* Washington, D.C.: Library of Congress, 1989.

Micheletti, Michele. "Swedish Corporatism at a Crossroads: The Impact of New Politics and New Social Movements." *West European Politics* 14, no. 3 (Jan. 1991): 144–65.

Mihut, Liliana. "The Emergence of Political Pluralism in Romania." *Communist and Post-Communist Studies* 27 (1994): 421.

Milbrath, Lester. *Environmentalists*. Albany, N.Y.: SUNY Press, 1984.

———. *Envisioning a Sustainable Society*. Albany, N.Y.: SUNY Press, 1989.

Miller, Alan. *Gaia Connections*. Maryland: Rowman and Littlefield, 1991.

Ministry of Environment. *Environmental White Paper*. Whankvoung Paekseol, Seoul: Iljisa, 1990, 1994.

Mir-Djalali, Elahe. "The Failure of Language to Communicate: A U.S.-Iranian Comparative Study." *International Journal of Intercultural Relations* 4 (1980): 307–28.

Mirici, Peter. *Canada-United States Trade and Economic Interdependence*. Montreal: C. D. Howe Research Institute, 1980.

———. *Trade Talks with Mexico: A Time for Realism*. Washington, D.C.: National Planning Assosciation, 1991.

Müller-Rommel, Ferdinand. "New Political Movements and 'New Politics' Parties." In Dalton and Kuechler, eds., 1990.

———, ed. *New Politics in Western Europe: The Rise and Success of Green Parties and Alternative Lists*. Boulder, Colo.: Westview Press, 1989.

Müller-Rommel, Ferdinand, and Geoffrey Pridham, eds. *Small Parties in Western Europe*. London: Sage, 1991.

Mumme, Stephen. "System Maintenance and Environmental Reform in Mexico: Salinas's Preemptive Strategy." *Latin American Perspectives* 19, no. 1 (winter 1992): 123–43.

Mumme, Stephen, Richard Bath, and Valerie Asseto. "Political Development and Environmental Policy in Mexico." *Latin American Research Review* 23, no. 1 (1988): 7–33.

Mumme, Stephen, and Roberto Sanchez. "Mexico's Environment under Salinas: Institutionalizing Policy Reform." Paper delivered at 15th Conference of Latin American Studies Association, Miami, Dec. 4–6, 1989.

Mungiu, Alina, and Andrei Pippidi. "Letter from Romania." *Government and Opposition* 29, no. 3 (winter 1994): 348–61.

Murti, T. R. V. *The Central Philosophy of Buddhism*. London: Unwin, 1987.

Myers, Norman. *The Primary Source*. New York: Norton, 1984.

NACLA Report on the Americas. (Mar.–Apr., 1981).

NACLA Report on the Americas. 23, no. 1 (1989): 12–38.

NACLA Report on the Americas. 28, no. 1 (July 1994).

National Action Plan for Agenda 21. Korea: Ministry of Environment, 1996.

National Resources Council (NRC). *Sustainable Agriculture and the Environment in the Humid Tropics*. Washington, D.C.: National Academy Press, 1993.

Nations, James and Daniel Komer. "Rainforests and the Hamburger Society." *Ecologist* 17, no. 4 (1989): 161–67.

Ng, F. S. P. "Ecological Principles of Tropical Lowland Rain Forest Conservation." In Sutton et al. eds., 1983.

Nove, Alec. *An Economic History of the U.S.S.R.* London: Penguin, 1989.

Nowshirvani, Vahid, and Patrick Clawson. "The State and Social Equality in Postrevolutionary Iran." In Weiner and Banuaziz, eds., 1994.

O'Connor, James. *The Fiscal Crisis of the State.* New York: St Martin's Press, 1973.

OECD. *Environmental Performance Reviews: Korea.* Paris, France: OECD Publications, 1997.

OECD. *Environmental Performance Reviews: Mexico.* Paris, France: OECD Publications, 1998.

Ophuls, William. *Requiem for Modern Politics.* Boulder, Colo.: Westview Press, 1997.

"Our Nature." President Sarney's speech, commission reports.

"Pacto de Grupos Ecologistas." Mexico. Offprint, Mar. 1991.

Paehlke, Robert. *Environmentalism and the Future of Progressive Politics.* New Haven: Yale University Press, 1989.

Palmer, David Scott, ed. *Shining Path of Peru.* New York: St. Martin's Press, 1994.

Papadakis, Elim. *The Green Movement in West Germany.* New York: St Martin's Press, 1984.

Paranjpye, Vijay. *Evaluating the Tehri Dam.* New Delhi, India: INTACH, 1988.

Parkin, Sara. *Green Parties: An International Guide.* London: Heretic Books, 1989.

Partide politice (Political parties). Bucharest: Rompres, 1993.

"Partido Verde Ecologista de México Declaración de Principios." Offprint. N.d.

Peet, Richard, and Michael Watts, eds. *Liberation Ecologies: Environment, Development, Social Movements.* London: Routledge, 1996.

Pelletier, Rejean, and Daniel Guerin. "Postmatérialisme et clivages partisans au Québec: Les partis sont-ils différents?" (Postmaterialism and partisan cleavages in Quebec: Are the parties different?). *Canadian Journal of Political Science* 29, no. 1 (Mar. 1996): 71–110.

Peritore, N. Patrick. "Brazilian Communist Opinion: A Q-Methodology Study of Ten Political Parties." *Journal of Developing Areas* 23, no. 1 (Oct. 1988): 105–36.

———. "Brazilian Party Left Opinion: A Q-Method Profile." *Political Psychology* 10, no.4 (Dec. 1989): 675–93.

———. "Environmental Attitudes of Indian Elites: Challenging Western Postmodernist Models." *Asian Survey* 33, no. 8 (Aug. 1993): 804–18.

———. "High-Tech Import Substitution: Brazil's Computer Policy and the Possibilities for Social Transformation." *Alternatives* 13 (1988): 27–54.

———. "India's Environmental Crisis and Chipko Andolan." *Asian Thought and Society* 17, no. 51 (Sept.–Dec. 1992): 205–11.

———. "Liberation Theology in the Brazilian Catholic Church: A Q-Methodology Study of the Diocese of Rio de Janeiro in 1985." *Luso-Brazilian Review* 26, no. 1 (summer 1989): 59–92.

———. "Reflections on Dangerous Fieldwork." *American Sociologist* 21, no. 4 (winter 1990): 359–72.

———. *Socialism, Communism, and Liberation Theology in Brazil.* Athens: Ohio University Press, 1990.

Peritore, N. Patrick, and Ana Karina Galve-Peritore. "Brazilian Agrarian Reform: A Q-Methodology Opinion Survey on a Conflicted Issue." *Journal of Developing Areas* 24, no. 3 (Apr. 1990): 377–406.

———. "Cleavage and Polarization in Mexico's Ruling Party: A Field Study of the 1988 Presidential Election." *Journal of Developing Areas* 28 (Oct. 1993): 67–88.

———, eds. *Biotechnology in Latin America: Politics, Impacts, and Risks*. Wilmington: Scholarly Resources, 1995.

Perot, Ross, and Pat Choate. *Save Your Job, Save Our Country*. New York: Hyperion, 1993.

Phillips, Dana. "Is Nature Necessary?" *Raritan* 13, no. 3 (winter 1994): 78–101.

Pierce, Jenny. *Under the Eagle: U.S. Intervention in Central America and the Caribbean*. Boston: South End Press, 1982.

Pierce, John. "The Hidden Layer of Political Culture: A Comment on 'Postmaterialist' Values and the Environment: A Critique and Reappraisal." *Social Science Quarterly* 78, no. 1 (Mar. 1997): 30–35.

Pierce, John, Nicholas Loverich, Taketsugu Tsurutani, and Takematsu Abe. "Environmental Belief Systems among Japanese and American Elites and Publics." *Political Behavior* 9, no. 2 (1987): 139–57.

Pierce, John, T. Tsurutani, and Nicholas Loverich. "Vanguards and Rearguards in Environmental Politics." *Comparative Political Studies* 18, no. 4 (1986): 419–47.

Piven, Frances Fox, ed. *Labor Parties in Postindustrial Societies*. Cambridge, Mass.: Polity Press, 1991.

Polanyi, Karl. *The Great Transformation*. Boston: Beacon Press, 1957.

Polanyi, Karl, Conrad Arensberg, and Harry Pearson, eds. *Trade and Market in Early Empires*. Chicago: Henry Regnery, 1971.

Pollard, Jane, and Michael Storper. "A Tale of 12 Cities: Metropolitan Employment Change in Dynamic Industries in the 1980s." *Economic Geography* 72, no. 1 (Jan. 1996): 1–22.

Poster, Mark, ed. *Jean Baudrillard: Selected Writings*. Palo Alto, Calif.: Stanford University Press, 1988.

Prance, G. T., W. Balee, B. M. Boom, and R. L. Carneiro. "Quantitative Ethnobotany and the Case for Conservation in Amazonia." *Conservation Biology* 1, no. 4 (1987): 296–310.

PREDA. *Industrial Newsletter* 17 (1976).

Princen, Thomas, and Matthias Finger. *Environmental NGOs in World Politics*. London: Routledge, 1994.

Puente, Sergio, and Jorge Legorreta. *Medio Ambiente y calidad de vida*. Mexico: P. y V. editores, 1988.

Puerto Rico. *Environmental Public Policy Act*. Law No. 9. June 18, 1970.

Puerto Rico-USA Foundation. Offprint, 1992.

Rabinow, Paul, ed. *The Foucault Reader*. New York: Pantheon, 1984.

Radio Free Europe. *Situation Report* 2 (Nov. 21, 1983): 18.

Rady, Martyn. *Romania in Turmoil*. London: I. B. Tauris, 1992.

Rainbow, Stephen. *Green Politics.* Auckland: Oxford University Press, 1993.

Ramos de Santiago, Carmen. *El desarrollo constitucional de Puerto Rico.* San Juan: Editorial UPR, 1985.

Readman, J. W., et al. "Oil and Combustion Product Contamination of the Gulf Marine Environment Following the War." *Nature* 358 (Aug. 20, 1992): 662–65.

Redclift, Michael. "Environmental Conflict and Development Policy in Rural Mexico." *Development and the Environmental Crisis.* London: Methuen, 1984.

———. "Mexico's Green Movements." *Ecologist* 17, no. 1 (1987): 44–46.

Reed, Paul, and David Rothenberg. *Wisdom in the Open Air: The Norwegian Roots of Deep Ecology.* Minneapolis: University of Minnesota Press, 1993.

Reid, David. *Sustainable Development.* London: Earthscan, 1995.

Reimer, Bo. "No Values—New Values? Youth and Postmaterialism." *Scandinavian Political Studies* 11, no. 4 (1988): 347–59.

Report to the UNCED. Governments of Brazil, Iran. Offprints, Rio de Janeiro, June 1–12, 1992.

Rhee, Hang Yul "The Economic Problems of the Korean Political Economy." In Kim and Kihl, eds., 1988.

Richardson, Dick, and Chris Rootes, eds. *The Green Challenge: The Development of Green Parties in Europe.* London: Routledge, 1995.

Ricklefs, Robert. *Ecology.* 3rd ed. New York: W. H. Freeman, 1990.

Robb, Peter. *Midnight in Sicily.* Boston: Faber and Faber, 1996.

Romania: Encyclopedic Survey. Government offprint, 1994.

Ross. *The Long Uphill Path: A Study of Puerto Rico's Program of Economic Development.* San Juan: San Juan Editorial, 1969.

Rothenberg, David. *Is It Painful to Think? Conversations with Arne Naess.* Minneapolis: University of Minnesota Press, 1993.

Roy, Kartik, et al., eds. *Economic Development and Environment.* Calcutta: Oxford University Press, 1992.

Roy, Ramashray. "India in 1993." *Asian Survey* 34, no. 2, (Feb. 1994): 205–6.

Rudig, Wolfgang. "Green Party Politics around the World." *Environment* 33 (Oct. 1991): 6–9, 25–31.

Rule, James. "Green Politics." *Dissent* 41, no. 2 (spring 1994): 21–23.

Russell, Phillip. *Mexico under Salinas.* Austin: Mexico Resource Center, 1994.

Ryan, Michael. *Marxism and Deconstruction.* Baltimore: Johns Hopkins University Press, 1982.

Sainteny, Guillaume. "Les dirigeants écologistes et le champ politique" (The ecological leaders and policies). *Revue Française de Science Politique* 37, no. 1 (Feb. 1987): 21–29.

San Juan Star. June 6, 1992.

Savage, James. "Postmaterialism of the Left and Right." *Comparative Political Studies* 17, no. 4 (Jan. 1985): 431–51.

Schmidheiny, Stephan. *Changing Course.* Cambridge, Mass.: MIT Press, 1993.

Schmink, Marianne, and Charles Wood. *Contested Frontiers in Amazonia.* New York: Columbia University Press, 1992.

Schneider, Stephen, and Randi Londer. *The Coevolution of Climate and Life.* San Francisco: Sierra Club, 1984.

Scientific American 271, no. 4 (Oct.1994): 120.

Scott, Allen, and Michael Storper. *Production, Work, Territory.* Boston: Allen and Unwin, 1986.

Secretaría do Meio-Ambiente. *Curso de Direito Ambiental—1997,* (Course on Environmental Law—1997). Offprint, 1997.

Sedesol. *México: Informe de la Situación General en Materia de Equilibrio Ecologico y Protección al Ambiente 1991–1992* (Mexico: Information on the general situation regarding ecological equilibrium and environmental protection 1991–1992). Mexico, SEDESOL, 1993.

Seger, Anthony. "Native Americans and the Conservation of Flora and Fauna in Brazil." In Hallsworth, ed., 1982.

SEMARNAP. *Informe de Labores 1995–1996.* Mexico: SEMARNAP, 1996.

———. *Ley General del Equilibrio Ecológico y la Protección al Ambiente.* Mexico: SEMARNAP, PROFEPA, 1997.

———. *México hacia el Desarrollo Sustentable: bases de la Transición.* México: SEMARNAP, 1996.

———. *Programa de Trabajo 1998.* Mexico: SEMARNAP, 1998.

Serrao, Emanuel Souza, and Alfredo Homma. "Brazil." In National Resources Council, 1993.

Shafir, Michael. "Romanian Local Elections Herald New Political Map." *RFE/ RL Research Report* (Mar. 13, 1992a): 30–31.

Shinn, Don. "Education and Quality of Life in Korea and the U.S.A: A Cross-Cultural Perspective." *Public Opinion Quarterly* 50 (1986): 360–70.

Shiva, Vandana. *Staying Alive.* London: Zed Books, 1990.

———. *The Violence of the Green Revolution.* Dehra Dun, India: Research Foundation for Science and the Environment, 1989.

Short, R. V., and E. Balaban, eds. *The Differences between the Sexes.* Cambridge: Cambridge University Press, 1994.

Shweder, Richard, and Robert LeVine, eds. *Culture Theory.* New York: Cambridge University Press, 1987.

Silverman, Bertran, ed. *Man and Socialism in Cuba: The Great Debate.* New York: Atheneum, 1973.

Singer, Paulo. *Economía política do trabalho* (Political economy of work). São Paulo, Brazil: Hucitec, 1977.

Singh, J. S., ed. *Environmental Regeneration in Himalaya.* Bombay, India: Asia Publishing House, 1986.

Singh, Tej Vir, and Jagdish Kaur, eds. *Himalayas: Mountains and Men.* Lucknow, India: Print House, 1983.

Sioli, Harald. *Amazônia: Fundamentos da Ecología da Maior Regi{at}o de Floresta Tropical* (Amazonia: The elements of ecology in the largest rain forest). Petropolis: Editora Vozes, 1985.

Sislin, John. "Revolution Betrayed? Romania and the National Salvation Front." *Studies in Comparative Communism* 24, no. 4 (Dec. 1991): 395–411.

Solis-Weiss, Vivianne. "Edenes productivos del litoral Méxicano: Arrecifes coralinos, manglares y pastos marinos." In Leff, ed., 1990.

Solis-Weiss, Vivianne, and Maria Nuria Mendez Ubach. "Los Recursos naturales de las lagunas costeras." In Leff, ed., 1990.

Stearman, Allyn MacLean. "Only Slaves Climb Trees: Revisiting the Myth of the Ecologically Noble Savage in Amazonia." *Human Nature* 5, no. 4 (1994): 339–57.

Steger, Mary Ann, John Pierce, Brent Steel, and Nicholas Loverich. "Political Culture, Postmaterial Values, and the New Environmental Paradigm." *Political Behavior* 2, no. 3 (1989): 233–54.

Steiguer, J. E. de. *Age of Environmentalism*. New York: McGraw-Hill, 1997.

Steinberg, David I. *The Republic of Korea: Economic Transformation and Social Change*. Boulder, Colo.: Westview Press, 1989.

Stephenson, William. *The Play Theory of Mass Communication*. Chicago: University of Chicago Press, 1967.

———. "The Quantimization of Psychological Events." *Operant Subjectivity* 12 (1988): 1–25.

———. "Quantum Theory of Subjectivity." *Integral Psychiatry* 6 (1989): 180–95.

———. *The Study of Behavior*. Chicago: University of Chicago Press, 1953.

———. "William James, Neils Bohr and Complementarity," pt 1. *Psychological Record* 36 (1986): 519–27.

———. "William James, Neils Bohr and Complementarity," pt. 2. *Psychological Record* 37 (1986): 529–43.

———. "William James, Neils Bohr and Complementarity," pt. 4. *Psychological Record* 37 (1987): 545–51.

Sterling, Claire. *Octopus: The Long Reach of the International Sicilian Mafia*. New York: Norton, 1990.

Sunoo, Harold Hakwon. *The South Korean Economy. Success or Failure? An Analysis of Export-Oriented Economic Policy*. Virginia Beach, Va.: Heritage Research House, 1989.

Sutton, S. L., T. C. Whitmore, and A. C. Chadwick, eds. *Tropical Rain Forest Ecology and Management*. Oxford: Blackwell, 1983.

Swain, Adhok. *Environmental Trap: The Ganges River Diversion, Bangladeshi Migration and Conflicts in India*. Sweden: Uppsala University Press, 1996.

Switzler, Jacqueline. *Green Backlash: The History and Politics of Environmental Opposition in the U.S.* Boulder, Colo.: Lynne Reiner Publishers, 1997.

Szalay, Lora, Hossein Moftakhar, and Elahe Mir-Djalali. *Environmental Politics*. London: Routledge, 1994.

———. "The Iranian Self-Image: Empirical Findings Compared with Laingen's Observations." *Political Psychology* (spring 1982): 1–23.

Szarka, Joseph. "Green Politics in France: The Impasse of Non-Alignment." *Parliamentary Affairs* 47, no. 3 (July 1994): 446–55.

Taeruik Research Institute. *National Poll on Environmental Preservation* [in Korean]. Seoul, Korea. Offprint, 1990.

Tainter, Joseph. *The Collapse of Complex Societies*. Cambridge: Cambridge University Press, 1988.

Tavares, Maria Conceição, and Mauricio Dias David. *A economía política da crise* (The political economy of crisis). Rio de Janeiro: IERJ, 1982.

Taylor, Dorceta. "Blacks and the Environment." *Environment and Behavior* 21, no. 2 (Mar. 1989): 175–205.

Tismaneanu, Vladimir. "The Revival of Politics in Romania." In Wessell, ed., 1991.

Trivers, Robert. "The evolution of reciprocal altruism." *Quarterly Review of Biology* 46 (1971): 35–57.

———. *Social Evolution*. Menlo Park, Calif.: Benjamin Cummings, 1985.

USDC. *Economic Study #1*. In Dietz, 1986.

Uusitalo, Lisa. "Are Environmental Attitudes and Behaviour Inconsistent? Findings from a Finnish Study." *Scandinavian Political Studies* 13, no. 2 (1990): 221–25.

Vallas, Steven, and John Beck. "Transformation of Work Revisited: The Limits of Flexibility in American Manufacturing." *Social Problems* 43, no. 3 (Aug. 1996): 339–62.

Van der Dennen, J. M. G., ed. *The Nature of the Sexes*. Groningen, The Netherlands: Origin Press, 1992.

Van Liere, Kent, and Riley Dunlap. "The Social Bases of Environmental Concern." *Public Opinion Quarterly* 44, no. 2 (1980): 181–97.

Van Parijs, Philippe. "A Revolution in Class Theory." *Politics and Society* 15, no. 4 (1986–87): 453–82.

Vauclair, Jacques. *Animal Cognition*. Cambridge: Harvard University Press, 1996.

Vedung, Evert. "The Formation of Green Parties: Environmentalism, State Response, and Political Entrepreneurship." In Hansen, ed., 1991.

Venkateswaran, Sandhya. *Environment, Development, and the Gender Gap*. New Delhi, India: Sage Publications, 1995.

Veja. "A morte ronda os indios na floresta" (Death surrounds Indians in the forest). *Veja* news magazine (São Paulo), Sept. 19, 1990, 70–83.

———. "Sinais de vida e morte no planeta verde" (Signs of life and death on the green planet). *Veja* news magazine (São Paulo), July 5, 1989, 60–109.

Verde Luz. 8, no. 1 (Marzo 1998): 1–2.

Vickers, William. "From Opportunism to Nascent Conservation: the Case of the Siona-Secoya." *Human Nature* 5, no. 4 (1994): 307–37.

Vohra, B. B. *The Greening of India*. New Delhi, India: INTACH, 1985.

Waller, Michael. "The Ecology Issue in Eastern Europe: Protest and Movements." *Journal of Communist Studies* 5 (1989): 303–27.

Wallerstein, Immanuel. *The Capitalist World Economy*. Cambridge: Cambridge University Press, 1980.

———. *The Modern World System*. 3 vols. New York: Academic Press, 1976–80.

———. *The Politics of the World Economy*. Cambridge: Cambridge University Press, 1984.

Warford, Gunther, and Jeremy Warford, eds. *Environmental Management and Economic Development*. Baltimore: Johns Hopkins University Press, 1989.

Weale, Albert. "The Greening of the European Polity?" *West European Politics* 14, no. 4 (Oct. 1991): 193–98.

Weiner, Myron, and Ali Banuaziz, eds. *The Politics of Social Transformation in Afghanistan, Iran, and Pakistan*. New York: Syracuse University Press, 1994.

Wenz, Peter. *Environmental Justice*. Albany, N.Y.: SUNY Press, 1988.

Wessell, Nils H., ed. *The New Europe: Revolution in East-West Relations*. New York: Academy of Political Science, 1991.

Wheelwright, E. L., and Bruce McFarlane. *The Chinese Road to Socialism*. New York: Monthly Review Press, 1970.

Williams, Richard, Joanne Heckman, and Jon Schneeberger. *Environmental Consequences of the Persian Gulf War 1990–1991*. National Geographic Society, 1991.

Wilson, E. O., ed. *Biodiversity*. Washington, D.C.: National Academy Press, 1989.

Winthrop, Stephen. "Debt for Nature Swaps: Debt Relief and Biosphere Preservation?" *S.A.I.S.* (School for Advanced International Studies) *Review, 9* (summer–fall 1989): 129–49.

Wolfson, Ze'ev. "The Caspian Sea: Latest Developments." *Environmental Policy Review* 7, no. 1 (1993): 14–21.

World Almanac. 1994.

World Commission on Environment and Development. *Our Common Future*. Oxford: Oxford University Press, 1987.

World Resources Institute. *The 1992 Information Please Environmental Almanac*. Boston: Houghton Mifflin, 1992.

———. *World Resources 1990–1991*. London: Oxford University Press, 1992.

Wyburd, G. "Case Study: Industry." In Berry, ed., 1993.

Yoon, Suk Hong. "National Interest and the Press in Korea." *Sungkok Journalism Review* 1 (1990): 37–55.

Zadeh, Iqtidar. "On the Ethics of Man's Interaction with the Environment: An Islamic Approach." *Environmental Ethics* 3 (spring 1981): 35–47.

Zekavat, Seid. "The State of the Environment in Iran." *Journal of Developing Societies* 13, no. 1 (1997): 49–72.

Ziegler, Charles. *Environmental Policy in the U.S.S.R.* Amherst: University of Massachusetts Press, 1987.

Zimmerman, Michael, et al., eds. *Environmental Philosophy*. N.J.: Prentice-Hall, 1993.

Zirker, Daniel, and Marvin Henberg. "Amazonia: Democracy, Ecology, and Brazilian Military Prerogatives in the 1992." *Armed Forces and Society* 20, no. 2 (winter 1994): 259–81.

Zvosec, Christine L. "Environmental Deterioration in Eastern Europe." *World Affairs* 147 (1984): 101–2.

Index

Acid rain, 96, 152–53, 195, 201, 210
Agriculture, 116, 149–51, 211, 217
Agrosilvapastoral culture, 71, 150–51
Air pollution, 95–97, 148, 152–54, 177, 195, 210
Andersen, Jorgen Goul, 29, 52–53
Attitudes, environmental, 1–3, 8–11, 12–13, 17–18, 229, 230, 233

Biodiversity, 100, 154–56, 212, 283
Biotechnology, 167, 171
Brown, Steven R., 12–18
Bureaucratic Nationalists, 11, 205–7, 221–22, 242, 283–84

Catholic Church, 127
Chipko Andolan, 65–70
Crime, organized, 24, 239
Cultural Traditionalists, 11, 186–87, 218–19, 242, 284

Dams, 77–78
Democracy, 25–26, 43, 130
Desertification, 149–51, 210
Development, 38, 69
Developmentalists, 10, 137–39, 203–5, 219–20, 241–42, 284–85
Dictatorship, 93–94, 114
Disorganized capitalism, 233–35, 285
Dunlap, Riley, 33, 35

Endemism, 100, 112, 154–56, 212–13
Environmental elites, 1–4, 7–8, 11–12, 15–17, 24, 26, 49, 128–29, 231–32, 236–39
Environmental groups, 25–26, 76, 101, 120, 125–28, 130, 159–61, 179, 197–98, 230–32
Environmental regulation, 96–97, 118–19, 163–64, 170–71, 244–45

Feminism, 285
Fisheries, 100–101, 148, 211
Fordism, 37–40, 176
Forests, 64–66, 69, 90, 100, 112–14, 116–17, 155, 211–12

Gandhi, Mohandas, 61–62, 65, 68, 81, 88–89
Gandhi, Rajiv, 63–64
Global North, ix
Global South, ix, x, 2, 11–12, 30–37, 41, 286
Global warming, 10
GNP, 10, 92, 103, 145–46, 286
Green capitalism, 2–3, 5–6, 287
Green economy, 70–72, 236, 287
Green parties, 80, 231–32, 238, 286
Green revolution, 72, 150, 287
Greens, 3–4, 8, 50–57, 79–81, 102–4, 129–32, 164–66, 172, 180–82, 239, 286–87

Hypercapitalism, 40, 44, 46, 236, 287

Import substitution, 38, 93, 287

Indians, American, 115–16, 126, 149, 150, 168
Inglehart, Ronald, 27–30, 34–35, 46–47

Khator, Renu, 73–76
Kitschelt, Herbert, 54
Knutsen, Oddbjorn, 28

Liberal capitalism, 233, 288
Lipietz, Alain, 37–38, 41

Maquiladoras, 151–52, 162–63, 288
Mercury Poisoning, 113
Ministry of Environment, 64, 73–76, 95, 119–24, 156–58, 176–77, 198, 201–3, 212–13
Modernism, 3, 19–20, 27–28, 50
Muller-Rommel, Ferdinand, 53

NAFTA, x, 161–64, 171, 288
Narmada Dam, 77–78
Nehru, Jawaharlal, 62–63
Neoliberalism, 36, 39–40, 57, 63–64, 94, 126–27, 158–59, 244–45
New Class, 45–50, 59
New Left, 19, 23, 48–49, 50
New Politics, x, 3, 23–26, 56–57, 59, 230–31, 233–39, 243–45, 288–89
New Right, 48–49
Nuclear Power, 99

OECD, 91

Political culture, 232
Political Greens, 8, 104–5, 166–67, 182–83, 239–41, 289
Population, 64, 113, 131, 210

Post-Fordism, ix, 37–44, 40, 44, 45, 58–59, 229, 287–88, 289
Postmaterialism, 27–30, 36, 57, 289–90
Postmodernism, ix, 19–26, 27, 30, 36, 37, 57–58, 228–29
Postmodern Managers, 10, 49, 84–86, 134–37, 169–72, 185–86, 241, 290
Postmodern philosophy, 19–26, 290

Q-Methodology, 12–18
Quartenary Sector, 229, 285–86, 291

Roy, Ramashray, 25

Shiite Islam, 214, 215–17, 218–19, 226
Statement set, 5–7, 14–15, 247–82
Surveys, 4, 16, 27–30, 31–34, 124–25, 177, 230
Sustainable Developers, 10, 81–4, 105–8, 132–34, 167–69, 183–85, 220–21, 241, 291
Sustainable Development, 115–18, 291
Swidden (slash and burn agriculture), 64, 113–14

Treaty regimes, 161–64, 213, 235

Waste, hazardous, 97–99, 151–52, 178–79, 210–11
Water pollution, 73, 99–100, 147–49, 210–11
Women's Rights, 10, 65, 68, 83, 85, 131, 238
WTO (World Trade Organization), 235–36, 291–92

N. Patrick Peritore has done field research in Mexico, Brazil, Cuba, Nicaragua, India, Romania, and New Zealand and written a number of articles and two books, *Socialism, Communism, and Liberation Theology in Brazil* (1990) and *Biotechnology in Latin America: Politics, Impacts, and Risks* (1995), with Karina Galve-Peritore. A professor at the University of Missouri, Columbia, he has taught at the University of Auckland and the University of Sibiu in Romania and has consulted in Mexico and New Zealand. His current research is in the biology of sex differences and politics.